Network Attacks and Defenses

A Hands-on Approach

Zouheir Trabelsi • Kadhim Hayawi
Arwa Al Braiki • Sujith Samuel Mathew

CRC Press
Taylor & Francis Group
Boca Raton   London   New York

CRC Press is an imprint of the
Taylor & Francis Group, an **informa** business
AN AUERBACH BOOK

CRC Press
Taylor & Francis Group
6000 Broken Sound Parkway NW, Suite 300
Boca Raton, FL 33487-2742

© 2013 by Taylor & Francis Group, LLC
CRC Press is an imprint of Taylor & Francis Group, an Informa business

No claim to original U.S. Government works

Printed in the United States of America on acid-free paper
Version Date: 20120827

International Standard Book Number: 978-1-4665-1794-3 (Hardback)

Visit the Taylor & Francis Web site at
http://www.taylorandfrancis.com

and the CRC Press Web site at
http://www.crcpress.com

Contents

Introduction

The importance of experimental learning has long been recognized and emphasized among pedagogical techniques. This book is designed to guide the reader through experiments in network security attacks and defenses using a simple step-by-step and hands-on approach. The intention of this book is to educate the reader on how to accomplish several well-known network attacks and implement the appropriate network security measures. This book is a catalyst for presenting an educational approach, which is based on only defensive techniques, to allow students to better anatomize and elaborate on both offensive and defensive techniques. It also describes model scenarios that educators can use to design and implement innovative hands-on security exercises.

Network security courses are often taught as concepts, at relatively abstract levels. A curriculum that covers the concepts of network security without giving suitable coverage to practical implementation deprives the student of the opportunity to experience the technologies and techniques required to ensure security. A hands-on approach to disseminating knowledge of network security will prepare the student for the complexities of conducting research and development in this field. Such an approach is rarely seen in most graduate and undergraduate courses. Even when the hands-on approach is advocated by some, it is usually dominated by exercises using defensive techniques. However, nowadays, offensive techniques originally developed by hackers are gaining widespread approval and interest. It is often criticized that offensive methods should not be taught to students as this only increases the population of "malicious hackers." Many educators in this field feel that hands-on courses that teach security attacks in detail are unethical and create the potential for some to use the tools and techniques in an irresponsible manner. The social implication is to restrict the injection of new hackers into society. However, others claim that teaching offensive techniques yields better security professionals than those who are taught only defensive techniques. It is important to note here that corporate businesses employ experts who use offensive techniques for penetration testing, to ensure their security. The use of offensive techniques to provide secure environments for large corporate entities has created a new genre of hackers, the "ethical hacker!" It is obvious that offensive techniques are central to better understanding security breaches and system failures. Teaching network attacks with hands-on experiments is a necessary component of education in network security. Moreover, we believe that security students need to experiment with attack techniques to be able to implement appropriate and efficient security solutions. This approach to education will enable the student to provide confidentiality, integrity, and availability of computer systems, networks, resources, and data. One cannot design perfectly or build defenses for attacks that one has not truly experienced first-hand. Offensive and defensive techniques must be taught with equal importance in IT (Information Technology) security courses. In addition, every course in IT security must be accompanied by discussions of the legal implications and cover the ethical responsibilities of the students toward their community and society at large.

Network security lacks sufficient contemporary textbooks and technical papers that describe in detail educational hands-on exercises that include both offensive and defensive techniques. To contribute toward filling this void in security education, this book proposes a series of comprehensive exercises that are indispensable to network security students.

This book does not pretend to include all offense and defense techniques. In contrast to other related security textbooks, this book discusses both the generation of several well-known network attacks and methods to implement the appropriate defense techniques. Practical processes involved in generating attacks are propagated to educate the reader on the complexity of the same rather than advocating the use of off-the-shelf security attack and penetration tools. The book is designed to accompany and complement existing trade or academic press texts, and can be offered to students enrolled in network security courses.

As a prerequisite for this book, the authors assume that the reader has knowledge of basic networking protocols and principles. The hardware network and security devices used in the exercises are from Juniper Networks and Cisco. However, the labs can easily be rebuilt using any available network and security devices or software from other vendors offering similar functionalities.

The book is organized as follows:

Chapter 1 describes the CAM (Content Addressable Memory) table poisoning attack on network switches. This attack intends to corrupt the entries in the switch's CAM table so that the network traffic will be redirected, causing a DoS (Denial-of-Service) attack situation. This chapter includes hands-on labs about the generation of the CAM table poisoning attack and the security features for preventing CAM table poisoning available on contemporary switches.

Chapter 2 deals with ARP (Address Resolution Protocol) cache poisoning attack. This attack is the malicious act by a host in a LAN (Local Area Network) of introducing a spurious IP address to MAC (Media Access Control) address mapping in another host's ARP cache. ARP cache poisoning is an easy attack to conduct, very harmful, and presents a very serious threat. ARP cache poisoning allows the generation of DoS and MiM (Man-in-the-Middle) attacks. A DoS attack consists of preventing a victim host from communicating with one or more host(s) in a LAN. A MiM attack is a common technique used to sniff network traffic in switched LANs. This chapter includes hands-on labs about the generation of DoS and MiM attacks using the ARP cache poisoning technique.

Chapter 3 covers the detection and prevention of abnormal ARP traffic. ARP cache poisoning is an example of attacks that use abnormal ARP traffic to corrupt target host ARP caches. Attacks based on abnormal ARP traffic are of interest because they are highly intentional and usually must be initiated, maintained, and controlled by humans. These attacks can be performed by novices or script kiddies, using widely available and easy-to-use tools specifically designed for that purpose. Due to the importance of this problem, several types of security solutions integrate mechanisms to cope with abnormal ARP traffic. This chapter evaluates common security solutions regarding their ability to detect abnormal ARP traffic and provides analysis based on heavy practical experiments. The chapter includes hands-on exercises about the detection and prevention of abnormal ARP traffic.

Chapter 4 discusses network traffic sniffing and the detection of Network Interface Cards (NICs) running in promiscuous mode. In LANs, sniffing activity with a malicious purpose can be very harmful. Network traffic sniffing allows malicious users to easily steal confidential data, passwords, and anyone's privacy. Using examples, this chapter explains how network traffic sniffing works. The chapter also discusses the concepts of the NICs hardware filter and system kernel's software filter, and describes a common technique for detecting NIC cards running in promiscuous mode. The chapter includes a hands-on exercise about how to generate and manually trap ARP request packets to detect NIC cards running in promiscuous mode.

Chapter 5 describes Internet Protocol-Based Denial-of-Service (IP-based DoS) attacks. A DoS attack is an attack that attempts to render a system unusable or significantly slow down the system for legitimate users by overloading the resources so no one else can access it. This chapter includes hands-on exercises about the generation and detection of four well-known DoS attacks, namely, Land attack, SYN flood attack, Teardrop attack, and UDP flood attack. In addition, this chapter presents a hands-on lab about the generation and prevention of abnormal IP traffic.

Chapter 6 discusses reconnaissance traffic. Before an attacker can run an exploit, he needs to understand the environment he is targeting. In doing so, he needs to gather preliminary information about the number of machines, types of machines, operating systems, and so forth. All the gathered information helps build a picture of the environment that is going to be tested or attacked. This chapter includes hands-on exercises about the generation and detection of four common reconnaissance activities, namely, IP address sweeping, TCP (Transmission Control Protocol) port scanning, remote OS (Operating System) identification, and Traceroute.

Chapter 7 considers network traffic filtering and inspection. Traffic filtering and inspection are a means to control access to networks. The concept consists of determining whether a packet is allowed to enter or exit an organization's network using a set of filtering rules that reflects and enforces the organization's security policy. Traffic filtering technology can be found in operating systems, software and hardware firewalls, and as a security feature of most routers and of some advanced switches. This chapter presents a series of hands-on exercises about filtering rules implementation for basic security policies, filtering of services running on nonstandard TCP and UDP (User Datagram Protocol) ports, verification of the consistency and efficiency of firewall filtering rules, packet content filtering, stateless and stateful packet filtering, and active and passive FTP (File Transfer Protocol) modes.

Chapter 8 introduces some of the common mechanisms used for router security and device hardening. The router represents a single point of entry for every network. Consequently, securing the border router is an important part of any network security solution. This chapter includes hands-on labs to demonstrate the following router security features: Authentication, Authorization, and Auditing (AAA) Model, management access security, traffic filtering using Access Control Lists (ACL), and stateful inspection. We put into practice traffic filtering based on the Internet Engineering Task Force (IETF) standard set by Request For Comments (RFC) and industry standards. The Cisco router is used because it is the most widespread device to forward packets among different networks. However, most of the security concepts and techniques explained here can be applied safely to other vendors' products.

Chapter 9 lays the foundations of Internet Protocol Security Virtual Private Network (IPsec VPN) security solution protocols, standards, types, and deployments. The IPsec VPN is an open standard defined by the IETF to provide secure communication between two endpoints on a public network using confidentiality, integrity, and authentication security technologies. IPsec VPN becomes an essential part of any enterprise network design; however, IPsec VPN implementation can be a very tedious and involved task, especially for beginners. This chapter guides the reader through easy-to-follow hands-on labs to deploy site-to-site IPsec VPN solutions using various illustrations, screen shots, and configuration steps.

Chapter 10 discusses the Remote Access IPsec VPN security solution architecture and describes its design, components, applications, and implementations. Remote Access VPN allows users to access private data and protected network resources of a central site through a secure IPsec

VPN tunnel. Because of the growing number of applications of Remote Access IPsec VPN, most of the operating system, firewall, and router vendors include VPN support in their products. This chapter includes hands-on lab implementations of the Remote Access IPsec VPN solution from two leaders in the field. The labs serve to expand the reader's knowledge of VPN best practices.

Chapter 1

Switch's CAM Table Poisoning Attack

1.1 Introduction

Local Area Networks (LANs) are configured to have switches that maintain a table called the Content Addressable Memory (CAM), which is used to map individual MAC (Media Access Control) addresses on the network to the physical ports on the switch. The CAM table allows the switch to direct data out of the physical port to exactly where the recipient is located, as opposed to indiscriminately broadcasting the data out of all ports like a hub. The advantage of this method is that data is bridged exclusively to the network segment containing the computer that the data is specifically destined for. The following screenshot shows an example of entries in the CAM table of a switch where four hosts are connected to the switch. For example, the first host (whose MAC address is 00:0F:1F:C0:EB:49) is connected to Port #1 (interface: Fast Ethernet 0/1) on the switch.

Interface Description ▽	Interface Type	Operational Status	Speed	MAC Address
FastEthernet0/1	ethernetCsmacd(6)	Up	100 Mbps	00:0F:1F:C0:EB:49
FastEthernet0/2	ethernetCsmacd(6)	Up	100 Mbps	00:08:74:04:BC:4A
FastEthernet0/3	ethernetCsmacd(6)	Up	100 Mbps	00:08:74:05:AD:20
FastEthernet0/4	ethernetCsmacd(6)	Up	100 Mbps	00:03:0D:38:79:57

When the switch receives a packet from a host, it extracts first the destination MAC address from the header of the Ethernet frame. Using this MAC address, the switch gets the corresponding port number from the CAM table. Then, the packet is sent only to the host connected to that port. Therefore, network traffic sniffing seems difficult to perform in a switched LAN. However, Chapter 2 elaborates on techniques to sniff network traffic in switched LANs.

The switch's CAM table poisoning attack is the malicious act of corrupting the entries in the switch's CAM table so that the network traffic will be redirected away from the intended hosts. This malicious activity may create a DoS (Denial-of-Service) situation, as the switch becomes unable to forward packets to their real and legitimate destinations.

This chapter includes two hands-on exercises. The first describes how to perform the CAM table poisoning attack. The second is about the implementation of the available security features on switches to prevent a CAM table poisoning attack.

The exercises use the following hardware devices and software tools:

◼ Cisco Catalyst 3650 Switch Series[*]
◼ CommView Visual Packet Builder[†]: Graphical User Interface (GUI) based packet generator

---

[*] http://www.cisco.com
[†] http://www.tamos.com

1.2 Lab Exercise 1.1: Switch's CAM Table Poisoning

1.2.1 Outcome

The learning objective of this hands-on exercise is for students to learn how to perform a switch's CAM table poisoning attack.

1.2.2 Description

The poisoning attack of a switch's CAM table intends to corrupt the entries in the table, so that the network traffic will be redirected. Consider two hosts connected to a switch, one on Port a and the other on Port b. The malicious host (connected to Port a) sends a fake packet, with the source MAC address in the packet's Ethernet header set to the MAC address of a target host (connected to Port b). The destination MAC address in the packet's header can be any MAC address. Once the switch receives the packet, it updates its CAM table. Therefore, the CAM table's entry for that target host's MAC address will be corrupted. Hence, the target host will be considered a host connected to Port a. Any packet sent to the target host (destination MAC address in the packet's Ethernet header is equal to the target host's MAC address) will be forwarded to Port a, that is, to the malicious host.

As an example of a CAM table poisoning attack, the previous figure shows that in the CAM table of a switch, there are four hosts connected to the switch. Host #1, the malicious host, attacks the switch's CAM table using three fake packets. The packets are almost the same but have different source MAC addresses in the Ethernet headers. The information of the packets is as follows:

1. First fake packet: Source MAC address in the Ethernet header = 00:08:74:04:BC:4A (Host #2).

2. Second fake packet: Source MAC address in the Ethernet header = 00:08:74:05:AD:20 (Host #3).
3. Third fake packet: Source MAC address in the Ethernet header = 00:03:0D:38:79:57 (Host #4).

After this attack, the switch's CAM table becomes corrupted, as shown in the following screenshot. The CAM table shows that all four hosts are connected to the switch's Port #1 (FastEthernet 0/1). Physically, however, only Host #1 is connected to Port #1.

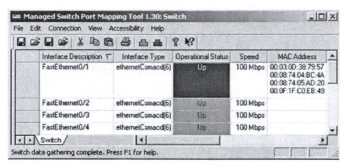

Once a packet is sent to one of these three victim hosts (Host #2, Host #3, or Host #4), the switch will forward it to Port #1, that is, to Host #1. This situation may create a DoS situation because the switch is not forwarding the packets, destined to these three hosts, to their legitimate destinations (see figure below).

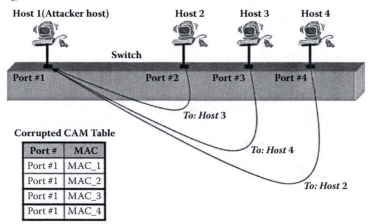

1.2.3 Experiment

The following experiment describes how to view and corrupt the contents of the CAM table. The network architecture used in the experiment is shown in the next figure. Three hosts are connected to a Cisco switch as follows:

1. Host A is connected to Port #2 on the switch.
2. Host B is connected to Port #4 on the switch.
3. Host C is connected to Port #6 on the switch.

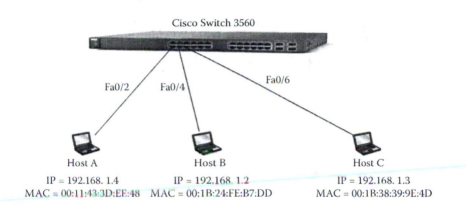

The experiment consists of the following steps:

Step 1: Assign static IP addresses to the network hosts.
Step 2: View the contents of the CAM table.
Step 3: Generate a malicious packet to corrupt the CAM table.

1.2.3.1 Step 1: Assign Static IP Addresses to the Network Hosts

The steps required to assign static IP addresses to hosts are very similar in most Windows and Linux operating systems.

For example, in Windows XP, to assign IP addresses to hosts, perform the following steps:

- Open the control panel and select "Network Connection."
- Double-click on the "Local Area Network connection" icon.
- Choose "Internet Protocol (TCP/IP)" and click on the "Properties" button.
- Choose "Use the following IP address" option and fill in the entries (see the following screenshot).

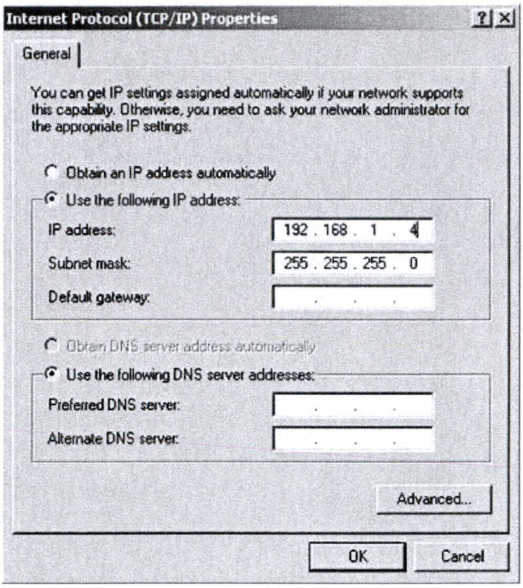

- Then click "OK."
- To verify the assigned static IP address, type the following command in the cmd window:

```
C:\>ipconfig/all
```

1.2.3.2 Step 2: View the Contents of the CAM Table

To view the contents of the CAM table, perform the following steps:

■ Connect a host to the console port on the switch.
■ Run the Terminal Application program (For example, HyperTerminal) in the host.
■ Under "Connect Using:" option, select one of the appropriate communication ports (COM1, COM2, etc.) that the console cable is attached to.
■ Select "OK" and a "Port Settings" window will pop up, prompting you to define the data rate and communication setting as defined by the vendor. (Most vendors have the following settings: 9600 Bits per second, 8 Data Bits, None-Parity, 1 Stop bits, and None Flow control.)
■ Select "OK." This will place you in the Terminal Window.
■ Depress the "Enter" key a few times until a menu from the switch appears in the Terminal Window.
■ If the menu appears, then you are ready to configure the switch as needed.
■ Type the following command to view the contents of the CAM table:

```
Switch> enable//enter the enable command to
access privileged EXEC mode
Switch# show mac-address-table
```

■ The content of the CAM table is shown in the next screenshot. Three hosts, whose MAC addresses are displayed, are connected on Port #2, Port #4, and Port #6, respectively.

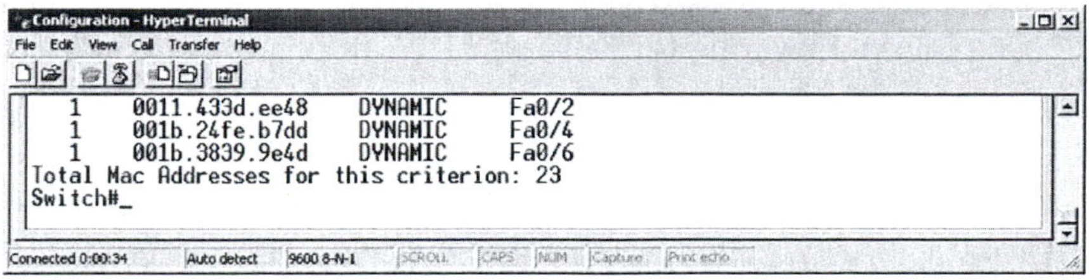

1.2.3.3 Step 3: Generate a Malicious Packet to Corrupt the CAM Table

Use any packet generator, such as CommView Visual Packet Builder, to generate a malicious packet whose MAC source in the Ethernet frame is equal to the MAC address of the victim host. For example, we assume that Host A generates a fake ICMP echo packet whose MAC source is equal to the MAC address of Host B. Using CommView Visual Packet Builder, the next screenshot provides a screenshot showing the contents of the fake ICMP echo packet.

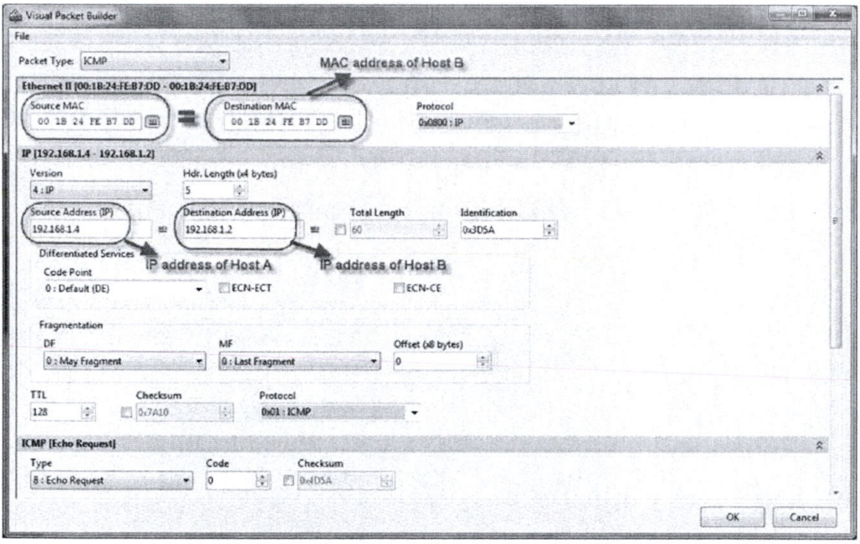

And the following screenshot is a screenshot of the content of the corrupted CAM table after sending the fake ICMP echo packet.

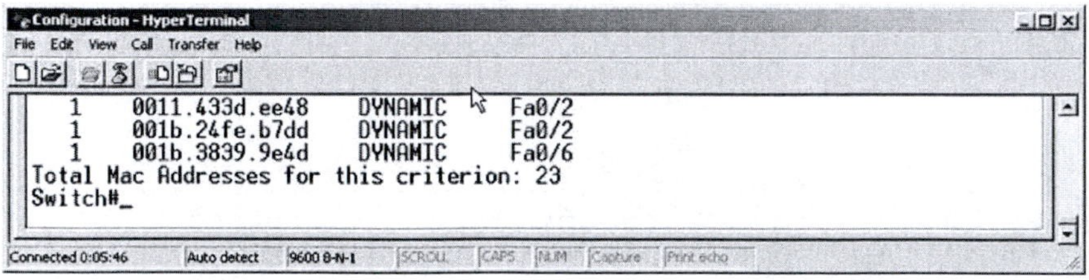

This screen shows that Host B is connected on Port #2. However, physically, Host B is still connected on Port #4. Consequently, when Host C sends packets to Host B, the switch will not forward them to Host B; they will be forwarded to Host A. This is a DoS attack situation, as Host C cannot communicate properly with Host B.

It is important to indicate that once Host B sends a packet to a destination, the switch automatically updates its CAM table. Consequently, the entry corresponding to Host B in the CAM table becomes uncorrupted. However, to keep the CAM table corrupted, the malicious Host A should keep injecting the fake ICMP echo packet.

1.2.3.4 MAC Flood Attack for Traffic Sniffing

An old attack technique for sniffing traffic in a switched LAN network is based on MAC flooding. MAC flooding is a technique employed to compromise the security of network switches. In a typical MAC flooding attack, a switch is fed many Ethernet frames, each containing a different source MAC address, by the attacker. The intention is to consume the limited memory set aside in the switch to store the CAM table. That is, when some CAM tables of old switch models overflow, the switches revert to broadcast mode (also known as hub mode or failopen mode). As a consequence, network traffic sniffing can be easily performed. Hence, after launching a successful MAC flooding attack, a malicious user can use a packet analyzer (a sniffer) to capture sensitive data being transmitted between other network's hosts, which would not be accessible when the switch is operating normally.

1.3 Lab Exercise 1.2: Prevention of CAM Table Poisoning Attack

1.3.1 Outcome

The learning objective of this hands-on exercise is for students to learn how to prevent the corruption of the content of the switch's CAM table.

1.3.2 Description

To prevent CAM table poisoning, security administrators usually rely on the presence of the "port security" feature of switches. Most switches can be configured to limit the number of MAC addresses that can be learned on ports connected to end stations. A smaller table of "secure" MAC addresses is maintained in addition to (and as a subset of) the traditional CAM table.

For example, Cisco Catalyst 3560 Series switches allow one to restrict the number of legitimate MAC addresses on a port (or an interface) using the port security feature. When that number is exceeded, a security violation would be triggered, and a violation action would be performed based on the mode configured on that port. Therefore, any unauthorized MAC address would be prevented from accessing and corrupting the CAM table of the switch. An interface can be configured for one of three violation modes, based on the action to be taken if a violation occurs:

1. Protect: When the number of secure MAC addresses reaches the maximum limit allowed on the interface, packets with unknown source MAC addresses are dropped until the switch administrator removes a sufficient number of secure MAC addresses to drop below the maximum value or increase the number of maximum allowable addresses. The switch administrator is not notified that a security violation has occurred.

2. Restrict: This mode is similar to the foregoing mode. However, in this mode, the switch administrator is notified that a security violation has occurred.
3. Shutdown: A port security violation causes the interface to shut down immediately. The switch administrator can bring it out of this state and can customize the time to recover. This is the default mode.

1.3.3 Experiment

The following experiment describes how to configure and test the port security features in Cisco Catalyst 3560 Series switches to prevent the corruption of the content of the CAM table. The experiment uses the same network architecture described in the previous lab and consists of the following steps:

Step 1: Assign static IP addresses to the network's hosts
Step 2: Configure the Restrict Mode Security Port in the switch
Step 3: Generate a malicious packet to corrupt the CAM table
Step 4: Configure the Shutdown Mode Security Port in the switch

1.3.3.1 Step 1: Assign Static IP Addresses to the Network's Hosts

Refer to Step 1 in the previous lab.

1.3.3.2 Step 2: Configure the Restrict Mode Security Port in the Switch

To configure the Restrict Mode Security Port:

■ Connect a host to the console port on the switch

■ Run the Terminal Application program in the host
■ Type the following commands:

```
Switch> enable//enter the enable command to
access privileged EXEC mode
Switch# Configure terminal
Switch(config)# interface fastethernet 0/2//
port security feature is applied on the host
connected on Port #2
Switch(config-if)# switchport mode access
Switch(config-if)# switchport port-security
Switch(config-if)# switchport port-security
violation restrict
Switch(config-if)# end
Switch# copy running-config startup-config
```

■ To display the port security mode, type the following command:

```
Switch# show port-security
```

The screenshot below shows the port security mode before the corruption attempt.

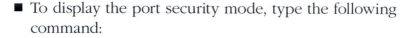

```
Configuration - HyperTerminal                                                    _|□|x|
File Edit View Call Transfer Help
□|🖙| 🖙|🕉| 🕮|🕮| 🕮|
Switch#show port-security
Secure Port   MaxSecureAddr   CurrentAddr   SecurityViolation   Security Action
              (Count)         (Count)       (Count)
--------------------------------------------------------------------------------
   Fa0/2          1              1                0             Restrict
--------------------------------------------------------------------------------
Total Addresses in System (excluding one mac per port)    : 0
Max Addresses limit in System (excluding one mac per port) : 6272
Connected 0:04:48    Auto detect   9600 8-N-1   SCROLL  CAPS  NUM  Capture  Print echo
```

1.3.3.3 *Step 3: Generate a Malicious Packet to Corrupt the CAM Table*

Use any packet generator, such as CommView Visual Packet Builder, to generate a malicious packet whose MAC source in the Ethernet header is set to a fake MAC address. For example, the same fake ICMP echo packet generated in the previous lab can be used.

■ Type the following command to view the CAM table content after the corruption attempt:

Switch# show `mac-address-table`.

The following screenshot clearly shows that the CAM table has not been corrupted.

```
Configuration - HyperTerminal                                        _ |□| x|
File  Edit  View  Call  Transfer  Help
D|☞| ☜|⑤| ☜|☟| ☞|
    1      0011.433d.ee48    STATIC     Fa0/2
    1      001b.24fe.b7dd    DYNAMIC    Fa0/4
    1      001b.3839.9e4d    DYNAMIC    Fa0/6
Total Mac Addresses for this criterion: 23
Switch#_

Connected 0:10:46    Auto detect   9600 8-N-1   SCROLL   CAPS  NUM   Capture   Print echo
```

■ Type the following command to display again the port security mode:

Switch# show `port-security`.

The screenshot below clearly shows that there have been twenty-seven packets that attempted to violate the security feature implemented on Port #2 (Fa0/2). These packets attempted to corrupt the CAM table; however, the switch has blocked them.

```
Configuration - HyperTerminal                                        _ |□| x|
File  Edit  View  Call  Transfer  Help
D|☞| ☜|⑤| ☜|☟| ☞|
Switch#show port-security
Secure Port  MaxSecureAddr  CurrentAddr  SecurityViolation  Security Action
               (Count)        (Count)        (Count)
----------------------------------------------------------------------------
    Fa0/2          1              1              27            Restrict
----------------------------------------------------------------------------
Total Addresses in System (excluding one mac per port)     : 0
Max Addresses limit in System (excluding one mac per port) : 6272
Switch#_

Connected 0:09:55    Auto detect   9600 8-N-1   SCROLL   CAPS  NUM   Capture   Print echo
```

1.3.3.4 Step 4: Configure the Shutdown Mode Security Port in the Switch

Type the following commands to configure the Shutdown Mode Security Port:

```
Switch(config)# interface fastethernet 0/2
Switch(config-if)# switchport mode access
Switch(config-if)# switchport port-security
Switch(config-if)# switchport port-security
violation shutdown
Switch(config-if)# end
```

Switch# copy running-config startup-config

■ Display the port security mode.

The following screenshot depicts the port security mode before the corruption attempt.

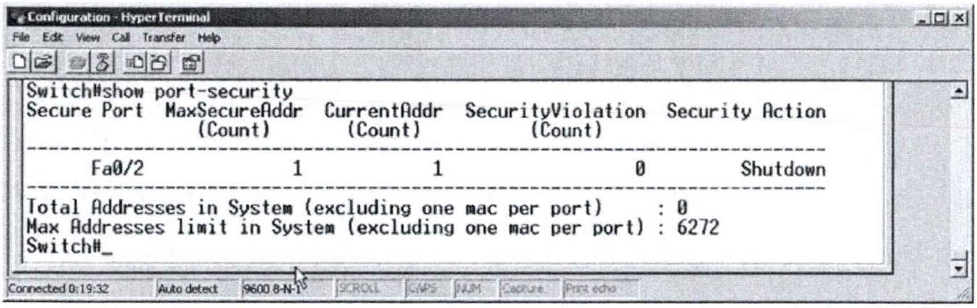

■ Generate the same fake ICMP packet of the previous test and then display the port security mode.

The next screenshot clearly shows that there has been a packet that attempted to violate the security feature implemented on Port #2. The switch has blocked the malicious packet and shut down the port.

```
🖳 Configuration - HyperTerminal                                          _□×
File  Edit  View  Call  Transfer  Help
 🗋🖻  🕮🕭  🕮🕭  🕮
┌─────────────────────────────────────────────────────────────────────────┐
│Switch#show port-security                                               ▲│
│Secure Port  MaxSecureAddr   CurrentAddr  SecurityViolation  Security Action│
│             (Count)         (Count)          (Count)                      │
│-----------------------------------------------------------------------    │
│    Fa0/2           1             0                 1          Shutdown     │
│-----------------------------------------------------------------------    │
│Total Addresses in System (excluding one mac per port)     : 0             │
│Max Addresses limit in System (excluding one mac per port) : 6272          │
│Switch#                                                                   ▼│
└─────────────────────────────────────────────────────────────────────────┘
Connected 0:33:42    Auto detect    9600 8-N-1    SCROLL  CAPS   NUM  Capture  Print echo
```

The following screenshot clearly shows that Host A has lost its connection to the switch (the interface 0/2 has been shut down), and a warning message has appeared on Host A's desktop.

1.4 Chapter Summary

This chapter describes the generation and prevention of the switch's CAM table poisoning attack. The attack is about corrupting the entries in the CAM table in order to create a DoS situation. After the attack, the target switch becomes unable to forward packets to their legitimate destinations. The chapter's hands-on exercises allow users to learn how to perform and prevent the switch's CAM table poisoning attack.

Chapter 2

ARP Cache Poisoning-Based MiM and DoS Attacks

2.1 Introduction

ARP (Address Resolution Protocol) cache poisoning is a technique used to perform Denial-of-Service (DoS) or Man-in-the-Middle (MiM) attacks. A DoS attack based on ARP cache poisoning prevents a host from communicating with other hosts in a LAN (Local Area Network). A MiM attack is used to sniff network traffic between hosts in a LAN. This attack is characterized by the rerouting (redirecting) of network traffic between hosts to a malicious host. To understand ARP cache poisoning-based attacks, it is important to first understand the ARP and ARP cache. A brief description of the ARP and ARP cache is presented here.

2.1.1 Address Resolution Protocol (ARP)

ARP is used to map an IP address to a given MAC (Media Access Control) address so that packets can be transmitted across a LAN. ARP messages are exchanged when one host knows the IP address (Internet Protocol address) of a remote host and wants to discover the remote host's MAC address. For example, in a LAN, to get the MAC address of Host 2, Host 1 needs to first send a broadcast ARP request message to all hosts in the network. Then, Host 2 will send a unicast ARP response message back to Host 1 containing its MAC address. An ARP message on an Ethernet/IP network has eight parameters, namely,

ARP Header
Operation code (1: for ARP request, 2: for ARP response)
Source IP address
Source MAC address
Destination IP address
Destination MAC address
Ethernet Header
Source MAC address
Destination MAC address
Ethernet Type (= 0x0806 for ARP message)

The ARP specifies no rules to maintain consistency between the ARP header and the Ethernet header. That means one can provide uncorrelated addresses between these two headers. For example, the source MAC address in the Ethernet header can be different from the source MAC address in the ARP header.

2.1.2 ARP Cache

Each host in a LAN segment has a table, called ARP cache, that maps IP addresses with their corresponding MAC addresses, as illustrated in the figure below.

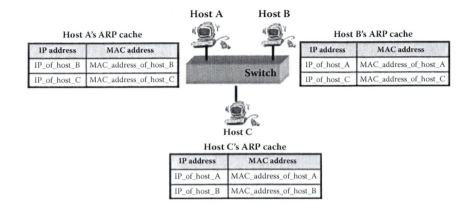

There are two types of entries in an ARP cache, namely, (1) *static entries*: depending on the operating system (OS), the entries remain permanently in the ARP cache, or until the system reboots; and (2) *dynamic entries*: the entries remain in the ARP cache for a few minutes (depending on the OS) and then they are removed if they are not referenced. Unfortunately, a static entries mechanism is used only in small LANs. However, in large networks, the deployment and updates of static entries in the ARP caches are not common practice.

Depending on the OS, in principle, ARP request or reply messages allow us to create new entries and to update existing entries in the ARP cache. That is, if an entry does not exist in the ARP cache, an ARP response message allows us to create the entry in the ARP cache. In addition, when a host receives an ARP request message, it believes that a connection is going to be performed. Hence, to minimize the ARP traffic, it creates a new entry in its ARP cache for the addresses provided in the ARP request message. If the entry already exists in the ARP cache, then ARP request or response messages allow its update by the addresses (the source MAC and IP addresses) provided in the ARP headers.

This chapter discusses three hands-on exercises. The first describes the ARP cache poisoning technique. The others are about implementing the DoS and MiM attacks, respectively, using the ARP cache poisoning technique.

The following hardware devices and software tools are used:

■ Cisco switch[*]
■ CommView tool[†]: Network monitor and analyzer tool (Sniffer)
■ CommView Visual Packet Builder[‡]: A Graphical User Interface (GUI) based packet generator

2.2 Lab 2.1: ARP Cache Poisoning Attack

2.2.1 Outcome

The learning objective of this exercise is for students to learn how to corrupt the ARP caches of hosts in a LAN.

2.2.2 Description

An ARP cache poisoning attack is the malicious act (by a host in a LAN) of introducing a spurious IP address to MAC address mapping in another host's ARP cache. This can be done by directly manipulating the ARP cache of a target host, independently of the ARP messages sent by the target host. To do that, the malicious host can either add a new fake entry in the target host's ARP cache or update an already-existing entry by fake IP and MAC addresses. These two methods are explained as follows:

1. **Create a new fake entry:** To do that, an ARP request message with fake source IP and MAC addresses in the ARP header is sent to a target host. When the target host

---

[*] http://www.cisco.net
[†] http://www.tamos.com
[‡] http://www.tamos.com

receives the ARP request message, it believes that a connection is going to be performed, and then creates a new entry in its ARP cache utilizing the fake source addresses (IP and/or MAC) provided in the message's ARP header. Consequently, the target host's ARP cache becomes corrupted with fake IP/MAC entries.

2. **Update an entry with fake addresses:** To do that, an ARP request or response message with fake IP and MAC addresses is sent to a target host. Thus, even if the entry already exists in the target host's ARP cache, it will be updated with the fake IP/MAC addresses.

2.2.3 Static ARP Cache Update

An efficient technique to protect an ARP cache against the poisoning attack is to use static entries in the ARP cache. The entries cannot be updated by ARP request and response packets and do not expire if they are static. However, this could provide a false sense of security under some OSs. In fact, there are OSs that mark static entries in their ARP caches, but authorize their updates by ARP request and response packets. Consequently, such entries cannot be considered static entries, but rather as permanent entries in the ARP caches. Several common OSs have been tested against the corruption of their static entries using ARP request and response messages. As examples, the following shows that only the ARP cache of Windows 2000 and SunOS Solaris 5.9 are vulnerable. Consequently, Windows 2000 and SunOS Solaris 5.9 do not prevent a malicious user from corrupting static entries. The remaining tested OSs prevented the corruption and update of static entries in the ARP caches. Therefore, in these OSs, a static entry is permanent and cannot be updated by ARP request and response messages.

Update of Static Entries in the ARP Caches Using ARP Request and Response Messages

	Can an ARP request update a static entry in the ARP cache?	Can an ARP response update a static entry in the ARP cache?	Status of the entry
Windows 7 Home Premium	No	No	Permanent and static
Windows Vista	No	No	Permanent and static
Windows XP	No	No	Permanent and static
Windows Server 2003 Enterprise Edition	No	No	Permanent and static
Windows 2000	Yes	Yes	Permanent but **not static**
Ubuntu 8.10, Kernel 2.6.27-7 generic	No	No	Permanent and static
Red Hat Enterprise 7.2, Kernel 2.4.9-e.12	No	No	Permanent and static
Free BSD 5.0	No	No	Permanent and static
SunOS Solaris 5.9	Yes	Yes	Permanent but **not static**

In principle, to corrupt the entries in the ARP cache of a target host, a malicious host generates ARP request or response messages, including fake IP and MAC addresses.

However, in practice, the success of this malicious activity depends on the OS of the target host. A malicious host may attempt to send fake ARP response messages to a target host even though the malicious host did not receive any ARP request message from the target host. If the OS of the target host accepts a fake ARP response message from the malicious host without checking whether or not an ARP request message was generated before, then the received ARP response message will corrupt the ARP cache of the target host. However, newer OSs are more robust and not vulnerable to this attack. Alternatively, the malicious host may attempt to send ARP request messages instead of ARP response messages. The following table gives the results of an experiment conducted on several common OSs. The objective of the experiment was to identify which OSs with dynamic entries in the ARP caches were vulnerable to the ARP cache poisoning attack.

Update of ARP Cache Entries Using ARP Request and Response Messages

Operating Systems	Windows Vista		Windows 7 Home Premium		Windows XP		Windows Server 2003 Enterprise Edition		Windows 2000	
Does the entry exist in the ARP cache?	Yes	No	Yes	No	Yes	No	Yes	No	Yes	No
ARP request	✓	✓	✓	✓	✓	✓	✓	✓	✓	✓
ARP reply	✓	X	✓	X	✓	X	✓	X	✓	✓

Update of ARP Cache Entries Using ARP Request and Response Messages

Operating Systems	Mac OS X Version 10.7.3		Red Hat Enterprise 7.2, Kernel 2.4.9-e.12		Ubuntu 8.10, Kernel 2.6.27-7 generic		Free BSD 5.0		SunOS Solaris 5.9	
Does the entry exist in the ARP cache?	Yes	No	Yes	No	Yes	No	Yes	No	Yes	No
ARP request	✓	✓	✓	✓	✓	✓	✓	✓	✓	✓
ARP response	✓	✓	✓	✓	✓	✓	✓	✓	✓	✓

Note: ✓ = the ARP request or response message is accepted by the system and therefore allows the update or the creation of an entry; and **X** = the ARP request or response message is rejected by the system and therefore does not allow the update and the creation of an entry.

The previous table clearly indicates that:

■ If the entry already existed in the ARP cache, all tested OSs allowed its update by ARP response (even in the absence of an ARP request) or request messages.
■ If the entry does not exist in the ARP cache, many tested OSs do not allow the creation of a new entry by an ARP response message. However, all tested OSs allow the creation of a new entry by an ARP request message.

Therefore, when using only ARP response messages, the ARP cache poisoning attack becomes difficult to realize against several OSs, as shown in the previous table.

However, it remains a possibility when using ARP request messages. In conclusion, most common OSs are still vulnerable to the ARP cache poisoning attack. Malicious users can use ARP request messages to create or update fake MAC/IP entries in the ARP caches of their target hosts. Also, ARP request or response massages can be used to maintain the existence of fake MAC/IP entries in the ARP caches of the target hosts.

2.2.4 Experiment

The following experiment describes how to corrupt the ARP cache of a target host. The experiment consists of the following steps:

Step 1: Assign static IP addresses to the network's hosts.
Step 2: View the ARP caches of the hosts.
Step 3: Build a malicious ARP request packet to corrupt a target host's ARP cache.

2.2.4.1 Network Architecture

The network architecture used in the experiment is shown in the following figure; the three hosts are connected to a Cisco switch.

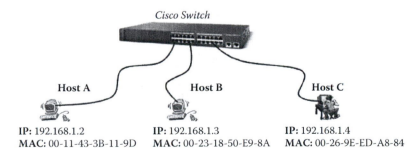

Cisco Switch

Host A
IP: 192.168.1.2
MAC: 00-11-43-3B-11-9D

Host B
IP: 192.168.1.3
MAC: 00-23-18-50-E9-8A

Host C
IP: 192.168.1.4
MAC: 00-26-9E-ED-A8-84

2.2.4.2 Step 1: Assign Static IP Addresses to the Network's Hosts

Refer to Chapter 1.

2.2.4.3 Step 2: View the ARP Caches of the Hosts

To display the ARP cache content of a host, type the online command: "*C:>arp –a*". For example, the screenshot below shows the ARP cache content of Host A (192.168.1.2).

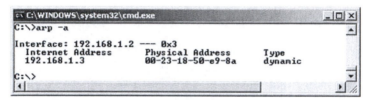

2.2.4.4 Build a Malicious ARP Request Packet to Corrupt a Target Host's ARP Cache

We assume that Host C wants to poison the ARP cache of Host A by inserting the following invalid entry: IP address of Host B <-> MAC address of Host C. Hence, Host C should send to Host A the following fake unicast ARP request:

ARP Header	
Operation code	1 (for ARP request)
Source IP address	**IP address of Host B**
Source MAC address	**MAC address of Host C**
Destination IP address	Any IP address
Destination MAC address	00:00:00:00:00:00
Ethernet Header	
Source MAC address	Any MAC address
Destination MAC address	**MAC address of Host A**
Ethernet Type	0x0806 for ARP message

Using any packet builder tool, the above fake ARP request can be easily built. CommView Visual Packet Builder provides a very friendly GUI interface to build ARP packets. The following screenshot shows the content of the fake unicast ARP request packet that is built to corrupt Host A's ARP cache.

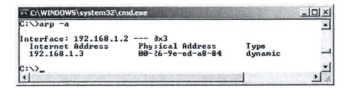

After sending the above fake ARP packet to Host A, the ARP cache of Host A becomes corrupted with the invalid entry, as shown below.

Consequently, as long as the ARP cache of Host A remains corrupted, all the traffic sent by Host A to Host B will be redirected to Host C. The following two exercises describe DoS and MiM attacks based on ARP cache poisoning.

2.3 Lab 2.2: DoS Attack Based on ARP Cache Poisoning

2.3.1 Outcome

The learning objective of this hands-on exercise is for students to learn how to perform a DoS attack, based on the ARP cache poisoning technique, in a LAN network.

2.3.2 DoS Attack Based on ARP Cache Poisoning

A DoS attack based on ARP cache poisoning consists of preventing a victim host from communicating with one or more hosts in a LAN. First, a malicious host corrupts the ARP cache of the victim host using the ARP cache poisoning technique (described in Lab 2.1). That is, the victim host's ARP cache is updated with fake entries (IP address and MAC address), corresponding to invalid association of IP addresses and nonexistent MAC addresses. Later, when the victim host attempts to send packets to a host, the packet will be sent to a nonexistent host, causing a DoS attack situation. Therefore, the victim host will be prevented from sending packets to the legitimate destination host.

The following figure shows the ARP cache of the victim Host A before the ARP cache poisoning attack.

Host A's ARP cache	
IP address	**MAC address**
IP_of_host_B	MAC_address_of_host_B
IP_of_host_C	MAC_address_of_host_C

And the next figure depicts the ARP cache of Host A after the ARP cache poisoning attack.

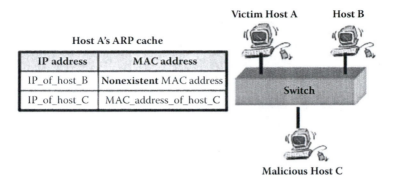

The cache includes a fake entry corresponding to the association of the IP address of Host B with a nonexistent MAC address. Consequently, any packet sent to Host B by Host A will be redirected to a nonexistent host. This is a DoS situation, as Host A's packets are prevented from reaching Host B. Hence, Host A and Host B cannot communicate properly unless the fake entry in the ARP cache of Host A is removed. This can be done when Host A refreshes its ARP cache content or by updating it when a legitimate ARP request or response packet is received. However, the malicious Host C may keep sending the fake ARP request to Host A, and consequently the fake entry remains in the ARP cache and the DoS situation will persist.

To poison Host A's ARP cache, the malicious Host C should send to the victim Host A the following fake unicast ARP request packet:

ARP Header	
Operation code	1 (for ARP request)
Source IP address	**IP address of Host B**
Source MAC address	**Nonexistent MAC address**
Destination IP address	Any IP address
Destination MAC address	00:00:00:00:00:00

Ethernet Header	
Source MAC address	Any MAC address
Destination MAC address	**MAC address of Host A**
Ethernet Type	0x0806 for ARP message

2.3.3 Experiment

This experiment describes how to practically perform DoS attacks based on the ARP cache poisoning technique. The experiment uses the same network architecture described in Lab 2.1. In addition, we assume that Host C is the malicious host and plans to deny Host A (victim) from communicating with Host B. To perform this DoS attack, Host C needs to corrupt the ARP cache of Host A by inserting a fake entry in Host A's ARP cache. The fake entry is the IP address of Host B associated with a nonexistent MAC address. The experiment consists of the following steps:

Step 1: Assign static IP addresses to the network's hosts.
Step 2: View Host A's ARP cache.
Step 3: Build the malicious ARP request packet.
Step 4: Test the DoS attack.

2.3.3.1 Step 1: Assign Static IP Addresses to the Network's Hosts

Refer to Chapter 1.

2.3.3.2 Step 2: View Host A's ARP Cache

The next screenshot shows the content of Host A's ARP cache before the ARP cache poisoning attack.

```
C:\WINDOWS\system32\cmd.exe                          _ □ x
C:\>arp -a

Interface: 192.168.1.2 --- 0x3
  Internet Address      Physical Address      Type
  192.168.1.3           00-23-18-50-e9-8a     dynamic

C:\>
```

2.3.3.3 *Step 3: Build the Malicious ARP Request Packet*

The malicious ARP packet issued from Host C intends to corrupt Host A's ARP cache. The fields of the headers of the malicious ARP request packet are set as follows:

ARP Header	
Operation code	1 (for ARP request)
Source IP address	**IP address of Host B**
Source MAC address	**AA:AA:AA:AA:AA:AA** **(Nonexistent fake MAC address)**
Destination IP address	Any IP address
Destination MAC address	00:00:00:00:00:00
Ethernet Header	
Source MAC address	Any MAC address
Destination MAC address	**MAC address of Host A**
Ethernet Type	0x0806 for ARP message

CommView Visual Packet Builder is used to build the malicious unicast ARP request packet to corrupt Host A's ARP cache. The next screenshot shows the content of the malicious unicast ARP request packet.

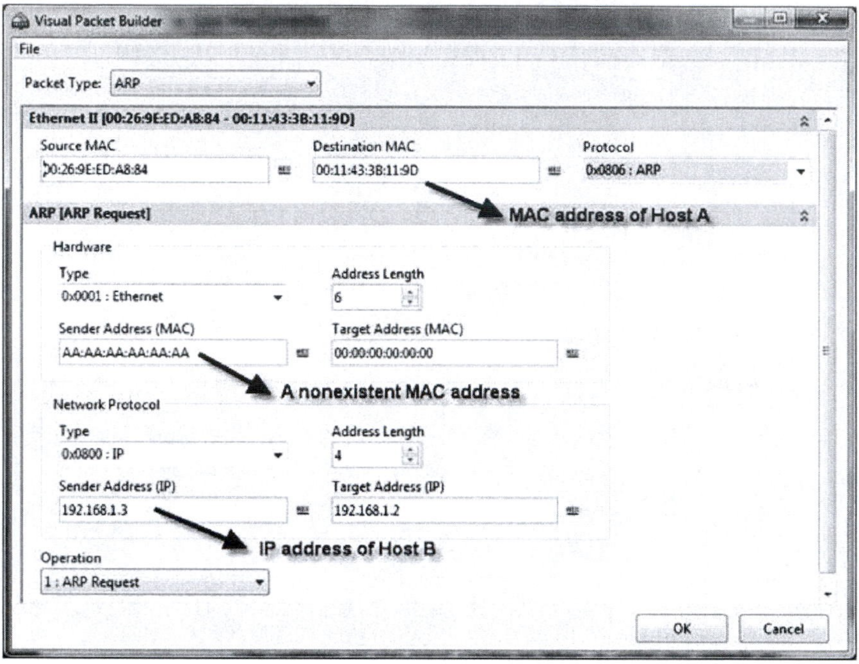

The following screenshot shows the corrupted content of Host A's ARP cache after the attack.

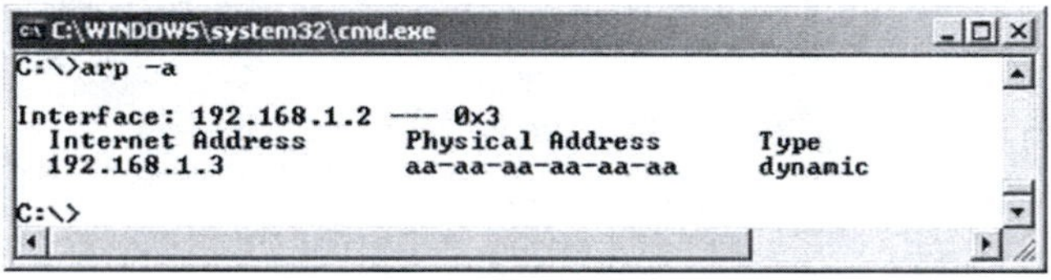

2.3.3.4 Step 4: Test the DoS Attack

To test the DoS attack, Host A pings Host B from the MS-DOS command window (C:\> ping 192.168.1.3). The following screenshot clearly shows that Host A is not getting any Ping response from Host B. This is not because Host B is not connected to the network or is denying Ping requests from Host A using a firewall. Rather, it is because the ARP cache of Host A is corrupted and the Ping request (the ICMP echo packet) did not reach Host B in order to generate the Ping response (the ICMP response packet). The Ping request has been sent to a nonexistent host whose MAC address is "aa-aa-aa-aa-aa-aa". Consequently, no ICMP response packet will be generated by Host B.

```
C:\WINDOWS\system32\cmd.exe - ping 12.168.1.3                _|□|×|
C:\>ping 12.168.1.3

Pinging 12.168.1.3 with 32 bytes of data:

Request timed out.
Request timed out.
Request timed out.
```

2.4 Lab 2.3: MiM Attack Based on ARP Cache Poisoning

2.4.1 Outcome

The learning objective of this hands-on exercise is for students to learn how to perform a MiM attack in LAN based on the ARP cache poisoning technique.

2.4.2 MiM Attack Based on ARP Cache Poisoning

A MiM attack is a common technique used to sniff network traffic in switched LANs and is based on fake ARP messages. This attack consists of rerouting (redirecting) the network traffic between two target hosts to a malicious host. Then, the malicious host will forward the received packets to the original destination, so that the communication between the two target hosts will not be interrupted and the two hosts' users will not notice that their traffic is being sniffed by a malicious user.

In this kind of attack, the malicious user first enables his host's IP packet routing, in order to act as a router and be able to forward the redirected packets, as illustrated in the following figure.

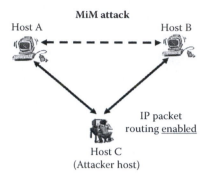

Then, using the ARP cache poisoning technique, the malicious user corrupts the ARP caches of the two target hosts, in order to force the two hosts to forward all their packets to the malicious host. This is extremely potent when we consider that not only can hosts be poisoned, but routers/gateways as well. All Internet traffic for a host could be intercepted by performing a MiM attack on the host and the LAN's router.

It is important to notice that if the malicious host corrupts the ARP caches of the two target hosts without enabling its IP packet routing, then the two hosts will not be able to exchange packets and it will be a DoS attack situation, as shown in the next figure. In this case, the malicious host does not forward the received packets to their legitimate destinations.

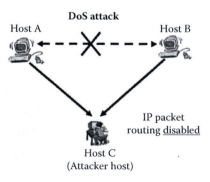

The MiM attack as shown above (i.e., second previous figure), where Host C is the malicious host and Hosts A and B are the two target hosts, is performed as follows. First, Host C enables its IP packet routing and then corrupts the ARP caches of Hosts A and B, using the ARP cache poisoning technique. The figure below shows the initial entries in the ARP caches of Hosts A and B before the ARP cache poisoning attack.

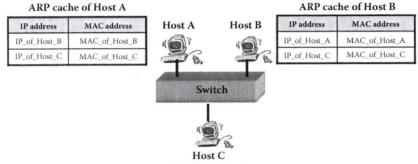

After the attack, the following figure shows the invalid entries in the ARP caches of Hosts A and B.

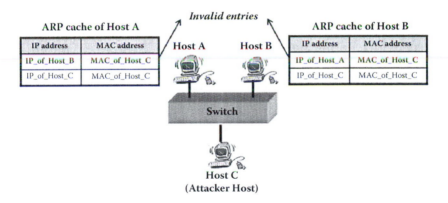

That is, Host A associates Host B's IP with Host C's MAC, and Host B associates Host A's IP with Host C's MAC. Consequently, all packets sent by Host A to Host B will first go to Host C. Then, Host C forwards them to Host B, as IP packet routing in Host C is enabled. Similarly, all packets sent by Host B to Host A will first go to Host C; then, Host C forwards them to Host A.

There are many easy-to-use tools that allow performing a MiM attack using mainly the above described technique. Examples of such tools are *ARP Spoof Tool*, *Winarp_mim*, *SwitchSniffer*, *WinArpSpoof*, *WinArpAttacker*, and *Cain & Abel*. However, using these ready-to-use tools, students will not be able to learn how a MiM attack is practically performed. Therefore, for educational purposes only, the experiment below describes the steps to perform the MiM attack.

As an example, the next screenshot provides a screenshot of the GUI interface of the *SwitchSniffer* tool. The user first scans the LAN to identify the connected hosts and then simply selects his target hosts. The tool will then corrupt the ARP caches of the selected target hosts, allowing the user to sniff their traffic.

2.4.3 Experiment

The following experiment describes how to practically perform a MiM attack using the ARP cache poisoning technique. The experiment uses the same network architecture described in Lab 2.1. In addition, we assume that Host C is the malicious host and intends to sniff the traffic exchanged between Host A and Host B, using a MiM attack. To perform this sniffing attack, Host C needs to corrupt the ARP caches of Hosts A and B by inserting fake entries in their ARP caches.

The experiment consists of the following steps:

Step 1: Assign static IP addresses to the network's hosts.
Step 2: Enable IP routing at Host C.
Step 3: View the ARP caches of Hosts A and B.
Step 4: Build two malicious ARP request packets.
Step 5: Test the MiM attack.
Step 6: Sniff and analyze the traffic between Hosts A and B.

2.4.3.1 Step 1: Assign Static IP Addresses to the Network's Hosts

Refer to Chapter 1.

2.4.3.2 Step 2: Enable IP Routing at Host C

By default, IP routing is disabled. The malicious Host C needs to enable IP packet routing in order to act as a router and be able to forward the redirected IP packets it receives.

The online command "*C:>ipconfig/all*" allows one to verify whether or not IP routing is enabled at a host. The following screenshot shows that IP routing is disabled at Host C.

We assume that Host C is running Windows XP or Windows 7. To enable IP routing, the value of the system registry related to IP routing needs to be modified, as follows:

1. From the Start menu, click Run.
2. Type regedt32.exe or regedit.exe, and then click OK.
3. In the registry editor, navigate to:

   HKEY_LOCAL_MACHINE \SYSTEM\CurrentControlSet\
   Services\Tcpip \Parameters

4. Select the *"IPEnableRouter"* entry (see the following screenshot for enabling IP routing In Windows XP or Windows 7).

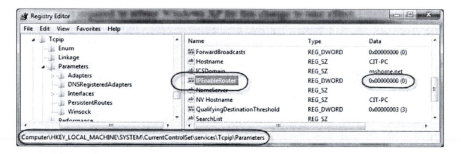

5. To enable IP routing, assign a value of 1 to the *"IPEnableRouter"* entry.
6. Close the registry editor.

It is necessary to reboot Host C for this change to take effect. The next screenshot shows that IP routing is enabled at Host C.

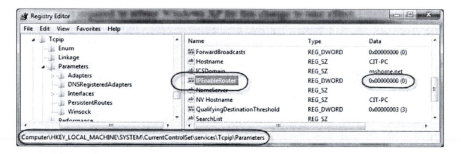

2.4.3.3 Step 3: View the ARP Caches of Host A and Host B

From Host A, ping Host B, and vice versa; then view their ARP caches. For example, the next screenshot shows the content of Host A's ARP cache.

2.4.3.4 Step 4: Build Two Malicious ARP Request Packets

To poison the ARP caches of Host A and Host B, two fake unicast ARP request packets are built, using CommView Visual Packet Builder. First, Host C sends a fake unicast ARP request packet to Host A to corrupt its ARP cache (as depicted in the following screenshot).

Then, Host C sends another fake unicast ARP request packet to Host B to corrupt its ARP cache (see screenshot below).

The following screenshots show the corrupted ARP caches of Hosts A (upper screen) and B (lower screen), respectively, after sending the above two fake unicast ARP request packets.

2.4.3.5 Step 5: Test the MiM Attack

If the previous steps are done properly, then when Host A pings Host B, Host A will normally get a ping response from Host B (ICMP response message). However, the traffic exchanged between Hosts A and B is first forwarded to Host C and then sent to its legitimate destination, all without their knowledge. This is because the ARP caches of Hosts A and B are corrupted.

2.4.3.6 Step 6: Sniff and Analyze the Traffic between Hosts A and B

Usually, when Host A pings Host B, an ICMP echo packet is sent by Host A to Host B. Then, Host B replies by sending to Host A an ICMP response packet. Hence, two packets are exchanged. However, in the MiM attack described in this hands-on exercise, four packets are exchanged. That is, the first packet is the ICMP echo packet sent by Host A to Host C. The second packet is the ICMP echo packet forwarded by Host C to Host B. The third packet is the ICMP response packet sent by Host B to Host C. The fourth packet is the ICMP response packet forwarded by Host C to Host A, as shown in the following figure.

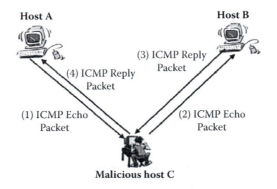

At Host C, *CommView sniffer* is used to capture the four exchanged packets. The analysis of the source and destination MAC addresses of the four captured packets clearly indicates that the exchanged ping traffic between Host A and Host B has been forwarded to Host C.

The following screenshot reveals that an ICMP echo packet (Packet #1) has been sent by Host A to Host C, although the destination IP address of the packet is the IP address of Host B.

The next screenshot shows that an ICMP echo packet (Packet #2) has been forwarded by Host C to Host B, although the source IP address of the packet is the IP address of Host A.

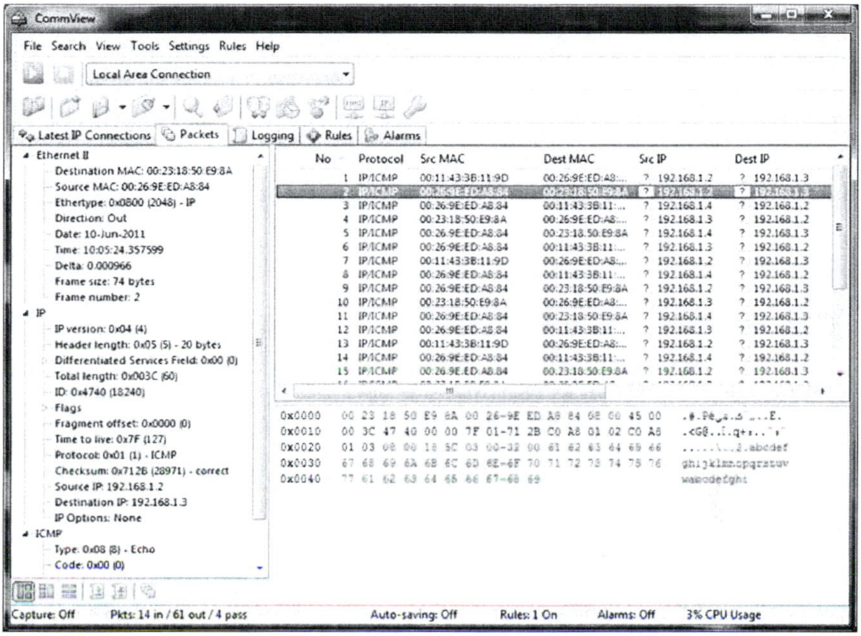

And the next screenshot shows that an ICMP response packet (Packet #4) has been sent by Host B to Host C, although the destination IP address of the packet is the IP address of Host A.

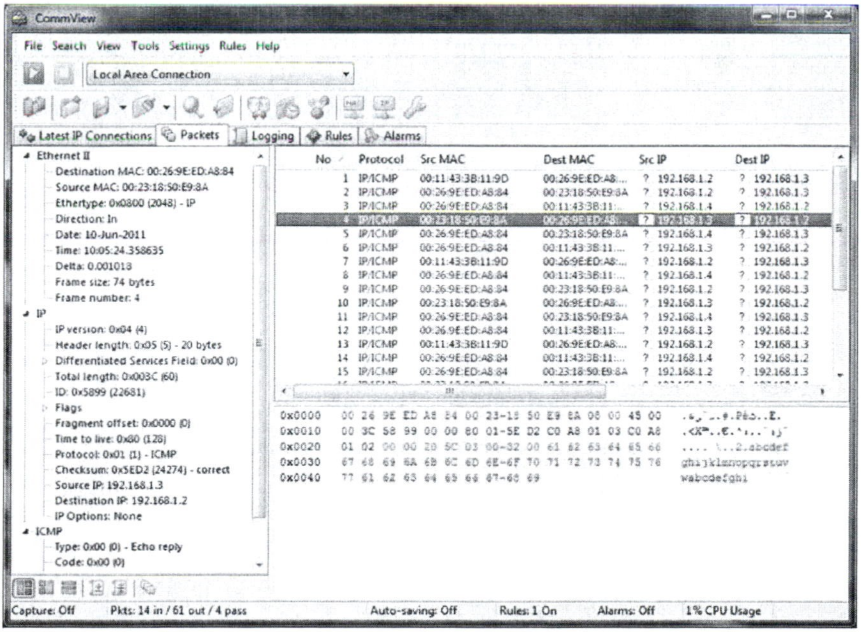

Below is a screenshot showing that an ICMP response packet (Packet #6) has been forwarded by Host C to Host A, although the source IP address of the packet is the IP address of Host B.

2.5 Chapter Summary

This chapter discussed the generation of DoS and MiM attacks based on the ARP cache poisoning technique. A DoS attack prevents a victim host from communicating with one or more hosts in a LAN. A MiM attack was used to sniff network traffic between hosts in a switched LAN. Students learned how to perform DoS and MiM attacks based on the ARP cache poisoning technique in switched LANs.

Chapter 3

Abnormal ARP Traffic Detection and Prevention

3.1 Introduction

Abnormal ARP (Address Resolution Protocol) packets are usually injected into a network to corrupt the ARP caches of target hosts. An ARP poisoning attack, described in Chapter 2, is an example of attacks that use abnormal ARP packets to eavesdrop and manipulate data flowing through a LAN (Local Area Network). Abnormal ARP packet based attacks are of special interest because they are highly intentional and are usually initiated, maintained, and controlled by humans. These attacks can be performed by novices, using widely available and easy-to-use tools specially designed for this purpose. More skillful users with malicious intent can use packet generators to build abnormal ARP packets to execute the attacks. Due to the high relevance of this problem, several security solutions, ranging from high-cost LAN switches, Intrusion Detection and Prevention (IDS/IPS) hardware appliances and software tools, to Unified Threat Management (UTM*) appliances, integrate mechanisms to cope with abnormal ARP traffic.

This chapter first evaluates common security solutions regarding their ability to detect and prevent abnormal ARP traffic. Then the chapter describes three hands-on labs. The first hands-on lab (Lab 3.1) is about the detection of abnormal ARP traffic using XArp 2. The second hands-on lab (Lab 3.2) is about the prevention of abnormal ARP traffic using the Dynamic ARP Inspection (DAI) security feature implemented on the Cisco Catalyst 3560 switch for Non-DHCP Environment. The third hands-on lab (Lab 3.3) is about the prevention of abnormal ARP traffic using the Dynamic ARP Inspection (DAI) and DHCP Snooping security features implemented on the Cisco Catalyst 3560 switch for DHCP Environment.

The hands-on exercises use the following hardware devices and software tools:

- Cisco Catalyst 3650 Switch†
- XArp 2‡: Abnormal ARP traffic detection tool
- CommView Visual Packet Builder§: A Graphical User Interface (GUI) based packet generator
- DHCP Turbo¶: a DHCP server tool

3.2 Abnormal ARP Packets

There are various types of abnormal ARP packets. Some packets are harmful and present very serious threats. Others are not as harmful but may have hidden content that is part of

---

* *UTM (Unified Threat Management):* is used to describe a security device that has many features in one box, including a firewall, an IDS or IPS system, e-mail spam filtering, anti-virus capability, and World Wide Web content filtering.
† http://www.cisco.com
‡ http://www.chrismc.de
§ http://www.tamos.com
¶ http://www.weird-solutions.com

potential malicious activities. Four possible types of abnormal ARP request packets and six possible types of abnormal ARP reply packets have been identified. Tables 3.1 and 3.2 list the identified types of abnormal ARP request and reply packets, respectively. The details are as follows.

- **P#1, P#5, and P#7**: Security devices should keep track of IP-to-MAC (Internet Protocol-to-Media Access Control) address mappings. Every ARP packet contains a mapping of the IP-to-MAC address. An ARP request packet contains the IP-MAC mapping of the sender. An ARP reply packet contains the IP-MAC mapping of the machine resolved. Every mapping is inserted into a database. If a monitored mapping breaks current mappings, an alert should be generated. An IP-to-MAC mappings database can be filled either automatically or manually.
- **P#2, P#6, and P#8**: ARP packets have special restrictions. In an ARP request and reply packet, the Ethernet source MAC address has to match the ARP source MAC address. In an ARP reply, the Ethernet destination MAC address has to match the ARP destination MAC address.
- **P#3**: A normal ARP request must be sent to the broadcast MAC address, and not to a Unicast MAC address. Such packets are used by ARP poisoning software to attack only a specific machine and not all machines in a LAN.
- **P#9**: A normal ARP reply packet must be sent to a Unicast MAC address, and not to the broadcast MAC address. Such packets are used by ARP poisoning software to attack all machines in a LAN.
- **P#4 and P#10**: There are fields in the ARP packet that have restrictions regarding the values they can adopt. These values should be checked for correctness. ARP mappings may not contain certain IP addresses. These include broadcast and multicast as well as null addresses.

Table 3.1   List of Possible Abnormal ARP Request Packets

Packet Identifier	P#1	P#2	P#3 (Unicast ARP request)	P#4 (Unexpected IP or MAC address in ARP request packets)
ARP Header				
ARP Operation	Request	Request	Request	Request
Source IP	IP address of a host A	IP address of a host A		0.0.0.0 255.255.255.255 Multicast Not in the network subnet
Source MAC	MAC address of a non-existent host	MAC address of a host A		00-00-00-00-00-00 ff-ff-ff-ff-ff-ff Multicast
Destination IP				0.0.0.0 255.255.255.255 Multicast Not in the network subnet
Destination MAC				
Ethernet Header				
Source MAC		MAC address of a nonexistent host		00-00-00-00-00-00 ff-ff-ff-ff-ff-ff Multicast MAC
Destination MAC			Unicast	00-00-00-00-00-00 Unicast or Multicast
Does the packet corrupt the ARP cache?	Yes	No	No	No

Table 3.2 List of Possible Abnormal ARP Reply Packets

Packet Identifier	P#5	P#6	P#7	P#8	P#9 (Broadcast ARP reply)	P#10 (Unexpected IP or MAC address)
ARP Header						
Operation	Reply	Reply	Reply	Reply	Reply	Reply
Source IP	IP address of a host A	IP address of a host A				0.0.0.0 255.255.255.255 Multicast Not in the network subnet
Source MAC	MAC address of a nonexistent host	MAC address of a host A				00-00-00-00-00-00 ff-ff-ff-ff-ff-ff Multicast
Destination IP			IP_B	IP_B		0.0.0.0 255.255.255.255 Multicast Not in the network subnet

(continued)

Table 3.2 List of Possible Abnormal ARP Reply Packets (Continued)

Packet Identifier	P#5	P#6	P#7	P#8	P#9 (Broadcast ARP reply)	P#10 (Unexpected IP or MAC address)
ARP Header						
Destination MAC			MAC address of a nonexistent host	MAC address of a host B		00-00-00-00-00-00 ff-ff-ff-ff-ff-ff Multicast
Ethernet Header						
Source MAC		MAC address of a nonexistent host				00-00-00-00-00-00 ff-ff-ff-ff-ff-ff Multicast
Destination MAC				MAC address of a nonexistent host	ff-ff-ff-ff-ff-ff	00-00-00-00-00-00 ff-ff-ff-ff-ff-ff Multicast
Does the packet corrupt the ARP cache?	Yes	No	No	No	No	No

Some MAC addresses in ARP packets are highly suspicious. For example, no IP-to-MAC mapping should have the MAC broadcast, multicast, or null address assigned. Every ARP packet's IP addresses must be in the same subnet. ARP packets with IP addresses that do not belong to the network interfaces subnet are suspicious and must be alerted.

Tables 3.1 and 3.2 show that only abnormal packets P#1 and P#5 can corrupt the ARP caches of target hosts, with fake IP-MAC entries. The remaining abnormal ARP packets do not corrupt ARP caches. However, they may still be harmful and hide potential attack activities, such DoS (Denial-of-Service) attacks. Therefore, the need to implement efficient security solutions that are able to detect all kinds of abnormal ARP packets becomes a must.

3.3 Experiments

Experiments were conducted extensively to evaluate the effectiveness of common security solutions in detecting and preventing abnormal ARP traffic. The selected security solutions are classified into four categories, namely,

- LAN switches
  - Cisco Switch 3560 Series
  - Juniper Switches EX3200 Series
- Software IDS/IPS
  - Snort IDS
  - XArp 2
  - Sax2 NIDS
- DS/IPS hardware appliances
  - Cisco IPS 4255 Series
  - TopLayer Model 5000
  - IBM ISS Proventia Model GX4004C
  - SourceFire
  - TippingPoint 50

■ Unified Threat Management (UTM) devices
  – Juniper Netscreen 50

Table 3.3 shows the security solutions that include ARP inspection mechanisms, regardless of the type of inspection.

In the experiments that follow, the "IPS TippingPoint 50" appliance is excluded because it includes ARP inspection that is not concerned with the detection of ARP cache poisoning activities. The appliance uses three ARP signatures to check whether or not the Hardware Type and Protocol Type fields in the Ethernet header contain valid values.

Among the security solutions that include ARP inspection mechanisms (Table 3.3), Table 3.4 shows the ones that can totally or partially detect the abnormal ARP packets listed in Tables 3.1 and 3.2. Using the data presented in Table 3.4, it is evident that no system offers an ideal solution for detecting ARP poisoning activities. Of the tested systems, XArp 2 is ideal in terms of the number of detected abnormal ARP packets. Snort IDS is a good alternative, but both of them perform only detection and are not able to prevent ARP poisoning attacks. The prevention or blocking systems, such as Cisco Switches 3560 Series or Juniper Switches EX3200 Series, are most ambitious but usually require complex installation procedures. In addition, the high cost of these switches makes this solution unaffordable for many companies. Cisco IPS is a prevention system and is a limited alternative solution because it can deal with few types of abnormal ARP packets (P#1 and P#5). Nevertheless, it is important to remember that packets P#1 and P#5 are the most used ARP packets during an ARP cache poisoning attack, as they are the only packets that can corrupt the ARP caches of target hosts.

Sax2 NIDS cannot detect any abnormal packet described in Tables 3.1 and 3.2. However, it can detect ARP request storm traffic and ARP scanning traffic. This type of attack traffic uses normal ARP packets.

Table 3.3   Security Solutions Performing ARP Inspection

	Type	Performing ARP Inspection? (Yes or No)	Detection or Prevention Solution?
Cisco 3560 Switch Series	Switch	Yes	Prevention
Juniper Switches EX3200 Series	Switch	Yes	Prevention
Snort IDS	IDS software tool	Yes	Detection
XArp 2	IDS software tool	Yes	Detection
Sax2 NIDS	IDS software tool	Yes	Detection
Cisco IPS 4425 Series	IPS appliance	Yes	Detection
TopLayer Model 5000	IPS appliance	No	Detection
IBM ISS Proventia			
Model GX4004C	IPS appliance	No	Detection
SourceFire	IPS appliance	No	Detection
TippingPoint 50	IPS appliance	Yes	Detection
Juniper Netscreen 50	UTM	No	Detection

In Table 3.4, *partially detected* means that the device detects all or some ARP request or reply packets that have unexpected IP and/or MAC source or destination addresses.

Table 3.4 Detection of Abnormal ARP Request and Reply Packets

	P#1	P#2	P#3	P#4	P#5	P#6	P#7	P#8	P#9	P#10
Cisco 3560 Switch Series	Detected	Detected	Not detected	Not detected	Detected	Detected	Detected	Detected	Not detected	Not detected
Juniper Switches EX3200 Series	Detected	Detected	Not detected	Not detected	Detected	Detected	Detected	Detected	Not detected	Not detected
Snort IDS	Detected	Detected	Detected	Not detected	Detected	Detected	Detected	Detected	Not detected	Not detected
XArp 2 tool	Detected	Detected	Detected	Partially detected	Detected	Detected	Detected	Detected	Detected	Partially detected
Sax2 NIDS	Not detected	Not detected	Not detected	Not detected	Not detected	Not detected	Not detected	Not detected	Not detected	Not detected
Cisco IPS Series 4255	Detected	Not detected	Not detected	Partially detected	Detected	Not detected	Detected	Not detected	Not detected	Partially detected

3.3.1 Cross-Layers ARP Inspection

To detect the abnormal ARP packets P#2, P#6, and P#8 described in Tables 3.1 and 3.2, the ARP inspection mechanism should be able to perform cross-layers ARP inspection between the Ethernet and ARP headers. In ARP request and reply packets, the Ethernet source MAC address must match the ARP source MAC address. However, in an ARP reply packet, the Ethernet destination MAC address must match the ARP destination MAC address. Table 3.5 lists security solutions that include cross-layers ARP inspection mechanisms.

3.3.2 ARP Stateful Inspection

ARP replies should normally follow ARP requests. A stateful detection process should remember all ARP requests and match them to ARP replies. Many ARP poisoning tools send ARP replies that are not requested. Table 3.6 shows the list of security solutions that perform ARP stateful inspections on ARP requests against ARP replies. ARP inspection mechanisms might give false detection reports in some cases as machines want to distribute their IP-to-MAC mapping to other machines

Table 3.5 Security Solutions Performing Cross-Layers ARP Inspection

	Performing Cross-Layers ARP Inspections?
Cisco Catalyst 3560 Switch Series	Yes
Juniper Switches EX3200 Series	Yes
Snort IDS	Yes
XArp 2	Yes
Sax2 NIDS	No
Cisco IPS 4425 Series	No

Table 3.6 Security Solutions Performing ARP Stateful Inspection

	Performing ARP Stateful Inspections?
Cisco Catalyst 3560 Switch Series	No
Juniper Switches EX3200 Series	No
Snort IDS	No
XArp 2	Yes
Sax2 NIDS	Yes
Cisco IPS 4425 Series	No

that did not request it. Among the above tested security solutions, the XArp 2 tool and Sax2 IDS are the only solutions that perform ARP stateful inspection.

3.3.3 ARP Request Storm and ARP Scan

3.3.3.1 ARP Request Storm

Dynamic ARP entries remain in the ARP cache for a few minutes and then they are removed if they are not referenced. Consequently, to keep the ARP cache of a target host corrupted with fake entries, malicious users may storm the target host with ARP request packets. In other words, the malicious host keeps sending fake ARP request packets continuously to the target host. If the number of ARP request packets per second exceeds the ARP request threshold, then this is an indication that an ARP request storm is taking place.

3.3.3.2 ARP Scan

The possible reason for ARP scanning in LANs is because of surveillance software that is active, or a virus performing ARP

Table 3.7   Security Solutions Including ARP Request Storm and/or ARP Scan Detection Mechanisms

	Detect ARP Request Storm?	Detect ARP Scan?
Cisco Catalyst 3560 Switch Series	No	No
Juniper Switches EX3200 Series	No	No
Snort IDS	No	No
XArp 2	No	No
Sax2 NIDS	Yes	Yes
Cisco IPS 4425 Series	No	No

scanning. Table 3.7 shows the security solutions that include mechanisms to detect ARP request storms and/or ARP scanning. Among the tested security solutions, Sax2 NIDS is the only solution that is able to detect ARP request storms and ARP scanning.

3.3.4 *Experimental Results Analysis*

The above experimental results show clearly that abnormal ARP traffic is not fully detected and prevented by the tested security solutions. It is evident that these solutions lack efficient detection and prevention mechanisms.

In addition to the basic abnormal ARP inspection features, security solutions should be able to

■ Perform cross-layers ARP inspection between the Ethernet and ARP headers. Among the tested security solutions, only Cisco Switch 3560 Series, Juniper Switch EX3200 Series, Snort IDS, and XArp 2 perform cross-layers ARP inspection.

- Perform ARP stateful inspection in order to remember ARP requests and match them to ARP replies. XArp 2 and Sax2 NIDS are the only security solutions that perform ARP stateful inspection.
- Cope with ARP request storm traffic and ARP scanning traffic. Sax2 NIDS is the only security solution that is able to detect ARP request storms and ARP scanning.

Based on the results from the above experiments, "XArp 2" is the most efficient available security solution to cope with abnormal ARP traffic. However, compared to the other tested security solutions, improvements can be made by adding security mechanisms to detect ARP request storms and ARP scanning. On the other hand, the Cisco Catalyst 3560 switch and Juniper EX3200 Series switches are examples of high-cost switches that use an efficient advanced security feature, called Dynamic ARP Inspection (DAI), for preventing abnormal ARP traffic.

3.4 Lab 3.1: Abnormal ARP Traffic Detection

3.4.1 Outcome

The learning objective of this hands-on exercise is for students to learn how to generate and detect abnormal ARP traffic using XArp 2 in a LAN.

3.4.2 XArp 2 Detection Tool

XArp 2 is an efficient tool that provides a security solution to detect abnormal ARP traffic. XArp 2 monitors Ethernet activities, keeps a database of Ethernet MAC address/IP address pairs, and detects unexpected MAC/IP association modifications and other abnormal ARP traffic. XArp 2 passively inspects the network traffic, searching for an indication of ARP attacks. XArp 2 presumes that the host running XArp 2 has access to a monitoring port on the switch (usually known as a SPAN port, or mirroring port).

There are other tools that include abnormal ARP traffic detection mechanisms. For example, Snort is an open source network intrusion detection system and is able to detect some types of abnormal ARP packets. Similar to XArp 2, Snort is a sensor that needs to have access to a monitoring port or be placed in a location where it can see all the network traffic. In short, solutions such as XArp 2 and Snort attempt to detect malicious behavior, rather than prevent it.

3.4.3 Experiment

The following experiment describes how to detect abnormal ARP packets using XArp 2 in a LAN. The experiment provides examples of XArp 2 alert messages generated after injecting different types of abnormal ARP packets.

The experiment consists of the following steps:

Step 1: Assign static IP addresses to the network's hosts.
Step 2: Install the XArp 2 tool.
Step 3: Configure a SPAN port in the Cisco switch.
Step 4: Generate and detect abnormal ARP packets.

3.4.3.1 Network Architecture

The network architecture used in the experiment is shown in the figure below. Three hosts are connected to a Cisco switch. XArp 2 is installed in Host C, and the switch port on which Host C is connected is a SPAN port (Fa0/9).

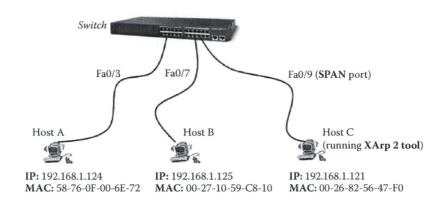

3.4.3.2 Step 1: Assign Static IP Addresses to the Network's Hosts

Refer to Chapter 1.

3.4.3.3 Step 2: Install the XArp 2 Tool

This step consists of installing XArp 2 in Host C and then selecting the aggressive security level, as shown in the next screenshot, in order to detect most types of abnormal ARP packets.

3.4.3.4 Step 3: Configure a SPAN Port in the Cisco Switch

The following steps show how to configure the Fa0/9 port in the switch as a SPAN port:

- Connect Host C to the console port on the switch.
- Start the configuration using the HyperTerminal tool. (Refer to Chapter 1 for further information on the HyperTerminal tool.)
- Type the following command to configure a SPAN port:

```
Switch> enable//enter the enable command to
access privileged EXEC mode
Switch# configure terminal
Switch(conf)#monitor session 1 source interface
fastethernet 0/3 both
Switch(conf)#monitor session 1 source interface
fastethernet 0/7 both
Switch(conf)#monitor session 1 destination
interface fastethernet 0/9
Switch(conf)#exit
Switch# copy running-config startup-config
```

After typing the above commands, all the traffic issued from Host A (Fa0/3) and Host B (Fa/07) will be sniffed by Host C (Fa0/9).

3.4.3.5 Step 4: Generate and Detect Abnormal ARP Packets

A packet issued from Host A is to be used to generate abnormal ARP packets. Because XArp 2 is monitoring Host A and Host B's traffic, the generated abnormal ARP packets are expected to be inspected by XArp 2. In this experiment, four types of abnormal ARP packets are generated using CommView Visual Packet Builder:

■ *Packet #1*: Host A sends a broadcast abnormal ARP request packet. The packet breaks the valid IP/MAC address mapping, as the source IP address/MAC address pair in the ARP header is invalid, as shown here:

ARP Header	
Operation code	1 (for ARP request)
Source IP address	**IP address of Host C**
Source MAC address	**MAC address of Host A**
Destination IP address	Any IP address
Destination MAC address	00:00:00:00:00:00
Ethernet Header	
Source MAC address	MAC address of Host A
Destination MAC address	Broadcast MAC address
Ethernet Type	0x0806 for ARP message

CommView Visual Packet Builder allows for generating the above abnormal ARP packet (Packet #1; see screenshot below).

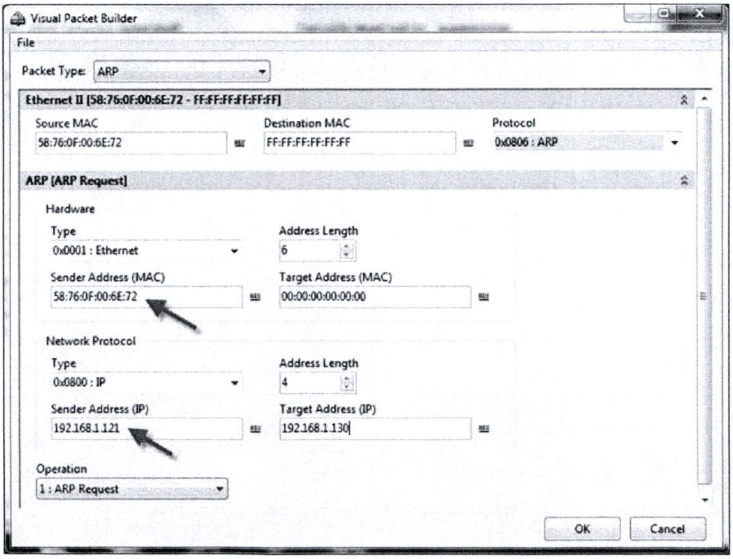

After injecting the abnormal ARP packet in the network, XArp 2 generated the tool's ChangeFilter alert message shown in the following screenshot.

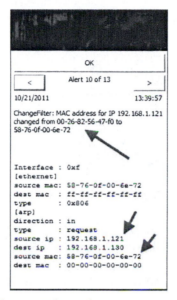

The XArp 2 ChangeFilter alert message indicates that the packet breaks current mappings. XArp 2 keeps track of IP-to-MAC address mappings. ARP requests contain the IP-MAC mapping of the sender. ARP replies contain the IP-MAC mapping of the host resolved. Every mapping is inserted into a database. If a monitored mapping breaks current mappings, an alert is generated.

■ *Packet #2*: Host A sends a broadcast abnormal ARP request packet. The packet has an Ethernet source MAC address that does not match the ARP source MAC address, as shown here:

ARP Header	
Operation code	1 (for ARP request)
Source IP address	IP address of Host B
Source MAC address	**MAC address of Host B**

ARP Header	
Destination IP address	Any IP address
Destination MAC address	00:00:00:00:00:00
Ethernet Header	
Source MAC address	**MAC address of Host A**
Destination MAC address	Broadcast MAC address
Ethernet Type	0x0806 for ARP message

CommView Visual Packet Builder allows for generating the above abnormal ARP packet (Packet #2; see screenshot below).

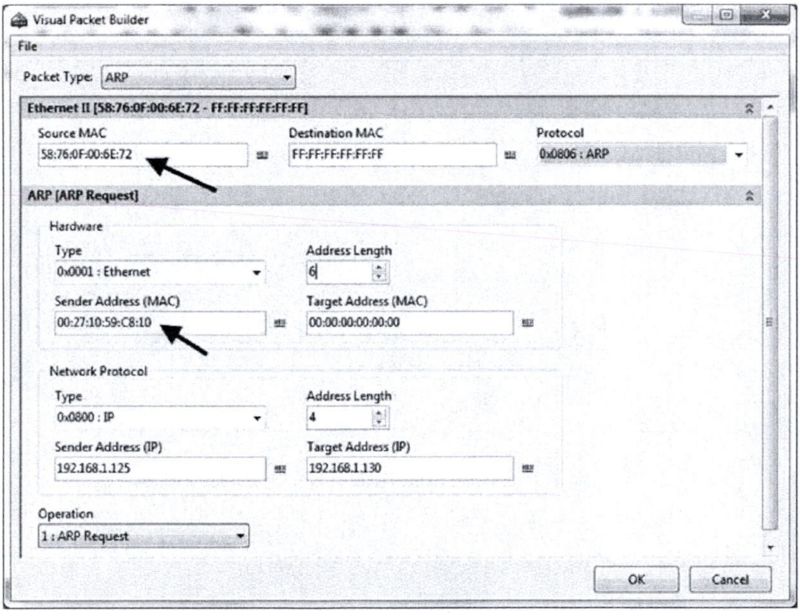

After injecting the above abnormal ARP packet in the network, XArp 2 generated the tool's CorruptFilter alert message shown in the following screenshot.

The XArp 2 CorruptFilter alert message indicates that the ARP packet includes incorrect values. That is, the Ethernet source MAC address does not match the ARP source MAC address. XArp 2 checks these values for correctness.

■ *Packet #3*: Host A sends an abnormal Unicast ARP request packet to Host B. An ARP request packet needs to be sent to the broadcast MAC address. However, in this experiment, the generated ARP request packet has been sent to a Unicast MAC address (MAC address of Host B), as shown here:

ARP Header	
Operation code	1 (for ARP request)
Source IP address	IP address of Host A
Source MAC address	MAC address of Host A
Destination IP address	Any IP address
Destination MAC address	00:00:00:00:00:00
Ethernet Header	
Source MAC address	MAC address of Host A
Destination MAC address	**MAC address of Host B**
Ethernet Type	0x0806 for ARP message

CommView Visual Packet Builder allows for generating the above abnormal Unicast ARP packet (Packet #3), as shown in the following screenshot.

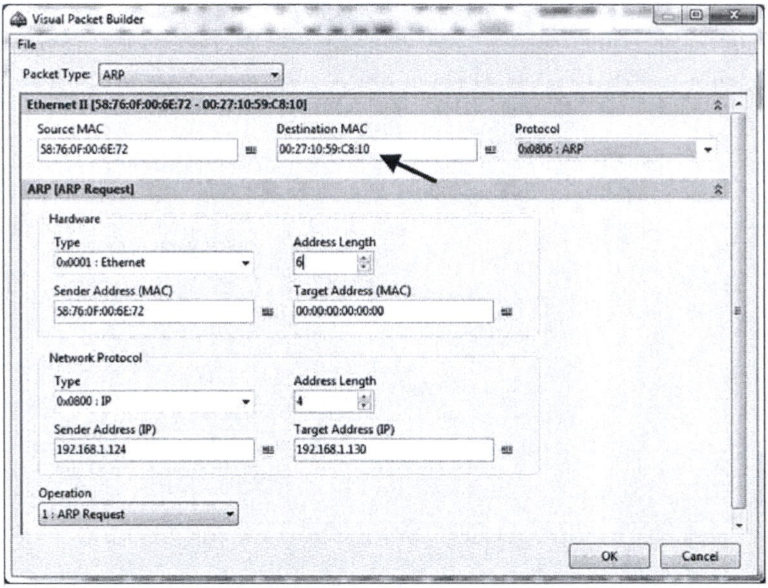

After injecting the above abnormal ARP request packet in the network, XArp 2 generated the tool's DirectedRequestFilter alert message as follows.

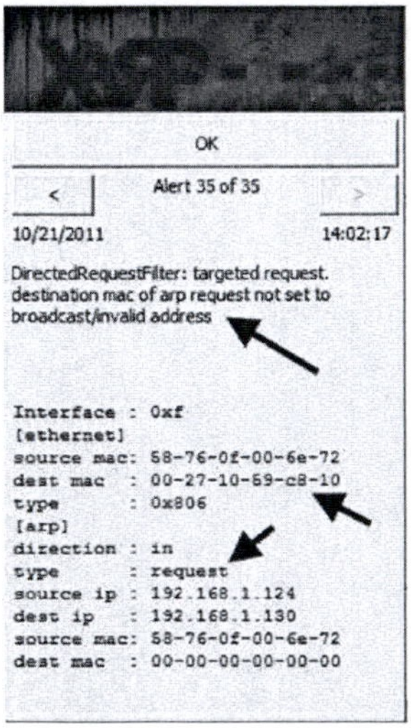

The XArp 2 DirectedRequestFilter alert message indicates that the ARP request packet is sent to a Unicast MAC address. However, ARP requests must be sent to the broadcast MAC address.

■ *Packet #4*: Host A sends an ARP reply packet that is not requested to Host B. That is, Host A sends an ARP reply packet to Host B, despite the fact that Host B did not send any ARP request packet. ARP replies should normally follow ARP requests. The following abnormal ARP reply packet that is not requested has been sent by Host A to Host B:

ARP Header	
Operation code	1 (for **ARP reply**)
Source IP address	IP address of Host A
Source MAC address	MAC address of Host A
Destination IP address	IP address of Host B
Destination MAC address	MAC address of Host B
Ethernet Header	
Source MAC address	MAC address of Host A
Destination MAC address	MAC address of Host B
Ethernet Type	0x0806 for ARP message

CommView Visual Packet Builder allows for generating the above abnormal ARP reply packet (Packet #4; see screenshot below).

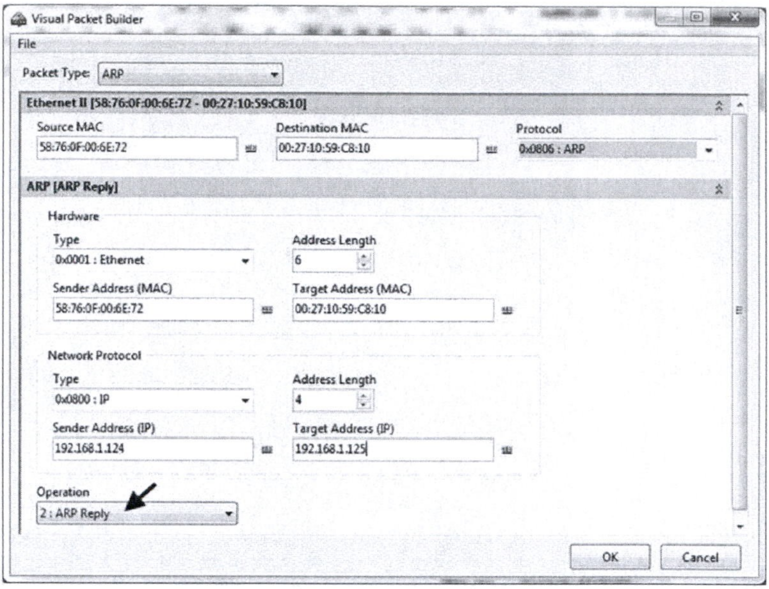

After injecting the above abnormal ARP request packet in the network, XArp 2 generated the tool's RequestedResponseFilter alert message shown in the following screenshot.

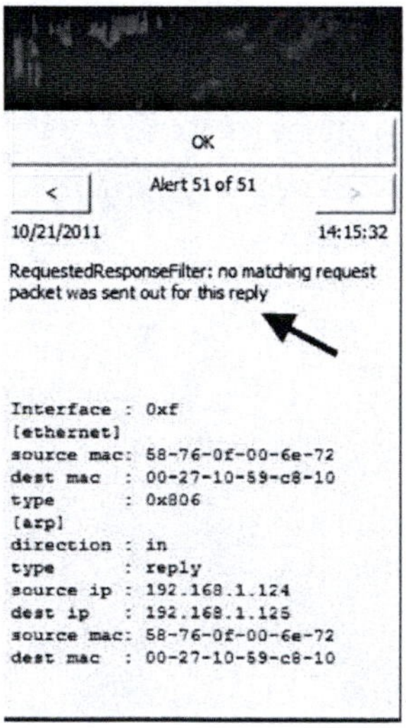

The XArp 2 RequestedResponseFilter alert message indicates that an ARP reply packet that is not requested has been generated. XArp 2 remembers all originating ARP requests and matches them to ARP replies.

3.5 Lab 3.2: Abnormal ARP Traffic Prevention Using Dynamic ARP Inspection for a Non-DHCP Network Environment

3.5.1 Outcome

The learning objective of this hands-on exercise is for students to learn how to prevent abnormal ARP traffic using the Dynamic ARP Inspection security feature for a non-DHCP environment in a LAN.

3.5.2 Dynamic ARP Inspection

Advanced switches, such as Cisco Catalyst 3560 switches and Juniper EX series switches, use a security feature called Dynamic ARP Inspection to discard abnormal ARP packets, mainly the ones with invalid IP-to-MAC address bindings. Dynamic ARP Inspection ensures that only valid ARP requests and responses are relayed. This feature helps prevent malicious attacks by not relaying invalid ARP requests and responses to other ports in the same LAN. This capability protects the network hosts from DoS and MiM attacks that use the ARP cache poisoning technique. Dynamic ARP Inspection relies on the use of an ARP Access Control List (ACL) that includes the valid IP-to-MAC address bindings. The ARP ACL list is created manually for a non-DHCP network environment and automatically for a DHCP network environment.

For example, we assume that four hosts (A, B, C, and D) are connected to a switch. In Cisco Catalyst 3560 switches, to protect the above hosts from an ARP cache poisoning attack, the following ARP ACL is created:

```
Permit ip host Sender-IP-A mac host Sender-MAC-A
Permit ip host Sender-IP-B mac host Sender-MAC-B
Permit ip host Sender-IP-C mac host Sender-MAC-C
Permit ip host Sender-IP-D mac host Sender-MAC-D
Deny ip any mac any log
```

Dynamic ARP Inspection can be also configured to drop ARP packets when the IP addresses are invalid or when the MAC addresses in the ARP header do not match the addresses specified in the Ethernet header.

It is important to mention that most switches use ARP ACLs to test only the validity of the source IP and MAC pair in the ARP header. They are not used to test the validity of the destination IP and MAC pair in the ARP header. This is because invalid destination IP and MAC pairs in the ARP header do not corrupt the ARP caches of target hosts.

3.5.3 Experiment

The following experiment describes how to prevent abnormal ARP packets using Dynamic ARP Inspection for a non-DHCP environment in a LAN.

3.5.3.1 Network Architecture

The network architecture used in the experiment is shown in the following figure. Three hosts are connected to a Cisco Catalyst 3560 switch.

The experiment consists of the following steps:

Step 1: Assign static IP addresses to the network's hosts.
Step 2: Configure Dynamic ARP Inspection for a non-DHCP environment in a Cisco Catalyst 3560 switch.
Step 3: Generate and prevent abnormal ARP packets.

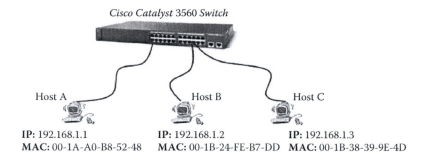

Cisco Catalyst 3560 Switch

Host A
IP: 192.168.1.1
MAC: 00-1A-A0-B8-52-48

Host B
IP: 192.168.1.2
MAC: 00-1B-24-FE-B7-DD

Host C
IP: 192.168.1.3
MAC: 00-1B-38-39-9E-4D

3.5.3.2 Step 1: Assign Static IP Addresses to the Network's Hosts

Refer to Chapter 1.

3.5.3.3 Step 2: Configure Dynamic ARP Inspection for a Non-DHCP Environment in a Cisco Catalyst 3560 Switch

- Connect Host A to the console port on the switch.
- Start the configuration using the HyperTerminal tool. (Refer to Chapter 1 for further information on using the HyperTerminal tool.)
- Type the following commands to create the ARP ACL list for the network shown in the previous figure:

```
Switch>enable //enter the enable command to
access privileged EXEC mode
Switch#configure terminal //enable global
configuration mode
Switch(config)# ip arp inspection vlan 1//
enable dynamic ARP inspection in vlan 1
Switch(config)# ip arp inspection vlan 1
logging acl-match matchlog //enable dynamic ARP
inspection on vlan 1, and ARP packets permitted
or denied by the ACL are logged.
Switch(config)#arp access-list ZouheirACL//
define an ARP ACL, and enter ARP access-list
```

```
configuration mode. For this example, the
access list name is "ZouheirACL"
Switch(config-arp-nacl)# permit ip host
192.168.1.1 mac host 00-1A-A0-B8-52-48 log
Switch(config-arp-nacl)# permit ip host
192.168.1.2 mac host 00-1B-24-FE-B7-DD log
Switch(config-arp-nacl)# permit ip host
192.168.1.3 mac host 00-1B-38-39-9E-4D log
Switch(config-arp-nacl)# deny ip any log
Switch(config-arp-nacl)# exit
Switch(config)# ip arp inspection filter
ZouheirACL vlan 1 static //apply the ARP ACL
(ZouheirACL) to the vlan 1
Switch(config)# exit
Switch# copy running-config startup-config//
this command allows us to save the configuration
```

It is important to indicate that the switch uses the ARP ACL
list to test only the source IP and MAC addresses of the sender
host in an ARP packet. It does not test the destination IP and
MAC addresses.

To verify the entries of the created ARP ACL list
« ZouheirACL », type the following command:

```
Switch# show arp access-list
```

The following screenshot shows the content of the ARP
ACL list « ZouheirACL ».

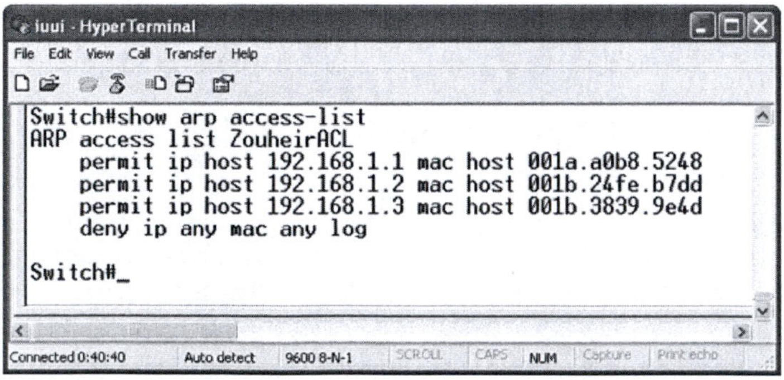

In addition, to configure the switch to perform additional checks on the source MAC address, the destination MAC address, the source IP address, and destination IP address, type the following commands:

```
Switch# configure terminal
Switch(config)# ip arp inspection validate src-mac
dst-mac ip
```

In the above command, the options "src-mac", "dst-mac", and "ip" allow the switch to perform additional checks, namely,

1. Option "src-mac" allows for checking the source MAC address in the Ethernet header against the source MAC address in the ARP header. This check is performed on both ARP requests and responses.
2. Option "dst-mac" allows for checking the destination MAC address in the Ethernet header against the destination MAC address in the ARP header. This check is performed for ARP responses.
3. Option "ip" allows for checking the ARP header for invalid and unexpected IP addresses. Addresses include 0.0.0.0, 255.255.255.255, and all IP multicast addresses. Source IP addresses are checked in all ARP requests and responses, and destination IP addresses are checked only in ARP responses.

Type the following command to specify the number of entries to be logged in the buffer:

```
Switch(config)# ip arp inspection log-buffer
entries 200
```

To display the configuration and the operating state of Dynamic ARP Inspection for the VLAN 1, type the following command:

```
Switch# show ip arp inspection vlan 1
```

The screenshot below shows the configuration and operating state of Dynamic ARP Inspection for VLAN 1.

```
ⁱiuui - HyperTerminal                                             _ □ ✕
File  Edit  View  Call  Transfer  Help
 D ☞ ⊜ ⅜ ⁰㝒 ☞

 Switch#show ip arp inspection vlan 1

 Source Mac Validation       : Enabled
 Destination Mac Validation  : Enabled
 IP Address Validation       : Enabled

   Vlan      Configuration    Operation   ACL Match       Static ACL
   ----      -------------    ---------   ---------       ----------
    1        Enabled          Active      ZouheirACL      Yes

   Vlan      ACL Logging      DHCP Logging
   ----      -----------      ------------
    1        Acl-Match        Deny
 Switch#_

Connected 0:46:05    Auto detect   9600 8-N-1    SCROLL   CAPS  NUM   Capture   Print echo
```

3.5.3.4 Step 3: Generate and Prevent Abnormal ARP Packets

We assume that Dynamic ARP Inspection is enabled at the Cisco switch. From Host A, four types of abnormal ARP packets are generated:

■ Packet #1: Host A sends the following broadcast abnormal ARP request packet. The packet breaks the valid IP/MAC address mapping, as the source IP address/MAC address pair in the ARP header is invalid, as shown here:

ARP Header	
Operation code	1 (for ARP request)
Source IP address	**IP address of Host C**
Source MAC address	**MAC address of Host A**
Destination IP address	Any IP address
Destination MAC address	00:00:00:00:00:00

Ethernet Header	
Source MAC address	MAC address of Host A
Destination MAC address	Broadcast MAC address
Ethernet Type	0x0806 for ARP message

The following screenshot shows the above-generated abnormal ARP packet using CommView Visual Packet Builder.

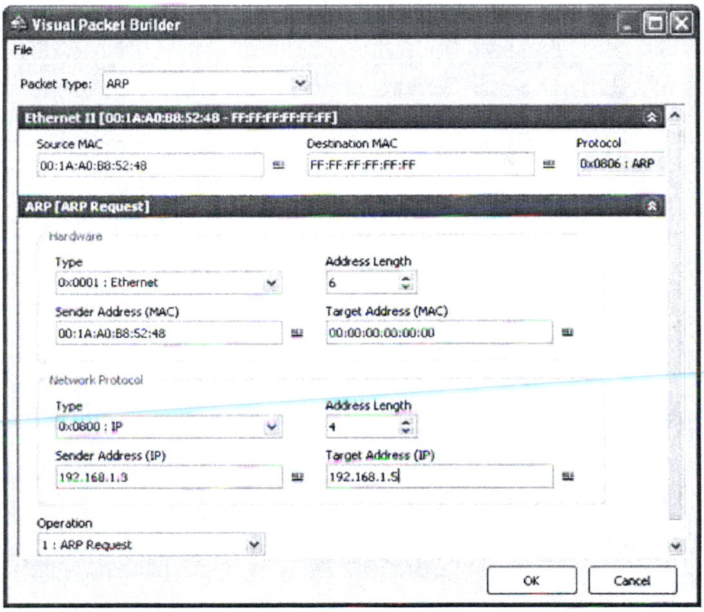

After injecting the above abnormal ARP request packet in the network, the Cisco switch discarded the packet. To display statistics about dropped ARP packets, type the following command:

```
Switch# show ip arp inspection statistics vlan 1
```

The following screenshot shows that the above-generated abnormal ARP request packet has been dropped by the Cisco switch's "ACL Drop" mechanism, because it contains an invalid source IP address/MAC address pair (192.168.1.3/00-11-43-3D-EE-48).

```
juui - HyperTerminal
File  Edit  View  Call  Transfer  Help

Switch#show ip arp inspection statistics vlan 1

 Vlan     Forwarded        Dropped      DHCP Drops      ACL Drops
 ----     ---------        -------      ----------      ---------
  1           0               1             0               1

 Vlan   DHCP Permits    ACL Permits    Source MAC Failures
 ----   ------------    -----------    -------------------
  1          0              0                  0

 Vlan   Dest MAC Failures   IP Validation Failures   Invalid Protocol Data
 ----   -----------------   ----------------------   ---------------------
  1           0                     0                        0
Switch#_

Connected 2:05:54      Auto detect    9600 8-N-1    SCROLL   CAPS   NUM   Capture   Print echo
```

■ Packet #2: Host A sends the following abnormal ARP request packet to Host B. The ARP packet has the source MAC address in the Ethernet header different from the source MAC address in the ARP header, as shown below:

ARP Header	
Operation code	1 (for ARP request)
Source IP address	IP address of Host A
Source MAC address	**MAC address of Host A**
Destination IP address	Any IP address
Destination MAC address	00:00:00:00:00:00
Ethernet Header	
Source MAC address	**MAC address of Host C**
Destination MAC address	Broadcast MAC address
Ethernet Type	0x0806 for ARP message

The following screenshot shows the above-generated abnormal ARP packet using CommView Visual Packet Builder.

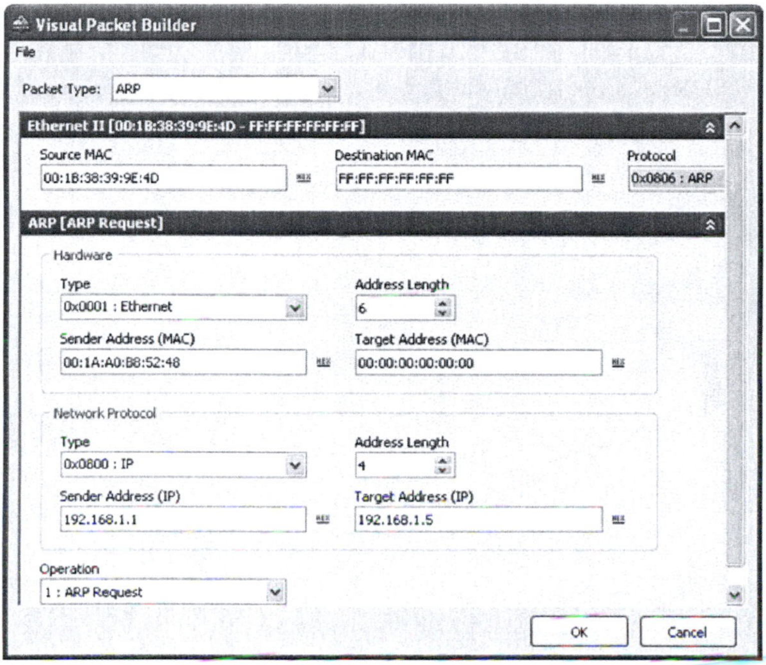

After injecting the above abnormal ARP request packet in the network, the Cisco switch discarded the packet. To display statistics about dropped ARP packets, type the following command:

```
Switch# show ip arp inspection statistics vlan 1
```

The screenshot below shows that the generated abnormal ARP packet was dropped by the Cisco switch's "Source MAC Failures" mechanism, because the sender MAC address in the Ethernet header does not correspond to the sender MAC address in the ARP header.

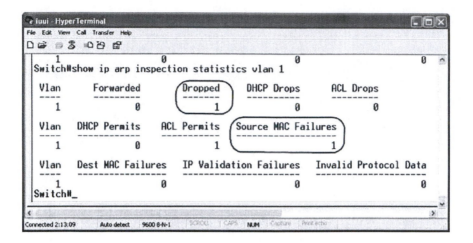

- Packet #3: Host A sends the following abnormal ARP reply packet to Host B. The ARP packet has the destination MAC address in the Ethernet header different from the destination MAC address in the ARP header, as shown here:

ARP Header	
Operation code	2 (for **ARP reply**)
Source IP address	IP address of Host A
Source MAC address	MAC address of Host A
Destination IP address	IP address of Host B
Destination MAC address	**MAC address of Host B**
Ethernet Header	
Source MAC address	MAC address of Host A
Destination MAC address	**MAC address of Host C**
Ethernet Type	0x0806 for ARP message

The following screenshot shows the above-generated abnormal ARP reply packet using CommView Visual Packet Builder.

After injecting the above abnormal ARP reply packet in the network, the Cisco switch discarded the packet. To display statistics about dropped ARP packets, type the following command:

```
Switch# show ip arp inspection statistics vlan 1
```

Below is a screenshot showing that the above-generated abnormal ARP reply packet has been dropped by the Cisco switch's "Dest MAC Failures" mechanism, because the destination MAC address in the Ethernet header does not correspond to the destination MAC address in the ARP header.

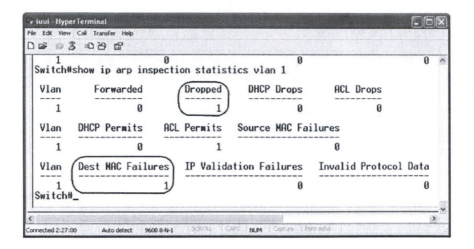

■ Packet #4: Host A sends the following abnormal ARP reply
packet. The packet contains invalid destination IP address
(255.255.255.255) in the ARP header, as shown below:

ARP Header	
Operation code	2 (for ARP reply)
Source IP address	IP address of Host A
Source MAC address	MAC address of Host A
Destination IP address	**255.255.255.255**
Destination MAC address	MAC address of Host C
Ethernet Header	
Source MAC address	MAC address of Host A
Destination MAC address	MAC address of Host C
Ethernet Type	0x0806 for ARP message

The switch uses the ARP ACL to test only the validity of
the source IP and MAC pair in the ARP packet header.
It does not test the validity of the destination IP and
MAC pair in the ARP packet header. This is because

invalid destination IP and MAC pairs do not corrupt the ARP caches of target hosts. However, the "IP Validation Failures" mechanism allows for verifying the ARP header for invalid and unexpected IP addresses, such as the IP address "255.255.255.255".

The next screenshot shows the above-generated abnormal ARP reply packet using CommView Visual Packet Builder.

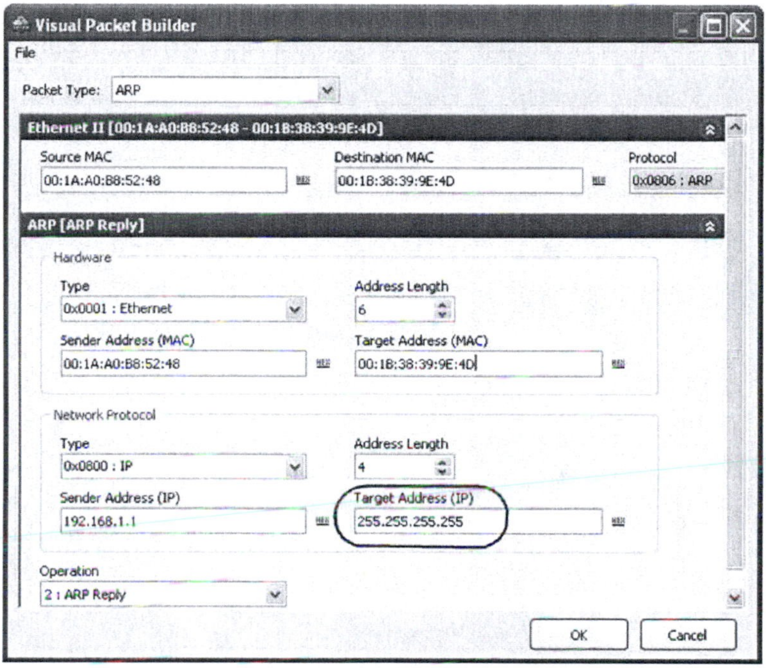

After injecting the above abnormal ARP reply packet in the network, the Cisco switch discarded the packet. To display statistics about dropped ARP packets, type the following command:

```
Switch# show ip arp inspection statistics vlan 1
```

Here is the screenshot showing that the generated abnormal ARP reply packet has been dropped by the Cisco switch's "IP Validation Failures" mechanism, because it contains an invalid destination IP address.

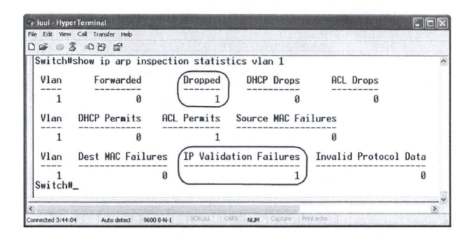

3.6 Lab 3.3: Abnormal ARP Traffic Prevention Using Dynamic ARP Inspection and DHCP Snooping for a DHCP Environment

3.6.1 Outcome

The learning objective of this hands-on exercise is for students to learn how to generate and prevent abnormal ARP traffic using Dynamic ARP Inspection and DHCP Snooping security features for a DHCP environment in a LAN.

3.6.2 DHCP Snooping

In a DHCP network environment, DHCP servers automatically assign IP addresses to hosts connected to the network, from a defined range of IP addresses. This is very often used in enterprise networks to reduce configuration efforts.

In a DHCP environment, the Dynamic ARP Inspection security feature in Cisco switches allows for determining the validity of ARP packets based on valid IP-to-MAC address bindings stored in a trusted database, the DHCP snooping binding database. This database is built by a mechanism called

DHCP snooping. When an ARP packet is received on a trusted interface, the switch forwards the packet without any check. On untrusted interfaces, the switch forwards the packet only if it is valid.

3.6.3 Experiment

The following experiment describes how to prevent abnormal ARP packets using Dynamic ARP Inspection and DHCP snooping for a DHCP environment in a LAN.

The experiment consists of the following steps:

Step 1: Enable DHCP snooping.
Step 2: Configure Dynamic ARP Inspection for a DHCP environment.
Step 3: Generate and prevent abnormal ARP packets.

3.6.3.1 Network Architecture

The network architecture used in the experiment is shown in the next figure. Two hosts are connected to a Cisco Catalyst 3560 switch on two untrusted ports. The third host hosts a DHCP server. The user can use any available DHCP server software. In this experiment, the DHCP Turbo server tool is used.

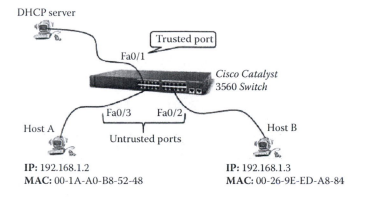

3.6.3.2 *Step 1: Enable DHCP Snooping*

To enable DHCP snooping and configure the Cisco Catalyst 3560 switch's port, on which the DHCP server is connected, as a trusted port (by default, the switch ports are untrusted), the following steps are required:

- Connect Host A to the console port on the switch.
- Start the configuration using the HyperTerminal tool (Refer to Chapter 1 for further information on using the HyperTerminal tool).
- Type the following commands:

```
Switch>enable//enter the enable command to
access privileged EXEC mode
Switch#configure terminal//enter global
configuration mode
Switch(config)#ip dhcp snooping//enable DHCP
snooping globally
Switch(config)#ip dhcp snooping vlan 1//enable
DHCP snooping on vlan 1
Switch(config)#interface FastEthernet 0/1//
enter interface configuration mode for
interface FastEthernet 0/1 (Port#1)
Switch(config-if)#ip dhcp snooping trust//
configure the interface as trusted. The
default is untrusted.
Switch(config-if)#end
Switch#copy running-config startup-config//save
the entries in the configuration file
```

Reboot the DHCP server and the Cisco switch to allow for building the DHCP snooping binding database. Then type the following command to display the contents of the DHCP snooping binding database:

Switch#show ip dhcp snooping binding

The following screenshot shows the content of the DHCP snooping database.

```
gb - HyperTerminal                                                          _ □ ×
File  Edit  View  Call  Transfer  Help
 □ ☞  ⊗ ⅜  ⬚ ⭧  ☞
Switch#show ip dhcp snooping binding
MacAddress          IpAddress        Lease(sec)  Type            VLAN  Interface
-----------------   -------------    ----------  -------------   ----  ----------
-----------
00:1A:A0:B8:52:48   192.168.1.2      258791      dhcp-snooping   1     FastEthern
et0/3
00:26:9E:ED:A8:84   192.168.1.3      258793      dhcp-snooping   1     FastEthern
et0/2
Total number of bindings: 2

Switch#_

Connected 0:26:17   Auto detect   9600 8-N-1   SCROLL  CAPS  NUM  Capture  Print echo
```

3.6.3.3 *Step 2: Configure Dynamic ARP Inspection for a DHCP Environment*

To configure the Dynamic ARP Inspection, type the following commands:

```
Switch>enable//enter the enable command to access
privileged EXEC mode
Switch#configure terminal//enter global
configuration mode
Switch(config)#ip arp inspection vlan 1//enable
dynamic ARP inspection on vlan 1
Switch(config)#end//return to privileged EXEC mode
Switch#show ip arp inspection vlan 1//verify the
dynamic ARP inspection configuration
Switch#show ip arp inspection statistics vlan 1//
check the dynamic ARP inspection statistics
Switch#configure terminal
Switch(config)#ip arp inspection validate src-mac
dst-mac ip//perform a specific check on incoming ARP
packets. Refer to Lab #3.2 for further information.
Switch(config)#ip arp inspection log-buffer entries
200//specify the number of entries to be logged in
the buffer. The range is 0 to 1024.
```

```
Switch(config)#ip arp inspection log-buffer logs 0
interval 1//this means that the entry is placed in
the log buffer, but a system message is not gener-
ated.
```

3.6.3.4 Step 3: Generate and Prevent Abnormal ARP Packet

Because DHCP snooping and Dynamic ARP Inspection are enabled, abnormal ARP packets with invalid IP/MAC address mapping are expected to be discarded by the switch. In this experiment, the user can use the same four abnormal ARP packets of the previous lab. As an example, we generate only the following abnormal ARP packet:

■ Packet#1: Host A sends the following broadcast abnormal ARP request packet. The packet breaks the valid IP/MAC address mapping, because the source IP address/MAC address pair in the ARP header is invalid, as shown here.

ARP Header	
Operation code	1 (for ARP request)
Source IP address	**IP address of Host B**
Source MAC address	**MAC address of Host A**
Destination IP address	Any IP address
Destination MAC address	00:00:00:00:00:00
Ethernet Header	
Source MAC address	MAC address of Host A
Destination MAC address	Broadcast MAC address
Ethernet Type	0x0806 for ARP message

The following screenshot shows the above abnormal ARP packet generated using CommView Visual Packet Builder.

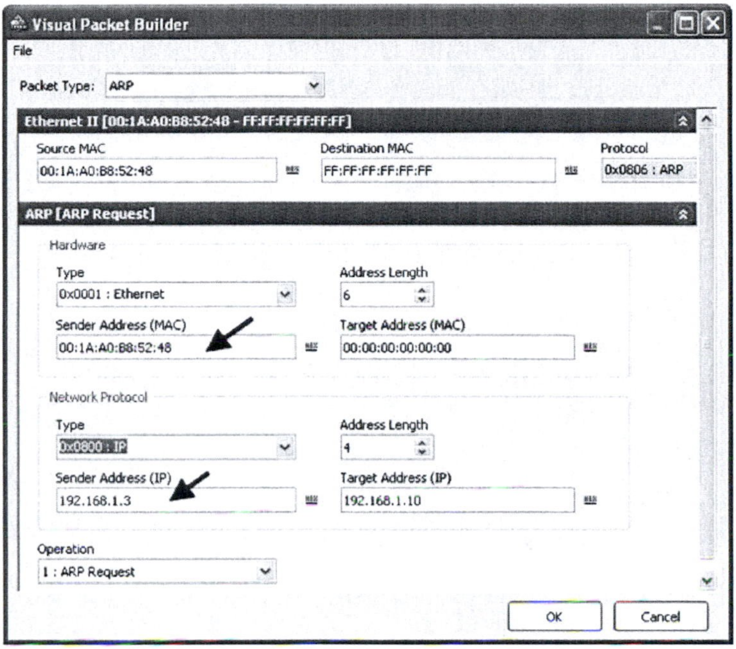

After injecting the above abnormal ARP request packet in the network, the Cisco switch discarded the packet. To display statistics about dropped ARP packets, type the following command:

```
Switch#show ip arp inspection statistics vlan 1
```

The next screenshot shows that the above-generated abnormal ARP request packet has been dropped by the Cisco switch's "DHCP Deny" mechanism, because it contains an invalid source IP address/MAC address pair (192.168.1.3/00-1A-A0-B8-52-48).

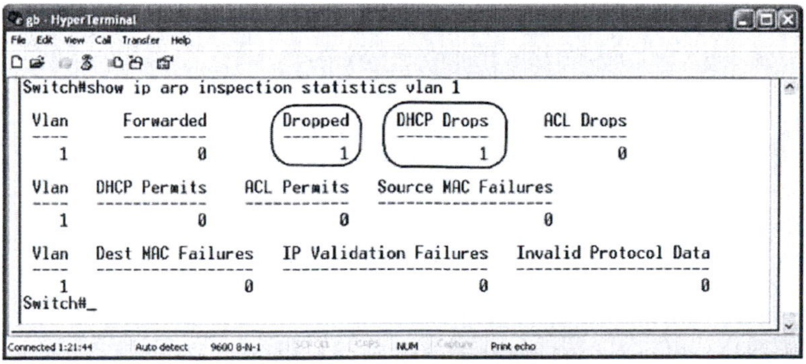

3.7 Chapter Summary

In this chapter, security solutions that detect and prevent abnormal ARP traffic were analyzed and evaluated based on practical experiments. It is clear that the detection and prevention of abnormal ARP traffic have not been given enough attention by most common security solutions, even though some abnormal ARP traffic may present serious threats.

This chapter described three hands-on exercises: (1) the detection of abnormal ARP traffic using XArp 2, (2) the prevention of abnormal ARP traffic using the Dynamic ARP Inspection (DAI) security feature for a non-DHCP environment in Cisco Catalyst 3560 switches, and (3) the prevention of abnormal ARP traffic using the Dynamic ARP Inspection and DHCP snooping security features for a DHCP environment in Cisco Catalyst 3560 switches.

Chapter 4

Network Traffic Sniffing and Promiscuous Mode Detection

4.1 Introduction

A sniffing attack is among the various types of attacks on Local Area Networks (LANs). It is an easy attack to perform and may be very harmful. Network traffic sniffing allows malicious users to easily steal confidential data, passwords, and anyone's privacy. Because many basic services, such as FTP (File Transfer Protocol), Telnet, and e-mail (SMTP/POP3), send passwords and data in cleartext, malicious users can easily spy on the network's users by analyzing the contents of the corresponding captured network traffic. For other services, a decryption program may be needed to pull passwords out of data streams. All unprotected network traffic can be vulnerable to sniffing.

Network traffic sniffing can be done by simply downloading a free sniffer program from the Internet and installing it on a computer. In addition, in a switched LAN (non-broadcast network), a sniffing attack requires that the sniffing host be either connected to a SPAN (Switched Port Analyzer) port on the network's switch or use a technique, such as a MiM (Man-In-the-Middle) attack, described in Chapter 2, to redirect the target traffic. However, in broadcast LANs, there is no need to redirect traffic to the sniffing host or to connect the sniffing host to a SPAN port, because the network traffic is broadcast to all the network's hosts.

Sniffers are programs that allow a host to capture and display the contents of any packet that passes through the host's Network Interface Card (NIC), also known as the network adapter, even if it is not destined to the host. This can be done by putting the host's NIC into a mode called "promiscuous mode." This mode allows the NIC to blindly receive any packet, not just packets intended for it, on the Ethernet network without checking its destination MAC (Media Access Control) address at all, and pass it to the system kernel. Hence, packets that are not supposed to arrive at the sniffing host are no longer blocked by the host's NIC. By default, NICs are set to a mode called "normal mode." When a host's NIC is in normal mode, it captures only packets destined to the host, using a filtering mechanism, known as the NIC's hardware filter. That is, the host's NIC accepts only packets whose destination MAC addresses are sent to the host NIC's MAC address. In fact, NICs are represented by a 6-byte hardware address (Ethernet MAC address). The cards' manufacturers assign a unique MAC address for each card, such that each MAC address is unique in the whole world. All communications on an Ethernet network are based on this unicast hardware MAC address. However, a NIC can set up additional hardware filters in order to receive different kinds of packets. In normal mode, the NIC filters packets based on the hardware filter that has been set up. The following are possible additional hardware filters:

- *Broadcast*: This filter allows the NIC to receive broad-cast packets that have a destination MAC address set to "*FF:FF:FF:FF:FF:FF*".
- *Multicast*: This filter allows the NIC to receive all packets that are specifically configured to arrive at some multicast group addresses. Only packets from the hardware multi-cast addresses registered beforehand in the multicast list can be received by the NIC. Multicast packets have a desti-nation MAC address set to "*01:00:5E:xx:xx:xx*".
- *All Multicast*: This filter allows the NIC to receive all multicast packets that have their group bit set to "*01:xx:xx:xx:xx:xx*".

The following three screenshots are examples of sniffing the password of an FTP session. The CommView sniffer is used to capture the FTP session traffic. The first screenshot shows the GUI (Graphical User Interface) of the LeapFTP tool (FTP client) connected to the FTP server (ftp.crcpress.com) using a username and a password.

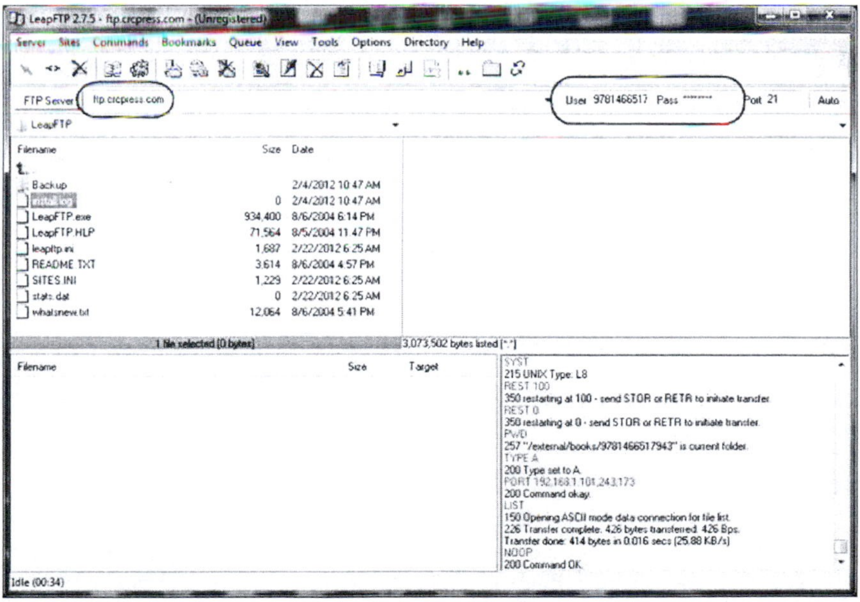

The next screenshot shows the username ("9781466517943") of the FTP session captured by the CommView sniffer.

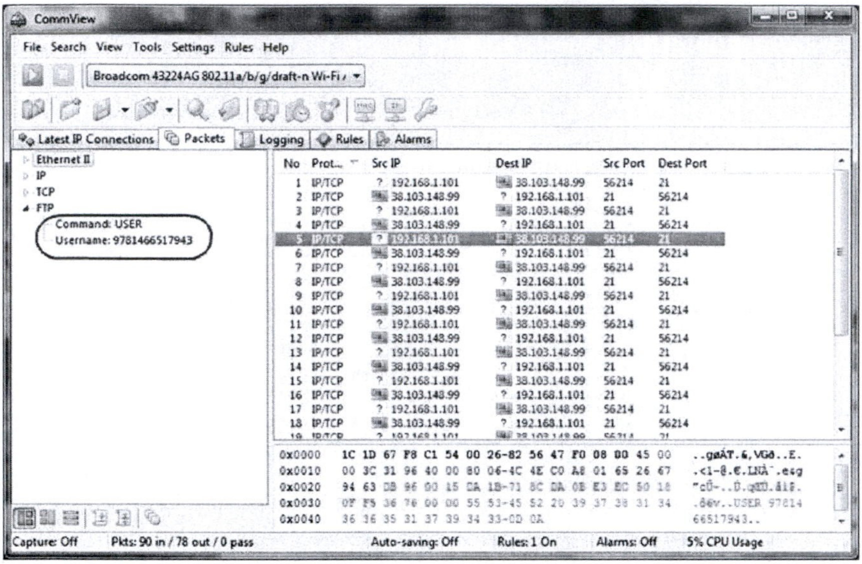

And the following screenshot shows the password of the FTP session captured by the CommView sniffer.

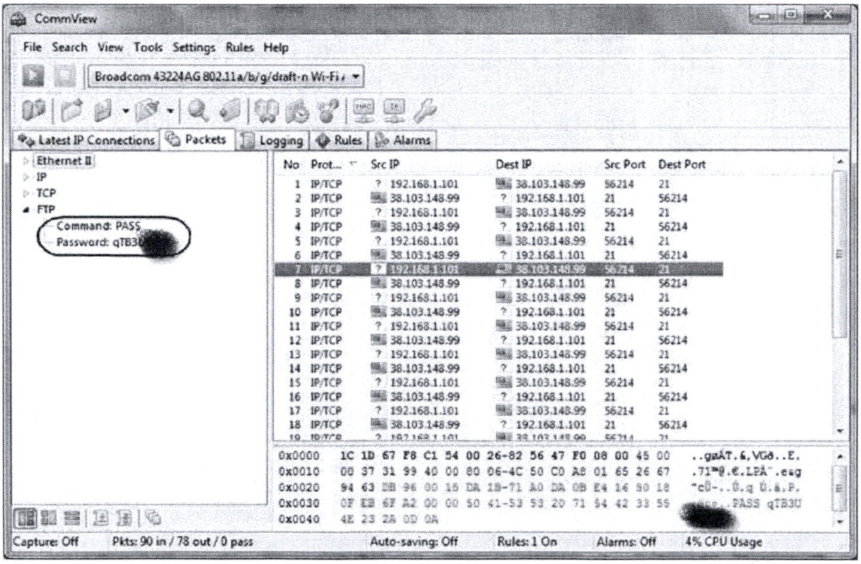

There are many available ready-to-use password sniffer programs that support password monitoring through FTP, POP3 (Post Office Protocol 3), SMTP (Simple Mail Transfer Protocol), HTTP (HyperText Transfer Protocol), and Telnet. Examples of password sniffers include Ace Password Sniffer (http://www.effetech.com/aps/), Password Sniffer (htt://www.packet-sniffer.net/password-sniffer.htm), and SniffPass (http://www.nirsoft.net/utils/password_sniffer.html). Password sniffers are, in general, small monitoring software that listens to networks, captures the passwords that pass through the network adapters, and displays them on the screen instantly. The next screenshot shows an example of sniffed passwords generated by the Ace Password Sniffer tool.

The sniffing attack on a network is usually difficult to detect because it does not interfere with the network traffic at all. In practice, the detection of sniffing hosts in a network consists of detecting the hosts with NICs running in promiscuous mode. Network hosts with NICs running in promiscuous mode can be considered suspicious hosts. It is important to note that some programs, once installed in a host, may set the host's NIC to the promiscuous mode without having the intention of performing any malicious sniffing activities. In addition, the host's user is unaware of the fact that his host's NIC has been set to the promiscuous mode by the installed program. Such a host will be identified as a suspicious host because its NIC is running in promiscuous mode. In such a case, it is up to the network administrator to take the appropriate actions.

This chapter discusses a hands-on exercise about how to detect a NIC running in promiscuous mode. The following software tools are used:

- NetScanTools Pro*: promiscuous detection tool
- PromiScan†: promiscuous detection tool
- CommView tool‡: network monitor and analyzer tool (sniffer)
- CommView Visual Packet Builder§: a Graphical User Interface (GUI)-based packet generator

4.2 Lab 4.1: Promiscuous Mode Detection

4.2.1 Outcome

The learning objective of this exercise is for students to learn how to detect NICb running in promiscuous mode.

4.2.2 Description

When a NIC is running in promiscuous mode, packets that are supposed to be filtered by the NIC's hardware filter are now passed to the system kernel. Therefore, if we configure an ARP (Address Resolution Protocol) request packet such that it does not have a broadcast MAC address as the destination MAC address in the packet's Ethernet header, send it to a suspicious host on the network, and discover that the host responds to it, then the host is running in promiscuous mode.

Hence, this detection technique consists of checking whether or not a suspicious host responds to trap ARP request

---

* http://www.netscantools.com
† http://www.securityfriday.com
‡ http://www.tamos.com
§ http://www.tamos.com

packets that are not supposed to be treated by the suspicious host. Because a sniffing host receives packets that are not targeting it, it may make mistakes such as responding to an ARP request packet, which originally is supposed to be filtered by the host NIC's hardware filter. Therefore, the detection is performed by checking the ARP response packets when ARP request packets are sent to a suspicious host on the network.

As an example, the trap ARP request packet's destination MAC address is set to a MAC address that does not exist, such as "00-00-00-00-00-01". When the NIC is running in normal mode, the trap ARP packet is considered to be "to other host" packet, and it is refused by the NIC's hardware filter. However, when the NIC is running in promiscuous mode, its hardware filter is disabled. Then, the trap ARP request packet will be able to pass to the system kernel. The system kernel assumes that the packet arrives because it has been allowed by the NIC's hardware filter, and consequently a response packet should be generated. However, this is not true. There exists some sort of additional software filter in the system kernel, called the software filter. After the hardware filter, packets are actually filtered again by the software filter of the system kernel. Therefore, when a NIC is running in normal mode, both the hardware and software filters are enabled. However, when the NIC is running in promiscuous mode, the hardware filter is disabled, but the system kernel's software filter remains enabled. The types of filters performed by the software filter depend on the operating system's (OS's) kernel.

4.2.3 Tests

The objective of the tests is to identify the filtering mechanisms used by the software filters of several common OSs' kernels. For each OS kernel, the tests consist of identifying special MAC addresses that will be used by trap ARP packets to detect NICs running in promiscuous mode. If an ARP response is received as a result of the test ARP request packet, then the special destination MAC address included in the ARP request packet can be used to identify NICs running in promiscuous mode. The following list includes the special MAC addresses used in the tests.

- FF:FF:FF:FF:FF:FF (Br): This is the broadcast MAC address that all hosts in a LAN should receive. This address is not filtered by the hardware and software filters. It is used to check whether or not a host supports the broadcast MAC address Br.
- FF:FF:FF:FF:FF:FE (Br47), FF:FF:00:00:00:00 (Br16), and FF:00:00:00:00:00 (Br8): These are fake broadcast MAC addresses. They are used to verify whether or not the software filter checks all bits of a given MAC address to classify it as a broadcast MAC address.
- 01:00:00:00:00:00 group bit address (Gr): This is a MAC address with only the group bit set. It is used to check whether or not the software filter considers it a multicast MAC address.
- 01:00:5E:00:00:00 multicast address 0 (M0): This multicast MAC address is usually not used. It is used to check whether or not the software filter considers it a multicast MAC address.
- 01:00:5E:00:00:01 multicast address 1 (M1): This is a multicast MAC address that all hosts in a LAN should receive. This address is not filtered by the hardware and software filters. It is used to check whether or not a host supports multicast MAC addresses.
- 01:00:5E:00:00:02 multicast address 2 (M2): This multicast MAC address is called the "All Routers" multicast group address. It addresses all routers on the same network segment. Therefore, it is an example of multicast MAC addresses that are not registered in the multicast lists of NICs. It is used to check whether or not the software filter considers it a multicast MAC address.

■ 01:00:5E:00:00:03 multicast address 3 (M3): This multicast MAC address is an example of multicast addresses that are not assigned. It is used to check whether or not the software filter considers it a multicast MAC address.

Table 4.1 and Table 4.2 show the tests results for several OSs. After sending an ARP request packet, if no ARP response packet is received, an "—" is placed in the column. If a legal ARP response packet is received, an "O" is placed in the column. However, if an illegal ARP response packet is received, an "X" is placed in the column. An ARP response is said to be illegal when its corresponding ARP request packet is supposed to be blocked by the hardware or software filters and consequently no ARP response packet should be received. However, when the NIC is running in promiscuous mode, the test results show that the tested OS kernel's software filters do not properly filter several types of MAC addresses, mainly Br47 and Br16 addresses.

As expected, all tested kernels respond only to the broadcast MAC address Br and the multicast MAC address M1 when the NIC is running in normal mode. However, when the NIC is running in promiscuous mode, the test results are OS dependent. That is,

■ In the case of Windows 7, Windows Vista, Mac OS 10.7.3, Ubuntu 8.10, Red Hat Enterprise 7.2, and FreeBSD 5.0, their system kernels responded to all fake broadcast MAC addresses (Br47, Br16, and Br8) and to the MAC addresses with the group bit set (Gr, M0, M2, and M3). Therefore, the foregoing MAC addresses can be used to identify NICs running in promiscuous mode. The broadcast MAC address Br and the multicast MAC address M1 are not considered, as they are addresses that all hosts in the LAN should receive. For the foregoing OSs, the following figure shows that the fake broadcast MAC addresses Br47, Br16, and Br8 are filtered by

Table 4.1 Promiscuous Mode Detection for Windows Operating Systems

MAC Addresses	Operating Systems	Windows 7 Home Premium		Windows XP		Windows Server 2003 Enterprise Edition		Windows Vista		Windows 2000/NT	
		Normal	Promiscuous	Normal	Promiscuous	Normal	Promiscuous	Normal	Promiscuous	Normal	Promiscuous
FF:FF:FF:FF:FF:FF	Br	O	O	O	O	O	O	O	O	O	O
FF:FF:FF:FF:FF:FE	Br47	—	X	—	X	—	X	—	X	—	X
FF:FF:00:00:00:00	Br16	—	X	—	X	—	X	—	X	X	X
FF:00:00:00:00:00	Br8	—	X	—	—	—	—	—	X	—	—
01:00:00:00:00:00	Gr	—	X	—	—	—	—	—	X	—	—
01:00:5E:00:00:00	M0	—	X	—	—	—	—	—	X	—	—
01:00:5E:00:00:01	M1	O	O	O	O	O	O	O	O	O	O
01:00:5E:00:00:02	M2	—	X	—	—	—	—	—	X	—	—
01:00:5E:00:00:03	M3	—	X	—	—	—	—	—	X	—	—

Note: O: legal response, X: illegal response, —: no response.

Table 4.2 Promiscuous Mode Detection for Other Operating Systems

MAC Addresses	Operating Systems	Mac OS X Version 10.7.3		Ubuntu 8.10, Kernel 2.6.27-7 generic		Red Hat Enterprise 7.2, Kernel 2.4.9-e.12		FreeBSD 5.0	
		Normal	Promiscuous	Normal	Promiscuous	Normal	Promiscuous	Normal	Promiscuous
FF:FF:FF:FF:FF:FF	Br	O	O	O	O	O	O	O	O
FF:FF:FF:FF:FF:FE	Br47	—	X	—	X	—	X	—	X
FF:FF:FF:00:00:00	Br16	—	X	—	X	—	X	—	X
FF:00:00:00:00:00	Br8	—	X	—	X	—	X	—	X
01:00:00:00:00:00	Gr	—	X	—	X	—	X	—	X
01:00:5E:00:00:00	M0	—	X	—	X	—	X	—	X
01:00:5E:00:00:01	M1	O	O	O	O	O	O	O	O
01:00:5E:00:00:02	M2	—	X	—	X	—	X	—	X
01:00:5E:00:00:03	M3	—	X	—	X	—	X	—	X

Note: O: legal response, X: illegal response, —: no response.

the hardware filter when the NIC is running in normal mode.

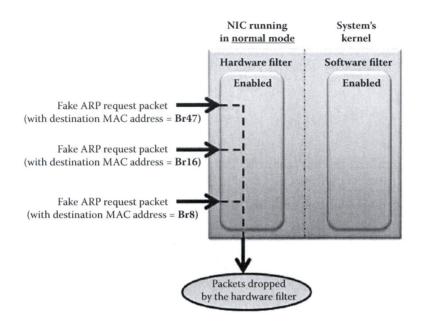

However, they are accepted and sent to the system kernel when the NIC is running in promiscuous mode, as shown in the figure below.

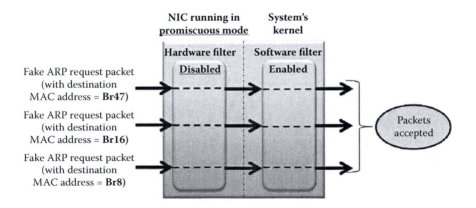

- In the case of Windows XP and Windows Server 2003, their system kernels responded only to the fake broadcast MAC addresses Br47 and Br16. Hence, the software filters determine the broadcast MAC address by checking only the first 2 bytes. Therefore, the addresses Br47 and Br16 can be used to identify whether or not a NIC is running in promiscuous mode.
- In the case of Windows 2000/NT, the system kernels responded only to the fake broadcast MAC addresses Br47 and Br16. Hence, the software filters of Windows 2000/NT identify the broadcast MAC address by checking only the first 2 bytes. It is important to notice that when the NIC is running in normal mode, Windows 2000/NT responded also to the fake MAC broadcast Br16. Therefore, only the fake broadcast MAC address Br47 can be used to identify whether or not a NIC is running in promiscuous mode.

4.2.4 Promiscuous Mode Detection Tools

A number of ready-to-use promiscuous detection tools are available, such as PMD (http://webteca.altervista.org/index.htm), PromiScan (http://www.securityfriday.com), Nmap (http://www.nmap.org), and NetScanTools Pro (http://www.netscantools.com). The tools are used to determine if there is a device listening to packets that should not be listening to packets. Most of these tools are based on the above-described detection technique. For example, the next two screenshots show the results of a promiscuous mode scanning of a target host using NetScanTools Pro and PromiScan tools, respectively. The MAC addresses used by these two tools are also shown. In NetScanTools Pro, the fake broadcast B31 corresponds to the fake broadcast Br47 (FF:FF:FF:FF:FF:FE).

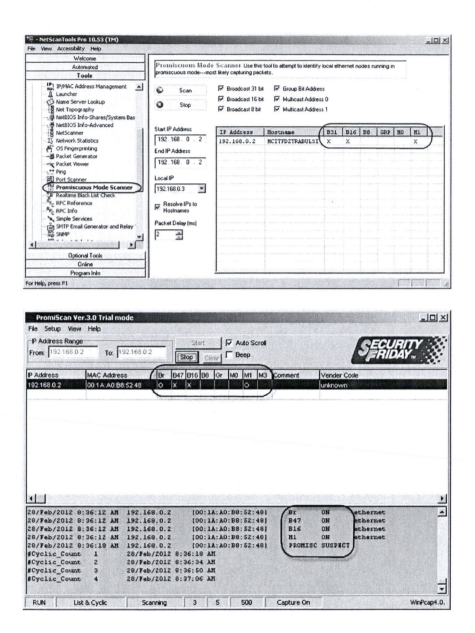

The major limitation of this detection technique is that if a sniffing host stops responding to ARP request messages while sniffing the network traffic, using, for example, a local firewall, then the technique becomes useless because it relies on the ARP response messages generated by the sniffing host.

4.2.5 Experiment

Because this book has an educational purpose, the following experiment describes how to manually generate trap ARP request packets to identify NICs running in promiscuous mode in a LAN.

4.2.6 Network Architecture

The network architecture used in the experiment is shown in the following figure. The two hosts, A and B, are connected to a switch and running the Windows 7 operating system.

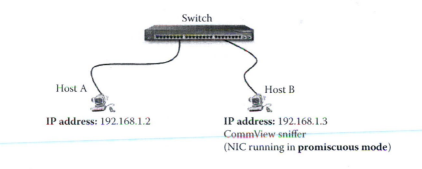

4.2.7 Experiment

The experiment consists of the following steps:

Step 1: Assign static IP addresses to the network's hosts.
Step 2: Run Host B's NIC in promiscuous mode.
Step 3: Generate trap ARP request packets.
Step 4: Analyze the ARP response packets.

4.2.7.1 Step 1: Assign Static IP Addresses to the Network's Hosts

Refer to Chapter 1.

4.2.7.2 Step 2: Run Host B's NIC in Promiscuous Mode

Install CommView sniffer (or any available sniffer tool) at Host B so that its NIC runs in promiscuous mode.

4.2.7.3 Step 3: Generate Trap ARP Request Packets

From Host A, tests are conducted to identify whether or not Host B's NIC is running in promiscuous mode. Hence, Host A will proceed to send a number of trap ARP request packets to Host B, using the fake broadcast MAC addresses Br47 and Br16, and the multicast MAC addresses M0, M2, and M3. The trap ARP request packets will look as follows:

ARP Header	
Operation code	1 (for ARP request)
Source IP address	IP address of Host A
Source MAC address	MAC address of Host A
Destination IP address	IP address of Host B
Destination MAC address	00:00:00:00:00:00
Ethernet Header	
Source MAC address	MAC address of Host A
Destination MAC address	Br47, Br16, M0, M2, M3
Ethernet type	0x0806 for ARP message

Using any packet builder tool, the above trap ARP requests can be easily built. CommView Visual Packet Builder provides a very friendly GUI to build ARP packets. The three screenshots that follow show the content of examples of trap ARP request packets with the destination MAC addresses Br47, Br16, and M0, respectively.

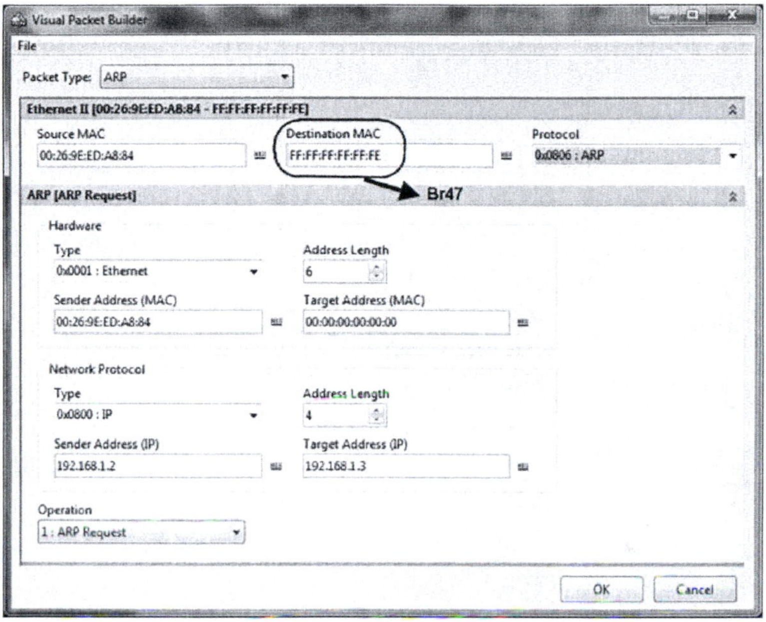
Visual Packet Builder
File
Packet Type: ARP
Ethernet II [00:26:9E:ED:A8:84 - FF:FF:FF:FF:FF:FE]
Source MAC
00:26:9E:ED:A8:84
Destination MAC
FF:FF:FF:FF:FF:FE
Protocol
0x0806 : ARP
Br47
ARP [ARP Request]
Hardware
Type
0x0001 : Ethernet
Address Length
6
Sender Address (MAC)
00:26:9E:ED:A8:84
Target Address (MAC)
00:00:00:00:00:00
Network Protocol
Type
0x0800 : IP
Address Length
4
Sender Address (IP)
192.168.1.2
Target Address (IP)
192.168.1.3
Operation
1 : ARP Request
OK
Cancel

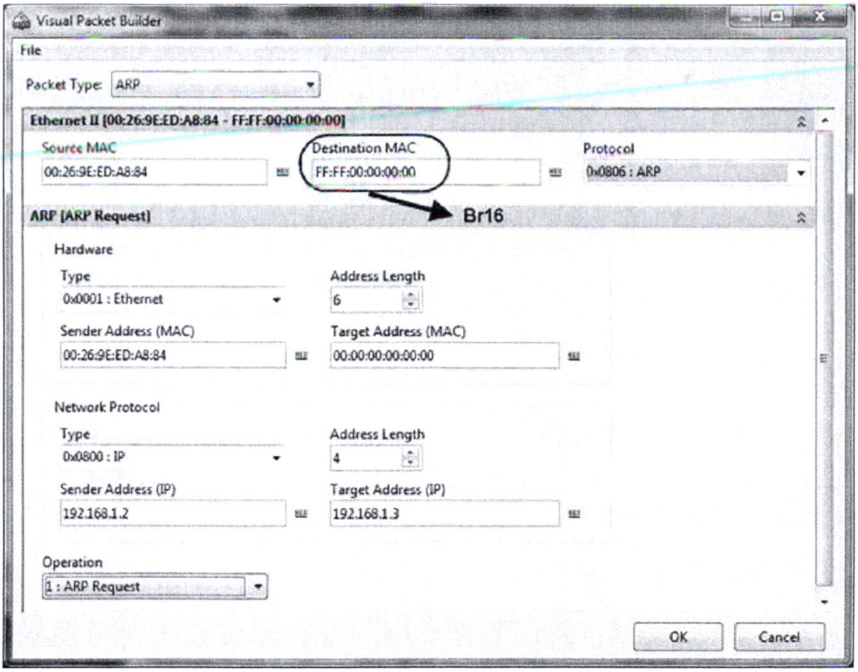
Visual Packet Builder
File
Packet Type: ARP
Ethernet II [00:26:9E:ED:A8:84 - FF:FF:00:00:00:00]
Source MAC
00:26:9E:ED:A8:84
Destination MAC
FF:FF:00:00:00:00
Protocol
0x0806 : ARP
Br16
ARP [ARP Request]
Hardware
Type
0x0001 : Ethernet
Address Length
6
Sender Address (MAC)
00:26:9E:ED:A8:84
Target Address (MAC)
00:00:00:00:00:00
Network Protocol
Type
0x0800 : IP
Address Length
4
Sender Address (IP)
192.168.1.2
Target Address (IP)
192.168.1.3
Operation
1 : ARP Request
OK
Cancel

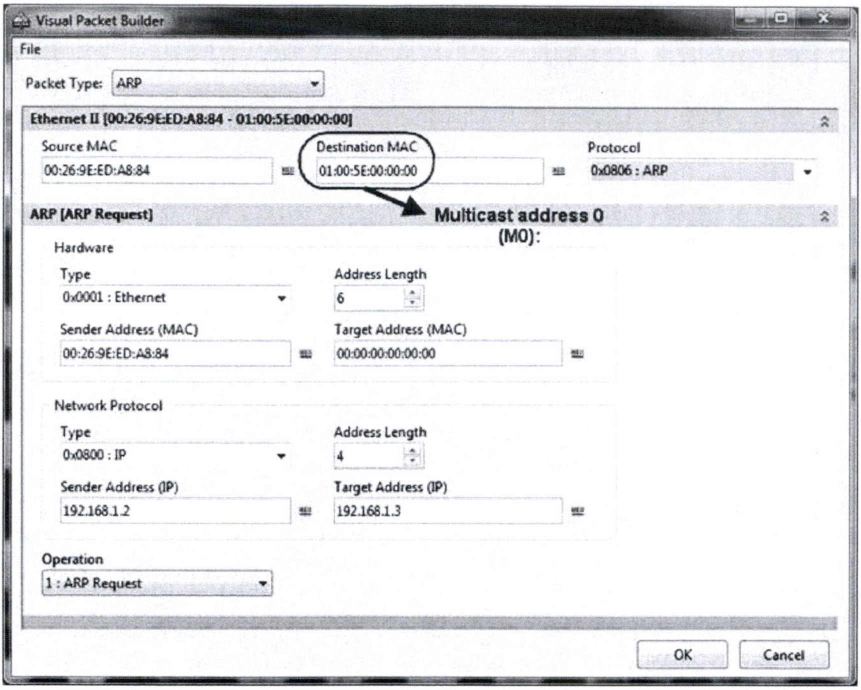

4.2.7.4 Step 4: Analyze the ARP Response Packets

Host A uses CommView sniffer to collect any ARP reply packets generated by Host B after receiving the trap ARP request packets. The next screenshot of the CommView sniffer shows the contents of the generated trap ARP request packet with the destination MAC address Br47. And the subsequent screenshot clearly shows that an ARP reply packet has been received from Host B after sending the foregoing trap ARP request packet.

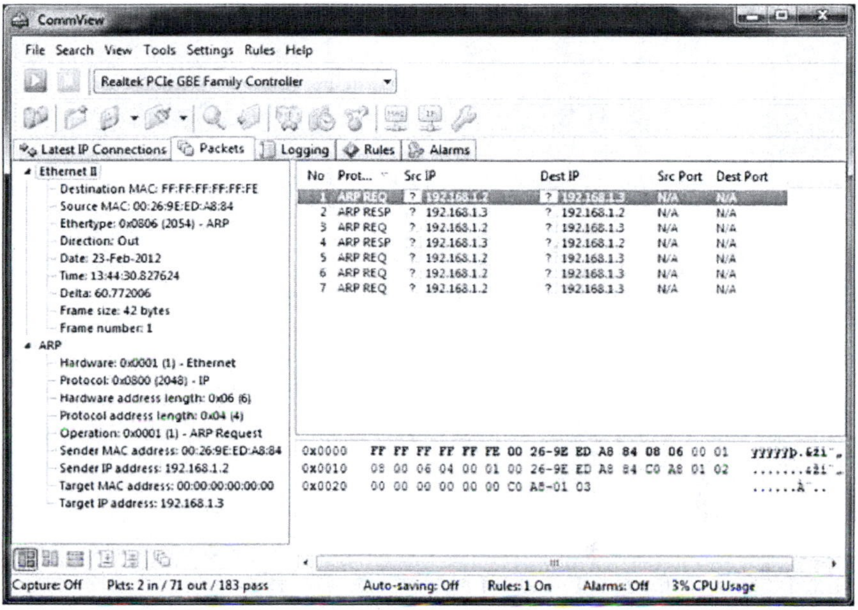

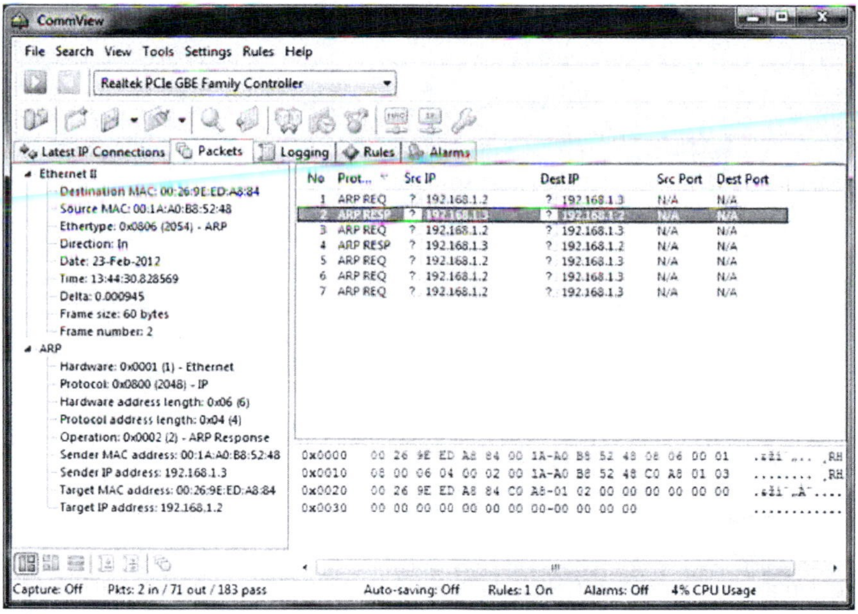

The next screenshot shows the contents of the generated trap ARP request packet with the destination MAC address Br16. And the subsequent screenshot shows that an ARP reply packet has been received from Host B after sending the foregoing trap ARP request packet.

However, the three following screenshots show that the CommView sniffer did not capture any ARP reply packet issued from Host B, after sending the trap ARP request packets with the destination multicast MAC addresses M0, M2, and M3, respectively.

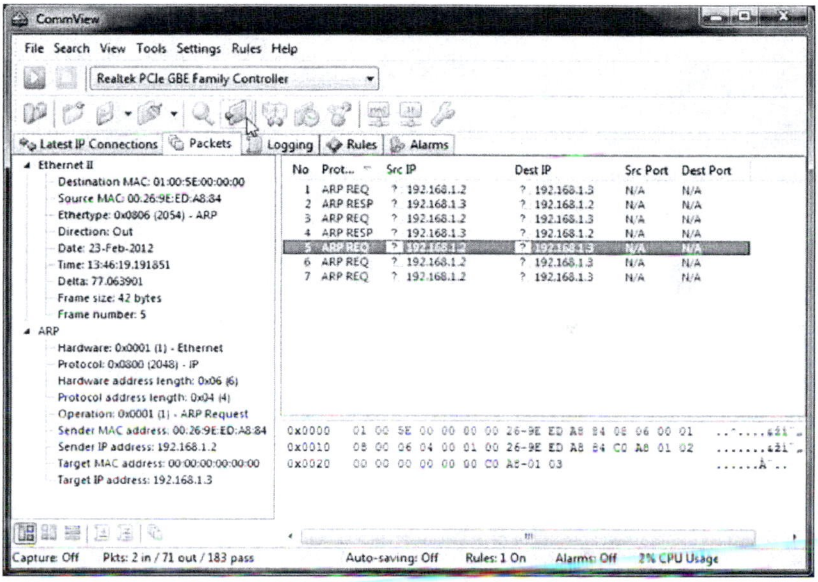

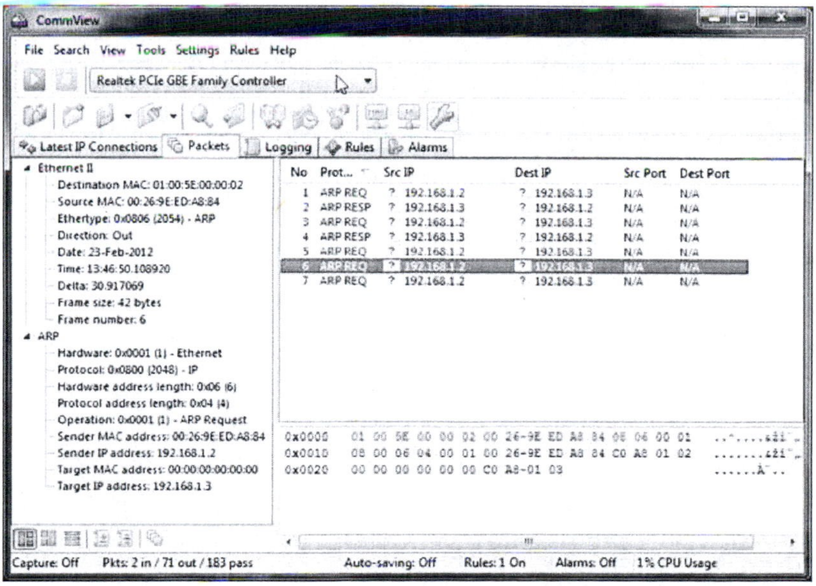

Consequently, Host B's system kernel responded to the fake broadcast MAC addresses Br47 and Br16, and did not respond to multicast MAC addresses M0, M1, and M2. Hence, based on the results shown in Tables 4.1 and 4.2, Host B's NIC is running in promiscuous mode and Host B's OS is mostly a Windows-based system.

4.2.8 Wireless Network Sniffing

In wireless local area networks (WLANs), wireless network cards do not support promiscuous mode, but can operate in six modes: Master (acting as an access point), Managed (client, also known as station), Ad-hoc, Mesh, Repeater, and RF Monitor modes.

The RF Monitor mode allows wireless network cards to captured packets without having to associate with an access point or an ad-hoc network first. RF Monitor mode also enables a wireless network card to passively capture packets without transmitting any packet. A wireless network sniffer can start monitoring wireless networks, only after setting the wireless card to the RF Monitor mode. When a wireless sniffer is running, the only thing required for monitoring a wireless network is being within the signal range. Then, the sniffer intercepts and displays wireless packets, and can show nodes, access points (APs), Service Set Identifier (SSIDs), signal strength, and other important network statics. In RF Monitor mode, the wireless card does not check to see if the cyclic redundancy check (CRC) values are correct for the packets captured, so some captured packets may be corrupted. Hackers can use the RF Monitor mode for malicious purposes, such as collecting traffic for WEP cracking.

The detection of wireless network cards running in the RF Monitor mode is a challenge that is different from the challenge of the detection of wired network cards running in the promiscuous mode. The difficulty comes from the fact that when configured in the RF Monitor mode, the wireless card stops transmitting data. Traditional detection techniques usually rely on the use of trap packets to identify wired network cards running in the promiscuous mode. However, when a wireless card does not transmit data, it becomes consequently difficult to detect whether or not it is sniffing the network and is set to the RF Monitor mode.

4.2.8.1 WEP Key Cracking and Network Traffic Decryption

Wired Equivalent Privacy (WEP) is a security protocol, specified in the IEEE Wireless Fidelity (Wi-Fi) standard, 802.11, that is designed to provide protection to WLANs. WEP adds security to 802.11 Wi-Fi networks at the data link layer (OSI model Layer 2). WEP seeks to establish similar protection to that offered by the wired network's physical security measures by encrypting data transmitted over the WLAN.

WEP uses the stream cipher RC4 for confidentiality and the CRC-32 checksum for integrity. WEP uses a 64-bit (or 128-bit) encryption key. The key is composed of a 24-bit initialization vector (IV) and a 40-bit (or 104-bit) WEP key. Due to the vulnerabilities of WEP, the WEP key can be easily cracked using open-source tools. WEP was depreciated in 2004 and was replaced by WPA.

WEP cracking involves the following steps: wardriving, sniffing the network traffic, cracking the WEP key, and decrypting the captured traffic using the crack WEP key.

4.2.8.1.1 Wardriving and Sniffing

Wardriving is a scanning process of discovering APs around a building or elsewhere with a computer. There are many available tools such as CommView for WiFi[*], Cain and Abel[†], KisMAC[‡], Kismet[§] and Wireshark[¶] that can be used to perform wardriving. Wardriving collects and logs such information as the SSIDs of the wireless networks, the security protocol used (e.g., WEP, WPA, etc.), the AP's MAC address and a list of clients currently connected to it along with their MAC addresses. For example, after performing a wardriving using CommView for the WiFi tool, the following screenshot shows the list of identified SSIDs, and the MAC addresses of the APs and station clients, per channels.

---

[*] http://www.tamos.com
[†] http://www.oxid.it/cain.html
[‡] http://kismac-ng.org
[§] http://www.kismetwireless.net
[¶] http: //www.Wireshark.org

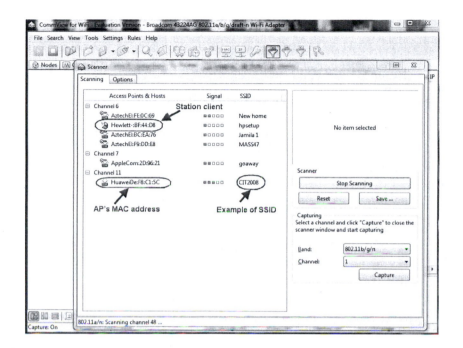

The following screenshot shows the security protocol used (e.g., WEP, WPA, etc.) for each AP of channel 6.

A wireless sniffer allows one to configure a network card onto a certain channel and collect all radio signals within the range of the network card. Examples of such sniffers include CommView for WiFi, Kismet, Wireshark and Airodump* (which is part of the Aircrack suite). The packets captured by

---

* http://www.aircrack-ng.org

using these sniffers are usually saved in files with the extension .cap. The data in the capture packets can be used in a number of attacks later. The following screenshot shows the encrypted packets captured by CommView for the WiFi tool for Channel 6.

4.2.8.1.2 WEP Key Cracking

When a sufficient amount of encrypted packets are collected through sniffing, the user can proceed to crack the WEP key. The IVs in the packets are needed for WEP key cracking. The number of captured IVs needed to crack the key depends on the AP's key size. For a 64-bit encryption, about 250,000 to 500,000 IVs are needed depending on the complexity of the key. The key consists of ten digits with values of A-F and 0-9. To crack a 128-bit encryption, about 500,000 to 1 million IVs are needed. Examples of programs that are capable of cracking WEP keys include KisMAC, Aircrack, and Cain and Abel, and AirSnort[*]. The following screenshot shows the GUI interface of the Aircrack-ng tool used to crack a WEP key.

---

[*] http://airsnort.shmoo.com

Example of file containing captured and encrypted packets

The following screenshot shows the result of cracking a WEP key using the Aircrack-ng tool. The WEP key found is "1F:1F:1F:1F:1F."

Cracked WEP key

4.2.8.1.3 Network Traffic Decryption

Once the WEP key is cracked, the user can use the key to decrypt the captured network traffic using a tool such as Airdecap-ng (part of the Aircrack suite). The following screenshot shows the GUI interface of the Airdecap-ng tool used to decrypt an encrypted file using the WEP key "1F:1F:1F:1F:1F."

4.3 Chapter Summary

This chapter discussed sniffing attacks and the detection of NIC running in promiscuous mode. In LANs, sniffing activity with malicious purpose can be very harmful. It allows malicious users to easily steal confidential data, passwords, and anyone's privacy. This chapter also explained the concepts of the NIC's hardware filter and system kernel's software filter, and described a common technique for detecting NICs in promiscuous mode. The chapter's hands-on exercise was concerned with the implementation of the detection technique and how to manually generate trap ARP request packets to detect NICs running in promiscuous mode.

Chapter 5

IP-Based Denial-of-Service Attacks

5.1 Introduction

It is a very frustrating experience when some services are not available and the unavailability is not explained. When a system has all its resources overloaded, it is rendered unusable or provides very low performance for legitimate users. This attack on system resources is called a Denial-of-Service (DoS) attack. DoS attacks may target a system to prevent network communication or may target an entire organization to prevent outgoing or incoming traffic to certain network services, such as an organization's Website or e-mail services.

The hard truth is: orchestrating these DoS attacks is much easier to accomplish when compared to remotely gaining access to a target system. Hence, DoS attacks have become very common on the Internet. They are either deliberate or accidental. A DoS attack is caused deliberately when an unauthorized user actively overloads a resource, and accidentally when an authorized user unintentionally does something that causes services to become unavailable.

DoS attacks can be broadly classified into two types. The first type causes a system crash or network crash. When an attacker directs data or packets to a system (the victim), it may cause the system to either crash or reboot. Consequently, the resources of the system are inaccessible. The second type of attack involves flooding the system or network with large amounts of information and thereby rendering it unresponsive. Consequently, when legitimate users try to connect to the system, they are denied access because all the resources have been exhausted. In the latter case, an attacker must constantly flood the system with information packets for the duration of the attack. After the flooding stops, the attack is over and the system resumes operation.

Unfortunately, DoS attacks cannot be totally prevented. There is always the possibility that an attacker sends excessive information to a system that it is not able to process. The threat of DoS attacks can be minimized by increasing the network's bandwidth and using vendor patches, firewalls, intrusion prevention systems (IPS), and proper network configurations. However, an attacker can always use additional resources to flood a target system or network and invent new types of DoS attacks.

Most DoS attacks rely on weaknesses in the TCP/IP protocols. The following are a few of the classic DoS attacks: Ping of Death, Land, Smurf, SYN Flood, UDP Flood, SSPing, ICMP Flood, ICMP Fragment, Large Size ICMP Packet, CPU Hog, Win Nuke, RPC Locator, Jolt2, and Bubonic.

5.1.1 Distributed Denial-of-Service (DDoS) Attack

A Distributed Denial-of-Service (DDoS) attack is a DoS attack that is mounted from a large number of locations across the network. The attacks are usually mounted from a number of compromised systems. These systems may have been compromised by a Trojan horse or a worm, or they might have been compromised by being manually hacked. These compromised systems are usually controlled with a fairly sophisticated piece of client/server software, such as Trinoo, Tribe Flood Network, Stacheldraht, TFN2K, or Shaft. DDoS attacks can be very difficult to defend.

This chapter includes four hands-on exercises about the generation and detection of four common DoS attacks, namely, Land attack, SYN Flood attack, Teardrop attack, and UDP Flood attack. In addition, this chapter includes a hands-on exercise about the generation and detection of abnormal IP packets that might contain hidden threats or DoS traffic.

These hands-on exercises use the following hardware devices and software tools:

- Juniper Networks SSG20 Wireless Appliance[*] (Juniper Networks device): Intrusion detection device
- CommView[†] Tool: Network monitor and analyzer tool (sniffer)
- CommView Visual Packet Builder[‡]: Graphical User Interface (GUI)-based packet generator
- FrameIP Packet Generator[§]: Online packet generator
- Advanced Port Scanner[¶]: Port scanner tool
- Fast Port Scanner[**]: Port scanner tool

---

[*] http://www.juniper.net
[†] http://www.tamos.com
[‡] http://www.tamos.com
[§] http://www.frameip.com
[¶] http://www.radmin.com
[**] http://www.globalwebmonitor.com

5.2 Lab 5.1: Land Attack

5.2.1 Outcome

The learning objective of this exercise is for students to learn how to generate and detect a Land attack.

5.2.2 Description

A Land attack occurs when an attacker sends spoofed TCP SYN packets (TCP = Transmission Control Protocol; SYN = synchronize) (connection initiation) with the same source and destination IP address, and the same source and destination port number. The target host responds by sending the SYN ACK packet to itself, creating an empty connection that lasts until the idle timeout value is reached. Flooding a system with empty connection requests will overwhelm it and cause it to deny the services that it offers, as illustrated in the following figure.

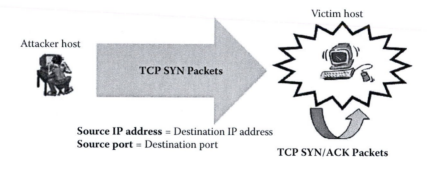

5.2.3 Experiment

To investigate how to generate and then detect a Land attack, an experiment is conducted using Juniper Networks device as the detection device. A stepwise description of the process is given below. The following figure illustrates the network architecture used in the experiment. An attacker host and a victim host are connected to the interfaces ethernet0/2 and ethernet0/3 of the Juniper Networks device, respectively.

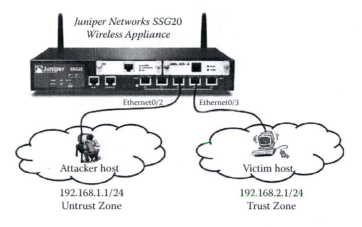

The experiment consists of the following steps:

Step 1: Configure the network interfaces in the Juniper Networks device.
Step 2: Set the security policies (filtering rules).
Step 3: Enable protection against the Land attack.
Step 4: Build Land attack packets.
Step 5: Sniff the generated traffic.
Step 6: View results in the Log file of the Juniper Networks device.

5.2.3.1 Step 1: Configure the Network Interfaces in the Juniper Networks Device

We assume that the attacker host is located in an Untrust zone/network (Network address: 192.168.1.1/24) and connected to the interface ethernet0/2 of the Juniper Networks device. The victim host is in a Trust zone/network (Network address: 192.168.2.1/24) and connected to the interface ethernet0/3, as depicted in the following screenshot, which illustrates the network interfaces configuration in the Juniper Networks device (see also previous figure).

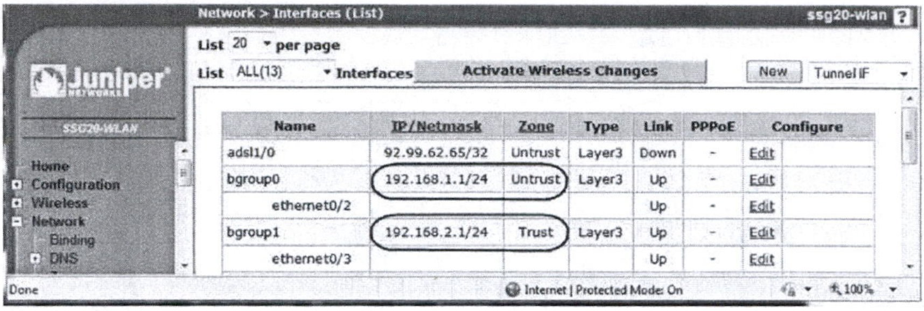

5.2.3.2 Step 2: Set the Security Policies (Filtering Rules)

Using the Web User Interface (WebUI) of the Juniper Networks device, the default policy between the two hosts is set to "Allow All/Permit" to allow all types of traffic between the two hosts, as shown in the next screenshot.

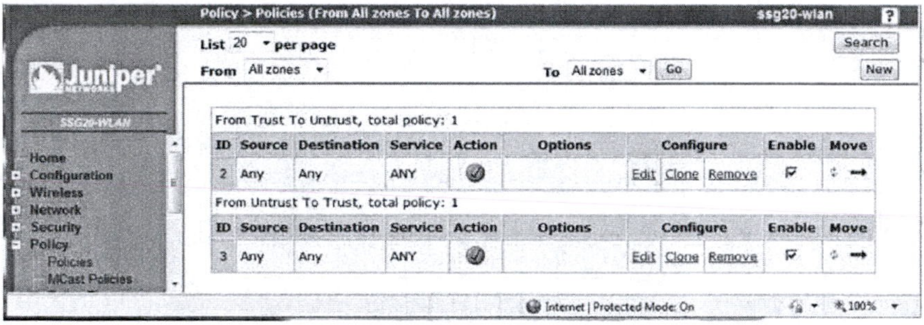

5.2.3.3 Step 3: Enable Protection against the Land Attack

To enable protection against the Land attack in the Juniper Networks device, do the following:

- Log in to the WebUI interface of the Juniper Networks device.
- Select Screening and set the following parameters as shown in the following screenshot.
- Set Zone to Untrust, because the Land attack traffic will be generated from an untrusted zone.

■ Select the Land Attack Protection option.
■ Then click "Apply."

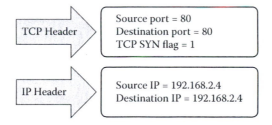

5.2.3.4 *Step 4: Build Land Attack Packets*

The Land attack is deployed by flooding a target system with spoofed SYN packets containing the IP address of the victim host as the destination and source IP addresses. In addition, such packets will have the same port number for both the source and destination ports. The figure below provides an example showing values of the main fields of a Land attack packet.

TCP Header ⟹ Source port = 80
Destination port = 80
TCP SYN flag = 1

IP Header ⟹ Source IP = 192.168.2.4
Destination IP = 192.168.2.4

The user can use a packet generator tool to build packets that produce the Land attack. For example, the user can use an online command tool, such as *FrameIP Packet Generator*, or a more friendly and easy to use GUI tool, such as *Engage Packet Builder** or *CommView Visual Packet Builder*.

---

* http://www.engagesecurity.com

5.2.3.4.1 CommView Visual Packet Builder

CommView Visual Packet Builder is used to generate a Land attack. The screenshot below shows how a spoofed TCP SYN packet is used to build a Land attack. The packet has the source IP address set to the destination IP address, the source port number set to the destination port number, and the destination MAC address set to the MAC address of the attacker host's gateway (192.168.1.1).

5.2.3.5 Step 5: Sniff the Generated Traffic

At the victim host, a sniffer program (network analyzer) can be used to capture the generated traffic. The aim of this step is to analyze and verify if the intended traffic has been generated adequately. For example, using CommView Sniffer, the next screenshot shows the Land attack packets generated in Step 4. It also shows that the victim host (192.168.2.4) is flooded with Land attack packets.

5.2.3.6 Step 6: View Results in the Log File of the Juniper Networks Device

The event log (as shown in the following screenshot) records the events in the Juniper Networks device after detecting the Land attack traffic. The steps to view the event log contents in the Juniper Networks device include:

■ Log in to the WebUI Interface of the Juniper Networks device.
■ In the left panel, expand the Reports, then expand System Log, and then select Event.

5.3 Lab 5.2: SYN Flood Attack

5.3.1 Outcome

The learning objective of this hands-on experiment is for students to learn how to generate and detect the SYN Flood attack.

5.3.2 Description

A SYN Flood attack occurs when a host becomes so overwhelmed by TCP SYN packets initiating incomplete connection requests that it can no longer process legitimate connection requests. When a client system attempts to establish a TCP connection to a system providing a service (the server), the client and server exchange a sequence of messages and the process is known as a three-way handshake.

The client system begins by sending a SYN (synchronization) message to the server. The server then acknowledges the SYN message by sending a SYN-ACK (acknowledgment) message to the client. The client then finishes establishing the connection by responding with an ACK message. The connection between the client and the server is then opened, and the service-specific data can be exchanged between the client and the server.

The potential for abuse arises at the point where the server has sent an acknowledgment (SYN-ACK) back to the client, but it has not yet received the final ACK message. This is referred to as a half-opened connection. The server has in its system memory a built-in data structure describing all pending connections. This data structure is of finite size, and it can be in a state of overflow by intentionally creating too many partially opened connections (as shown in the next figure). Creating a half-opened connection is easily accomplished with IP spoofing. The attacker's system sends SYN messages to the victim's server that appear to be legitimate, but in fact the source address is spoofed to a system that is not connected to the network. This means that the final

ACK message is never sent to the victim's server. Because the source address is spoofed, it is very difficult to determine the identity of the true attacker when the packet arrives at the victim's system.

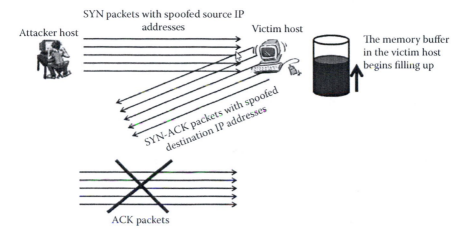

5.3.3 *Experiment*

To determine how to generate and detect the SYN Flood attack, an experiment is conducted using the Juniper Networks device as a detection device. This experiment uses the same network architecture described in the Land attack exercise above (Lab 5.1).

The experiment consists of the following steps:

Step 1: Configure the network interfaces in the Juniper Networks device.
Step 2: Set the security policies (filtering rules).
Step 3: Enable protection against the SYN Flood attack.
Step 4: Build SYN Flood attack packets.
Step 5: Sniff the generated traffic.
Step 6: View results in the Log file of the Juniper Networks device.

Steps 1 and 2 are similar to the ones described in the experiment of the Land attack hands-on lab (Lab 5.1).

5.3.3.1 Step 3: Enable Protection against the SYN Flood Attack

To enable protection against the SYN Flood attack on the Juniper Networks device, do the following:

- Log in to the WebUI interface of the Juniper Networks device.
- Select Screening and set the following parameters as shown in the next screenshot.
- Set Zone to Untrust, because the SYN Flood attack traffic is generated from untrusted zones.
- Select the SYN Flood Protection option.
- There are a number of threshold values that can be set but the main threshold is concerned with the number of SYN packets per second permitted to pass through the Juniper Networks device (see next screenshot). The user must select minimum threshold values so that the SYN Flood attack is detected quickly.
- Then click "Apply."

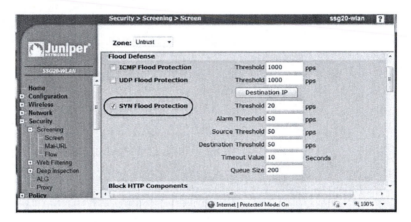

5.3.3.2 Step 4: Build SYN Flood Attack Packets

There are many available ready-to-use SYN Flood attack tools. However, considering the educational context of this book, we urge users to learn to build their own SYN Flood attack packets.

The TCP and IP headers of SYN Flood attack packets should be set to the values shown in the following figure, where an example SYN Flood attack packet is illustrated. The source IP address should be set to a spoofed or random IP address. The destination port should be set to a number of an open TCP port in the victim host.

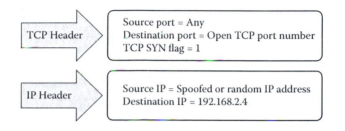

The attacker can use any port scanner tool to identify the list of open TCP ports at the victim host. Then the attacker can select one open TCP port number and use it as the target destination port number in the SYN Flood attack packets. For example, the following screenshot shows the result of a TCP port scanning of a target host, using the *Advanced Port Scanner tool.*

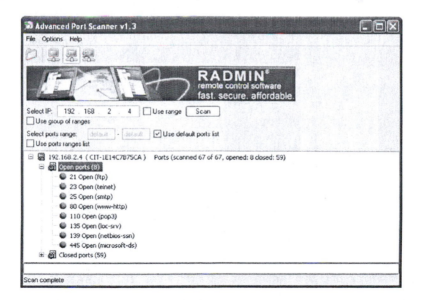

To build SYN Flood attack packets, the packet builder tool should allow including spoofed or random source IP addresses in the IP header.

5.3.3.2.1 FrameIP Packet Generator

The FrameIP Packet Generator is an example of tools that allow for sending TCP SYN packets with random source ports numbers and/or random source IP addresses. The screenshot that follows depicts the online command of *FrameIP* that allows generating TCP SYN flood traffic to the destination port 80 of the target host with IP address 192.168.2.4. Each generated TCP SYN packet will have a random fake source port number and a random fake source IP address.

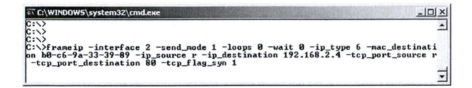

```
C:\WINDOWS\system32\cmd.exe                                          _|□|x|
C:\>
C:\>
C:\>
C:\>frameip -interface 2 -send_mode 1 -loops 0 -wait 0 -ip_type 6 -mac_destinati
on b0-c6-9a-33-39-89 -ip_source r -ip_destination 192.168.2.4 -tcp_port_source r
 -tcp_port_destination 80 -tcp_flag_syn 1
```

The following screenshot shows FrameIP's generated TCP SYN Flood traffic that results from executing the above FrameIP's online command.

```
C:\WINDOWS\system32\cmd.exe                                          _|□|x|
The frame was sent from 12.49.53.66 to 192.168.2.4 with 69 Bytes
The frame was sent from 10.65.118.120 to 192.168.2.4 with 69 Bytes
The frame was sent from 231.60.162.50 to 192.168.2.4 with 69 Bytes
The frame was sent from 255.172.61.114 to 192.168.2.4 with 69 Bytes
The frame was sent from 154.206.74.3 to 192.168.2.4 with 69 Bytes
The frame was sent from 152.123.225.174 to 192.168.2.4 with 69 Bytes
The frame was sent from 146.41.210.123 to 192.168.2.4 with 69 Bytes
The frame was sent from 211.82.161.4 to 192.168.2.4 with 69 Bytes
The frame was sent from 57.34.126.149 to 192.168.2.4 with 69 Bytes
The frame was sent from 15.134.50.41 to 192.168.2.4 with 69 Bytes
The frame was sent from 185.99.218.5 to 192.168.2.4 with 69 Bytes
The frame was sent from 187.132.19.87 to 192.168.2.4 with 69 Bytes
The frame was sent from 117.117.41.99 to 192.168.2.4 with 69 Bytes
The frame was sent from 209.235.187.31 to 192.168.2.4 with 69 Bytes
The frame was sent from 103.56.124.122 to 192.168.2.4 with 69 Bytes
The frame was sent from 140.238.252.225 to 192.168.2.4 with 69 Bytes
The frame was sent from 159.201.119.92 to 192.168.2.4 with 69 Bytes
The frame was sent from 12.211.246.86 to 192.168.2.4 with 69 Bytes
The frame was sent from 159.16.52.86 to 192.168.2.4 with 69 Bytes^C
D:\Documents and Settings\Administrator\Desktop\Tools\FrameIP>
```

The parameters for the command depicted above are as follows:

Command's Parameters	Description
-interface 2	Interface used (see tool's help)
-send_mode 1	Type of library used (see tool's help)
-loops 0	Number of loops (0 = no stop)
-wait 0	Time to wait after each packet
-ip_type 6	Type of packet (6 = TCP packet)
-mac_destination	MAC address of the gateway interface
-ip_source r	Random source IP address (r = random address)
-ip_destination 192.168.2.4	Destination IP address
-tcp_port_source r	Random TCP source port numbers
-tcp_port_destination 80	TCP destination port number
-tcp_flag_syn 1	TCP SYN flag bit set

5.3.3.3 Step 5: Sniff the Generated Traffic

At the victim host, a sniffer can be used to capture the generated traffic. The aim of this step is to analyze and verify that the intended traffic has been generated adequately. For example, using CommView Sniffer, the following screenshot shows that the victim host (192.168.2.4) is under the SYN Flood attack and the target TCP port is 80.

5.3.3.4 Step 6: View Results in the Log File of the Juniper Networks Device

The Juniper Networks device writes an alarm in the event log when the number of SYN packets from one or more sources to a single destination exceeds the thresholds. The next screenshot shows the event log contents after detecting SYN Flood attack traffic.

5.4 Lab 5.3: Teardrop Attack

5.4.1 Outcome

The learning objective of this hands-on experiment is for students to learn how to generate and detect the Teardrop attack.

5.4.2 Description

The Teardrop attack targets the process of reassembling fragmented IP packets. Fragmentation is necessary when IP datagrams are larger than the maximum unit of transmission (MUT) of a network segment across which the datagrams must travel. To successfully reassemble packets at the receiving end, the IP header for each fragment includes an offset to identify the fragment's position in the original unfragmented packet. In a Teardrop attack, packet fragments are deliberately fabricated with overlapping offset fields, causing the host to hang or crash when it tries to reassemble them.

The next figure shows that the second fragment packet (Packet #2) purports to begin 20 bytes earlier (at 40) than the first fragment packet (Packet #1) ends (at 60). The offset of Packet #2 is not in accord with the packet length of Packet #1. This discrepancy can cause some systems to crash during the reassembly attempt.

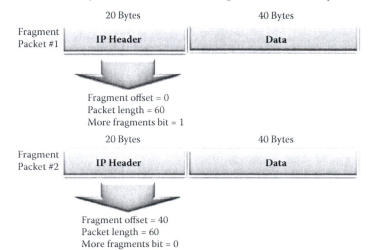

5.4.3 Experiment

To determine how to generate and detect the Teardrop attack, an experiment is conducted using the Juniper Networks device as a detection device. Below is a description and the steps of the experiment. The experiment uses the same network architecture described in the Land attack hands-on lab (Lab 5.1) and consists of the following steps:

Step 1: Configure the network interfaces in the Juniper Networks device.
Step 2: Set the security policies (filtering rules).
Step 3: Enable protection against the Teardrop attack.
Step 4: Build Teardrop attack packets.
Step 5: View results in the Log file of the Juniper Networks device.

Steps 1 and 2 are similar to the ones described in the experiment of the Land attack hands-on lab above (Lab 5.1).

5.4.3.1 Step 3: Enable Protection against the Teardrop Attack

To enable protection against the Teardrop attack in the Juniper Networks device, do the following:

■ Log in to the WebUI interface of Juniper Networks device.
■ Select Screening and set the following parameters as shown in the following screenshot to enable protection against the Teardrop attack.

Security > Screening > Screen   ssg20-wlan **?**

Juniper
NETWORKS

SSG20-WLAN

Home
Configuration
Wireless
Network
Security
  Screening
    Screen
    Mal-URL
    Flow

Zone: Untrust ▼

Denial of Service Defense
☐ **Ping of Death Attack Protection**
☑ **Teardrop Attack Protection**
☐ **ICMP Fragment Protection**
☐ **ICMP Ping ID Zero Protection**
☐ **Large Size ICMP Packet (Size > 1024) Protection**
☐ **Block Fragment Traffic**
☐ **Land Attack Protection**
☐ **SYN-ACK-ACK Proxy Protection**   Threshold 512   Connections

Done   Internet | Protected Mode: On   100%

- Set Zone to Untrust because the Teardrop attack traffic will be generated from an untrusted zone.
- Select the Teardrop Attack Protection option.
- Then click "Apply."

5.4.3.2 Step 4: Build Teardrop Attack Packets

To generate a Teardrop attack, two fragmented packets must be built. The packets belong to the same original packet and have the same IP's Identification (ID). The field ID includes an identifying value assigned by the sender host to aid in assembling the fragments of a datagram. However, the two fragmented packets have overlapping offset values. As an example, the IP header values of two Teardrop attack packets are illustrated in the next figure.

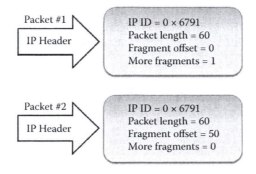

Packet #1
IP Header
→ IP ID = 0 × 6791
Packet length = 60
Fragment offset = 0
More fragments = 1

Packet #2
IP Header
→ IP ID = 0 × 6791
Packet length = 60
Fragment offset = 50
More fragments = 0

5.4.3.2.1 CommView Visual Packet Builder

Using the CommView Visual Packet Builder, the following two screenshots show the first and second fragmented packets with overlapped offset values leading to the Teardrop attack.

5.4.3.3 Step 5: View Results in the Log File of the Juniper Networks Device

The event log contents in the Juniper Networks device after detecting Teardrop attack traffic are shown in the next screenshot.

5.5 Lab 5.4: UDP Flood Attack

5.5.1 Outcome

The learning objective of this hands-on exercise is for students to learn how to generate and detect UDP Flood attack.

5.5.2 Description

UDP (User Datagram Protocol) is a connectionless protocol and does not require any connection set-up procedure to transfer data. A UDP Flood attack is possible when an attacker floods target ports on a victim system with UDP packets. When the victim system receives a UDP packet, it determines what application is waiting on the destination UDP port. Two possibilities exist. First, if there is no application waiting on the port (closed UDP port), the victim host will generate an ICMP error packet (destination unreachable) to the forged source address. Second, if there is an application running on the destination UDP port, then the application handles the UDP packet. In both cases, if enough UDP packets are delivered to destination UDP ports, the victim host or application may slow down or go down. The scenario is shown in the next figure.

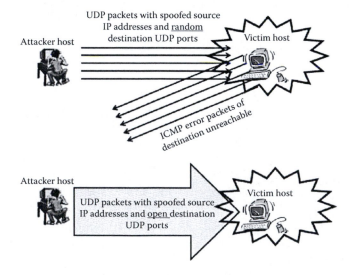

5.5.3 Experiment

To determine how to generate and detect the UDP Flood attack, an experiment is conducted using the Juniper Networks device as a detection device. This experiment uses the same network architecture described in the Land attack hands-on lab above (Lab 5.1).

The experiment consists of the following steps:

Step 1: Configure the network interfaces in the Juniper Networks device.
Step 2: Set the security policies (filtering rules).
Step 3: Enable protection against the UDP Flood attack.
Step 4: Build UDP Flood attack packets.
Step 5: Sniff the generated traffic.
Step 6: View results in the Log file of the Juniper Networks device.

Steps 1 and 2 are similar to the ones described in the experiment of the Land attack hands-on lab above (Lab 5.1).

5.5.3.1 Step 3: Enable Protection against the UDP Flood Attack

To enable protection against the UDP Flood attack in the Juniper Networks device, do the following:

■ Log in to the WebUI interface of the Juniper Networks device.
■ Select Screening and set the following parameters as shown in the following screenshot to enable protection against the UDP Flood attack.

Security > Screening > Screen   ssg20-wlan ?

Juniper
NETWORKS

Zone: Untrust ▾

SSG20-WLAN

Home
⊞ Configuration
⊞ Wireless
⊞ Network
⊟ Security
  ⊟ Screening
    Screen

☐ Generate Alarms without Dropping Packet
☐ Apply Screen to Tunnel
Flood Defense
☐ ICMP Flood Protection   Threshold 1000   pps
☑ UDP Flood Protection   Threshold 100   pps
                                 Destination IP

Done   🖼 🌐 Internet | Protected Mode: On   🔍 ▾ 🔍 100% ▾

- Set Zone to Untrust, because the UDP Flood attack traffic will be generated from untrusted zones.
- Select the UDP Flood Protection option.
- Set the threshold. The threshold is the number of UDP packets per second that the Juniper Networks device can accept before a UDP Flood attack is detected and logged. The default threshold value is 1,000 packets per second. The user must set a threshold value so that the UDP Flood attack is detected quickly.
- Then click "Apply."

5.5.3.2 *Step 4: Build UDP Flood Attack Packets*

There are many available ready-to-use UDP Flood attack tools. However, considering the educational context of this book, we urge users to learn to build their own UDP Flood packets.

In a UDP Flood attack packet, the source IP address should be set to a spoofed or random IP address. The destination port should be set to a number of an open UDP port in the victim host (see next figure).

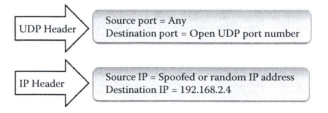

UDP Header → Source port = Any
Destination port = Open UDP port number

IP Header → Source IP = Spoofed or random IP address
Destination IP = 192.168.2.4

The attacker can use any port scanner tool to identify the list of open UDP ports at the victim host. Then, one open UDP port number is selected and is used as the destination port number in the UDP Flood attack packets. The example in the next screenshot shows the result of a UDP port scanning of a target host using the Fast Port Scanner tool.

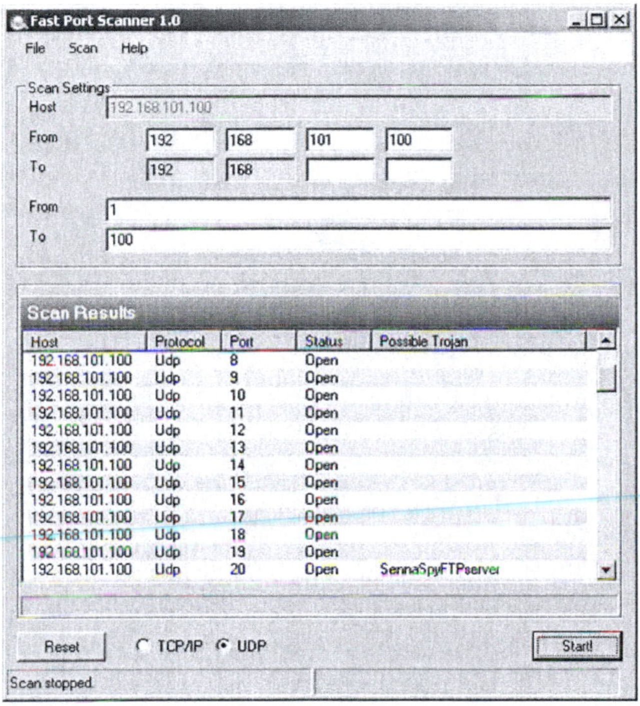

To build UDP Flood attack packets, the user must use a packet builder tool that allows for including spoofed or random IP addresses in the source IP field of the IP header. Random or spoofed source IP addresses allow hiding the real source IP address of the attacker host.

5.5.3.2.1 FrameIP Packet Generator

The FrameIP Packet Generator has the ability to generate UDP packets with random or spoofed source IP addresses. The following screenshot is that of the online command of *FrameIP* that allows generating UDP flood traffic to the destination UDP port 53 of the target host with IP address 192.168.2.4.

```
C:\WINDOWS\system32\cmd.exe                                        _|□|×|
C:\>
C:\>
C:\>
C:\>frameip -interface 2 -send_mode 1 -loops 0 -wait 0 -ip_type 17 -mac_destinat
ion b0-c6-9a-33-39-89 -ip_source r -ip_destination 192.168.2.4 -udp_port_source
r -udp_port_destination 53
```

where

Command's Parameters	Description
-interface 2	Interface used (see tool's help)
-send_mode 1	Type of library used (see tool's help)
-loops 0	Number of loops (0 = no stop)
-wait 0	Time to wait after each packet
-ip_type 17	Type of packet (17 = UDP packet)
-mac_destination	MAC address of the gateway interface
-ip_source r	Random source IP address (r = random address)
-ip_destination 192.168.2.4	Destination IP address
-udp_port_source r	Random UCP source port numbers
-udp_port_destination 53	UCP destination port number

5.5.3.3 Step 5: Sniff the Generated Traffic

At the victim host, a sniffer can be used to capture the generated traffic. For example, using CommView sniffer, the next screenshot shows that the victim host (192.168.2.4) is under UDP Flood attack and the target UDP port is 53.

5.5.3.4 Step 6: View Results in the Log File of the Juniper Networks Device

The Juniper Networks device writes an alarm in the event log when the number of UDP packets from one or more sources to a single destination exceeds the threshold. The event log contents in the Juniper Networks device after detecting UDP Flood attack traffic are shown in the next screenshot.

5.6 Lab 5.5: Abnormal IP Packets

5.6.1 Outcome

The learning objective of this hands-on exercise is for students to learn how to generate and detect abnormal IP packets that might contain hidden threats or DoS traffic.

5.6.2 Description

Attackers can send abnormal packets that might contain hidden threats or cause a DoS situation at the target system. In most cases, it is unclear what the intent of generating abnormal packets is. However, abnormal packets are usually a strong indication of the existence of malicious activities. Therefore, it is important to block abnormal packets from reaching their targets. Usually, abnormal packets are packets that include unexpected field values, have unexpectedly large sizes, or are fragmented packets that normally should not be fragmented. Three examples of abnormal packets are presented here.

5.6.2.1 ICMP Fragmented Packet

ICMP packets are used to send error and control messages. For example, when a packet is dropped by a router, usually an ICMP error packet is sent to the source host. An ICMP echo packet is a control packet and is used to identify a live remote host.

ICMP packets are small in size because they contain very short messages. Therefore, there is no legitimate reason for ICMP packets to be fragmented. An ICMP packet is considered a fragmented packet when its "More Fragments" flag is set or it has an offset value indicated in the offset field. It is unusual to see fragmented ICMP packets.

5.6.2.2 Large ICMP Packet

As noted, ICMP packets are small because they contain very short messages. Therefore, there is no legitimate reason for large ICMP packets to exist. It is unusual to see large ICMP packets. If an ICMP packet is so large, then something is amiss. It also might indicate some other kind of questionable activity.

5.6.2.3 Unknown Protocol Packet

The Protocol field in the IP header identifies the higher-layer protocol (generally either a transport layer protocol or encapsulated network layer protocol) carried in the datagram. The values of this field were originally defined by the IETF (Internet Engineering Task Force) "Assigned Numbers" standard, RFC 1700, and are now maintained by the Internet Assigned Numbers Authority (IANA). These higher-layer protocols with ID numbers of 137 or greater are reserved and undefined at this time. Therefore, in a normal situation, packets that use unknown protocols (with an ID number of 137 or greater) are suspicious and should be blocked from entering the network unless the network makes use of nonstandard protocols.

5.6.3 Experiment

To learn how to generate and detect the foregoing three abnormal IP packets, an experiment is conducted using the Juniper Networks device as a detection device. Below is a description and steps of the experiment. This experiment uses the same network architecture described in the Land attack hands-on lab above (Lab 5.1).

The experiment consists of the following steps:

Step 1: Configure the network interfaces in the Juniper Networks device.
Step 2: Set the security policies (filtering rules).

Step 3: Enable protection against the three abnormal packets.

Step 4: Generate the three abnormal packets.

Step 5: View results in the Log file of the Juniper Networks device.

Steps 1 and 2 are similar to the ones described in the experiment of the Land attack hands-on lab above (Lab 5.1).

5.6.3.1 Step 3: Enable Protection against the Three Abnormal Packets

To enable protection against ICMP fragmented packets, large ICMP packets, and unknown protocol packets in the Juniper Networks device, do the following:

- Log in to the WebUI interface of the Juniper Networks device.
- Select Screening and set the following parameters.
- Set Zone to Untrust, because the abnormal packets are generated from an untrusted zone.
- Set ICMP Fragmentation Protection, Large ICMP Protection, Unknown Protocol Protection, as shown in the next two screenshots. The first screenshot illustrates protection against ICMP Fragmented packets and Large size packets, while the second screenshot illustrates protection against Unknown protocol packets.
- Then click "Apply."

5.6.3.2 *Step 4: Generate the Three Abnormal Packets*

Using CommView Visual Packet Builder, the next three screen-shots show the three abnormal IP packets: ICMP Fragmented packet, Large size ICMP packet, and Unknown protocol packet, respectively.

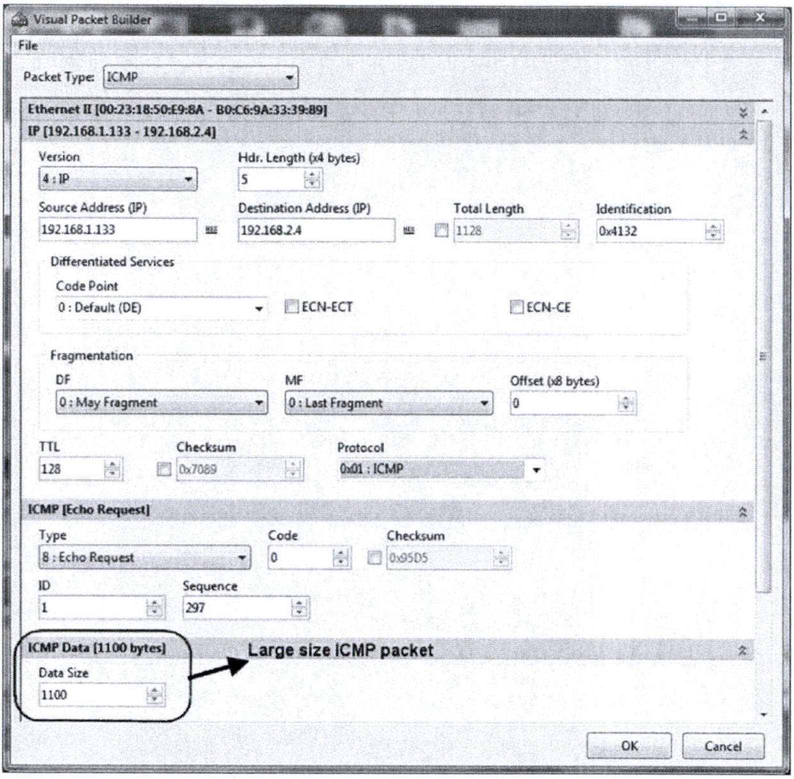

Visual Packet Builder
File
Packet Type: ICMP
Ethernet II [00:23:18:50:E9:8A - B0:C6:9A:33:39:89]
IP [192.168.1.133 - 192.168.2.4]
Version
4 : IP
Hdr. Length (x4 bytes)
5
Source Address (IP)
192.168.1.133
Destination Address (IP)
192.168.2.4
Total Length
1128
Identification
0x4132
Differentiated Services
Code Point
0 : Default (DE)
ECN-ECT
ECN-CE
Fragmentation
DF
0 : May Fragment
MF
0 : Last Fragment
Offset (x8 bytes)
0
TTL
128
Checksum
0x7089
Protocol
0x01 : ICMP
ICMP [Echo Request]
Type
8 : Echo Request
Code
0
Checksum
0x95D5
ID
1
Sequence
297
ICMP Data [1100 bytes]
Large size ICMP packet
Data Size
1100
OK
Cancel

Visual Packet Builder
File
Packet Type:
Ethernet II [00:23:18:50:E9:8A - B0:C6:9A:33:39:89]
Source MAC
00:23:18:50:E9:8A
Destination MAC
B0:C6:9A:33:39:89
Protocol
0x0800 : IP
IP [192.168.1.133 - 192.168.2.4]
Version
4 : IP
Hdr. Length (x4 bytes)
5
Source Address (IP)
192.168.1.133
Destination Address (IP)
192.168.2.4
Total Length
21
Identification
0x4132
Differentiated Services
Code Point
0 : Default (DE)
ECN-ECT
ECN-CE
Fragmentation
DF
0 : May Fragment
MF
1 : More Fragments
Offset (x8 bytes)
0
TTL
128
Checksum
0x0000
Protocol
0x8A
Unknown protocol
(0x8A = 138)
OK
Cancel

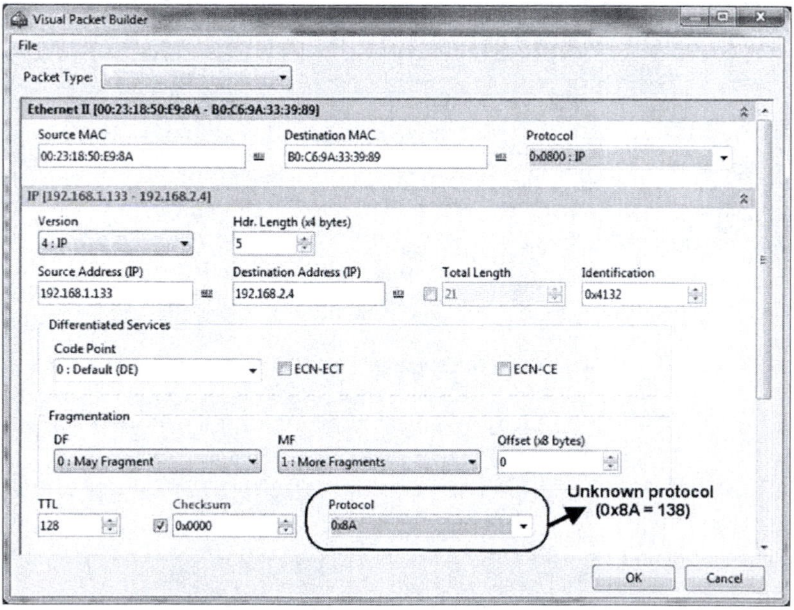

5.6.3.3 Step 5: View Results in the Log File of the Juniper Networks Device

The contents of the event log in the Juniper Networks device after the detection of the above three abnormal packets is shown in the following screenshot.

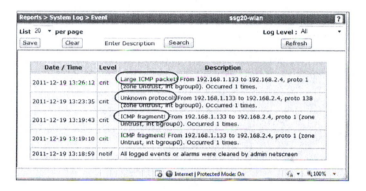

5.7 Chapter Summary

In a DoS attack, the attacker attempts to prevent legitimate users from accessing information or services. By targeting computers and networks, attackers prevent legitimate users from accessing e-mail, websites, online accounts (banking), or other services that rely on the affected computers and networks. This chapter presented hands-on exercises for four well-known IP-based DoS attacks, namely, Land attack, SYN Flood attack, Teardrop attack, and UDP Flood attack. In addition, an exercise about abnormal IP packets that might contain hidden threats or DoS traffic was discussed. The learning objective of the chapter's hands-on labs is for students to learn how to generate and detect the four well-known DoS attacks, as well as three types of abnormal IP packets. There are many available ready-to-use attack tools. However, considering the educational context of this book, we demonstrated to the users how to practically build and test their own attack traffic.

Chapter 6

Reconnaissance Traffic

6.1 Introduction

Every attacker does a study of the targeted environment prior to an exploit. The attacker collects some preliminary information such as the number of systems, the configurations of the systems, and the operating systems (OSs) that are used. All the information gathered builds a clear picture of the environment that is targeted. Retrospectively, it is therefore extremely important for an organization to know what information an attacker can acquire about itself and secure it so as to minimize the potential loss of this critical information.

Attackers use various tools to get information about a targeted environment; some are listed here:

1. Social information about the domain names, domain holder details, and contact information such as names, phone numbers, and postal and e-mail addresses. The Whois and Nslookup tools allow collecting such information.
2. Tools to ping active hosts allow identifying them.

3. Port scanning tools, such as Nmap, Nessus, and NetScanTools Pro, allow identifying open ports on target hosts.
4. Nmap, NetScanTools Pro, Xprobe2, and GFI LANguard scanner are some of the tools that allow identifying remote OSs.
5. Traceroute command and VisualRoute tool are examples of tools that allow mapping out target networks.

In this chapter we take a look at some of the above tools and examine how systems and networks can be protected from reconnaissance traffic. The hands-on exercises discuss four common reconnaissance activities, namely, IP address sweeping, TCP port scanning, remote OS identification, and Traceroute.

The exercises use the following hardware devices and software tools:

■ Juniper Networks SSG20 Wireless Appliance[*]: intrusion detection device
■ CommView Tool[†]: network monitor and analyzer tool (sniffer)
■ Advanced Port Scanner[‡]: port scanner tool
■ Advanced IP Scanner[§]: IP scanner tool
■ NetScanTools Pro[¶]: network exploration tool and security scanner
■ Nmap[**]: network exploration tool and security scanner.
■ VisualRoute[††]: Traceroute tool

---

[*] http://www.juniper.net
[†] http://www.tamos.com
[‡] http://www.radmin.com
[§] http://www.radmin.com
[¶] http://www.netscantools.com
[**] http://www.nmap.org
[††] http://www.visualroute.com

6.2 Lab 6.1: IP Address Sweeping

6.2.1 Outcome

The learning objective of this exercise is for students to learn how to perform and detect IP address sweeping.

6.2.2 Description

IP address sweeping consists of scanning a range of IP addresses with ICMP ping packets looking for active devices. That is, each target IP address is sent ICMP echo request ping packets. ICMP echo reply packets allow locating active devices and gathering information about them. It is usually used in conjunction with port scanning for a full accounting of each IP address.

6.2.3 Experiment

To determine how to generate and detect an IP address sweeping attack, an experiment is conducted using the Juniper Networks device, as an example of a detection device, and Advanced Port Scanner as a tool for generating IP address sweeping attacks. Below is a description and steps of the experiment. This experiment uses the same network architecture described in the Land attack hands-on exercise of Chapter 5 (Lab 5.1).

The experiment consists of the following steps:

Step 1: Configure the network interfaces in the Juniper Networks device.
Step 2: Set the security policies (filtering rules).
Step 3: Enable protection against IP address sweeping.
Step 4: Perform IP address sweeping.
Step 5: Sniff the generated traffic.
Step 6: View results in the Log file of the Juniper Networks device.

Steps 1 and 2 are similar to the ones described in the experiment of the Land attack hands-on exercise of Chapter 5 (Lab 5.1).

6.2.3.1 Step 3: Enable Protection against IP Address Sweeping

To enable protection against IP address sweeping in the Juniper Networks device, do the following:

■ Log in to the WebUI interface of Juniper Networks device.
■ Select Screening and set the following parameters as shown in the following screenshot.

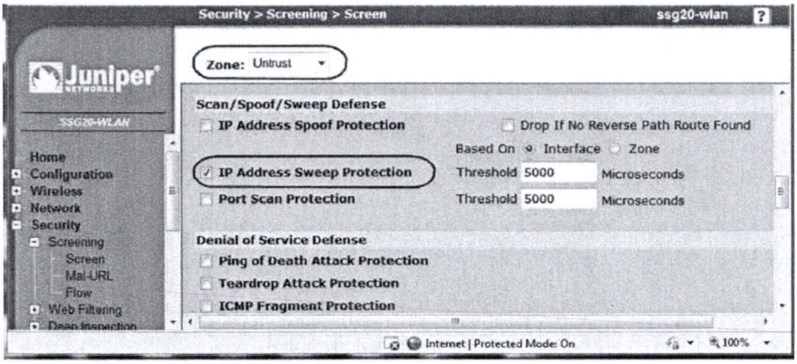

■ Set Zone to Untrust, because the IP address sweeping traffic will be generated from an untrusted zone.
  – Select the IP Address Sweep Protection option.
  – Set the threshold values: In the Juniper device, an IP address sweeping occurs when one source IP address sends ten ICMP packets to different hosts within a defined interval. The security device internally logs the number of ICMP packets to different addresses from one remote source. If a remote host sends ICMP traffic to ten addresses using the default settings, then in 0.005 seconds (5,000 microseconds),

the security device flags this as an address sweep attack and rejects all further ICMP echo requests from that host for the remainder of the specified threshold time period. The user should select a threshold value to ensure that IP address sweeping will be detected quickly.

■ Then click "Apply."

6.2.3.2 *Step 4: Perform IP Address Sweeping*

At the attacker host, the Advanced IP Scanner tool is used to perform IP address sweeping. For example, the following screenshot shows the hosts that are alive and dead.

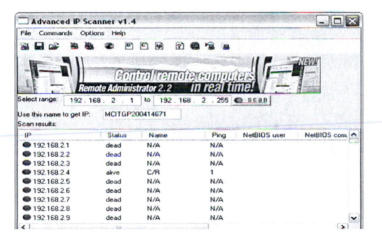

6.2.3.3 *Step 5: Sniff the Generated Traffic*

At the attacker host, a sniffer can be used to capture the generated traffic. Using CommView sniffer, the following screenshot shows that the attacker host (192.168.1.133) is performing IP address sweeping by sending ICMP echo request packets to a range of IP addresses (192.168.2.1–192.168.2.254).

6.2.3.4 Step 6: View Results in the Log File of the Juniper Networks Device

The next screenshot shows the event log contents in the Juniper Networks device after detecting IP address sweeping traffic.

6.3 Lab 6.2: TCP Port Scanning

6.3.1 Outcome

The learning objective of this hands-on exercise is for students to learn how to perform and detect TCP port scanning.

6.3.2 Description

TCP port scanning is a popular reconnaissance technique used by attackers to discover services to break into. All systems connected to a network run services that listen to well-known and not so well-known ports. A port scan helps the attacker find which ports are available (i.e., what service might be listening to a port). Essentially, a port scan consists of sending a message to each port, one at a time. The kind of response received indicates whether the port is used and can therefore be probed further for weaknesses.

There are a number of different methods to perform the actual port scans by setting different TCP (Transmission Control Protocol) flags or sending different types of TCP packets. The port scan mainly locates open ports. For example, a SYN scan will tell the port scanners which ports are listening and which are not, depending on the type of response generated. A FIN scan will generate a response from closed ports, but ports that are open and listening will not send a response, so the port scanner will be able to determine which ports are open and which are not.

Port scanning software, in its most basic state, simply sends out a request to connect sequentially to the target computer on each port and makes a note of which ports responded or seem open to more in-depth probing.

If the port scan is being done with malicious intent, the intruder would generally prefer to go undetected. Network security applications can be configured to alert administrators if connection requests are detected across a broad range of ports from a single host. To get around this, the intruder can do the port scan in strobe or stealth mode. Strobing limits the ports to a smaller target set rather than blanket scanning all 65,536 ports. Stealth scanning uses techniques to slow down the scan. By scanning the ports over a much longer period of time, the intruder reduces the chance that the target will trigger an alert.

6.3.3 Experiment

To experiment with how to perform and detect a port scanning attack, an experiment is conducted using the Advanced Port Scanner as the port scanner and the Juniper Networks device as the detection device. This experiment uses the same network architecture described in the Land attack hands-on exercise of Chapter 5 (Lab 5.1).

The experiment consists of the following steps:

Step 1: Configure the network interfaces in the Juniper Networks device.
Step 2: Set the security policies (filtering rules).
Step 3: Enable protection against TCP port scanning.
Step 4: Perform TCP port scanning.
Step 5: Sniff the generated traffic.
Step 6: View results in the Log file of the Juniper Networks device.

Steps 1 and 2 are similar to the ones described in the experiment of the Land attack hands-on exercise of Chapter 5 (Lab 5.1).

6.3.3.1 Enable Protection against Port Scanning

To enable protection against port scanning in the Juniper Networks device, do the following:

■ Log in to the WebUI interface of the Juniper Networks device.
■ Select "Screening" and set the following parameters as shown in the next screenshot:
  – Set Zone to "Untrust," because the port scanning traffic will be generated from an untrusted zone.

- Select the "Port Scan Protection" option.
- Set the value of Threshold: In the Juniper Networks device, a port scan occurs when one source IP address sends IP packets containing TCP SYN segments to ten different ports at the same destination IP address within a defined interval. If a remote host sends ICMP traffic to ten addresses using the default settings, in 0.005 seconds (5,000 microseconds), then the device flags this as a port scan attack and rejects all further packets from the remote source for the remainder of the specified timeout period. The user should select a threshold value to ensure that TCP port scanning traffic will be detected quickly.
■ Then click "Apply."

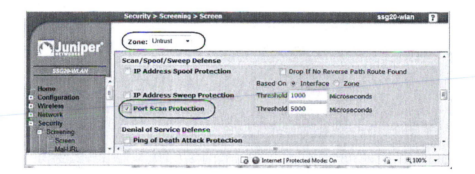

6.3.3.2 *Step 4: Perform TCP Port Scanning*

At the attacker host, the Advanced Port Scanner tool is used to perform TCP port scanning on the victim host (192.168.2.4). The next screenshot shows the identified opened and closed TCP ports in the targeted system.

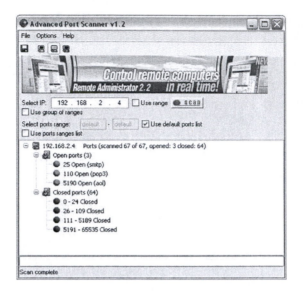

6.3.3.3 Step 5: Sniff the Generated Traffic

At the attacker host, a sniffer can be used to capture the generated traffic. For example, using the CommView sniffer, the next screenshot shows that the attack host (192.168.1.133) is performing TCP port scanning on the victim host (192.168.2.4).

6.3.3.4 Step 6: View Results in the Log File of the Juniper Networks Device

The event log contents in the Juniper Networks device after detecting the TCP port scan attack are provided in the next screenshot.

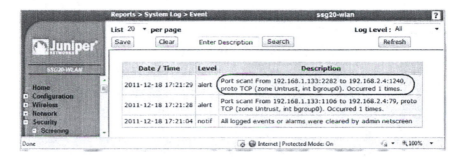

6.4 Lab 6.3: Remote Operating System Identification

6.4.1 Outcome

The learning objective of this hands-on exercise is for students to learn how to prevent remote operating system (OS) identification attacks.

6.4.2 Description

The knowledge of a system's OS helps an attacker in launching attacks. It is valuable information for both penetration testers and hackers because when vulnerabilities are found, they are normally dependent on the OS version. Before launching an exploit, an attacker might try to probe the targeted host to learn its OS.

Remote OS identification is done by actively sending packets to the remote host and analyzing the responses. There are tools, such as NetscanTools Pro, Nmap, Xprobe2, and GFI LANguard scanner, that can perform remote

OS identification. They take responses and form a fingerprint that can be queried against a signature database of known OSs. The packets sent to the remote host are unusual packets because they are not specified in the RFC. Each OS handles them differently, and by parsing the output, the attacker is able to identify what type of device is accessed and which OS is running. As an example, one type of packet used is one with the SYN and FIN bits both set. In normal operation, this type of packet should not occur so when the OS responds to this packet, it does so in a predictable fashion, which enables the program to determine which OS the host is running. The sequence numbers used with TCP also have various levels of randomness, depending on which OS is running. The tools also use this information to make a best guess at what the remote OS is. The following section describes in more detail the techniques used by the NetScanTools Pro and Nmap tools.

6.4.2.1 NetScanTools Pro

NetScanTools Pro is an integrated collection of Internet information-gathering utilities. To identify a remote OS, this tool relies on sending four basic ICMP packet types to the target:

1. Standard ICMP Echo Request (Ping) packets
2. ICMP Timestamp Request packets
3. ICMP Information Request packets
4. ICMP Subnet Mask Request packets

Then the tool looks at the response and sends further variations of the four basic packet types. The responses of the target OS are noted and used to classify the type of target OS. It is important to indicate that if some or all the above four inbound ICMP packets are blocked by a firewall, so that they cannot reach the target remote host, the OS identification mechanism will not be able to work properly and its output result is definitely not accurate. The following screenshot shows the output that results from running NetScanTools Pro with the OS fingerprint option turned on.

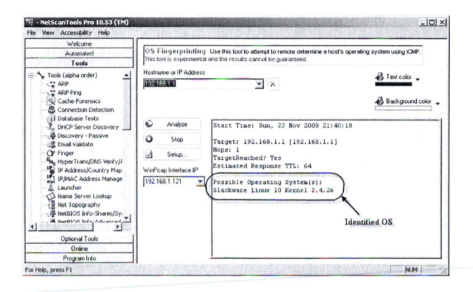

6.4.2.2 Nmap Tool

Nmap is a network exploration tool and security scanner. It is designed to allow users to scan networks to determine which hosts are up and what services they offer. Nmap also includes features such as remote OS identification, parallel scanning, port filtering detection, and timing options.

Nmap OS fingerprinting works by sending up to 16 TCP, UDP, and ICMP probes to known open and closed ports of the targeted system. These probes are specially designed to exploit various ambiguities in the standard protocol RFCs. Then Nmap listens for responses. Dozens of attributes in

those responses are analyzed and combined to generate a
fingerprint. Every probe packet is tracked and resent at least
once if there is no response. All of the packets are IPv4
with a random IP ID value. Probes to an open TCP port are
skipped if no such port has been found. For closed TCP or
UDP ports, Nmap will first check if such a port has been
found. If not, Nmap will just pick a port at random and hope
for the best.

The following are examples of TCP probe packets sent by
Nmap to a remote host:

- T1: The first packet sends a TCP packet with the SYN and
  ECN-Echo flags enabled to an open TCP port.
- T2: The second packet sends a TCP null (no flags set)
  packet with the IP DF bit set and a window field of 128 to
  an open port.
- T3: The third packet sends a TCP packet with the SYN,
  FIN, URG, and PSH flags set and a window field of 256 to
  an open port. The IP DF bit is not set.
- T4: The fourth packet sends a TCP ACK packet with IP
  DF and a window field of 1024 to an open port.
- T5: The fifth packet sends a TCP SYN packet without IP
  DF and a window field of 31,337 to a closed port.
- T6: The sixth packet sends a TCP ACK packet with IP DF
  and a window field of 32,768 to a closed port.
- T7: The seventh packet sends a TCP packet with the FIN,
  PSH, and URG flags set and a window field of 65,535 to a
  closed port. The IP DF bit is not set.

The website <http://nmap.org> describes in detail all the TCP/
IP probe packets used by Nmap.

The following screenshot shows the output that results from
running Nmap with the OS fingerprint option turned on, using
the Zenmap interface (the official Nmap GUI interface).

Some network security devices, such as Juniper Networks, are capable of blocking some OS probe packets so that the OS probe tool cannot identify the target remote OS, or the OS identification result will not be accurate.

6.4.3 Experiment

To determine how to prevent the Nmap tool from identifying a remote OS, an experiment is conducted using the Juniper Networks device. Three TCP probe packets can be blocked by the Juniper Networks device, namely,

1. *TCP packet without flags (T2):* A normal TCP packet header has at least one flag control set. A TCP packet with no control flags set is an anomalous event.

Because different OSs respond differently to such anomalies, the response (or lack of response) from the targeted device can provide a clue as to the type of OS it is running.

2. *TCP packet with SYN and FIN flags set (T3):* Both the SYN and FIN control flags are not normally set in the same TCP segment header. The SYN flag synchronizes sequence numbers to initiate a TCP connection. The FIN flag indicates the end of data transmission to finish a TCP connection. Their purposes are mutually exclusive. A TCP header with the SYN and FIN flags set is anomalous TCP behavior, causing various responses from the recipient, depending on the OS.

3. *TCP packet with FIN flag and without ACK (T7):* Normally, TCP packets with the FIN flag set also have the ACK flag set (to acknowledge the previous packet received). Because a TCP header with the FIN flag set but the ACK flag unset is anomalous TCP behavior, there is no predictable response to this. The OS might respond by sending a TCP packet with the RST flag set. Another might completely ignore it. The victim's response can provide the attacker with a clue as to its OS.

This experiment uses the same network architecture described in the Land attack hands-on exercise of Chapter 5 (Lab 5.1).

The experiment consists of the following steps:

Step 1: Configure the network interfaces in the Juniper Networks device.

Step 2: Set the security policies (filtering rules).

Step 3: Enable protection against the three TCP probe packets.

Step 4: Generate the three TCP probe packets.

Step 5: Sniff the generated traffic.

Step 6: View results in the Log file of the Juniper Networks device.

Steps 1 and 2 are similar to the ones described in the experiment of the Land attack hands-on exercise of Chapter 5 (Lab 5.1).

6.4.3.1 Step 3: Enable Protection against the Three TCP Packets

To enable protection against the three TCP probe packets in the Juniper Networks device, do the following:

■ Log in to the WebUI interface of the Juniper Networks device.
■ Select "Screening" and set the following parameters as shown in the following screenshot.
  – Set Zone to Untrust, because the Land attack traffic will be generated from an untrusted zone.
  – Select:
    • TCP Packet Without Flag Protection
    • SYN and FIN Bits Set Protection
    • FIN Bit With No ACK in Flags Protection
■ Then click "Apply."

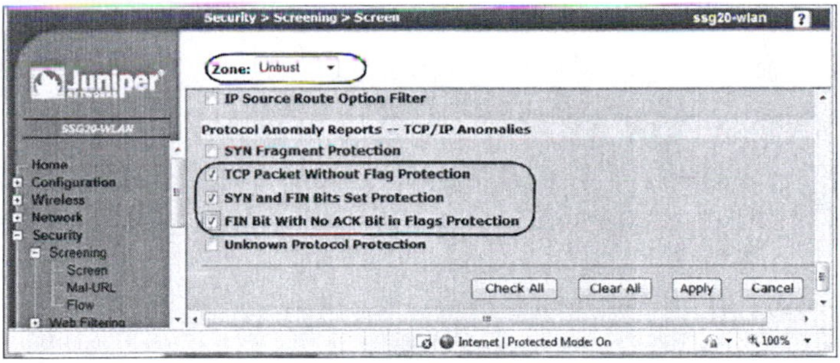

6.4.3.2 Step 4: Generate the Three TCP Probe Packets

By running the Nmap tool, the three probe TCP packets (T2, T3, and T7) are sent to a remote OS.

6.4.3.3 Step 5: Sniff the Generated Traffic

At the attacker host where Nmap is running, a CommView sniffer is used to capture the generated traffic. The next three screenshots show the T2 (TCP packet without flags), T3 (TCP packet with SYN and FIN flags set), and T7 (TCP packet with FIN flag and without ACK) packets, respectively.

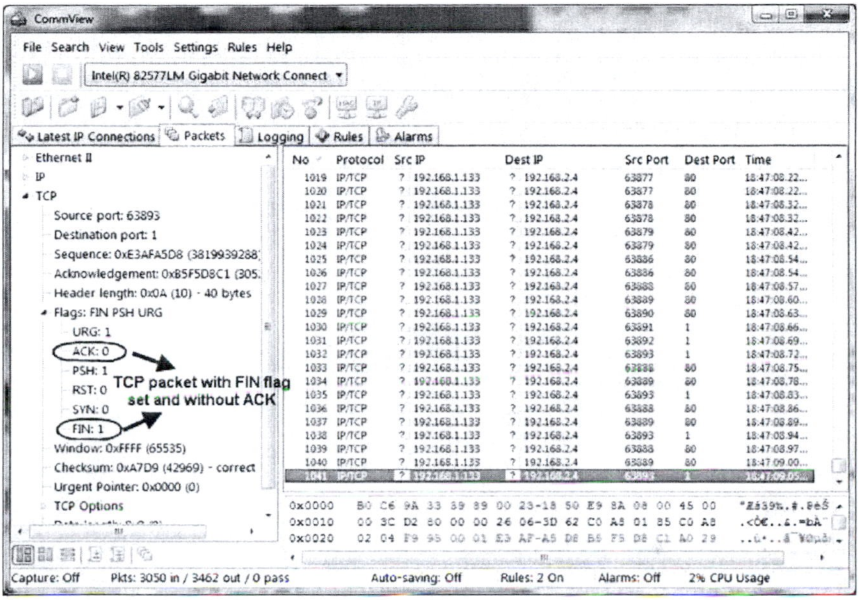

6.4.3.4 Step 6: View Results in the Log File of the Juniper Networks Device

The following screenshot shows the event log contents in the Juniper Networks device after detecting the three unusual probe TCP packets.

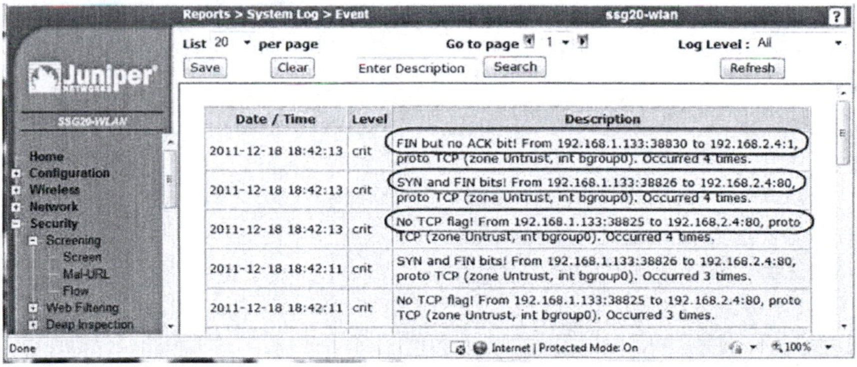

Based on the results of the tests performed by the Nmap tool, an OS signature could not be built because the three probe TCP packets generated by Nmap have been blocked by the Juniper Networks device. Therefore, Nmap could not identify the OS of the remote host (192.168.2.4), as shown in the next screenshot.

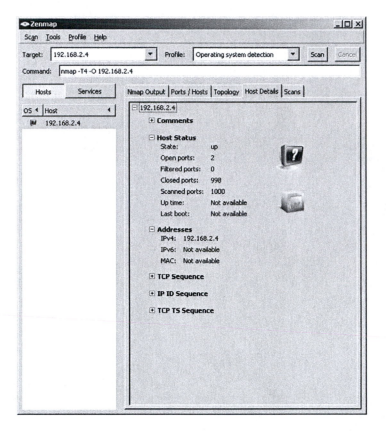

6.5 Lab 6.4: Traceroute

6.5.1 Outcome

The learning objective of this hands-on exercise is for students to learn how to analyze traceroute traffic and prevent the gathering of information about remote hosts and networks using traceroute.

6.5.2 Description

Traceroute is the program that shows the route over the network between two systems, listing all the intermediate routers a connection must pass through to get to its destination. Traceroute is a popular reconnaissance technique.

Traceroute works by causing each router along a network path to return an ICMP error message. An IP packet contains a Time-To-Live (TTL) value that specifies how long it can go on its search for a destination before being discarded. Each time a packet passes through a router, its TTL value is decremented by one; when it reaches zero, the packet is dropped, and an ICMP Time-To-Live Exceeded error message is returned to the sender.

The Traceroute program sends its first group of packets with a TTL value of 1. The first router along the path will therefore discard the packet (its TTL is decremented to 0) and return the ICMP TTL Exceeded error message. Thus, the first router on the path is found. Packets can then be sent with a TTL of 2, and then 3, and so on, causing each router along the path to return an ICMP TTL error message, identifying it to the sender. Eventually, either the final destination is reached or the maximum value is reached, and the traceroute ends.

At the final destination, a different ICMP error message is returned. Most Linux versions of Traceroute work by sending UDP datagrams to some random high-numbered port where nothing is likely to be listening. When that final system is reached, because nothing is answering on that port, an ICMP Port Unreachable error message is returned, and the Traceroute program finishes (see the following figure for the operation steps of the Linux version of Traceroute).

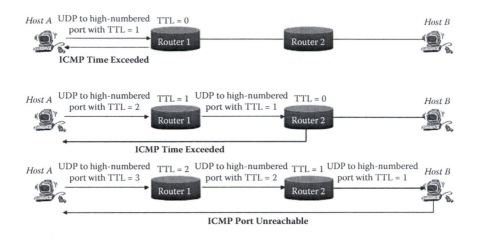

The Windows version of Traceroute uses ICMP Echo Request packets (ping packets) rather than UDP datagrams; refer to the next figure for operation steps for the Windows version of Traceroute. A few versions of Traceroute, such as the one on Solaris, allow choosing either method (high-port UDP or ICMP echo requests).

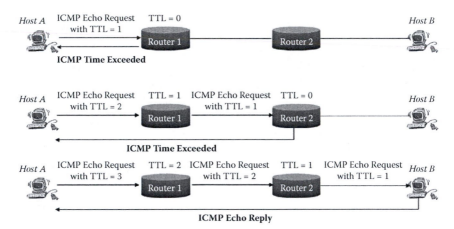

To perform traceroute, usually the online commands *Tracert* or *Traceroute* are used in a Windows environment or Linux/Unix environment, respectively. There are also GUI-based traceroute tools, such as NetScanTools Pro and VisualRoute tools. The following screenshot provides an example of a traceroute output using the NetScanTools Pro tool. There are two hops between the source host and the destination host (213.42.4.30), as two ICMP Time Exceeded packets and one ICMP Echo Reply packet have been received.

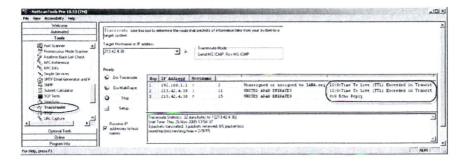

6.5.3 *Preventing Techniques*

To prevent gathering information when using Traceroute, there are two methods that can be used:

■ The first method uses a firewall to block outgoing ICMP Time Exceeded, ICMP Echo Reply, and ICMP Destination Unreachable-Port packets. To block such ICMP traffic, the following filtering rules should be implemented at the firewalls or routers:

Rule Name	Direction	Source IP	Destination IP	Protocol	Type	Code	Action
Block_ICMP_ Time_ Exceeded	Outgoing	Any	Any	ICMP	11	0	Deny
Block_ICMP_ Echo_Reply	Outgoing	Any	Any	ICMP	0	0	Deny
Block_ICMP_ Port_ Unreachable	Outgoing	Any	Any	ICMP	3	3	Deny

■ The second method uses a predefined firewall filtering rule to block traceroute traffic. Most firewall appliances include a predefined filtering rule to deny Traceroute traffic.

The following two sections describe two experiments. The first shows how to capture and analyze the packets generated by the *Tracert* command. The second shows how to prevent traceroute using a predefined filtering rule in the Juniper Networks device.

6.5.3.1 Experiment 6.4.1: Analyze Traffic Generated by the Tracert Command

The objective of this experiment is to analyze the *Tracert* command traffic. The next screenshot shows the result (output) of the execution of the *Tracert* command. It shows that there is only one hop (192.168.1.1) between the source host and the target host (192.168.2.4).

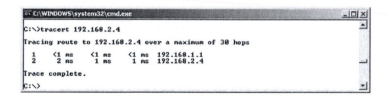

The CommView sniffer is used to capture the generated traffic. The following four screenshots show the four ICMP packets exchanged between the attacker host (source host) and the target host:

1. The first ICMP Echo Request packet with TTL = 1 sent by the source host to the target host:

2. After receiving this packet, the first router sends an ICMP Time Exceeded packet to the source host. The packet in this screenshot also shows the IP and ICMP headers of the original packet in the previous screenshot.

3. The second ICMP Echo Request packet with TTL = 2 sent by the source host to the target host:

4. The ICMP Echo Reply sent by the target host to the source host:

6.5.3.2 Experiment 6.4.2: Deny Traceroute Traffic

6.5.3.2.1 Network Architecture

This experiment uses the same network architecture described in the Land attack hands-on exercise of Chapter 5 (Lab 5.1).

6.5.3.2.2 Experiment steps:

Steps in the experiment are as follows:

Step 1: Configure the network interfaces in the Juniper Networks device.

Step 2: Create a filtering rule to deny traceroute traffic.

Step 3: Execute the *Tracert* command.

Step 4: View results in the log file of the Juniper Networks device.

6.5.3.2.2.1 Step 1: Configure the network interfaces in the Juniper Networks device

Step 1 is similar to the one described in the experiment of the Land attack hands-on lab of Chapter 5 (Lab 5.1)

6.5.3.2.2.2 Step 2: Create a filtering rule to deny traceroute traffic

In the Juniper Networks device, to create a filtering rule that allows denying traceroute, do the following:

■ Log in to the WebUI interface of the Juniper Networks device.

■ Select "Policies", then create the filtering rule as shown below.

6.5.3.2.2.3 Step 3: Execute *Tracert* command

In cases where a trace either fails to reach its destination or no ICMP Time Exceeded messages are returned, the output shows an asterisk in each of the three time columns where the round-trip time is usually displayed and a "Request timed out." The screenshot below shows that the *Tracert* command is unable to identify the list of hops between the source host and the destination host. This is because the traceroute traffic has been filtered by the filtering rule of the previous screenshot.

6.5.3.2.2.4 Step 4: View results in the log file of the Juniper Networks device

The event log contents in the Juniper Networks device after detecting and blocking traceroute traffic are shown below.

6.6 Chapter Summary

Attackers need to gather information about targeted systems and networks prior to performing their exploits. There are many available, easy-to-use techniques and tools to collect information about a targeted environment. Retrospectively, it is extremely important for an organization to know what information an attacker can acquire about itself so as to secure and minimize the potential loss of critical information. This chapter discussed some reconnaissance techniques and described how practically systems and networks can be protected from reconnaissance traffic. The hands-on exercises discussed four common reconnaissance techniques, namely, IP address sweeping, TCP port scanning, remote OS identification, and Traceroute.

Chapter 7

Packet Filtering and Inspection

7.1 Introduction

Most organizations control the traffic that crosses into and out of their networks to prevent attacks against their computer systems and to conform with various policy choices.

Network packet filtering and inspection are means to control access to networks and systems. The concept consists of determining whether a packet is allowed to enter or exit a network by comparing the packet's payload data and/or some fields' value located in the packet's header to predefined values. Packet filtering and inspection technology is found in operating systems, firewalls, intrusion detection and prevention systems, and as a security feature of most routers and of some advanced switches.

Firewalls control access into and from the network, based on a set of filtering rules that reflect and enforce the organization's security policies. Within a network, the firewall is typically the first filtering device that encounters packets that attempt to enter an organization's network from the outside, and it is typically the last device to see exiting packets. It is the firewall's job to make filtering decisions on every packet that crosses it: either to let it pass or to drop it.

This chapter discusses a series of hands-on exercises about filtering and inspecting common network traffic and standard/nonstandard services using firewall filtering rules. The chapter includes an exercise about the consistency and efficiency verification of firewall filtering rules. The exercises use the following hardware devices and software tools:

- Juniper Networks SSG20 Wireless Appliance* (Juniper Networks device): as a firewall device
- Cisco ASA 5520 Adaptive Security Appliance†: as a firewall device
- CommView Tool‡: network monitor and analyzer tool (sniffer)
- CommView Visual Packet Builder§: Graphical User Interface (GUI)-based packet generator
- LiteServe¶: Web, FTP, e-mail, and Telnet server software
- FirePAC**: stand-alone software tool for verifying the inconsistency and inefficiency of a filtering rule set

7.2 Lab 7.1: Basic Packet Filtering

7.2.1 Outcome

The learning objective of this hands-on exercise is for students to learn how to implement firewall filtering rules for basic security policies.

---

* http://www.juniper.net
† http://www.cisco.com
‡ http://www.tamos.com
§ http://www.tamos.com
¶ http://www.cmfperception.com
** http://www.athenasecurity.com

7.2.2 Basic Packet Filtering

Basic packet filtering is the selective passing or blocking of packets as they pass through a network interface. The criteria that packet filtering uses when inspecting packets are based on the Layer 3 (IPv4 and IPv6) and Layer 4 [TCP (Transmission Control Protocol), UDP (User Datagram Protocol), ICMP (Internet Control Message Protocol), and ICMPv6] headers of the OSI (Open Systems Interconnection) model. The most often used criteria are source and destination IP addresses, source and destination TCP/UDP ports, TCP flag bits, type and code fields in an ICMP header, and the protocol field of the Layer 4 header.

Firewall filtering rules specify the criteria that a packet must match and the resulting action. The action is either *Pass* (Let the packet through), *Block* (Do not forward the packet), or *Reject* (same as Drop, except that a special ICMP packet is sent back to the sender informing it that the packet was filtered). Filtering rules are evaluated in sequential order, first to last. There is an implicit *"Pass all"* or *"Deny all"* at the end of a filtering rule set, meaning that if a packet does not match any filtering rule, the resulting action will be to pass or deny. The recommended practice when implementing filtering rules is to take a "default deny" approach. That is, to deny *everything* and then selectively allow certain traffic through the firewall. This approach is recommended because it errs on the side of caution and also makes writing a rule set easier.

For example, to filter out all Ping traffic coming to the network, block all incoming ICMP echo request packets (Type = 8 and Code = 0). To filter out all incoming requests to access internal FTP servers, block all incoming traffic that is directed at TCP port 21. For these two security policies, filtering rules should be defined and implemented in the selected packet filtering technology (firewall, router, switch, operating system, etc.). The following two filtering rules (R1 and R2) reflect the above two security policies:

Rule	Direction	Source IP Address	Destination IP Address	Protocol	Type	Code	Action
R1	Incoming	Any	Any	ICMP	8	0	Deny

Rule	Direction	Source IP Address	Destination IP Address	Protocol	Source Port	Destination Port	Action
R2	Incoming	Any	Any	TCP	Any	21	Deny

7.2.3 Experiment

This experiment consists of implementing filtering rules in the Juniper Networks device for a variety of security policies. The security policies allow applying filtering rules on network traffic exchanged between client hosts and servers.

7.2.4 Network Architecture

The following figure illustrates the network architecture used in the experiment. The traffic exchanged between the three networks goes through the Juniper Networks device, where it is filtered and inspected by a set of filtering rules.

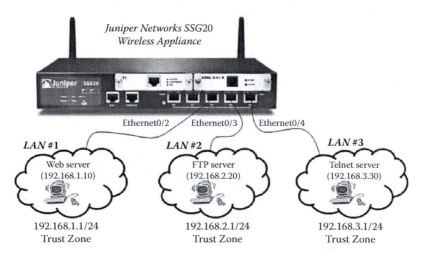

7.2.5 *Experiment Steps*

The experiment consists of the following steps:

Step 1: Configure the network interfaces in the Juniper
   Networks device.
Step 2: Set up Web, FTP, and Telnet servers.
Step 3: Implement filtering rules for security policies.
Step 4: Test the filtering rules and view the results in the
   Log file of the Juniper Networks device.

7.2.5.1 *Step 1: Configure the Network Interfaces in the Juniper Networks Device*

Using the WebUI interface of the Juniper Networks
device, configure the interfaces *ethernet0/2, ether-net0/3,* and *ethernet0/4,* as shown in the next screenshot.
LAN #1 (192.168.1.1/24), LAN #2 (192.168.2.1/24), and LAN #3
(192.168.3.1/24) are connected to the network interfaces *ether-net0/2, ethernet0/3,* and *ethernet0/4,* respectively.

Name	IP/Netmask	Zone	Type	Link
bgroup0	192.168.1.1/24	Trust	Layer3	Up
ethernet0/2				Up
bgroup1	192.168.2.1/24	Trust	Layer3	Up
ethernet0/3				Up
bgroup2	192.168.3.1/24	Trust	Layer3	Up
ethernet0/4				Up
bgroup3	0.0.0.0/0	Null	Unused	Down

7.2.5.2 *Step 2: Set Up Web, FTP, and Telnet Servers*

There are many available server software programs on the
Internet that can be downloaded and used to set up Web,
FTP, and Telnet servers. For example, if you are using a

Windows-based computer, you can use the built-in Internet Information Services (IIS). It is a set of Internet-based services for servers created by Microsoft for use with Microsoft Windows. The services provided currently include FTP (File Transfer Protocol), FTPS (File Transfer Protocol Secure), SMTP (Simple Mail Transfer Protocol), NNTP (Network News Transfer Protocol), and HTTP/ HTTPS (HyperText Transfer Protocol/HyperText Transfer Protocol Secure).

In this hands-on lab, the *LiteServe* tool is used to set up the Web, FTP, and Telnet servers (see next screenshot). The servers are set up as follows:

- In LAN #1, a host with IP address 192.168.1.10 hosts a Web server.
- In LAN #2, a host with IP address 192.168.2.20 hosts an FTP server.
- In LAN #3, a host with IP address 192.168.3.30 hosts a Telnet server.

7.2.5.3 Step 3: Implement Filtering Rules for Security Policies

In the Juniper Networks device, to implement a filtering rule for a security policy, do the following:

- Log in to the WebUI interface of the device.
- Select "Policy"; then specify the zones of the networks involved in the filtering rule, as shown next:

- Click on the "New" button and set the values of the fields of the filtering rule. For example, the following screenshot of a filtering rule shows that all hosts in LAN #1 (192.168.1.1/24) are allowed to Ping all hosts in LAN #2 (192.168.2.1/24). In addition, the traffic exchanged between the hosts will be logged.

The following are examples of security policies and their corresponding filtering rules:

1. *Security Policy #1 (SP#1):* LAN #1's hosts are allowed to ping LAN #2 and LAN #3's hosts. However, LAN #2 and LAN #3's hosts are not allowed to Ping LAN #1's hosts. The default security policy is "Deny all". The following screenshot shows the filtering rules implemented in the Juniper Networks device and corresponds to the security policy SP#1:

Policy > Policies (From All zones To All zones)										ssg20-wlan	🔲

List 20 ▾ **per page**   Search
From All zones ▾   **To** All zones ▾ Go   New

Trust Intra-zone policy, total policy: 3

ID	Source	Destination	Service	Action		Options		Configure			Enable	Move
1	192.168.1.1/24	192.168.2.1/24 192.168.3.1/24	PING	✅	🔳			Edit	Clone	Remove	☑	↕ →
2	192.168.2.1/24 192.168.3.1/24	192.168.1.1/24	PING	❌	🔳			Edit	Clone	Remove	☑	↕ →
3	Any	Any	ANY	❌				Edit	Clone	Remove	☑	↕ →

- The rule with ID 1 allows LAN #1's hosts (192.168.1.1/24) to ping LAN #2's hosts (192.168.2.1/24) and LAN #3's hosts (192.168.3.1/24).
- The rule with ID 2 does not allow LAN #2's hosts and LAN #3's hosts to ping LAN #1's hosts.
- The rule with ID 3 is the default security.

2. *Security Policy #2 (SP#2):* LAN #3's hosts are allowed to access the Web site (192.168.1.10/32) in LAN #1. However, LAN #2's hosts are not allowed to access the Web site. The next screenshot shows the filtering rules implemented in the Juniper Networks device and corresponds to the security policy SP#2:

Policy > Policies (From All zones To All zones)										ssg20-wlan	🔲

List 20 ▾ **per page**   Search
From All zones ▾   **To** All zones ▾ Go   New

Trust Intra-zone policy, total policy: 2

ID	Source	Destination	Service	Action		Options		Configure			Enable	Move
1	192.168.3.1/24	192.168.1.10/32	HTTP	✅				Edit	Clone	Remove	☑	↕ →
2	192.168.2.1/24	192.168.1.10/32	HTTP	❌	🔳			Edit	Clone	Remove	☑	↕ →

- The rule with ID 1 allows LAN #3's hosts (192.168.3.1/24) to access the Web site (192.168.1.10/32) in LAN #1.
- The rule with ID 2 does not allow LAN #2's hosts (192.168.2.1/24) to access the Web site (192.168.1.10/32) in LAN #1.

3. *Security Policy #3 (SP#3):* The only host in LAN #1 that is allowed to telnet the host (192.168.3.30) in LAN #3 is the host (192.168.1.10). The following screenshot shows the filtering rules implemented in the Juniper Networks device and corresponds to the security policy SP#3:

Policy > Policies (From All zones To All zones)   ssg20-wlan   ?

List 20 ▾ per page   Search

From All zones ▾   To All zones ▾ Go   New

Trust Intra-zone policy, total policy: 2

ID	Source	Destination	Service	Action	Options	Configure			Enable	Move
1	192.168.1.10/32	192.168.3.30/32	TELNET	✅		Edit	Clone	Remove	☑	↕ →
2	192.168.1.1/24	192.168.3.30/32	TELNET	❌	🔲	Edit	Clone	Remove	☑	↕ →

- The rule with ID 1 allows the host (192.168.1.10/32) in LAN #1 to access the Telnet server (192.168.3.30/32) in LAN #3.
- The rule with ID 2 does not allow LAN #1's hosts (192.168.1.1/24) to access the Telnet server (192.168.3.30/32) in LAN #3.

4. *Security Policy #4 (SP #4):* LAN #1's hosts are allowed to access any FTP server in LAN #2. However, LAN #3's hosts are not allowed to access any FTP server in LAN #2. The next screenshot shows the filtering rules implemented in the Juniper Networks device and corresponds to the security policy SP #4:

Policy > Policies (From All zones To All zones)   ssg20-wlan   ?

List 20 ▾ per page   Search

From All zones ▾   To All zones ▾ Go   New

Trust Intra-zone policy, total policy: 2

ID	Source	Destination	Service	Action	Options	Configure			Enable	Move
1	192.168.1.1/24	192.168.2.1/24	FTP	✅		Edit	Clone	Remove	☑	↕ →
2	192.168.3.1/24	192.168.2.1/24	FTP	❌	🔲	Edit	Clone	Remove	☑	↕ →

- The rule with ID 1 allows LAN #1's hosts (192.168.1.1/24) to access any FTP server in LAN #2 (192.168.2.1/24).
- The rule with ID 2 does not allow LAN #3's hosts (192.168.3.1/24) to access any FTP server in LAN #2 (192.168.2.1/24).

7.2.5.4 Step 4: Test the Filtering Rules and View the Results in the Log File of the Juniper Networks Device

Each security policy is easily tested by generating the appropriate traffic and then checking the content of the log event in the Juniper Networks device. For example, to test the filtering rules corresponding to the security policy SP#1, we assume that a host in LAN #2 tries to Ping a host in LAN #1. However, the event log of the Juniper Networks device (next screenshot) shows that the Ping traffic has been denied by the filtering rule with ID 2.

To test the filtering rules corresponding to the security policy SP#2, we assume that a host in LAN #2 tries to access the Web site (192.168.1.10) in LAN #1. However, the event log of the Juniper Networks device (next screenshot) shows that the Web (HTTP) traffic has been denied by the filtering rule with ID 2.

Reports > Policies > Traffic Log					ssg20-wlan	

List 20 ▾ per page

[Save] [Clear] [Refresh]

Traffic log for policy :	ID	Source	Destination	Service	Action	
	2	Trust/192.168.2.1/24	Trust/192.168.1.10/32	HTTP	Deny	

Date/Time	Source Address/Port	Destination Address/Port	Translated Source Address/Port	Translated Destination Address/Port	Service	Duration	Bytes Sent	Bytes Received	Close Reason
2011-11-21 23:13:48	192.168.2.20:1087	192.168.1.10:80	0.0.0.0:0	0.0.0.0:0	HTTP	0 sec.	0	0	Traffic Denied
2011-11-21 23:13:42	192.168.2.20:1087	192.168.1.10:80	0.0.0.0:0	0.0.0.0:0	HTTP	0 sec.	0	0	Traffic Denied
2011-11-21 23:13:39	192.168.2.20:1087	192.168.1.10:80	0.0.0.0:0	0.0.0.0:0	HTTP	0 sec.	0	0	Traffic Denied

7.3 Lab 7.2: Nonstandard Services Filtering

7.3.1 Outcome

The learning objective of this hands-on exercise is for students to learn how to implement firewall filtering rules for services running on nonstandard TCP and UDP ports.

7.3.2 Nonstandard Services Filtering

Standard services usually run on standard ports. For example, the standard ports for HTTP and FTP services are 80 and 21, respectively. Client programs, such as Web browsers, usually do not require the user to specify the ports on which standard services are running. They require just the IP address (or domain name) of the target server hosting the service. However, for a given reason, such as for security reasons or the unavailability of the standard ports, standard services can be run on alternative ports. In such a case, client programs require that the user provide the alternative port number of the target service. Otherwise, the client program will not be able to connect to the service, because it is running on an unknown port. For example, to access a Web server running on port 3000 and located in a host with IP 192.168.1.1, the user needs to enter the URL http://192.168.1.1:3000 in the Web browser.

Therefore, filtering rules that filter services running on standard ports are useless for filtering services running on nonstandard ports. For example, if you want to prevent external hosts from accessing any internal nonstandard Web server running on port 3000, then the following filtering rule will not work for this security policy:

Rule	Direction	Source IP Address	Destination IP Address	Protocol	Source Port	Destination Port	Action
R1	Incoming	Any	Any	TCP	Any	80	Deny

However, the following filtering rule works because it prevents hosts from accessing any internal nonstandard Web server running on port 3000:

Rule	Direction	Source IP Address	Destination IP Address	Protocol	Source Port	Destination Port	Action
R1	Incoming	Any	Any	TCP	Any	3000	Deny

Firewalls usually include predefined rules to filter standard services and are unable to filter nonstandard services unless the user provides the firewall with the TCP or UDP ports of the nonstandard services. In practice, this is achieved by creating a new service profile for the nonstandard service and specifying its corresponding TCP or UDP port number.

7.3.3 Experiment

This experiment consists of creating a nonstandard service and then implementing the appropriate filtering rule to filter traffic targeting the service, using the Juniper Networks device.

7.3.4 Network Architecture

This experiment uses the same network architecture described in the previous hands-on exercise (Lab 7.1).

7.3.5 Experiment Steps

The experiment consists of the following steps:

Step 1: Configure the network interfaces in the Juniper Networks device.

Step 2: Set up a nonstandard Web server running on port 3000.

Step 3: Create a nonstandard service profile in the Juniper Networks device.

Step 4: Implement filtering rules to filter traffic targeting the nonstandard service.

Step 5: Test the filtering rules and view the results in the event log of the Juniper Networks device.

7.3.5.1 Step 1: Configure the Network Interfaces in the Juniper Networks Device

Step 1 is similar to the previous hands-on lab's (Lab 7.1) Step 1.

7.3.5.2 Step 2: Set Up a Nonstandard Web Server Running on Port 3000

The *LiterServe* tool is used to set up the nonstandard Web server. The next screenshot shows that a Web server is set to run on the nonstandard port 3000.

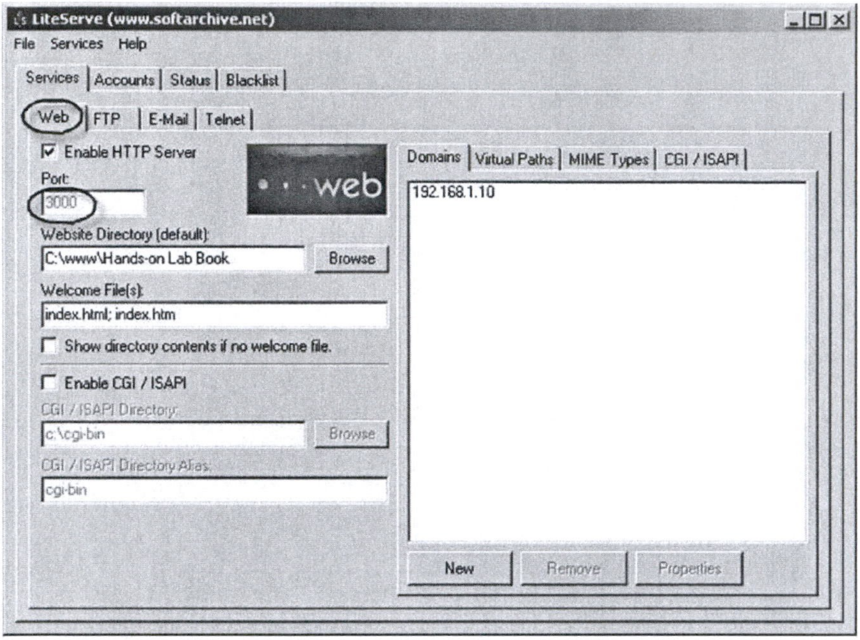

7.3.5.3 Step 3: Create a Nonstandard Service Profile in the Juniper Networks Device

In the Juniper Networks device, to create a new profile for a nonstandard service, do the following:

- Log in to the WebUI interface of the Juniper Networks device.
- Select "Objects" = > "Services" = > "Custom" as shown in the following screenshot.
- Select a name for the nonstandard service (for example, Web server (3000)).
- Select "TCP" for the Layer 4 transport protocol.
- Because the nonstandard service will run on port 3000, set the value of the destination port to 3000.
- Click on the "OK" button.

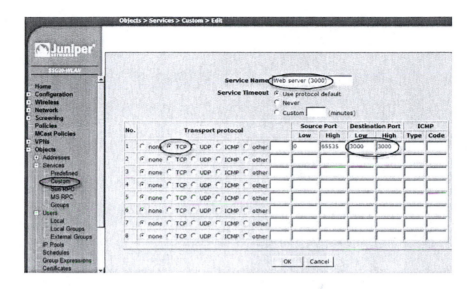

7.3.5.4 Step 4: Implement Filtering Rules to Filter Traffic Targeting the Nonstandard Service

As an example, we assume that we want to create a filtering rule for the following security policy:

- LAN#3's hosts (192.168.3.1/24) are not allowed to access the nonstandard Web server (192.168.1.10) in LAN #1.

The following steps and screenshot show how to create a filtering rule for the above security policy in the Juniper Networks device:

- Log in to the WebUI interface of the device.
- Select "Policies"; then specify the zones of the networks related to the security policy.
- Set *Source address* to 192.168.3.1/24.
- Set *Destination address* to 192.168.1.10/32.
- Set *Service* to "Web server (3000)".
- Set *Action* to *Deny*.
- Select *Logging*.

7.3.5.5 Step 5: Test the Filtering Rules and View the Results in the Event Log of the Juniper Networks Device

To test the above filtering rule, from a host in LAN #3, open a Web browser and enter the following URL: "http://192.168.1.10:3000". Then open the event log corresponding to the above filtering rule in the Juniper Networks device. The next screenshot shows that the Juniper Networks device has denied the traffic coming from host 192.168.3.30 and destined to port 3000 on host 192.168.1.10.

7.4 Lab 7.3: Consistency and Efficiency Verification of Firewall Filtering Rules

7.4.1 Outcome

The learning objective of this hands-on exercise is for students to learn how to verify the consistency and efficiency of firewall filtering rules.

7.4.2 Consistency and Efficiency of Filtering Rules

Firewalls play an important role in the enforcement of access control policies in contemporary networks. Network perimeter security policy is generally described by the implemented filtering rules in a firewall. Generating such rules is considered a formidable task, due to the network complexity (many network segments), the diversity of the network's equipment (personal computer, servers, routers, etc.), and the large number of vulnerabilities within such equipment.

However, firewalls are effective only if they are configured correctly, such that their filtering rules are consistent and implemented according to the intended security policies. Unfortunately, due to the potentially large number of rules and their complex relationships with each other, the task of firewall configuration is notoriously error prone. In practice, firewalls are often misconfigured, leaving security holes in the protection system. In addition, because the majority of firewalls are custom-configured devices, manual generation of firewall filtering rules, which is subject to human error, can produce faults that can be transformed into anomalies that alter the normal operation of the filtering process. That is, weak or ill-defined filtering rules can modify the expected and desired responses of the firewall and, as a consequence, may increase the possibility of the firewall allowing undesired packets to enter or leave the network. Misconfiguration errors result in inconsistencies in the firewall. An example of a critical inconsistency is when all the packets that are intended to be denied by a given filtering rule are accepted by some preceding rules. Therefore, the intended effect of the Deny rule is cancelled by the preceding Accept rules.

The consistencies and effectiveness of a firewall are strongly dependent on the ability of the administrator to develop well-defined and coherent filtering rules and to be able to continuously clean and verify the correctness of these rules. It is important to mention that in cases where there are dozens or hundreds of filtering rules, inconsistent and inefficient filtering rules with anomalies might not be easy to spot.

We consider three types of inconsistencies—*shadowing, generalization,* and *correlation*—and one inefficiency—*redundancy.* The definitions of these inconsistencies and the inefficiency follow:

- **Shadowing:** A rule is shadowed by a preceding rule if it is a subset of the preceding rule and the two rules define different actions. That is, an upper rule shadows a lower rule when the upper rule matches all the packets that are also matched by the lower rule, such that the lower rule will never be reached by the firewall. A firewall performs rule lookup, starting from the top of the filtering rule list. When it finds a match for traffic received, it stops the rule lookup in the filtering rule list. Shadowing is a critical error in the security policy, as the lower filtering rule never takes effect. The upper rule is called the shadowing rule. The lower rule is called the shadowed rule. The next table shows an example of shadowing rules. To correct this situation, simply remove one of the filtering rules or reverse the order of the two filtering rules, putting the more specific one (shadowed rule) first.

Rule	Direction	Source IP address	Destination IP address	Protocol	Source Port	Destination Port	Action
R1	Incoming	Any	Any	TCP	Any	80	**Allow**
R2	Incoming	192.168.3.30	Any	TCP	Any	80	**Deny**

Shadowing is a critical inconsistency because it is likely that the rule with the denial action is there to stop some well-known malicious traffic. However, due to the shadowing, that traffic is not actually stopped by the firewall. Such inconsistencies can easily occur when the firewall has a distributed implementation and/or when it is managed by multiple administrators, both being frequent cases in large organizations.

■ ***Generalization:*** A rule is a generalization of a preceding rule if it is a superset of the preceding rule and the two rules define different actions. The next table shows an example of generalization rules. Generalization is often used by firewall administrators to make a rule set compact. Nevertheless, it may be the case that some of the generalizations are not intentional, in which case it is useful to detect them and let the administrator decide whether or not they are harmful.

Rule	Direction	Source IP address	Destination IP address	Protocol	Source Port	Destination Port	Action
R1	Incoming	192.168.3.30	Any	TCP	Any	25	**Deny**
R2	Incoming	Any	Any	TCP	Any	25	**Allow**

■ ***Correlation:*** Two rules correlate if their intersection is not empty, they are not related by the superset or subset relations, and they define different actions. Packets that match the intersection will take the action of the preceding rule. The next table is an example of correlation rules.

Rule	Direction	Source IP address	Destination IP address	Protocol	Source Port	Destination Port	Action
R1	Incoming	192.168.3.30	Any	TCP	Any	Any	**Deny**
R2	Incoming	Any	Any	TCP	Any	25	**Allow**

■ ***Redundancy:*** A redundant rule performs the same action on the same packets as another rule such that its removal would not affect the operation of the firewall. A redundant rule may not contribute to making the filtering decision, but it adds to the size of the filtering rule list and might increase the search time and space requirements. There are two types of redundancy: masked redundancy and partially masked redundancy. In the case of masked redundancy, the successor rule is unnecessary. However, in the case of partially masked redundancy, the preceding rule is unnecessary. The next two tables provide examples of masked redundancy and partially masked redundancy, respectively.

Rule	Direction	Source IP address	Destination IP address	Protocol	Source Port	Destination Port	Action
R1	Incoming	Any	Any	TCP	Any	80	**Deny**
R2	Incoming	192.168.3.30	Any	TCP	Any	80	**Deny**

Rule	Direction	Source IP address	Destination IP address	Protocol	Source Port	Destination Port	Action
R1	Incoming	Any	Any	TCP	Any	25	**Allow**
R2	Incoming	Any	Any	TCP	Any	Any	**Allow**

Note that not all these inconsistencies and redundancies are equally critical. Usually, only shadowing is considered a configuration error, while generalization and correlation are, in fact, often used by firewall administrators to make a rule set compact. Nevertheless, it may be the case that some of the generalizations and correlations are not intentional, in which case it is useful to detect them and let the administrator decide whether or not they are harmful. Redundancy is not considered a serious configuration error either, but redundant rules are clearly useless; therefore, it is worth identifying and removing them and increasing the efficiency of filtering by doing so.

7.4.3 Importance of the Filtering Rules Order

The order of filtering rules is a crucial and important factor during the filtering process. In fact, any reorganization of the filtering rules can change completely the filtering process results. The example illustrated in the next three tables shows clearly how the reordering of the filtering rules may alter the whole expected filtering results for some packets.

The first table shows two filtering rules and their order (AB). The firewall uses the two rules to filter all incoming and outgoing packets. The second table shows the results of the filter process of two packets (Packet 1 and Packet 2). While filtering the two packets, the filtering process keeps the order specified by the first table, which is "AB". The second table shows clearly that the filter process results (*Real action*) are similar to the expected results (*Desired action*). However, the third table shows that when the order of the filtering rules changes to "BA", the filtering process generates a *Real* action (Deny), which is not similar to the *Desired* action (Allow).

Rules	Source IP	Destination IP	Action
A	10.*.*.*	172.16.6.*	ALLOW
B	10.1.99.*	172.16.*.*	DENY

Packet	Source IP	Target IP	Desired action	Real action
1	10.1.99.1	172.16.1.1	DENY	DENY(B)
2	10.1.99.1	172.16.6.1	ALLOW	ALLOW(A)

Packet	Source IP	Target IP	Desired action	Real action
1	10.1.99.1	172.16.1.1	DENY	DENY (B)
2	10.1.99.1	172.16.6.1	ALLOW	DENY (B)

Checking a large firewall (i.e., hundreds of filtering rules) for inconsistencies and inefficiencies is difficult and prone to errors when it is done manually and in an ad hoc manner. Thus, automated tools are required to assume such a task. However, very few firewalls integrate the inconsistency and inefficiency verification capabilities of the filtering rule set. For example, the Juniper Networks device provides a simple online command that identifies redundant and shadowed rules. There are also very few stand-alone software tools, such as the *FirePAC* tool and Firesec,* that are able to verify the inconsistency and inefficiency of filtering rules set. The FirePAC tool analyzes firewall configuration files for security risks, identifies problem rules in the configuration, determines redundant and unused rules, and summarizes the services allowed by the filtering rules. FirePAC also provides the firewall's administrator with recommendations on how to correct the situation. Reversing the order of some filtering rules or removing some of them are examples of recommendations. It is then the administrator's responsibility to correct the situation. Firesec is a solution for firewall filtering rules analysis. It addresses the problems inherent with large rule sets and helps purge and update a rule base as per network requirements. Firesec analyzes the rule base to address instances of two or more rules that match the same traffic and perform the

---

* http://www.niiconsulting.com

same action, or two or more rules that match the same traffic but perform opposite actions, or rules that can be combined by creating object groups. Firesec provides multiple functions such as removing redundant rules, grouping similar rules, and searching for vulnerable rule patterns.

The following two experiments show the steps used to verify the consistency and efficiency of firewall filtering rules using the Juniper Networks device and the FirePAC tool, respectively.

7.4.4 Experiment: Juniper Networks device

This experiment consists of using the Juniper Networks device to verify the consistency and efficiency of a set of firewall filtering rules.

7.4.5 Network Architecture

This experiment uses the same network architecture described in the Packet Filtering lab (Lab 7.1).

7.4.6 Experiment Steps

The experiment consists of the following steps:

Step 1: Configure the network interfaces in the Juniper Networks device.
Step 2: Implement inconsistent and inefficient filtering rules.
Step 3: Verify the consistency and efficiency of the filtering rules.

7.4.6.1 Step 1: Configure the Network Interfaces in the Juniper Networks Device

Step 1 is similar to the one of the experiment of the Packet Filtering lab (Lab 7.1).

7.4.6.2 Step 2: Implement Inconsistent and Inefficient Filtering Rules

Log in to the WebUI interface of the Juniper Networks device, select "Policy", and then implement the following inconsistent and inefficient filtering rules (see next screenshot):

- Rules R1 and R2 are Shadowing rules.
- Rule R3 and R4 are Generalization rules.
- Rule R5 and R6 are Correlation rules.
- Rules R7 and R8 are Masked redundancy rules.
- Rules R9 and R10 are Partially masked redundancy rules.

7.4.6.3 Step 3: Verify the Consistency and Efficiency of the Filtering Rules

The Juniper Networks device provides an online command that allows verifying the consistency and efficiency of filtering rules. To perform this task, connect a host to the Juniper Networks device using a console cable and Microsoft Hyper Terminal; then type the online command "exec policy verify". The screenshot below shows the results of the execution of this online command.

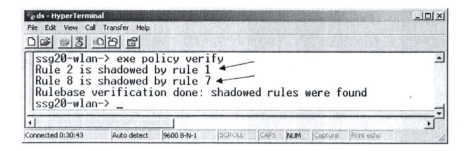

The Juniper Networks device was able to identify that Rule 2 is shadowed by Rule 1, and Rule 8 is shadowed by Rule 7. Hence, the Juniper Networks device classifies Masked redundancy rules as Shadowed rules. However, the Juniper Networks device was unable to detect the presence of Generalization rules (R3 and R4), Correlation rules (R5, and R6), and the Partially masked redundancy rules (R9 and R10) among the list of filtering rules. It is clear that the Juniper Networks device does not include a powerful mechanism for verifying the consistency and efficiency of filtering rules.

7.4.7 Experiment: FirePAC Tool

This experiment consists of using the FirePAC tool to verify the consistency and efficiency of the same set of firewall filtering rules (Section 7.4.6.2). The FirePAC tool requires as input data the firewall configuration file, which includes the set of filtering rules.

7.4.8 Experiment Steps

The experiment consists of the following steps:

Step 1: Acquire the firewall configuration file.
Step 2: Verify the consistency and efficiency of the filtering rules.
Step 3: Analysis of the FirePAC tool's findings.

7.4.8.1 Step 1: Acquire the Firewall Configuration File

The following are the steps to collect the configuration file of the Juniper Networks device:

- Connect to the Juniper Networks device using a console cable and the Microsoft Hyper Terminal tool.
- From the bar menu of Microsoft Hyper Terminal tool, select "Transfer", then "Capture Text…" (screenshot below).

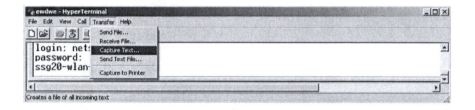

- Select a folder and a name for the firewall configuration file (screenshot below).

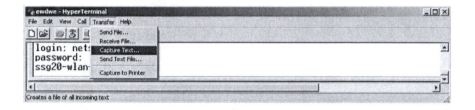

- Enter the command "set console page 0", then the command "get config" (screenshot below).

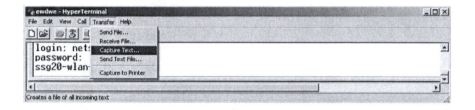

7.4.8.2 Step 2: Verify the Consistency and Efficiency of the Filtering Rules

The following are the steps employed to verify the consistency and efficiency of the filtering rules shown in Section 7.4.6.2, but using the FirePAC tool:

- Run the FirePAC tool.
- Select "UPDATE" from the GUI interface of the FirePAC tool (screenshot below) and follow the steps.
- Select "REPORT" from the GUI interface of the FirePAC tool to generate a report showing any inconstancy and/or inefficiency among the filtering rules (screenshot below).

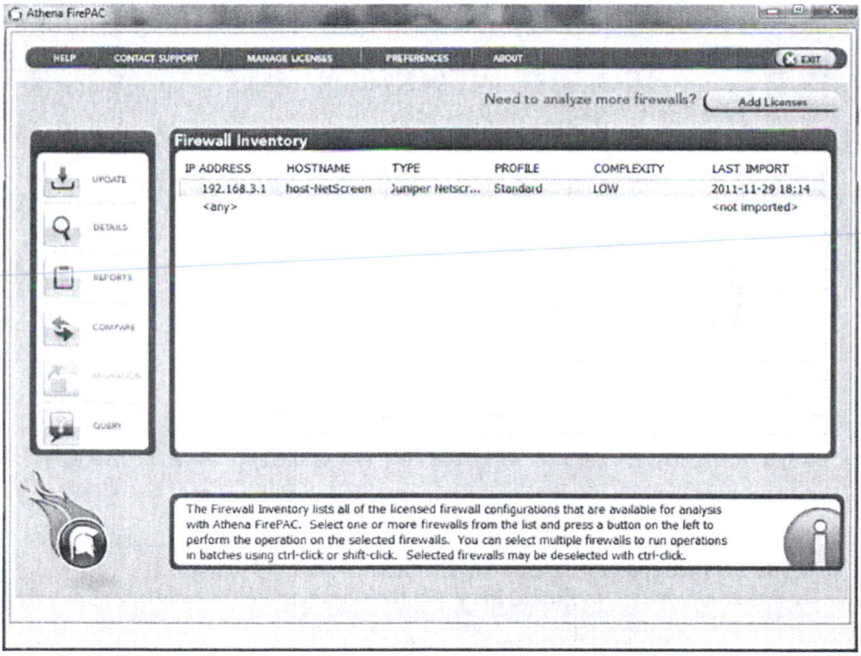

7.4.8.3 Step 3: Analysis of the FirePAC Tool's Findings

The FirePAC tool produces reports regarding the results of the analysis of the input filtering rules set. The following screen shows the part of the report related to the identified inconsistencies and inefficiencies within the input filtering rules. The report shows mainly that:

- Three redundant and shadowed rules have been identified.
- Three order-dependency rules have been identified.

ATHENA FirePAC

Firewall Analysis Summary

Host name:host-NetScreen

Completed on Tue Nov 29 18:17:58 GST 2011

Firewall Name: host-NetScreen
Device Model: Juniper Netscreen

Rule Analysis

This report provides an analysis of the firewall acl rules based on rule relationships, rule usage obtained from firewall traffic log data, and checks for potentially dangerous services.

Configuration Summary

We found a total of 30.0% of rules (3 out of 10) that can potentially be removed from the rule base.

ACL Rules	10
Network Group Objects	0
Network Objects	12
Service Group Objects	6
Service Objects	138

Rule Cleanup

Redundant and Shadowed Rules	3
Unused Rules	0
Rules without Logging enabled	10

Rule Optimization

Most Used Rules	0
Rule Order Dependency	3
Optimized Rule Order	

The next screen provides a more detailed report about the finding of the FirePAC tool, that is

- Rule 2 (Line 169) is shadowed by rule 1 (Line 166).
- Rule 8 (Line 187) is redundant to rule 7 (Line 184).
- Rule 9 (Line 190) is shadowed by rule 10 (Line 193).

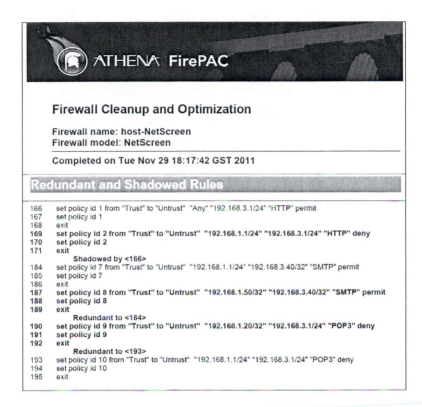

Firewall Cleanup and Optimization

Firewall name: host-NetScreen
Firewall model: NetScreen

Completed on Tue Nov 29 18:17:42 GST 2011

Redundant and Shadowed Rules

```
166    set policy id 1 from "Trust" to "Untrust"  "Any" "192.168.3.1/24" "HTTP" permit
167    set policy id 1
168    exit
169    set policy id 2 from "Trust" to "Untrust"  "192.168.1.1/24" "192.168.3.1/24" "HTTP" deny
170    set policy id 2
171    exit
             Shadowed by <166>
184    set policy id 7 from "Trust" to "Untrust"  "192.168.1.1/24" "192.168.3.40/32" "SMTP" permit
185    set policy id 7
186    exit
187    set policy id 8 from "Trust" to "Untrust"  "192.168.1.50/32" "192.168.3.40/32" "SMTP" permit
188    set policy id 8
189    exit
             Redundant to <184>
190    set policy id 9 from "Trust" to "Untrust"  "192.168.1.20/32" "192.168.3.1/24" "POP3" deny
191    set policy id 9
192    exit
             Redundant to <193>
193    set policy id 10 from "Trust" to "Untrust"  "192.168.1.1/24" "192.168.3.1/24" "POP3" deny
194    set policy id 10
195    exit
```

Among the list of rules shown in the previous screen, the next screen shows the order-dependent rules:

■ Rule 2 (Line 169) is order dependent to rule 1 (Line 166).
■ Rule 4 (Line 175) is order dependent to rule 3 (Line 172).
■ Rule 6 (Line 181) is order dependent by rule 5 (Line 178).

A rule that is order dependent on another rule (those rules marked bold in the following screen) has overlapping matching ranges with the other rule and hence cannot be moved above the source of dependency without changing the behavior of the firewall. Similarly, a rule that is the source of a dependency cannot be moved below the dependent rule. Thus, a rule order dependency limits rule movement.

The FirePAC tool provides more detailed analysis of the filtering rule set and generates more detailed reports than the Juniper Networks device. For example, the Juniper Networks device did not make any difference between redundant and shadowed rules and was unable to identify partially masked redundancy rules (rules 9 and 10). Also, it did not identify order-dependent rules, such as rules 3 and 4. In addition, the FirePAC tool provides recommendations on how to clean and optimize the input set of filtering rules.

7.5 Lab 7.4: Packet Content Filtering

7.5.1 Outcome

The learning objective of this hands-on exercise is for students to learn how to perform packet content filtering.

7.5.2 Packet Content Filtering

Packet content filtering, known also as Deep Packet Inspection (DPI), is a form of network packet filtering that examines the data part (Payload data) and possibly also the headers of a packet as it passes an inspection point, such as a firewall. Usually, packet content filtering searches for protocol noncompliance, viruses, spam, intrusions, or pre-defined criteria to decide if the packet can pass or if it needs to be routed to a different destination, or for the purpose of collecting statistical information. Packet content filtering enables advanced network management and security functions as well as Internet datamining, eavesdropping, and censorship.

In classic packet filtering, the protocol, destination port, source port, destination IP, and source IP fields are inspected. However, in the packet content filtering process, all the packet's fields, mainly the payload data, are inspected to detect whether they contain malicious signatures (usually malicious strings); see the next figure. The packet content filtering process uses a set of signatures, usually created by the firewall administrator. For example, you might want to prevent your network's users from receiving e-mails from a specific e-mail address. You may also want to block access to any Web page that contains the word "Bomb" or a URL that includes the word "sex".

The application layer in the TCP/UDP model contains the fields and payload data of the services. Examples of common TCP services are Web (HTTP), e-mail (SMTP/POP3), and FTP. For example, in an e-mail, the body (content text) is always preceded by header lines that identify particular routing information of the message, including the sender, recipient, date, and subject. Some headers are mandatory, such as the FROM, TO, and DATE headers. Others are optional, but very commonly used, such as SUBJECT and CC. Other headers include the sending timestamps and the receiving timestamps of all mail transfer agents that have received and sent the message. In other words, any time a message is transferred from one user to another (i.e., when it is sent or forwarded), the message is date/timestamped by a mail transfer agent (MTA), a computer program or software agent that facilitates the transfer of e-mail messages from one computer to another. This date/timestamp, like FROM, TO, and SUBJECT, becomes one of the many headers that precede the body of an e-mail.

The figure below shows an example of a full e-mail header.

Return-Path: <naoufel.kraiem@topnet.tn>
Received: from topnetmail20.outgw.tn (topnetmail20.outgw.tn
[196.203.220.20])
*   by fmc.antispam.uaeu.ac.ae id pAGFshNZ001352-*
pAGFshNa001352; Wed, 16 Nov 2011 19:54:44 +0400
Received: from smtp23.topnet.tn (unknown [41.226.21.40])
*   by topnetmail20.outgw.tn (Postfix) with SMTP id*
3C0182570001
*   for <trabelsi@uaeu.ac.ae>; Wed, 16 Nov 2011 16:54:43 +0100*
(CET)
Received: (qmail 21172 invoked by uid 89); 16 Nov 2011 16:37:49 -0000
Received: from unknown (HELO smtp13.topnet.tn) (41.226.22.47)
* by smtp23.topnet.tn with SMTP; 16 Nov 2011 16:37:49 -0000*
Received: (qmail 18962 invoked by uid 89); 16 Nov 2011 15:19:50 -0000
Received: from unknown (HELO as21.topnet.tn) (41.226.21.42)
* by smtp13.topnet.tn with SMTP; 16 Nov 2011 15:19:50 -0000*
Received: from (unknown [41.226.21.46]) by as21.topnet.tn with smtp
*   id 0766_51df_3b68a1f4_1069_11e1_b80d_00219b8e91e0;*
*   Wed, 16 Nov 2011 16:39:54 +0100*
Received: (qmail 19194 invoked by uid 89); 16 Nov 2011 16:37:45 -0000
Received: from unknown (HELO ?192.168.1.2?) (197.0.49.239)
* by smtp22.topnet.tn with SMTP; 16 Nov 2011 16:37:47 -0000*
Subject: Information
From: "Naoufel.kraiem" <naoufel.kraiem@topnet.tn>
Content-Type: text/plain; charset=utf-8
Message-Id: <03849B41-2BA5-4F81-B7D0-D96406885BC1@topnet.tn>
Date: Wed, 16 Nov 2011 11:27:53 +0100
To: "trabelsi@uaeu.ac.ae" <trabelsi@uaeu.ac.ae>
Content-Transfer-Encoding: quoted-printable
Mime-Version: 1.0 (iPad Mail 8J2)
X-Mailer: iPad Mail (8J2)
X-FEAS-DNSBL: zen.spamhaus.org / 197.0.49.239
X-FE-ORIG-ENV-FROM: naoufel.kraiem@topnet.tn

7.5.3 Experiment

This experiment consists of using the Juniper Networks device to implement packet content filtering for a variety of security policies.

7.5.4 Network Architecture

The next figure shows the network architecture used in the experiment. Three networks (LAN #1, LAN #2, and LAN #3) are connected to the Juniper Networks device. The traffic exchanged between the three networks goes through the Juniper Networks device, where it is filtered by a set of filtering rules.

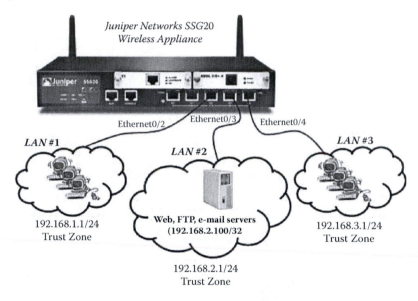

7.5.5 Experiment Steps

The experiment consists of the following steps:

Step 1: Configure the network interfaces in the Juniper Networks device.
Step 2: Set up Web, FTP, and e-mail servers.
Step 3: Implement filtering rules for security policies.
Step 4: Test the filtering rules and view the results in the log file of the Juniper Networks device.

7.5.5.1 Step 1: Configure the Network Interfaces in the Juniper Networks Device

Step 1 is similar to the one of the experiment of the Packet Filtering lab (Lab 7.1).

7.5.5.2 Step 2: Set Up Web, FTP, and E-Mail servers

The *LiterServe* tool is used to set up Web, FTP, and e-mail servers. The three servers are installed in a host with IP address 192.168.2.100, in LAN #2, as shown above.

7.5.5.3 Step 3: Implement Filtering Rules for Security Policies

The following are examples of security policies and their corresponding filtering rules implemented using the WebUI interface of the Juniper Networks device. The security policies are concerned with the inspection of the payload data in the exchanged Web, FTP, and e-mail traffic. The corresponding filtering rules are implemented using the packet contents inspection capability (Deep Inspection) of the Juniper Networks device.

1. **Security Policy #1 (SP#1):** LAN #1's hosts are not allowed to access any Web server in LAN #2 with Web pages containing the word "bomb." This security policy is concerned with the inspection of the payload data of Web traffic. In the Juniper Networks device, to implement the appropriate filtering rules for this security policy using Deep Inspection, an attack signature should be created first, as follows:
   - Log in to the WebUI interface of the device.
   - Select "Security" -> "Deep Inspection" -> "Attacks" -> "custom" as shown in the screenshot below.

- Next, create an attack signature, as shown in the following screenshot. An attack signature indicates the part of the payload data which the Deep Inspection will be applied. For the security policy (SP#1), the attack signature states that the payload data of the Web (HTTP) traffic is inspected to verify whether it contains the word "bomb." The attack context (which is the part of the payload data that will be inspected) is *"HTTP Text and HTML Data"*, and the attack pattern *(.*bomb.*)* is any string that contains the word "bomb."

- Next, create an attack group, as shown in the screenshot below. An attack group includes all the attack signatures that the Deep Inspection process will use in a given filtering rule. Therefore, an attack group may include more than one attack signature. In the case of the above security policy (SP#1), only one attack signature is used.

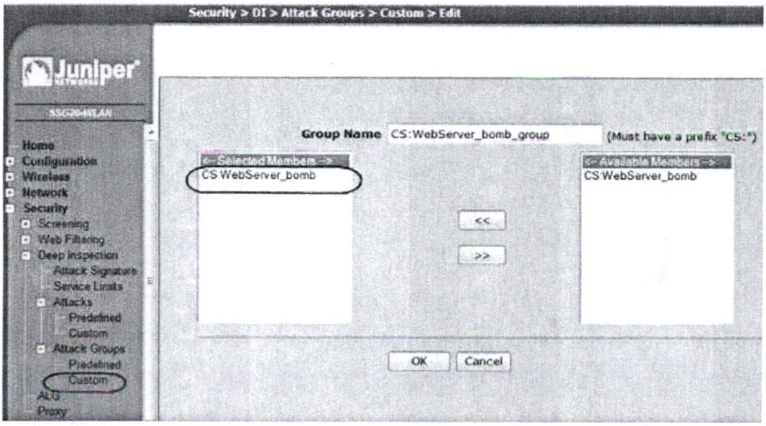

- Select "Policy" and then define LAN #1's hosts as the source hosts and LAN #2's hosts as the destination hosts.
- Click on "Deep Inspection" to select the appropriate attack group for this security policy, as shown in the screenshot below.

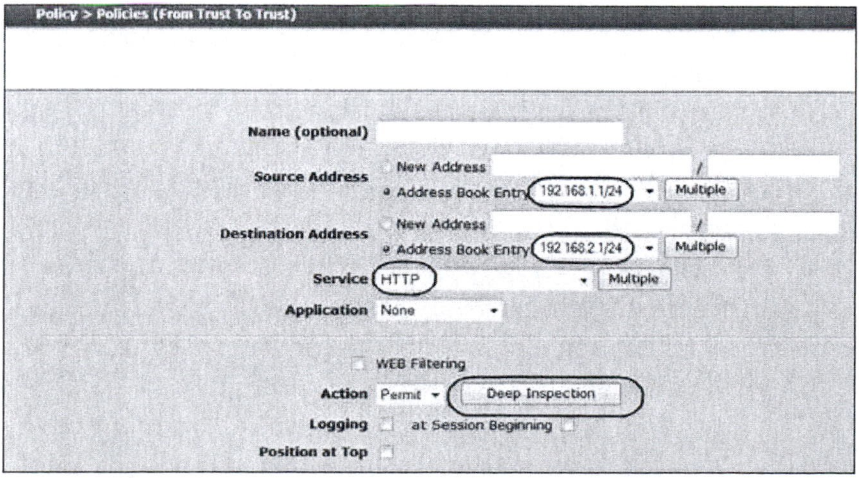

– Select the appropriate "Attack group," as shown below.

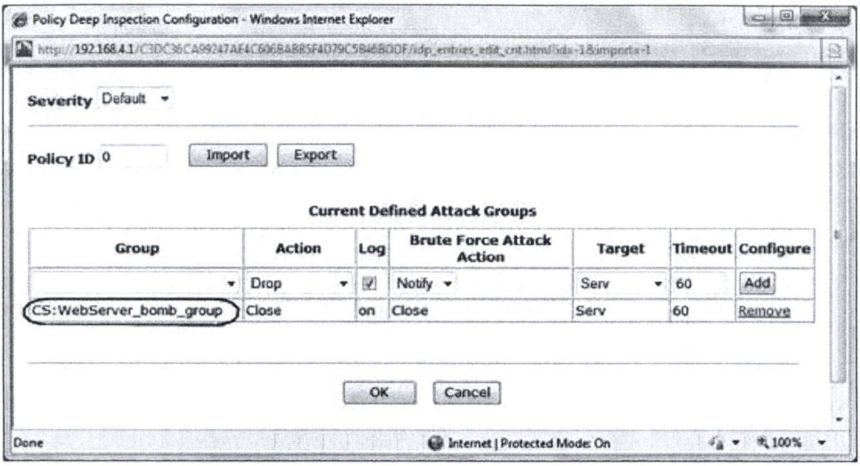

– The next screenshot shows the filtering rule implemented in the Juniper Networks device for the security
policy (SP#1). The "Action" column indicates that the
rule uses Deep Inspection.

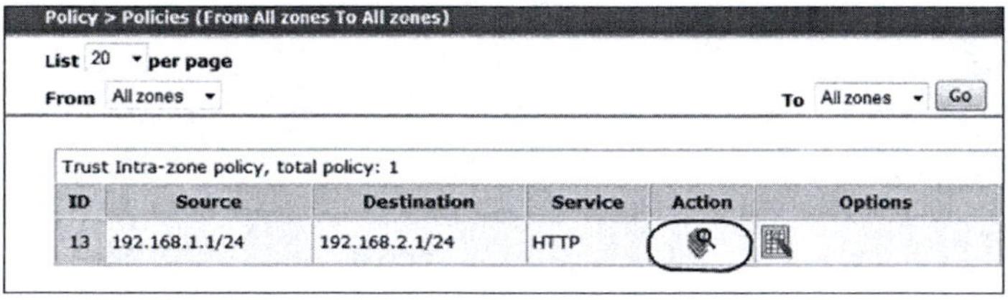

7.5.5.4 Step 4: Test the Filtering Rules and View the Results in the Log File of the Juniper Networks Device

We assume that the Web pages of the Web server running on
Host (192.168.2.100) contains the word "bomb," as shown in
the following screenshot.

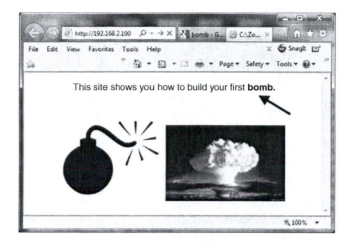

We also assume that host (192.168.1.2) in LAN #1 attempts to access the Web pages of the Web server (192.168.2.100). The subsequent screenshot shows the event log for the previous filtering rule. The following screenshot shows that host (192.168.1.2) has been denied access to the Web server (192.168.2.100). This is due to the fact that the filtering rule uses Deep Inspection to deny access to Web pages that contain the word "bomb."

Reports > Policies > Traffic Log										ssg20-wlan
List 20 ▾ per page										

| | | | | | | | Save | | | Clear | | | Refresh |

Traffic log for policy :

ID	Source	Destination	Service	Action
13	Trust/192.168.1.1/24	Trust/192.168.2.1/24	HTTP	Permit

Date/Time	Source Address/Port	Destination Address/Port	Translated Source Address/Port	Translated Destination Address/Port	Service	Duration	Bytes Sent	Bytes Received	Close Reason
2003-01-21 12:11:02	192.168.1.2:59411	192.168.2.100:80	192.168.1.2:59411	192.168.2.100:80	HTTP	1 sec.	0	0	Creation

2. **Security Policy #2 (SP#2):** LAN #3's hosts are not allowed to access any FTP server in LAN #2, using "anonymous" as the user name or "12345678" as the password. This security policy is concerned with the inspection of the payload data of FTP traffic.
   – For this security policy (SP#2), two attack signatures are required. The first attack signature states that

the payload data of FTP traffic is inspected to verify whether the FTP username includes the word "anonymous." Therefore, the attack context is "FTP User Name" and the attack pattern is "anonymous" (see screenshot below).

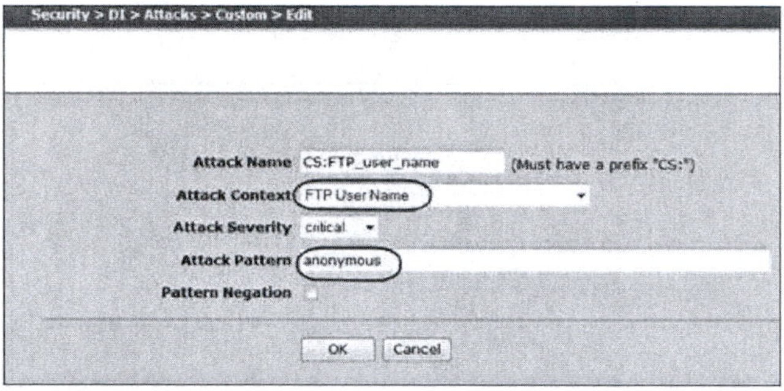

- The second attack signature states that the payload data of FTP traffic is inspected to verify whether the FTP user password is "12345678." Therefore, the attack context is "FTP User Password" and the attack pattern is "12345678" (screenshot below).

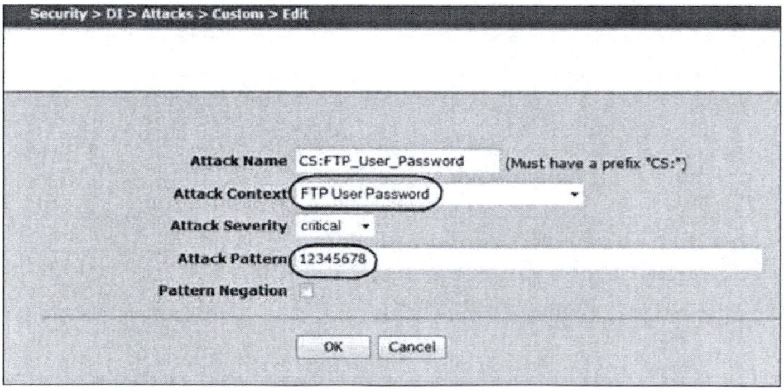

- Then, an attack group that includes the two attack signatures is created, as shown below.

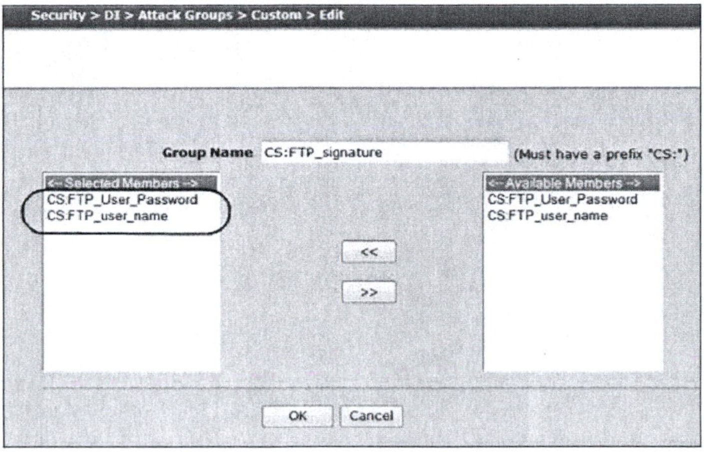

Security > DI > Attack Groups > Custom > Edit

Group Name CS:FTP_signature   (Must have a prefix "CS:")

<--Selected Members -->
CS:FTP_User_Password
CS:FTP_user_name

<--Available Members -->
CS:FTP_User_Password
CS:FTP_user_name

<<

>>

OK   Cancel

– The next screenshot shows the filtering rule implemented in the Juniper Networks device for the security
policy (SP#2). The "Action" column indicates that the
rule uses Deep Inspection:

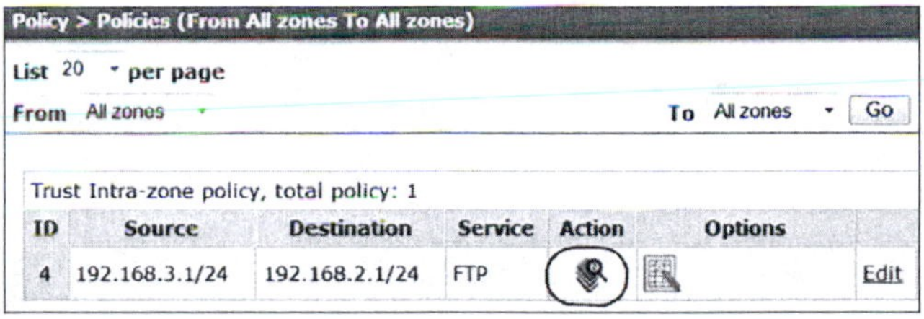

Policy > Policies (From All zones To All zones)

List 20 ▾ per page

From All zones ▾   To All zones ▾   Go

Trust Intra-zone policy, total policy: 1

ID	Source	Destination	Service	Action	Options	
4	192.168.3.1/24	192.168.2.1/24	FTP	🛡	🖼	Edit

3. **Security Policy #3 (SP#3):** LAN #1's hosts are not
   allowed to send e-mails that contain the string "hacker" in
   any e-mail header line. This security policy is concerned
   with the inspection of the payload data of e-mail (SMTP)
   traffic.
   – For this security policy (SP#3), one attack signature is
   required. The attack signature states that the payload
   data of SMTP traffic is inspected to verify whether
   the e-mail header lines contain the string "hacker."
   Therefore, the attack context is "SMTP Any Header

Line" and the attack pattern is ".*hacker.*" (screenshot below).

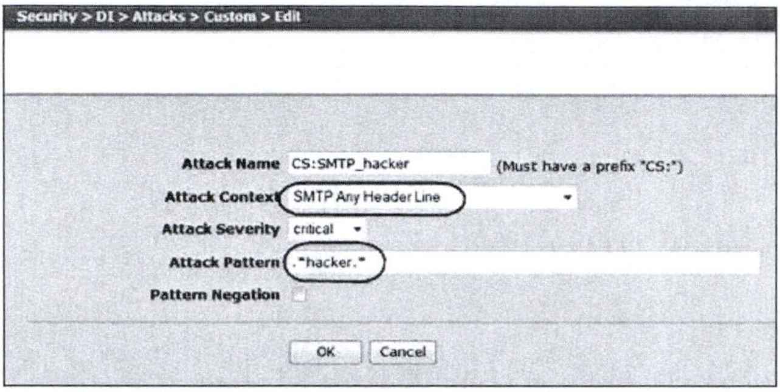

– Then, an attack group that includes the above attack signature is created, as shown below.

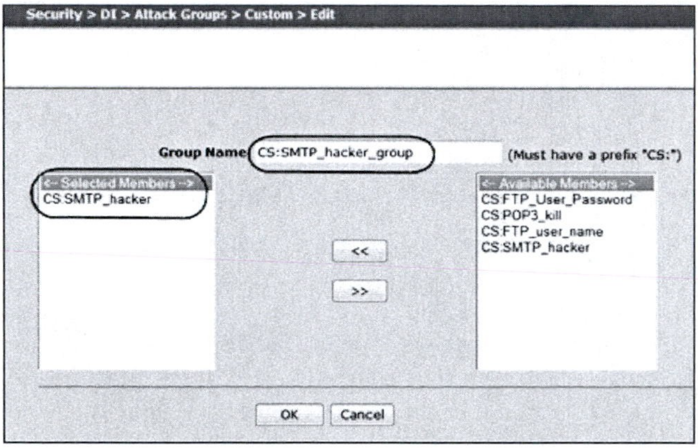

■ The following screenshot shows the filtering rule implemented in the Juniper Networks device for the security policy (SP#3). The "Action" column indicates that the rule uses Deep Inspection.

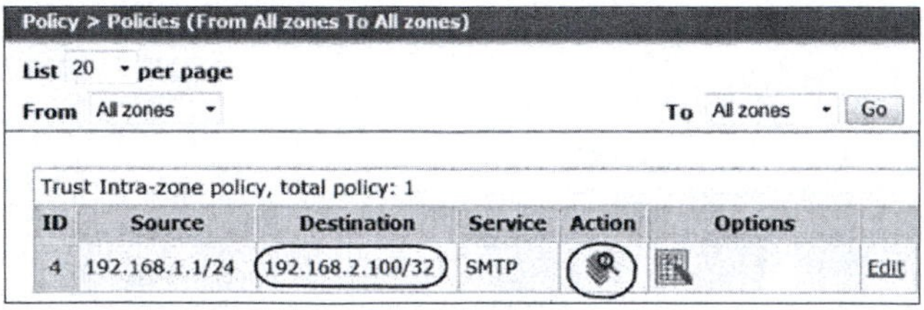

4. ***Security Policy #4 (SP #4):*** LAN #3's hosts are not allowed to receive e-mails that contain the string "kill" in the subject header line. This security policy is concerned with the inspection of the payload data of e-mail (POP3) traffic.
   - For this security policy (SP#4), one attack signature is required. The attack signature states that the payload data of POP3 traffic is inspected to verify whether the e-mail subject header line contains the string "kill." Therefore, the attack context is "PO3 Subject Header" and the attack pattern is ".*kill.*" (screenshot below).

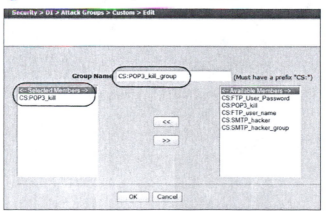

   - Then, an attack group that includes the above attack signature is created, as shown below.

   - The following screenshot shows the filtering rule implemented in the Juniper Networks device for the security policy (SP#4). The "Action" column indicates that the rule uses Deep Inspection.

Policy > Policies (From All zones To All zones)						
List 20 ▾ per page						
From All zones ▾				To All zones ▾	Go	
Trust Intra-zone policy, total policy: 1						
ID	**Source**	**Destination**	**Service**	**Action**	**Options**	
4	192.168.3.1/24	(192.168.2.100/32)	POP3	🖐	📋	Edit

7.6 Lab 7.5: Stateless versus Stateful Packet Filtering

7.6.1 Outcome

The learning objective of this hands-on exercise is for students to better anatomize the concept of stateless and stateful packet filtering through examples and experiments.

7.6.2 Security Issues with Stateless Packet Filtering

Client/server technology-based Internet services (such as Web, FTP, and e-mail) are bi-directional. Obviously, filtering rules related to a bi-directional service must allow both traffic directions to cross the firewall. The combinations of packets going in both directions in TCP and UDP services are called TCP and UDP sessions, respectively. A TCP or UDP session has a client, which is the computer that initiates the session, and a server, which is the computer hosting the service. For example, the following single filtering rule is expected to allow bi-directional traffic between the Web clients with IP addresses 192.168.1.1/24 and the Web servers with IP addresses 192.168.2.1/24 to cross the firewall:

Rule	Direction	Source IP	Destination IP	Protocol	Source Port	Destination Port	Action
R1	Client-to-Server	192.168.1.1/24	192.168.2.1/24	TCP	Any	HTTP (80)	Allow

A TCP or UDP session is characterized by four attributes, namely, the IP address of the client, the IP address of the server, the client port (known as the source port), and the server port (known as the destination port). Usually, the server port number allows identifying the nature of the offered service. For example, a Web session and a Telnet session are almost always on TCP ports 80 and 23, respectively. However, the client port is usually chosen dynamically at runtime by the operating system of the client host, and it is bigger than 1023. Therefore, the client port number is essentially unpredictable. It is important to notice that because the client port is unpredictable, the firewall should allow any session flow with any source port to cross the firewall. Consequently, in basic packet filtering, this would introduce a very serious security vulnerability that allows malicious hosts to flood the target servers with unwanted traffic that may cause a DoS (Denial of Service) attack situation. To better anatomize this security problem, we assume the following two security policies:

- Security policy (SP#1): We want to allow our internal hosts at IP addresses 192.168.1.1/24 to access any outside Web server (listening on TCP port 80) at IP addresses 192.168.2.1/24.
- Security policy (SP#2): In addition, we want to deny any external host (192.168.2.1/24) from establishing TCP connections with our internal hosts (192.168.1.1/24).

The first security policy (SP#1) allows the internal hosts to establish Web connections with any external server. However, the second security policy (SP#2) prevents external hosts from establishing TCP connections on the internal servers, and consequently protects the internal servers from TCP SYN flooding attacks. Also, in the case that internal hosts are infected with remote-controlled program-based viruses, such as Trojan horses, the second security policy prevents malicious users from remotely connecting to the infected internal host. Remote-controlled program-based viruses are a very serious threat because they allow malicious users to fully control remote victim hosts.

The packets exchanged between the Web clients and servers will look like this:

> Client-to-server packets:
> *Source IP = 192.168.1.1/24, Destination IP = 192.168.2.1/24, Source port = Y, Destination port = 80,*
> where 192.168.1.1/24 is the possible IP addresses of the Web clients, 192.168.2.1/24 is the possible IP addresses of the Web servers, and Y is an arbitrary port number selected by the Web client.

On the other hand, return traffic from the Web servers to the Web clients (server-to-client) swaps IP addresses and port numbers, and looks like this:

> *Source IP = 192.168.2.1/24, Destination IP = 192.168.1.1/24, Source port = 80, Destination port = Y.*

Before writing the appropriate filtering rules for the above two security policies, it is important to understand the *three-way handshake* mechanism used to establish a TCP session. In fact, the process of establishing a TCP connection involves the following steps (see next figure):

- The client sends a SYN message and goes into the SYN_SENT state.
- The server sends a message that combines an ACK for the client's SYN and contains the server's SYN, and goes into the SYN_RCVD state.
- The client sends an ACK for the server's SYN and goes into the ESTABLISHED state.
- After receiving the ACK message, the server goes into the ESTABLISHED state.

TCP Connection Establishment Process and States:

Three-way Handshake

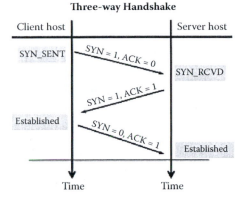

After a TCP connection has been established, all the exchanged packets will have the flag ACK set and the flag SYN unset (figure below).

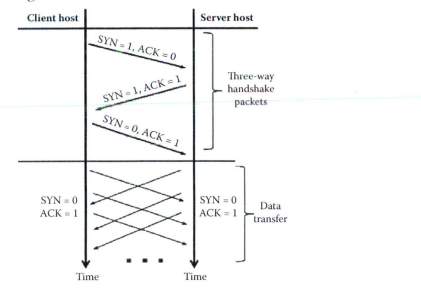

Therefore, if we consider only the SYN and ACK flags, there are only four types of TCP packets exchanged in a TCP connection:

■ Client-to-server packet: TCP packet with the flag SYN set and the flag ACK unset.
■ Server-to-client packet: TCP packet with the flags SYN and ACK set.

- Client-to-server packet: TCP packet with the flag SYN unset and the flag ACK set.
- Server-to-client packet: TCP packet with the flag SYN unset and the flag ACK set.

Consequently, in a TCP connection, to allow bi-directional service traffic through the firewall, the firewall should allow the above four types of TCP packets to pass through.

For example, the filtering rules for the above two security policies SP#1 and SP#2, respectively, are

Rule	Direction	Source IP	Destination IP	Protocol	Source port	Destination port	SYN	ACK	Action
R1	Client-to-Server	192.168.1.1/24	192.168.2.1/24	TCP	Y	80	1	0	Allow
R2	Server-to-Client	192.168.2.1/24	192.168.1.1/24	TCP	80	Y	1	1	Allow
R3	Client-to-Server	192.168.1.1/24	192.168.2.1/24	TCP	Y	80	0	1	Allow
R4	Server-to-Client	192.168.2.1/24	192.168.1.1/24	TCP	80	Y	0	1	Allow

Rule	Direction	Source IP	Destination IP	Protocol	Source port	Destination port	SYN	ACK	Action
R5	Client-to-Server	192.168.2.1/24	192.168.1.1/24	TCP	Y	Z	1	0	Deny

Regrettably, an attacker may exploit rules 2 and 4 to conduct DoS attacks, as the two rules match packets based on their source ports. Remember that the source port is under the packet sender's control. The attacker on any host at spoofed IP address 192.168.2.1/24 can build fake packets with source port 80, destination any host at IP address 192.168.1.1/24, and a destination port of his choice. Fake packets crafted this way will cross the firewall because they match either rule 2, if their flags SYN and ACK are set, or rule 4, if their flag SYN is unset and their flag ACK is set. For example, the following shows an example of a TCP packet that is rejected by the firewall since the packet attempts to establish a Web connection with an internal host. The packet is rejected by rule 5 of the above filtering rule list (previous screenshot).

Packet	Source IP	Destination IP	Protocol	Source port	Destination port	SYN	ACK
Packet #1	192.168.2.20	192.168.1.10	TCP	6000	80	1	0

However, what follows shows an example of a malicious TCP packet that is allowed by the firewall to pass. The malicious TCP packet pretends that the TCP connection with source port 9000 has been established already, as its flag SYN is unset and its flag ACK is set.

Packet	Source IP	Destination IP	Protocol	Source port	Destination port	SYN	ACK
Packet #2	192.168.2.20	192.168.1.10	TCP	80	9000	0	1

Based on the above filtering rule list, the firewall will allow the malicious packet to pass. Consequently, flooding a target internal host with such malicious TCP packets may create a DoS attack situation at the target host (see figure below).

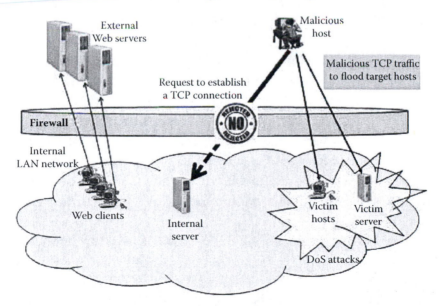

Therefore, this simple example demonstrates the limitations of basic packet filtering, although the filtering rules for security policy SP#1 and SP#2 above allow internal hosts to establish TCP connections with external Web servers and prevent external hosts from establishing TCP connections with internal servers. However, the major weakness of the filtering rules is that they allow malicious users to flood internal hosts with malicious TCP packets, which may create a DoS attack situation at the internal hosts, as shown in the previous figure.

In basic packet filtering, this DoS attack may occur easily because firewalls do not use mechanisms that allow deciding whether or not a given TCP packet belongs to an already established session. In fact, firewalls do not keep track of the state of the ongoing TCP connection sessions and do not remember what source port numbers the sessions' clients selected.

7.6.3 Stateful TCP Packet Filtering

To address the above security issue in basic packet filtering, firewalls keep track of established TCP connections. Practically, firewalls keep an entry, in a cache, for each open TCP connection. An entry of a TCP connection includes the client and server IP addresses, and the client and server port numbers. The client port number information was not fully known when the firewall administrator wrote the rules. However, when the connection is being set up, both port numbers are known, as they are listed in the packet's TCP header. All the packets that belong to an existing TCP connection, in both directions, are allowed to cross the firewall. This type of firewall is called a *stateful firewall*.

The entries of the state cache of established TCP connections are created using a simple mechanism. That is, when the first packet (SYN packet) of a new TCP connection reaches the firewall, the firewall matches it against the set of filtering rules. If there is a filtering rule that allows the packet across, the firewall inserts a new entry into the cache, and the TCP connection state is set to the SYN_RCVD state. Once the two other remaining packets of the three-way handshake process are received, the TCP connection state transits to the ESTABLISHED state. Therefore, the first packet (SYN packet) of a TCP connection effectively opens a hole in the firewall, and the cache mechanism allows the return traffic to go through this hole.

After the TCP connection has been established, the decision as to whether or not to allow subsequent TCP packets is based on the contents of the state cache. That is, when a subsequent TCP packet, with the flag SYN unset and the flag ACK set, reaches the firewall, the firewall checks whether an entry for the TCP connection it belongs to already exists in the cache. If the connection is listed in the cache, the packet is allowed through immediately. If no such connection exists, then the packet is rejected. The following provides an example of a SYN packet of a new TCP connection:

Packet	Source IP	Destination IP	Protocol	Source port	Destination port	SYN	ACK
Packet #1	192.168.1.5	192.168.2.10	TCP	1200	80	1	0

When the above first packet (Packet #1) is seen by the firewall, the firewall matches it against the set of filtering rules. Because Rule 1 (as shown in the screenshot above for the firewall filtering rules for the security policy SP#1) allows the packet across, the firewall inserts a new entry into the state cache, and the TCP connection state is SYN_RCVD (see below).

TCP connection	Client IP	Server IP	Client port	Server port	Connection State
Connection #1	192.168.1.5	192.168.2.10	1200	80	SYN_RCVD

Once the three-way handshake process is completed, the TCP connection state transits to the ESTABLISHED state (as shown below).

TCP connection	Client IP	Server IP	Client port	Server port	Connection State
Connection #1	192.168.1.5	192.168.2.10	1200	80	ESTABLISHED

When the TCP connection is terminated, the firewall removes the cache entry, thereby blocking the connection. Typically, the firewall also has a timeout value; if a TCP connection becomes inactive for too long, the firewall evicts the entry from the cache and blocks the connection.

7.6.4 Stateful UDP Packet Filtering

The tracking of a UDP session state is a complicated process, as UDP is a connectionless transport protocol and, unlike TCP, has no sequence numbers or flags (such as the six TCP flags: SYN, ACK, FIN, PSH, URG, and FIN). The only items that a tracking process can use are the IP addresses and port numbers of the client and server involved in a UDP session.

In addition, UDP has no mechanism that announces a session's end. Consequently, a UDP session's state table entries must be cleared after reaching a predefined timeout value. Otherwise, a malicious user may exploit this limitation in the UDP protocol to fill in the UDP session state table with fake sessions, resulting in a DoS attack situation.

On the other hand, UDP relies entirely on ICMP as its error handler. Therefore, ICMP is an important part of a UDP session to be considered when tracking its overall state. For example, in a UDP session, the client or server host may not have sufficient buffer space to process the receiving packets. Consequently, the host may become unable to keep up with the speed at which it is receiving packets. In such a situation, the receiving host can send an ICMP source quench message (Type = 4, Code = 0), which requests that the sender host decrease the rate of the sent packets. However, if the firewall blocks the ICMP source quench message because it is not part of the normal UDP session, the host that is sending packets too quickly does not know that an issue has come up, and it continues to send at the same speed, resulting in lost packets or a DoS attack situation at the receiving host (next figure).

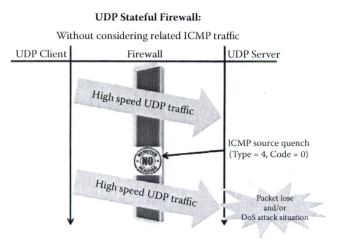

UDP Stateful Firewall:

Without considering related ICMP traffic

Therefore, a stateful firewall that tracks a UDP session state must consider such related ICMP traffic when deciding what traffic should be returned to protected hosts (see figure below).

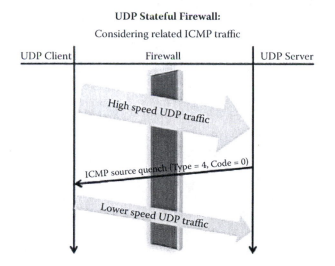

UDP Stateful Firewall:

Considering related ICMP traffic

7.6.5 Stateful ICMP Packet Filtering

ICMP is an error reporting and diagnostic protocol and is considered a required part of any IP implementation. There are two types of ICMP packets: error-reporting and control packets. ICMP error-reporting packets are used to return error messages and involve one-way communications. They are always reported to the original source IP address of the originating packet. However, ICMP control packets are used by hosts to send request messages and receive back corresponding reply messages. Hence, ICMP error messages involve two-way communication, or request/reply-type messages. ICMP, like UDP, is not a stateful protocol. However, like UDP, it also has attributes that allow its connections to be tracked. The ICMP attributes are usually the Type, Code, Identifier, and Sequence number fields in the ICMP header.

Examples of ICMP error messages are the ICMP source quench message (described in the previous section) and the ICMP time exceeded message. In an ICMP time exceeded message, the Type field must be set to 11. The Code field, which specifies the reason for the time exceeded message, includes the following:

Code	Description
0	Time-to-live exceeded in transit
1	Fragment reassembly time exceeded

An ICMP time exceeded message with the Code field unset is generated by a gateway to inform the source of a discarded packet that the time-to-live field reached zero. That is, every machine (such as an intermediate router) that forwards an IP datagram has to decrement the time-to-live (TTL) field of the

IP header by one. If the TTL reaches 0, an ICMP time-to-live exceed-in-transit message is sent to the source of the datagram. An ICMP time exceeded message with the Code field set is sent by a host if it fails to reassemble a fragmented datagram within its time limit.

An example of an application that is based on ICMP request/reply-type messages is Ping. It was created to verify whether a specific computer on a network or the Internet exists and is connected. Ping is a program that sends a series of ICMP echo requests (Type = 8, Code = 0) over a network or the Internet to a specific computer in order to generate ICMP echo responses (Type = 0, Code = 0) from that computer.

The tracking of ICMP traffic that involves one-way communication is complicated, as ICMP error messages are precipitated by requests by other protocols (TCP, UDP). Because of this multiprotocol issue, figuring ICMP messages into the state of an existing UDP or TCP session can be confusing and difficult to manage.

However, ICMP sessions that involve two-way communications are less complicated to track, as for each ICMP response message, there should be an ICMP request message that has been sent previously. That is, an ICMP session is tracked based on the source/destination addresses, Type, Code, Identifier, and Sequence number of the request and reply messages. In an ICMP session, the Identifier, Sequence number, and Data fields should be returned to the sender unaltered. The Identifier and Sequence number may be used by the echo request sender to aid in matching the replies with the echo requests. The Identifier might be used like a port in TCP or UDP to identify a session, and the Sequence number might be incremented on each echo request sent. The echoing node returns these same values in the echo reply.

This tracking method is about the only way ICMP can enter into a state table.

For example, after receiving the ICMP echo request packet shown below,

Packet	Source IP	Destination IP	Type	Code	Identifier	Sequence number
Packet #1	192.168.1.5	192.168.2.10	8	0	200	1

the stateful firewall creates a new entry in its ICMP session's cache as shown below.

ICMP session	Source IP	Destination IP	Type	Code	Identifier	Sequence number	Session State
Session #1	192.168.1.5	192.168.2.10	1200	80	**200**	1	**Request**

Therefore, the ICMP echo reply packet that follows will be accepted by the stateful firewall, as it includes the same attributes values as the ICMP echo request packet.

Packet	Source IP	Destination IP	Type	Code	Identifier	Sequence number
Packet #2	192.168.2.10	192.168.1.5	0	0	**200**	1

However, the following fake ICMP echo reply packet is rejected, as there has been no ICMP echo request message including the same attribute values.

Packet	Source IP	Destination IP	Type	Code	Identifier	Sequence number
Packet #3	192.168.2.10	192.168.1.5	0	0	**300**	1

Another issue with ICMP is that, like UDP, it is connection-less; therefore, it must base the retention of a state table entry on a predetermined timeout because ICMP also does not have a specific mechanism to end its communication sessions.

7.6.6 Experiment

This experiment consists of describing a set of steps allowing users to test whether or not the Cisco ASA 5520 Adaptive Security Appliance (firewall) offers stateful or stateless TCP and ICMP packet filtering. The same steps can be used to test any other firewall.

7.6.7 Network Architecture

The following figure shows the network architecture used in the experiment. We assume that a host (Host #1) with IP address 192.168.2.20 and a host (Host #2) with IP address 192.168.3.30 are connected to the GigabitEthernet0/0 and GigabitEthernet0/1 interfaces of the Cisco ASA 5520, respectively. We assume also that

- Host #1 is a Web client host.
- Host #2 is a Web server host (LiteServer is the Web server software).
- Both hosts use CommView sniffer to capture the exchanged network traffic.

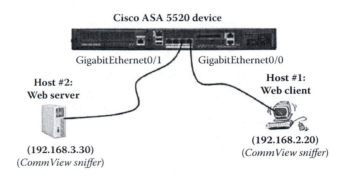

Cisco ASA 5520 device

GigabitEthernet0/1   GigabitEthernet0/0

Host #2:   Host #1:
Web server   Web client

(192.168.3.30)   (192.168.2.20)
(CommView sniffer)   (CommView sniffer)

The following screenshot shows the configuration of GigabitEthernet0/0 (192.168.2.1/24) and GigabitEthernet0/1 (192.168.3.1/24) interfaces of the Cisco ASA 5520.

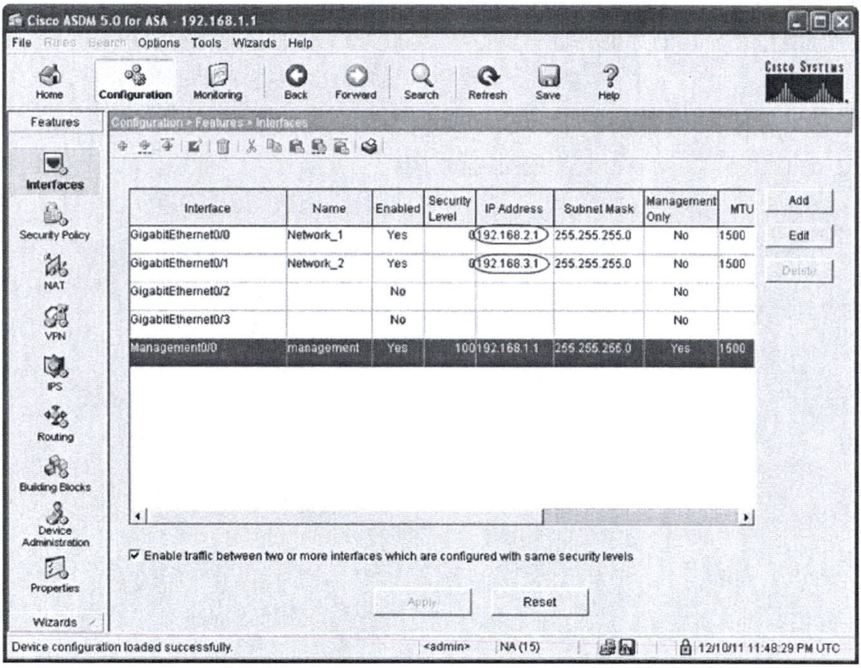

7.6.8 Experiment Steps

The experiment includes two parts to test whether or not the Cisco ASA 5520 offers stateful packet filtering for TCP traffic and ICMP traffic, respectively.

7.6.8.1 Part 1: Stateful TCP Packet Filtering Testing

This experiment consists of testing whether or not the Cisco ASA 5520 offers stateful TCP packet filtering capability. The following are the steps of the experiment:

1. First, to allow standard Web traffic (TCP/80) between the Web client host (Host #1) and the Web server host (Host #2), two filtering rules are implemented using the GUI interface of the Cisco ASA 5520, as shown below.

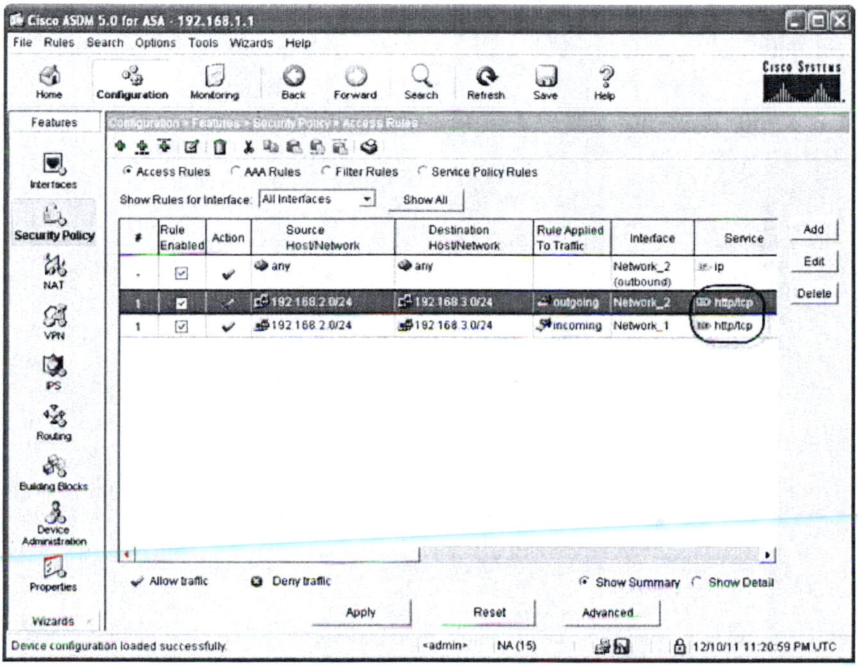

2. Then, from Host #1, a Web browser is used to connect to the Web server at Host #2.
3. At Host #1, CommView sniffer is used to capture the three-way handshake TCP packets of the Web session, as shown below.

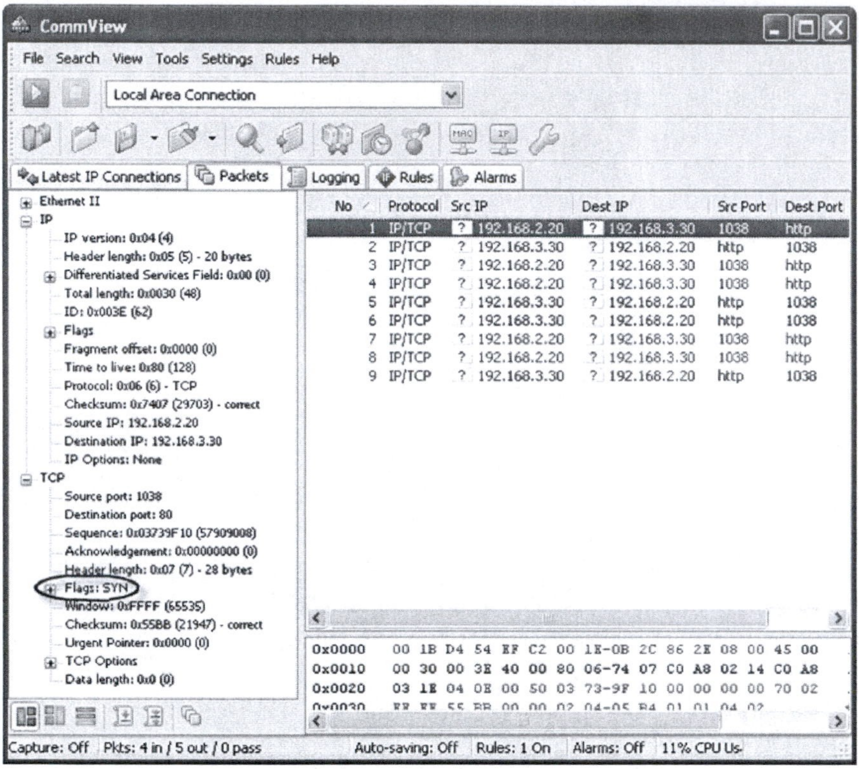

4. The values of the main fields of the three-way handshake packets characterizing the Web session are

Packet number as displayed in CommView sniffer	Source IP	Destination IP	Source port	Destination port	SYN	ACK
1	192.168.2.20	192.168.3.30	1038	80	0	1
2	192.168.3.30	192.168.2.20	80	1038	1	1
3	192.168.2.20	192.168.3.30	1038	80	0	1

5. Then, CommView Visual Packet Builder is used to send from Host #1 to Host #2 a fake TCP packet pretending that a TCP connection on port 80 is already established (SYN = 0 and ACK = 1). The fake TCP packet includes the same source and destination IP addresses, but includes a source port different from the source port of the current active Web session, as shown below.

Source IP	Destination IP	Source port	Destination port	SYN	ACK
192.168.2.20	192.168.3.30	**7000**	80	0	1

6. The following screenshot shows the fields of the above fake TCP packet built using CommView Visual Packet Builder.

After sending the fake TCP packet, CommView sniffer did not capture the sent fake TCP packet at Host #2. This is because the fake TCP packet was blocked by the Cisco ASA 5520. Consequently, the Cisco ASA 5520 is a stateful firewall for TCP-related traffic, as it denies TCP packets that do not belong to established TCP sessions. It is important to indicate that if CommView sniffer was able to capture the fake TCP packet at the Web server host (Host #2), then the Cisco ASA 5520 would be a stateless firewall.

7.6.9 Part 2: Stateful ICMP Packet Filtering Testing

This experiment consists of testing whether or not the Cisco ASA 5520 offers stateful ICMP packet filtering capability. The following are the steps of the experiment:

1. First, to allow Host #1 to ping Host #2, two filtering rules are implemented using the GUI interface of the Cisco ASA 5520, as shown below.

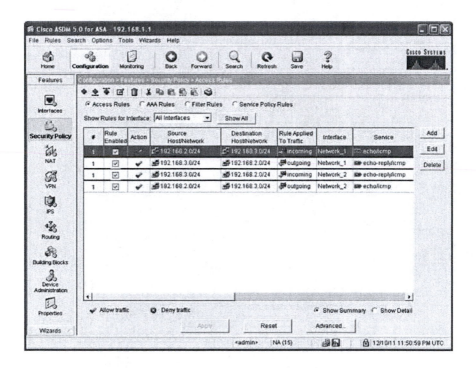

2. Then, Host #1 pings Host #2.
3. At Host#1, CommView sniffer is used to capture the exchanged ICMP packets. The next screenshot shows the ICMP echo request packet sent from Host #1 to Host #2.

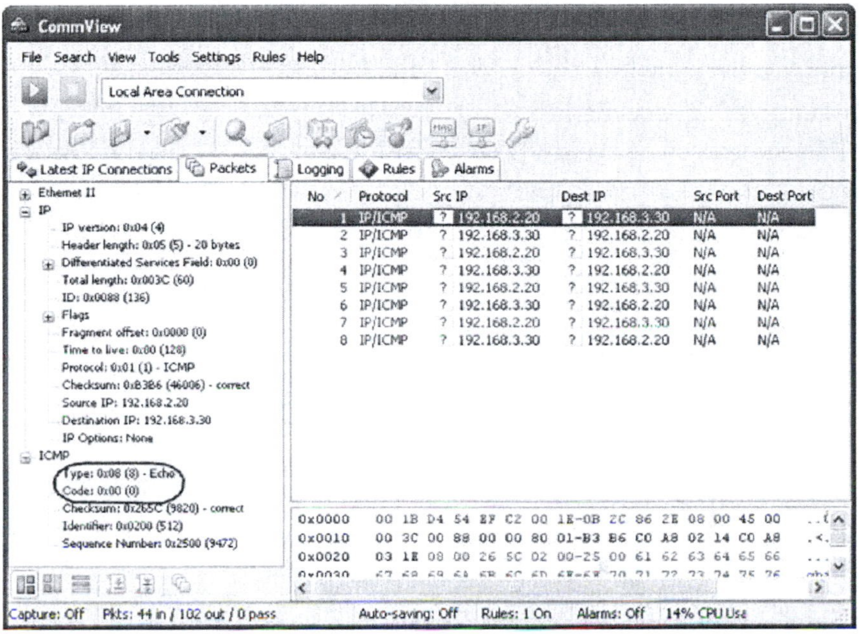

The next screenshot shows the ICMP echo reply packet sent from Host #2 to Host #1.

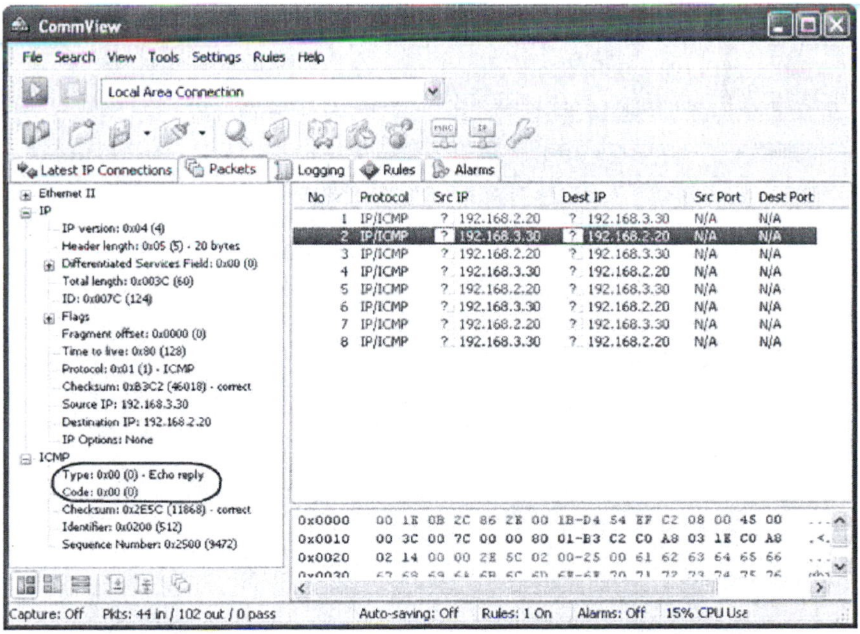

4. The values of the main fields of the two ICMP packets characterizing the Ping traffic are:

Packet number as displayed in CommView	Source IP	Destination IP	Type	Code	Identifier	Sequence Number
1	192.168.2.20	192.168.3.30	8	0	512	9472
2	192.168.3.30	192.168.2.20	0	0	512	9472

5. Then, CommView Visual Packet Builder is used to send from Host #2 to Host #1 a fake ICMP echo reply packet, pretending that an ICMP echo request packet has been received before from Host #1. The fake ICMP echo reply packet includes the same source and destination IP addresses, but includes a different Identifier and Sequence number, as shown below.

Source IP	Destination IP	Type	Code	Identifier	Sequence Number
192.168.3.30	192.168.2.20	0	0	512	8000

6. Following is a screenshot showing the fields of the fake ICMP echo reply packet, built using CommView Visual Packet Builder.

After sending the fake ICMP echo reply packet, CommView sniffer succeeded in capturing the fake packet. Consequently, the Cisco ASA 5520 is a stateless firewall for ICMP-related traffic, as it did not deny the fake ICMP echo reply packet. It is important to indicate that if CommView sniffer had not captured the fake ICMP echo reply packet at Host #1, then the Cisco ASA 5520 would have been a stateful firewall for ICMP-related traffic.

7.7 Lab 7.6: Active and Passive FTP Modes

7.7.1 Outcome

The learning objective of this hands-on lab exercise is for students to better anatomize the concept of Active and Passive FTP modes through examples and experiments.

7.7.2 Active and Passive FTP Modes

FTP is a service that is based on TCP client/server architecture. FTP is an unusual service in that it uses two communication channels, called the Command channel (also known as the Control channel) and the Data channel. FTP utilizes two ports at the server side: a Command port (21) and a Data port (usually 20 or 1024-65535). In addition, FTP offers two connection modes, namely, the Active FTP mode (also known as the Normal FTP mode) and the Passive FTP mode. The following subsections describe the two modes.

7.7.2.1 Active FTP Mode

In Active FTP mode, the FTP client connects from a random port $(X > 1023)$ to the FTP server's command port, port 21. Then, the client starts listening to port X+1 and sends the command "PORT X+1" to the server. The value "X+1" represents the port number of the Data channel at the client side. The server will then initiate the Data channel. That is, the server connects back to the client's specified data port from its local data port, which is port 20 or a random port $(Y > 1023)$.

The next figure shows the two TCP channels of an Active FTP connection. In Step 1, the FTP client's command port (X > 1023) contacts the server's command port (21) and sends the command PORT (X+1). In Step 2, the server then sends an ACK back to the client's command port. In Step 3, the server initiates a connection on its local data port (Y) to the data port (X+1) specified earlier by the client. Finally, the client sends an ACK back, as shown in Step 4.

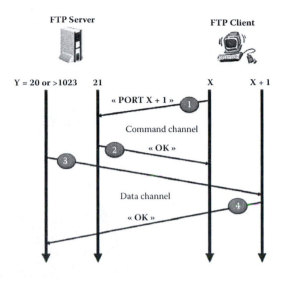

7.7.2.2 Active FTP Traffic Filtering

To allow Active FTP traffic to pass through the firewall, filtering rules should be implemented to allow the traffic of both the Command and the Data channels.

The next figure shows the different TCP packets exchanged in an Active FTP session. The Command session is initiated by the FTP client, while the Data session is initiated by the FTP server.

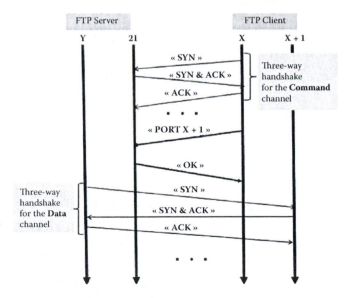

In addition, because FTP uses TCP-based channels, for each channel, four filtering rules are required to allow the corresponding traffic to pass through the firewall. For example, if the FTP client is an internal host and the FTP server is an external host, then the two subsequent tables list all the necessary filtering rules for the Command and Data channels, respectively.

Filtering Rules for the Command Channel in an Active FTP Session

Direction	Source IP	Destination IP	Protocol	Source port	Destination port	SYN	ACK	Action
Outgoing	FTP client	FTP server	TCP	1024–65535	21	1	0	Allow
Incoming	FTP server	FTP client	TCP	21	1024–65535	1	1	Allow
Outgoing	FTP client	FTP server	TCP	1024–65535	21	0	1	Allow
Incoming	FTP server	FTP client	TCP	21	1024–65535	0	1	Allow

Filtering Rules for the Data Channel in an Active FTP Session

Direction	Source IP	Destination IP	Protocol	Source port	Destination port	SYN	ACK	Action
Incoming	FTP server	FTP client	TCP	20, 1024–65535	1024–65535	1	0	Allow
Outgoing	FTP client	FTP server	TCP	1024–65535	20, 1024–65535	1	1	Allow
Incoming	FTP server	FTP client	TCP	20, 1024–65535	1024–65535	0	1	Allow
Outgoing	FTP client	FTP server	TCP	1024–65535	20, 1024–65535	0	1	Allow

7.7.2.3 Filtering Rules Implementation for Active FTP Traffic

Most firewalls include predefined filtering rules to allow and support Active FTP traffic. However, for educational purposes, to manually implement the filtering rules shown in the two tables above in a firewall, the firewall should allow for manipulating the values of the TCP flags while creating a filtering rule. For example, the Jetico Personal

Firewall* offers such a capability and allows specifying the values of the filtering rule's fields shown in the two tables above. Using Jetico Personal Firewall's GUI interface, the following screenshot shows the implementation of the height filtering rules from the above tables required to allow Active FTP traffic. We assume that the IP addresses of the internal FTP client and the external FTP server are 192.168.1.101 and 192.168.1.104, respectively. The default security policy is "Deny All".

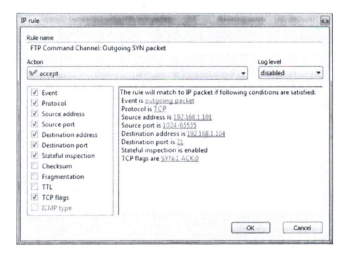

The following figures show the detailed contents of the filtering rules shown in the above screenshot.

A. Filtering rules for the Command channel in an Active FTP session:

1. Outgoing SYN packets for the Command channel:

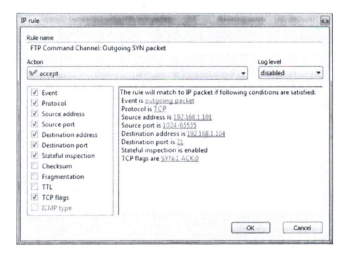

---

* http://www.jetico.com

2. Incoming SYN-ACK packets for the Command channel:

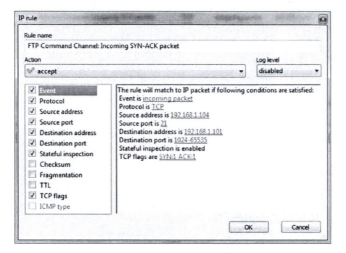

3. Outgoing ACK packets for the Command channel:

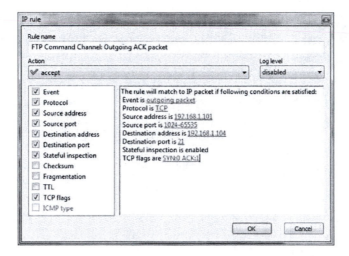

4. Incoming ACK packets for the Command channel:

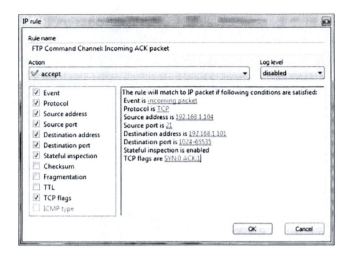

B. Filtering rules for the Data channel in an Active FTP session:

1. Incoming SYN packets for the Data channel:

2. Outgoing SYN-ACK packets for the Data channel:

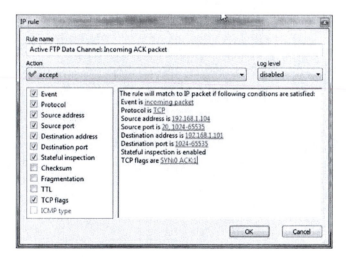

3. Incoming ACK packets for the Data channel:

4. Outgoing ACK packets for the Data channel:

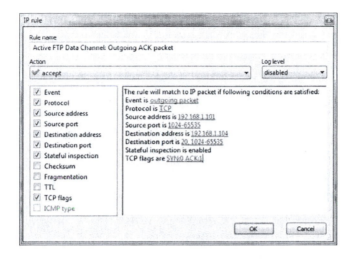

7.7.2.4 Security Issue with Active FTP Mode

Commonly, in a TCP client/server session, the client hosts initiate the session. However, in an Active FTP session, the FTP client initiates the Command session, and the FTP server initiates the Data session. This is a major security issue because, for the firewall, outside hosts are allowed to initiate TCP sessions on internal hosts. This type of connection is usually blocked because it allows malicious external hosts to generate attacks against the internal hosts. That is, in an Active FTP session, a malicious host can exploit the filtering rules corresponding to the Data channel to establish TCP connections with the internal hosts. This vulnerability would allow the malicious host to easily attack the internal hosts. DoS attacks or remote-controlled program-based attacks (such as Trojan horses) are examples of attacks that malicious hosts can perform against the internal hosts. Therefore, Active FTP is beneficial to the FTP server administrator, but detrimental to the client-side administrator.

7.7.3 Passive FTP Mode

To resolve the security issue with the Active FTP mode, a different method for FTP connections was developed. This is known as the Passive FTP mode. In this mode, the FTP client initiates both the Command and Data channels, hence solving the security issue with the Active FTP mode. The FTP client uses the command "PASV" to tell the server that the FTP session will be in Passive mode.

The following figure shows the two TCP channels of a Passive FTP connection. When opening an FTP connection, the client opens two random ports locally (X > 1023 and X+1). The first port contacts the server on port 21, then the client issues the "PASV" command (Step 1). The result of this is that the server then opens a port Y (20 or a random port (Y > 1023)) and sends the command "PORT Y" back to the client (Step 2). The client then initiates the connection from port "X+1" to port Y on the server to transfer data (Step 3). Finally, in Step 4, the server sends back an ACK to the client's data port.

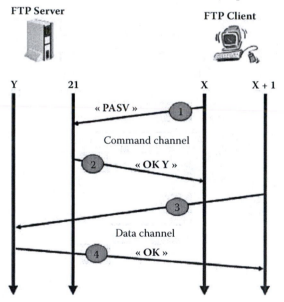

7.7.3.1 Passive FTP Traffic Filtering

To allow Passive FTP traffic to pass through the firewall, filtering rules should be implemented to allow the traffic of both the Command and the Data channels.

The next figure shows the different TCP packets exchanged in a Passive FTP session. The Command and Data sessions are both initiated by the FTP client.

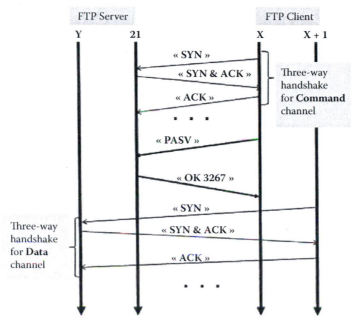

In addition, because FTP uses TCP-based channels, for each channel, four filtering rules are required to allow the corresponding traffic to pass through the firewall. For example, if the FTP client is an internal host and the FTP server is an external host, then the following table provides all the filtering rules for the Command and Data channels, respectively.

Filtering Rules for the Command and Data Channels in a Passive FTP Session

Direction	Source IP	Destination IP	Protocol	Source Port	Destination Port	SYN	ACK	Action
Outgoing	FTP client	FTP server	TCP	1024–65535	21, 20, 1024–65535	1	0	Allow
Incoming	FTP server	FTP client	TCP	21, 20, 1024–65535	1024–65535	1	1	Allow
Outgoing	FTP client	FTP server	TCP	1024–65535	21, 20, 1024–65535	0	1	Allow
Incoming	FTP server	FTP client	TCP	21, 20, 1024–65535	1024–65535	0	1	Allow

7.7.3.2 Filtering Rules Implementation for Passive FTP Traffic

Using Jetico Personal Firewall's GUI interface, the following screenshot shows the implementation of the four filtering rules from the above table, required to allow Passive FTP traffic.

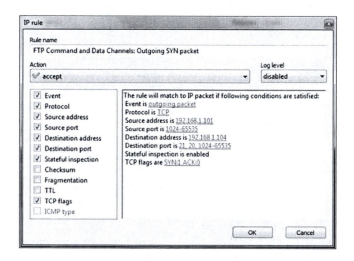

The following screenshots show the detailed contents of the filtering rules shown in the above screenshot.

1. Outgoing SYN packets for the Command and Data channels:

2. Incoming SYN-ACK packets for the Command and Data channels:

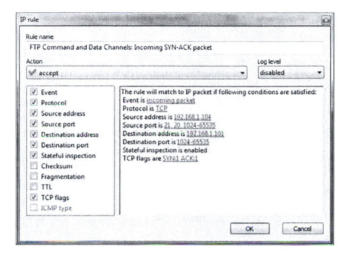

3. Outgoing ACK packets for the Command and Data channels:

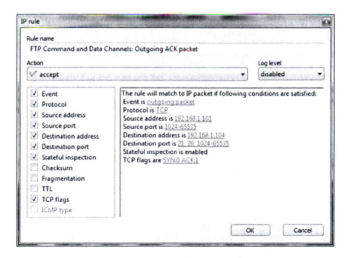

4. Incoming ACK packets for the Command and Data channels:

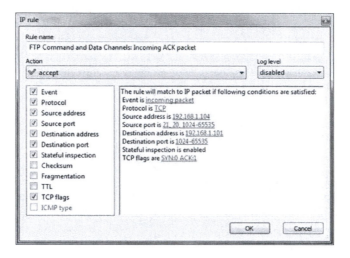

7.7.3.3 Security Issue with the Passive FTP Mode

It is unquestionable that the Passive FTP mode is a more secure mode compared to the Active FTP mode. However, the major security issue with the Passive FTP mode is that FTP client hosts are allowed to initiate connections to high-numbered ports on the FTP server. This may open up a whole range of problems on the FTP server side. However, because administrators of FTP servers will need to make their servers accessible to the greatest number of clients, they will almost certainly need to support Passive FTP. The security issue with the Passive FTP mode can be minimized using FTP servers that allow administrators to specify a limited port range for the FTP servers to use. In addition, firewalls will block any port that does not belong to that range. Therefore, Passive FTP is beneficial to the client, but detrimental to the FTP server administrator.

On the other hand, the use of the Passive FTP mode within a network involves supporting and troubleshooting clients that do (or do not) support the Passive FTP mode.

In addition, nowadays, users prefer to use their Web browsers as an FTP client. If the firewall is configured to allow only the Passive FTP mode, then the browsers should be configured to connect in the Passive FTP mode. This requires additional support work and troubleshooting for clients. For example, to change Internet Explorer 8 to connect in the Passive FTP mode, do the following:

1. Open Internet Explorer; click "Tools – Internet Options" and select "Advanced" tab.
2. Under "Browsing", clear the checkbox "Enable folder view for FTP sites". This is required, as keeping this box checked will override the passive option.
3. Select the checkbox for "Use Passive FTP (for firewall and DSL modem compatibility)", as shown in the next screenshot.
4. Click "Apply" and then the "OK" button.

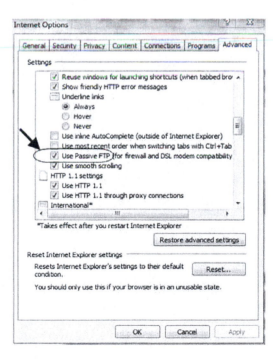

7.7.4 Experiment: Active FTP Traffic Sniffing and Analysis

The experiment is concerned with the sniffing and analysis of Active and Passive FTP traffic. The experiment includes two parts. The first one is about Active FTP traffic, while the second one is about Passive FTP traffic.

7.7.5 Network Architecture

The network architecture used in the experiment is shown in the following figure. Two hosts (Host #1 and Host #2) are connected to a Cisco switch. Host #1 is running LeapFTP tool as the FTP client. Host #2 is running LiteServe software as the FTP server.

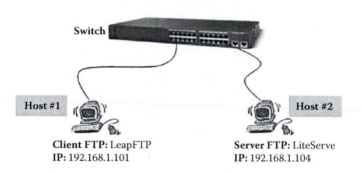

7.7.6 Experiment Steps—Part 1: Active FTP Session

The following experiment describes how to sniff and analyze the packets of an Active FTP session. The experiment consists of the following steps:

    Step 1: Connect to the FTP server using the Active FTP mode and sniff the session packets.
    Step 2: Analyze the Active FTP session packets.

7.7.6.1 Step 1: Connect to the FTP Server Using the Active FTP Mode and Sniff the Session Packets

From Host #1 and using LeapFTP, connect to the FTP server of Host #2. By default, LeapFTP uses the Active FTP mode. Then, using CommView sniffer at Host #1 or Host #2, capture the session packets.

7.7.6.2 Step 2: Analyze the Active FTP Session Packets

The following screenshots show the detailed contents of the main packets of the Command and Data sessions:

A. For the Command channel in the Active FTP session:
1. The first packet (SYN packet) of the three-way handshake of the Command channel in the Active FTP session:

2. The second packet (SYN-ACK packet) of the three-way handshake of the Command channel in the Active FTP session:

3. The third packet (ACK packet) of the three-way handshake of the Command channel in the Active FTP session:

4. The TCP packet of the Command channel in the Active FTP session that includes the port number for the Data channel (PORT Y = 49495):

Log Viewer [Active FTP session packets.ncf]

File   Search   Rules

Ethernet II
IP
- IP version: 0x04 (4)
- Header length: 0x05 (5) - 20 bytes
- Differentiated Services Field: 0x00 (0)
- Total length: 0x0043 (67)
- ID: 0x29CA (10698)
- Flags
- Fragment offset: 0x0000 (0)
- Time to live: 0x80 (128)
- Protocol: 0x06 (6) - TCP
- Checksum: 0x4CCD (19661) - correct
- Source IP: 192.168.1.101
- Destination IP: 192.168.1.104
- IP Options: None

TCP
- Source port: 49494
- Destination port: 21
- Sequence: 0xB6CC2E30 (3066834480)
- Acknowledgement: 0xAC86D300 (289451699)
- Header length: 0x05 (5) - 20 bytes
- Flags: PSH ACK
- Window: 0x10E1 (4321)
- Checksum: 0x3815 (15125) - correct
- Urgent Pointer: 0x0000 (0)
- TCP Options: None

FTP
- Command: PORT
- IP: 192.168.1.101
- Port: 49495

No	Protocol	Src IP	Dest IP	Src Port	Dest Port
1	IP/TCP	? 192.168.1.101	? 192.168.1.104	49494	21
2	IP/TCP	? 192.168.1.104	? 192.168.1.101	21	49494
3	IP/TCP	? 192.168.1.101	? 192.168.1.104	49494	21
4	IP/TCP	? 192.168.1.104	? 192.168.1.101	21	49494
5	IP/TCP	? 192.168.1.101	? 192.168.1.104	49494	21
6	IP/TCP	? 192.168.1.104	? 192.168.1.101	21	49494
7	IP/TCP	? 192.168.1.101	? 192.168.1.104	49494	21
8	IP/TCP	? 192.168.1.104	? 192.168.1.101	21	49494
9	IP/TCP	? 192.168.1.101	? 192.168.1.104	49494	21
10	IP/TCP	? 192.168.1.104	? 192.168.1.104	21	49494
11	IP/TCP	? 192.168.1.101	? 192.168.1.104	49494	21
12	IP/TCP	? 192.168.1.104	? 192.168.1.101	21	49494
13	IP/TCP	? 192.168.1.101	? 192.168.1.104	49494	21
14	IP/TCP	? 192.168.1.104	? 192.168.1.101	21	49494
15	IP/TCP	? 192.168.1.101	? 192.168.1.104	49494	21
16	IP/TCP	? 192.168.1.104	? 192.168.1.101	21	49494
17	IP/TCP	? 192.168.1.101	? 192.168.1.104	49494	21
18	IP/TCP	? 192.168.1.104	? 192.168.1.101	21	49494
19	IP/TCP	? 192.168.1.101	192.168.1.104	49494	21
20	IP/TCP	? 192.168.1.104	? 192.168.1.101	21	49494
21	IP/TCP	? 192.168.1.101	? 192.168.1.104	49494	21
22	IP/TCP	? 192.168.1.104	? 192.168.1.104	1074	49495
23	IP/TCP	? 192.168.1.101	? 192.168.1.104	49495	1074
24	IP/TCP	? 192.168.1.104	? 192.168.1.104	1074	49495
25	IP/TCP	? 192.168.1.104	? 192.168.1.101	21	49494
26	IP/TCP	? 192.168.1.104	? 192.168.1.101	1074	49495
27	IP/TCP	? 192.168.1.101	? 192.168.1.104	1074	49495
28	IP/TCP	? 192.168.1.101	? 192.168.1.104	49495	1074

```
0x0000   00 90 4B C8 F9 59 00 26-82 56 47 F0 08 00 45 00   .K£üY.&,VGð..E
0x0010   00 43 29 CA 40 00 80 06-4C CD C0 A8 01 65 C0 A8   .C)Ê£.€.LÍÀ .eÀ
0x0020   01 68 C1 56 00 15 B6 CC-2E 30 AC 86 D3 00 50 18   .hÁV..¶Ì.0¬†Ó.P.
0x0030   10 E1 3B 15 00 00 50 4F-52 54 20 31 39 32 2C 31   .á;...PORT 192,1
0x0040   36 38 2C 31 2C 31 30 31-2C 31 39 33 2C 38 37 0D   68,1,101,193,87.
0x0050   0A
```

B For the Data channel in the Active FTP session:

1. The first packet (SYN packet) of the three-way handshake of the Data channel in the Active FTP session:

Log Viewer [Active FTP session packets.ncf]

File   Search   Rules

Ethernet II
IP
- IP version: 0x04 (4)
- Header length: 0x05 (5) - 20 bytes
- Differentiated Services Field: 0x00 (0)
- Total length: 0x0030 (48)
- ID: 0x0333 (819)
- Flags
- Fragment offset: 0x0000 (0)
- Time to live: 0x80 (128)
- Protocol: 0x06 (6) - TCP
- Checksum: 0x7377 (29559) - correct
- Source IP: 192.168.1.104
- Destination IP: 192.168.1.101
- IP Options: None

TCP
- Source port: 1074
- Destination port: 49495
- Sequence: 0x4E88DB3F (1317591871)
- Acknowledgement: 0x00000000 (0)
- Header length: 0x07 (7) - 28 bytes
- Flags: SYN
- Window: 0x4000 (16384)
- Checksum: 0xCFAF (53167) - correct
- Urgent Pointer: 0x0000 (0)
- TCP Options
- Data length: 0x0 (0)

No	Protocol	Src IP	Dest IP	Src Port	Dest Port
9	IP/TCP	? 192.168.1.101	? 192.168.1.104	49494	21
10	IP/TCP	? 192.168.1.104	? 192.168.1.101	21	49494
11	IP/TCP	? 192.168.1.101	? 192.168.1.104	49494	21
12	IP/TCP	? 192.168.1.104	? 192.168.1.104	21	49494
13	IP/TCP	? 192.168.1.101	? 192.168.1.104	49494	21
14	IP/TCP	? 192.168.1.104	? 192.168.1.104	21	49494
15	IP/TCP	? 192.168.1.101	? 192.168.1.104	49494	21
16	IP/TCP	? 192.168.1.104	? 192.168.1.101	21	49494
17	IP/TCP	? 192.168.1.101	? 192.168.1.101	49494	21
18	IP/TCP	? 192.168.1.104	? 192.168.1.101	21	49494
19	IP/TCP	? 192.168.1.101	? 192.168.1.104	49494	21
20	IP/TCP	? 192.168.1.104	? 192.168.1.101	21	49494
21	IP/TCP	? 192.168.1.101	? 192.168.1.104	49494	21
22	IP/TCP	192.168.1.104	? 192.168.1.101	1074	49495
23	IP/TCP	? 192.168.1.101	? 192.168.1.104	49495	1074
24	IP/TCP	? 192.168.1.104	? 192.168.1.104	1074	49495
25	IP/TCP	? 192.168.1.104	? 192.168.1.101	21	49494
26	IP/TCP	? 192.168.1.104	? 192.168.1.101	1074	49495
27	IP/TCP	? 192.168.1.101	? 192.168.1.104	1074	49495
28	IP/TCP	? 192.168.1.101	? 192.168.1.104	49495	1074
29	IP/TCP	? 192.168.1.101	? 192.168.1.104	49495	1074
30	IP/TCP	? 192.168.1.101	? 192.168.1.104	49495	1074
31	IP/TCP	? 192.168.1.104	? 192.168.1.101	1074	49495
32	IP/TCP	? 192.168.1.101	? 192.168.1.104	49494	21

```
0x0000   00 26 82 56 47 F0 00 90-4B C8 F9 59 08 00 45 00   .&,VGð..K£üY..E
0x0010   00 30 03 33 40 00 80 06-73 77 C0 A8 01 68 C0 A8   .0.3@.€.swÀ .hÀ
0x0020   01 65 04 32 C1 57 4E 88-DB 3F 00 00 00 00 70 02   .e.2ÁWNˆÛ?....p.
0x0030   40 00 CF AF 00 00 02 04-05 B4 01 01 04 02         @.Ï¯.....´....
```

2. The second packet (SYN-ACK packet) of the three-way handshake of the Data channel in the Active FTP session:

3. The third packet (ACK packet) of the three-way handshake of the Data channel in the Active FTP session:

7.7.7 Experiment Steps—Part 2: Passive FTP Mode

The following experiment describes how to sniff and analyze the packets of a Passive FTP session. The experiment consists of the following steps:

Step 1: Configure LeapFTP as a Passive FTP client.
Step 2: Connect to the FTP server and sniff the session packets.
Step 3: Analyze the Passive FTP session packets.

7.7.7.1 Step 1: Configure LeapFTP as a Passive FTP Client

To configure LeapFTP as a Passive FTP client, do the following:

- From the GUI interface of LeapFTP, go to:
  - Options -> Preferences ->General -> Proxy.
- Select "Use PASV mode"; then click "OK" (as shown in the screenshot below).

7.7.7.2 Step 2: Connect to the FTP Server and Sniff the Session Packets

From Host #1 and using LeapFTP, connect to the FTP server running at Host #2. Then, using CommView sniffer, sniff the session packets.

7.7.7.3 Step 3: Analyze the Passive FTP Session Packets

The following screenshots show the detailed contents of the main packets of the Command and Data channels of the Passive FTP session:

A. For the Command channel in the Passive FTP session:
   1. The first packet (SYN packet) of the three-way hand-shake of the Command channel in the Passive FTP session:

   2. The second packet (SYN-ACK packet) of the three-way handshake of the Command channel in the Passive FTP session:

Log Viewer [Passive FTP session packets.ncf]

File   Search   Rules

▷ Ethernet II
▲ IP
　IP version: 0x04 (4)
　Header length: 0x05 (5) - 20 bytes
　▷ Differentiated Services Field: 0x00 (0)
　Total length: 0x0034 (52)
　ID: 0x03C6 (966)
　▷ Flags
　Fragment offset: 0x0000 (0)
　Time to live: 0x80 (128)
　Protocol: 0x06 (6) - TCP
　Checksum: 0x72E0 (29408) - correct
　Source IP: 192.168.1.104
　Destination IP: 192.168.1.101
　IP Options: None
▲ TCP
　Source port: 21
　Destination port: 49568
　Sequence: 0x5D655990 (1566923152)
　Acknowledgement: 0x7A89C7E9 (2055849961)
　Header length: 0x08 (8) - 32 bytes
　Flags: SYN ACK
　Window: 0x4470 (17520)
　Checksum: 0xEB5B (60251) - correct
　Urgent Pointer: 0x0000 (0)
　▷ TCP Options
　Data length: 0x0 (0)

No	Protocol	Src IP	Dest IP	Src Port	Dest Port
1	IP/TCP	? 192.168.1.101	? 192.168.1.104	49568	21
2	IP/TCP	? 192.168.1.104	? 192.168.1.101	21	49568
3	IP/TCP	? 192.168.1.101	? 192.168.1.104	49568	21
4	IP/TCP	? 192.168.1.101	? 192.168.1.104	21	49568
5	IP/TCP	? 192.168.1.101	? 192.168.1.104	49568	21
6	IP/TCP	? 192.168.1.104	? 192.168.1.101	21	49568
7	IP/TCP	? 192.168.1.101	? 192.168.1.104	49568	21
8	IP/TCP	? 192.168.1.104	? 192.168.1.101	21	49568
9	IP/TCP	? 192.168.1.101	? 192.168.1.104	49568	21
10	IP/TCP	? 192.168.1.104	? 192.168.1.101	21	49568
11	IP/TCP	? 192.168.1.101	? 192.168.1.104	49568	21
12	IP/TCP	? 192.168.1.104	? 192.168.1.101	21	49568
13	IP/TCP	? 192.168.1.101	? 192.168.1.104	49568	21
14	IP/TCP	? 192.168.1.104	? 192.168.1.101	21	49568
15	IP/TCP	? 192.168.1.101	? 192.168.1.104	49568	21
16	IP/TCP	? 192.168.1.104	? 192.168.1.101	21	49568
17	IP/TCP	? 192.168.1.101	? 192.168.1.104	49568	21
18	IP/TCP	? 192.168.1.104	? 192.168.1.101	21	49568
19	IP/TCP	? 192.168.1.101	? 192.168.1.104	49568	21
20	IP/TCP	? 192.168.1.104	? 192.168.1.101	21	49568
21	IP/TCP	? 192.168.1.104	? 192.168.1.101	49569	1078
22	IP/TCP	? 192.168.1.104	? 192.168.1.101	1078	49569
23	IP/TCP	? 192.168.1.101	? 192.168.1.104	49569	1078
24	IP/TCP	? 192.168.1.101	? 192.168.1.104	49568	21
25	IP/TCP	? 192.168.1.104	? 192.168.1.101	21	49568

```
0x0000   00 26 82 56 47 F0 00 90-4B C8 F9 59 08 00 45 00   .&.VG6.KËÙY..E
0x0010   00 34 03 C6 40 00 80 06-72 E0 C0 A8 01 68 C0 A8   .4.Æ@...rà À..hÀ.
0x0020   01 65 00 15 C1 A0 8D 6B-89 90 7A 89 C7 E9 60 12   .e..Á  .k..zëÇé`.
0x0030   44 70 EB 5B 00 00 02 04-05 B4 01 03 93 00 01 01   Dpë[......
0x0040   04 02
```

3. The third packet (ACK packet) of the three-way hand-shake of the Command channel in the Passive FTP session:

Log Viewer [Passive FTP session packets.ncf]

File   Search   Rules

▷ Ethernet II
▲ IP
　IP version: 0x04 (4)
　Header length: 0x05 (5) - 20 bytes
　▷ Differentiated Services Field: 0x00 (0)
　Total length: 0x0028 (40)
　ID: 0x305F (12383)
　▷ Flags
　Fragment offset: 0x0000 (0)
　Time to live: 0x80 (128)
　Protocol: 0x06 (6) - TCP
　Checksum: 0x4653 (18003) - correct
　Source IP: 192.168.1.101
　Destination IP: 192.168.1.104
　IP Options: None
▲ TCP
　Source port: 49568
　Destination port: 21
　Sequence: 0x7A89C7E9 (2055849961)
　Acknowledgement: 0x5D655991 (1566923153)
　Header length: 0x05 (5) - 20 bytes
　Flags: ACK
　Window: 0x111C (4380)
　Checksum: 0x5F7B (24443) - correct
　Urgent Pointer: 0x0000 (0)
　TCP Options: None
　Data length: 0x0 (0)

No	Protocol	Src IP	Dest IP	Src Port	Dest Port
1	IP/TCP	? 192.168.1.101	? 192.168.1.104	49568	21
2	IP/TCP	? 192.168.1.104	? 192.168.1.101	21	49568
3	IP/TCP	? 192.168.1.101	? 192.168.1.104	49568	21
4	IP/TCP	? 192.168.1.104	? 192.168.1.101	21	49568
5	IP/TCP	? 192.168.1.101	? 192.168.1.104	49568	21
6	IP/TCP	? 192.168.1.104	? 192.168.1.101	21	49568
7	IP/TCP	? 192.168.1.104	? 192.168.1.101	21	49568
8	IP/TCP	? 192.168.1.101	? 192.168.1.104	49568	21
9	IP/TCP	? 192.168.1.104	? 192.168.1.101	21	49568
10	IP/TCP	? 192.168.1.104	? 192.168.1.101	21	49568
11	IP/TCP	? 192.168.1.101	? 192.168.1.104	49568	21
12	IP/TCP	? 192.168.1.104	? 192.168.1.101	21	49568
13	IP/TCP	? 192.168.1.101	? 192.168.1.104	49568	21
14	IP/TCP	? 192.168.1.104	? 192.168.1.101	21	49568
15	IP/TCP	? 192.168.1.101	? 192.168.1.104	49568	21
16	IP/TCP	? 192.168.1.104	? 192.168.1.101	21	49568
17	IP/TCP	? 192.168.1.101	? 192.168.1.104	49568	21
18	IP/TCP	? 192.168.1.101	? 192.168.1.104	49568	21
19	IP/TCP	? 192.168.1.101	? 192.168.1.104	49568	21
20	IP/TCP	? 192.168.1.101	? 192.168.1.104	21	49568
21	IP/TCP	? 192.168.1.101	? 192.168.1.104	49569	1078
22	IP/TCP	? 192.168.1.101	? 192.168.1.104	1078	49569
23	IP/TCP	? 192.168.1.101	? 192.168.1.104	49569	1078
24	IP/TCP	? 192.168.1.101	? 192.168.1.104	49568	21
25	IP/TCP	? 192.168.1.104	? 192.168.1.101	21	49568

```
0x0000   00 90 4B C8 F9 59 00 26-82 56 47 F0 08 00 45 00   ..KÈùY.&.VG6..E
0x0010   00 28 30 5F 40 00 80 06-46 53 C0 A8 01 65 C0 A8   .(0_@...FSÀ..eÀ.
0x0020   01 68 C1 A0 00 15 7A 89-C7 E9 5D 65 59 91 60 10   .hÁ ..zÇé]eY`.
0x0030   11 1C 5F 7B 00 00                                 .._{..
```

4. The TCP packet of the Command channel in the Passive FTP session that includes the request "PASV":

Log Viewer [Passive FTP session packets.ncf]

File   Search   Rules

Ethernet II

▲ IP
  - IP version: 0x04 (4)
  - Header length: 0x05 (5) - 20 bytes
  ▷ Differentiated Services Field: 0x00 (0)
  - Total length: 0x002E (46)
  - ID: 0x3067 (12391)
  ▷ Flags
  - Fragment offset: 0x0000 (0)
  - Time to live: 0x80 (128)
  - Protocol: 0x06 (6) - TCP
  - Checksum: 0x4645 (17989) - correct
  - Source IP: 192.168.1.101
  - Destination IP: 192.168.1.104
  - IP Options: None

▲ TCP
  - Source port: 49568
  - Destination port: 21
  - Sequence: 0x7A59C8S1 (2055850033)
  - Acknowledgement: 0x5D655A7D (1566923388)
  - Header length: 0x05 (5) - 20 bytes
  ▷ Flags: PSH ACK
  - Window: 0x10E1 (4321)
  - Checksum: 0xADD2 (44498) - correct
  - Urgent Pointer: 0x0000 (0)
  - TCP Options: None

▲ FTP
  - Command: PASV

No	Protocol	Src IP	Dest IP	Src Port	Dest Port
1	IP/TCP	? 192.168.1.101	? 192.168.1.104	49568	21
2	IP/TCP	? 192.168.1.104	? 192.168.1.101	21	49568
3	IP/TCP	? 192.168.1.101	? 192.168.1.104	49568	21
4	IP/TCP	? 192.168.1.104	? 192.168.1.101	21	49568
5	IP/TCP	? 192.168.1.101	? 192.168.1.104	49568	21
6	IP/TCP	? 192.168.1.104	? 192.168.1.101	21	49568
7	IP/TCP	? 192.168.1.101	? 192.168.1.104	49568	21
8	IP/TCP	? 192.168.1.104	? 192.168.1.101	21	49568
9	IP/TCP	? 192.168.1.101	? 192.168.1.104	49568	21
10	IP/TCP	? 192.168.1.104	? 192.168.1.101	21	49568
11	IP/TCP	? 192.168.1.101	? 192.168.1.104	49568	21
12	IP/TCP	? 192.168.1.104	? 192.168.1.101	21	49568
13	IP/TCP	? 192.168.1.101	? 192.168.1.104	49568	21
14	IP/TCP	? 192.168.1.104	? 192.168.1.101	21	49568
15	IP/TCP	? 192.168.1.101	? 192.168.1.104	49568	21
16	IP/TCP	? 192.168.1.104	? 192.168.1.101	21	49568
17	IP/TCP	? 192.168.1.101	? 192.168.1.104	49568	21
18	IP/TCP	? 192.168.1.104	? 192.168.1.101	21	49568
19	IP/TCP	? 192.168.1.101	? 192.168.1.104	49568	21
20	IP/TCP	? 192.168.1.104	? 192.168.1.101	21	49568
21	IP/TCP	? 192.168.1.101	? 192.168.1.104	49569	1078
22	IP/TCP	? 192.168.1.104	? 192.168.1.101	1078	49569
23	IP/TCP	? 192.168.1.101	? 192.168.1.104	49569	1078
24	IP/TCP	? 192.168.1.104	? 192.168.1.101	49568	21
25	IP/TCP	? 192.168.1.104	? 192.168.1.101	21	49568
26	IP/TCP	? 192.168.1.104	? 192.168.1.101	1078	49569
27	IP/TCP	? 192.168.1.104	? 192.168.1.101	1078	49569

```
0x0000   00 90 4B C8 F9 59 00 26-82 56 47 F0 08 00 45 00   .ÉùY.&,VGð..E
0x0010   00 2E 30 67 40 00 80 06-46 45 C0 A8 01 65 C0 A8   ..0g@.€.FEÀ¨.é
0x0020   01 68 C1 A0 00 15 7A 69-C8 31 5D 65 5A 7D 50 18   .hÁ ..zÉ1]eZ}
0x0030   10 E1 AD D2 00 00 50 41-53 56 0D 0A                .áÒ..PASV..
```

5. The TCP packet of the Command channel in the Passive FTP session that sends the port number of the Data channel at the server side. The PORT command is formatted as a series of six numbers separated by commas. The first four octets are the FTP server's IP address, while the last two octets comprise the port that will be used for the data connection. To find the actual port, multiply the fifth octet by 256 and then add the sixth octet to the total. Thus, in the example below, the port number is ((4*256)+54), or 1078.

Log Viewer [Passive FTP session packets.ncf]

File Search Rules

Ethernet II
IP
- IP version: 0x04 (4)
- Header length: 0x05 (5) - 20 bytes
- Differentiated Services Field: 0x00 (0)
- Total length: 0x0058 (88)
- ID: 0x03CF (975)
- Flags
- Fragment offset: 0x0000 (0)
- Time to live: 0x80 (128)
- Protocol: 0x06 (6) - TCP
- Checksum: 0x72B3 (29363) - correct
- Source IP: 192.168.1.104
- Destination IP: 192.168.1.101
- IP Options: None
TCP
- Source port: 21
- Destination port: 49568
- Sequence: 0x5D65SA7D (1566923389)
- Acknowledgement: 0x7A89C837 (2055850039)
- Header length: 0x05 (5) - 20 bytes
- Flags: PSH ACK
- Window: 0x4472 (17442)
- Checksum: 0xE0A7 (57511) - correct
- Urgent Pointer: 0x0000 (0)
- TCP Options: None
FTP
- Status: 227
- Comment: Entering Passive Mode (192,168,1,104,4,54)

No	Protocol	Src IP	Dest IP	Src Port	Dest Port
1	IP/TCP	? 192.168.1.101	? 192.168.1.104	49568	21
2	IP/TCP	? 192.168.1.104	? 192.168.1.101	21	49568
3	IP/TCP	? 192.168.1.101	? 192.168.1.104	49568	21
4	IP/TCP	? 192.168.1.104	? 192.168.1.101	21	49568
5	IP/TCP	? 192.168.1.101	? 192.168.1.104	49568	21
6	IP/TCP	? 192.168.1.104	? 192.168.1.101	21	49568
7	IP/TCP	? 192.168.1.101	? 192.168.1.104	49568	21
8	IP/TCP	? 192.168.1.104	? 192.168.1.101	21	49568
9	IP/TCP	? 192.168.1.101	? 192.168.1.104	49568	21
10	IP/TCP	? 192.168.1.104	? 192.168.1.101	21	49568
11	IP/TCP	? 192.168.1.101	? 192.168.1.104	49568	21
12	IP/TCP	? 192.168.1.104	? 192.168.1.101	21	49568
13	IP/TCP	? 192.168.1.101	? 192.168.1.104	49568	21
14	IP/TCP	? 192.168.1.104	? 192.168.1.101	21	49568
15	IP/TCP	? 192.168.1.101	? 192.168.1.104	49568	21
16	IP/TCP	? 192.168.1.104	? 192.168.1.101	21	49568
17	IP/TCP	? 192.168.1.101	? 192.168.1.104	49568	21
18	IP/TCP	? 192.168.1.104	? 192.168.1.101	21	49568
19	IP/TCP	? 192.168.1.101	? 192.168.1.104	49568	21
20	IP/TCP	? 192.168.1.104	? 192.168.1.101	21	49568
21	IP/TCP	? 192.168.1.101	? 192.168.1.104	49569	1078
		1.104	192.168.1.101	1078	49569
		1.101	192.168.1.104	49569	1078
		1.101	192.168.1.104	49568	21
		1.104	192.168.1.101	21	49568
		1.104	192.168.1.101	1078	49569
		1.104	192.168.1.101	1078	49569
		1.101	192.168.1.104	49569	1078

The port number of the Data channel at the server side = 4*256 + 54 = 1078

```
0x0000  00 26 82 56 47 F0 00 4B C8 F9 59 08 00 45 00   .&.VG6.KE0Y..E.
0x0010  00 58 03 CF 40 00 80 06-72 B3 C0 A8 01 68 C0 A8   .X.I@.ε.rΑ^..hΑ
0x0020  01 65 00 15 C1 A0 5D 65-5A 7D 7A 89 C8 37 50 18   .e..Å .]eZ]zE79 
0x0030  44 72 E0 A7 00 00 32 32-37 20 45 6E 74 65 72 69   Dʳáṣ..227 Enteri
0x0040  6E 67 20 50 61 73 73 69 76 65 20 4D 6F 64 65 20   ng Passive Mode 
0x0050  28 31 39 32 2C 31 36-38-2C 31 2C 31 30 34 2C 34   (192,168,1,104,4
```

B. For the Data channel in the Passive FTP session:
1. The first packet (SYN packet) of the three-way handshake of the Data channel in the Passive FTP session:

Log Viewer [Passive FTP session packets.ncf]

File Search Rules

Ethernet II
IP
- IP version: 0x04 (4)
- Header length: 0x05 (5) - 20 bytes
- Differentiated Services Field: 0x00 (0)
- Total length: 0x0034 (52)
- ID: 0x3068 (12392)
- Flags
- Fragment offset: 0x0000 (0)
- Time to live: 0x80 (128)
- Protocol: 0x06 (6) - TCP
- Checksum: 0x463E (17982) - correct
- Source IP: 192.168.1.101
- Destination IP: 192.168.1.104
- IP Options: None
TCP
- Source port: 49569
- Destination port: 1078
- Sequence: 0x78F40213 (2029257235)
- Acknowledgement: 0x00000000 (0)
- Header length: 0x08 (8) - 32 bytes
- Flags: SYN
- Window: 0x2000 (8192)
- Checksum: 0x8A19 (35353) - correct
- Urgent Pointer: 0x0000 (0)
- TCP Options
- Data length: 0x0 (0)

No	Protocol	Src IP	Dest IP	Src Port	Dest Port
1	IP/TCP	? 192.168.1.101	? 192.168.1.104	49568	21
2	IP/TCP	? 192.168.1.104	? 192.168.1.101	21	49568
3	IP/TCP	? 192.168.1.101	? 192.168.1.104	49568	21
4	IP/TCP	? 192.168.1.104	? 192.168.1.101	21	49568
5	IP/TCP	? 192.168.1.101	? 192.168.1.104	49568	21
6	IP/TCP	? 192.168.1.104	? 192.168.1.101	21	49568
7	IP/TCP	? 192.168.1.101	? 192.168.1.104	49568	21
8	IP/TCP	? 192.168.1.104	? 192.168.1.101	21	49568
9	IP/TCP	? 192.168.1.104	? 192.168.1.101	21	49568
10	IP/TCP	? 192.168.1.101	? 192.168.1.104	49568	21
11	IP/TCP	? 192.168.1.101	? 192.168.1.104	49568	21
12	IP/TCP	? 192.168.1.104	? 192.168.1.101	21	49568
13	IP/TCP	? 192.168.1.101	? 192.168.1.104	49568	21
14	IP/TCP	? 192.168.1.104	? 192.168.1.101	21	49568
15	IP/TCP	? 192.168.1.101	? 192.168.1.104	49568	21
16	IP/TCP	? 192.168.1.104	? 192.168.1.101	21	49568
17	IP/TCP	? 192.168.1.101	? 192.168.1.104	49568	21
18	IP/TCP	? 192.168.1.104	? 192.168.1.101	21	49568
19	IP/TCP	? 192.168.1.101	? 192.168.1.104	49568	21
20	IP/TCP	? 192.168.1.104	? 192.168.1.101	21	49568
21	IP/TCP	? 192.168.1.101	? 192.168.1.104	49569	1078
22	IP/TCP	? 192.168.1.104	? 192.168.1.101	1078	49569
23	IP/TCP	? 192.168.1.101	? 192.168.1.104	49569	1078
24	IP/TCP	? 192.168.1.101	? 192.168.1.104	49568	21

```
0x0000  00 90 4B C8 F9 59 00 26-82 56 47 F0 08 00 45 00   .ÉKÈ.ʑ.&.VG6..E.
0x0010  00 34 30 68 40 00 80 06-46 3E C0 A8 01 65 C0 A8   .40h@.ε.F>Α^.eA
0x0020  01 68 C1 A1 04 36 78 F4-02 13 00 00 00 00 80 02   .hA;.6xô......€ 
0x0030  20 00 8A 19 00 00 02 04-05 B4 01 03 03 02 01 01   .Š.....´......
0x0040  04 02                                              ..
```

2. The second packet (SYN-ACK packet) of the three-way handshake of the Data channel in the Passive FTP session:

3. The third packet (ACK packet) of the three-way hand-shake of the Data channel in the Passive FTP session:

7.8 Chapter Summary

An enterprise with an intranet that allows its workers to access the wider Internet installs a firewall to prevent outsiders from accessing its own private data resources and for controlling what outside resources its own users have access to. Basically, a firewall examines each network packet to determine whether or not to forward it toward its destination. Therefore, firewalls play an important role in the enforcement of access control policies in contemporary networks.

This chapter discussed a series of hands-on exercises about filtering rules implementation for basic security policies, filtering of services running on nonstandard TCP and UDP ports, verification of the consistency and efficiency of firewall filtering rules, packet content filtering, stateless and stateful packet filtering, and active and passive FTP modes.

Chapter 8

Router Security

8.1 Introduction

An essential measure of securing any network is to ensure safe traffic across its borders. The router is a device that connects one or more networks together and hence is a point of entrance to a network. Consequently, the router enforces security solutions that are vital to the safety of any network.

This chapter discusses the implementation of the following security features on a router:

- *Authentication, Authorization, and Accounting (AAA) model:* The AAA (triple A) model adopts a modular approach and is a scalable security solution. It executes Authentication, Authorization, and Accounting policies in a flexible manner. The model first defines the security service method and then applies it to different lines or consoles. By doing so, it promotes usability, reusability, and scalability.
- *Network services security:* One of the most important router security hardening tasks is to disable network

services that are not needed and to secure the needed services, especially those that are used for device management (e.g., Telnet and HTTP). A sniffing attack is utilized to exploit the vulnerabilities of the cleartext network services, namely, Telnet and HTTP. Later, these vulnerable services are replaced by the encrypted text services SSH (Secure Shell) and HTTPS.

■ *Packet filtering, using Access Control Lists (ACLs):* The Internet Engineering Task Force (IETF) standard set by Request for Comment (RFC) 1918 and RFC 2827 is used to describe filtering policies. RFC 1918 defines private addresses that are not allowed on the Internet. RFC 2827 discusses network ingress filtering to prevent IP spoofing attacks. In addition, a variety of packet filtering rules are configured to allow and deny different types of traffic based on the defined policy.

■ *Stateful inspection:* Common routers support stateful packet filtering inspection. This feature allows returning traffic to the protected network to pass through the router based on state information derived from past communications. This is achieved by opening a dynamic hole in the security policy, which is executed using a mechanism known as Context Based Access Control (CBAC) on Cisco routers.

This chapter includes hands-on exercises about AAA model implementation, secure network services, and stateful packet filtering on a border router. Cisco routers are widely used in practical implementations. Hence, the hands-on exercises use Cisco devices to implement the discussed security concepts. Nonetheless, such security concepts can be applied to products from other vendors offering the same functionalities. The following hardware devices and software tools are used for the exercises:

■ Cisco router*: network router
■ CommView Tool†: network monitor and analyzer tool (sniffer)

8.2 Lab 8.1: AAA Model Basics

8.2.1 Outcome

The learning objective of this exercise is for students to learn the security features of the Cisco router by configuring the basic AAA model.

8.2.2 Description

Managing access to the resources of a network device is of prime importance when considering network security. Earlier measures for securing access include line password, ENABLE password, and local username. However, these only provide a basic level of authentication that identifies the users who are logged in to a router or other network device. On the other hand, the AAA model is a generalized policy-based framework that satisfies most of the common problems in network access control. It addresses the three main security services of any access control system—namely, Authentication, Authorization, and Accounting—as independent security functions.

Authentication must precede authorization and accounting, and involves two steps: identification and verification. First, the user is identified by submitting credentials such as username and password through a series of challenges and responses. Next, these credentials are verified to confirm the user's identity from an authorized database. The database can be a local

---

* HTTP://www.cisco.com
† HTTP://www.tamos.com

database that is stored on a network device or it can be the router itself. The database could be a remote database residing on a dedicated remote AAA server. The two prominent security protocols used to communicate with a remote AAA server are Cisco TACAS + (Terminal Access Controller Access-Control System Plus) and RADIUS (Remote Authentication Dial-In User Service) specified in RFC 2865.

Authorization follows the authentication process to enforce specific policies for network resources. It provides more granular control on the user privileges for accessing network resources. The main resources available for access control on Cisco routers are the Internetwork Operating System (IOS) commands. Based on the authorization policy, users are assigned to a certain privilege level ranging from 0 to 15. With a privilege level of 0, a user cannot execute any IOS command on the router. A privilege level of 1 represents "User EXEC" mode, which is assigned by default to a user who logs in to the router. A privilege level of 15, which is the default privilege level of the "Privileged EXEC" mode (Enable mode) of the router, gives a user the ability to perform all IOS commands. Following the principle of least privilege, which requires users to have access only to necessary resources for their purpose and no more, the remaining privilege levels are assigned to different users, depending on their job specifications. Authorization policies can be defined locally on the router itself or remotely using AAA servers.

Accounting is the process of collecting and recording information about user actions and network events that can be used for auditing purposes. Accounting comes after completing authentication and authorization. Accounting information can be stored on the router itself or remotely on AAA servers. Examples of accounting information are login session events, issued IOS commands, and number of packets.

This hands-on exercise focuses on explaining AAA model authentication and authorization methods using the Cisco IOS router. The exercise provides a step-by-step approach to

implement authentication and authorization methods that protect management access to the Cisco router. A local database
of the authentication and authorization policies has been
configured on the router to assign users the right privilege
level. The methods used to manage the router are the console
line and Telnet, which have been secured by the AAA model.
Additionally, non-AAA accounting methods have been implemented to show the different logging levels that are available
on the Cisco IOS router.

8.2.3 Experiment

The steps in the following experiment are conducted using
Cisco router 2800 running OS 12.4 to configure the authentication and authorization methods.

8.2.4 Network Architecture

The next figure illustrates the network architecture of the
experiment. A management station is connected to the router
through a console cable to make the required configuration.

Cisco Router 2800   Management Station

8.2.5 Experiment Steps

The experiment consists of the following steps:

    Step 1: Basic router set-up commands.
    Step 2: Configure the loopback interface.
    Step 3: Console default authentication and authorization.
    Step 4: Telnet default authentication and authorization.
    Step 5: Configure AAA model: Authentication.
    Step 6: Apply authentication to VTY.

Step 7: Apply authentication to the console.

Step 8: Test the console and Telnet authentication.

Step 9: Configure AAA model: Authorization.

Step 10: Apply authorization to VTY.

Step 11: Apply authorization to the console.

Step 12: Test the console and Telnet authorization.

Step 13: Configure console logging.

8.2.5.1 Step 1: Basic Router Set-Up Commands

First, connect a laptop to the serial console of the router. Type "enable" for the router to move to the privileged user EXEC mode. Next, to disable the DNS lookup, type: "no ip domain lookup" in the global configuration mode. Finally, to synchronize the logging messages and set the console timeout to infinity, issue the following commands:

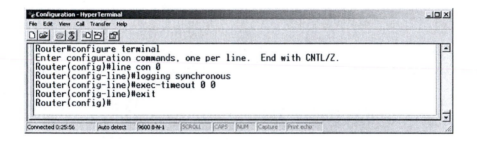

Use the "alias" command to make the configuration easier, as shown in the following:

```
Router(config)#alias exec c configure terminal
Router(config)#alias exec s show run
Router(config)#alias exec p ping
Router(config)#alias exec t telnet
Router(config)#alias exec b show ip int brief
Router(config)#alias exec be sh ip int brief | ex una
Router(config)#alias exec bu sh ip int brief | in up_
```

For example, type the alias command "do b" to display a brief representation of the interfaces.

```
Configuration - HyperTerminal                                             _ |□| x|
File  Edit  View  Call  Transfer  Help
D|☞| ☎|⑧| ▫|₴| ☞|
Router(config)#do b                                                              ▲
Interface              IP-Address      OK? Method Status            Prot
ocol
FastEthernet0/0        unassigned      YES unset  administratively down down

FastEthernet0/1        unassigned      YES unset  administratively down down

Serial0/2/0            unassigned      YES unset  administratively down down

Serial0/2/1            unassigned      YES unset  administratively down down

Router(config)#_
                                                                                 ▼
Connected 0:36:39    Auto detect   9600 8-N-1   SCROLL   CAPS   NUM   Capture   Print echo
```

To exclude the unassigned interfaces, enter the following command:

```
Configuration - HyperTerminal                                             _ |□| x|
File  Edit  View  Call  Transfer  Help
D|☞| ☎|⑧| ▫|₴| ☞|
                                                                                 ▲
Router(config)#do be
Interface              IP-Address      OK? Method Status            Prot
ocol
Router(config)#_
                                                                                 ▼
Connected 0:37:33    Auto detect   9600 8-N-1   SCROLL   CAPS   NUM   Capture   Print echo
```

8.2.5.2 Step 2: Configure the Loopback Interface

The loopback interface is used for Telnet testing. To create the loopback interface, issue the following commands:

```
Configuration - HyperTerminal                                             _ |□| x|
File  Edit  View  Call  Transfer  Help
D|☞| ☎|⑧| ▫|₴| ☞|
Router(config)#int loopback 0                                                    ▲
Router(config-if)#
*May  3 05:21:16.831: %LINEPROTO-5-UPDOWN: Line protocol on Interface Loopback0,
 changed state to up
Router(config-if)#ip address 150.1.1.1 255.255.255.0
Router(config-if)#_
                                                                                 ▼
Connected 0:41:23    Auto detect   9600 8-N-1   SCROLL   CAPS   NUM   Capture   Print echo
```

Next, to display the loopback interface that was created, issue the following commands:

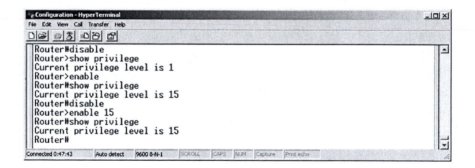

```
Configuration - HyperTerminal                                              _|□|×|
File  Edit  View  Call  Transfer  Help
 D|☞| ☞|ℨ| □|🖻| 🖻|
Router(config-if)#do b
Interface                  IP-Address      OK? Method Status              Prot
ocol
FastEthernet0/0            unassigned      YES unset  administratively down down

FastEthernet0/1            unassigned      YES unset  administratively down down

Serial0/2/0                unassigned      YES unset  administratively down down

Serial0/2/1                unassigned      YES unset  administratively down down

Loopback0                  150.1.1.1       YES manual up                   up

Router(config-if)#end
Router#
*May  3 05:23:06.687: %SYS-5-CONFIG_I: Configured from console by console
Router#_
Connected 0:42:51    Auto detect   9600 8-N-1    SCROLL   CAPS   NUM   Capture   Print echo
```

8.2.5.3 Step 3: Console Default Authentication and Authorization

To show the privilege levels of different users who are logged in, type the "show privilege" command. Notice that the default privilege level of the ENABLE mode is 15.

```
Configuration - HyperTerminal                                              _|□|×|
File  Edit  View  Call  Transfer  Help
 D|☞| ☞|ℨ| □|🖻| 🖻|
Router#disable
Router>show privilege
Current privilege level is 1
Router>enable
Router#show privilege
Current privilege level is 15
Router#disable
Router>enable 15
Router#show privilege
Current privilege level is 15
Router#
Connected 0:47:43    Auto detect   9600 8-N-1    SCROLL   CAPS   NUM   Capture   Print echo
```

8.2.5.4 Step 4: VTY (Telnet) Default Authentication and Authorization

To check the default authentication and authorization of the VTY line, use the following command, which shows that a password is required for the Telnet connection to work:

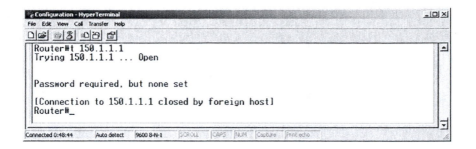

8.2.5.5 Step 5: Configure the AAA Model: Authentication

Configuration of authentication requires the username, the password, and the type of database. In this example, the database is a local instance. The name of the AAA method used for Authentication is ANN.

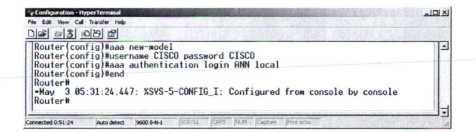

8.2.5.6 Step 6: Apply Authentication to VTY

To apply the authentication method ANN created in Step 5 to VTY, issue the following command:

```
Router(config)#line vty 0 4
Router(config-line)#login authentication ANN
Router(config-line)#exit
Router(config)#_
```

8.2.5.7 *Step 7: Apply Authentication to the Console*

The following commands describe how to apply the authentication configuration, created in Step 5, to the console line.

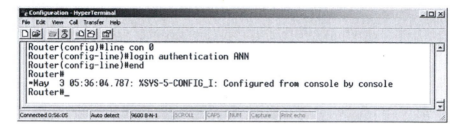

8.2.5.8 *Step 8: Test the Console and Telnet Authentication*

Using the "exit" command, the *User Access Verification* message appears because the authentication for the console has been configured. Enter "CISCO" as the username and password, as specified in the creation of the local database.

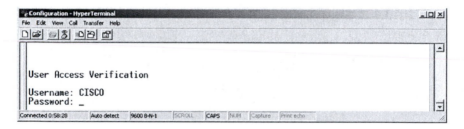

Next, telnet 150.1.1.1, which results in a *User Access Verification* message because the authentication has been configured for Telnet. Then, enter "CISCO" as username and password.

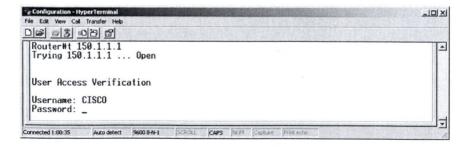

To display users who are logged in to the router, enter the command "show users". The command indicates that two users have logged in. One is logged in through the console line and the other is the Telnet user.

```
Configuration - HyperTerminal                                    _|□|×|
File  Edit  View  Call  Transfer  Help
D|☞| ⏺|⑤| □|🖺| ☎|

Router>show users
     Line        User        Host(s)              Idle        Location
     0 con 0     CISCO       150.1.1.1            00:00:00
   * vty 194     CISCO       idle                 00:00:00  150.1.1.1

     Interface   User                     Mode      Idle      Peer Address

Router>_

Connected 1:01:57     Auto detect   9600 8-N-1    SCROLL   CAPS   NUM   Capture   Print echo
```

8.2.5.9 Step 9: Configure the AAA Model: Authorization

The configuration of the authorization requires the specification of the method, the type of database, the username, and the privilege level, which is 15, as in the following commands. The name of the authorization method used is ARR.

```
Configuration - HyperTerminal                                    _|□|×|
File  Edit  View  Call  Transfer  Help
D|☞| ⏺|⑤| □|🖺| ☎|

Router#c
Enter configuration commands, one per line.  End with CNTL/Z.
Router(config)#aaa authorization exec ARR local
Router(config)#username CISCO privilege 15
Router(config)#

Connected 1:07:27     Auto detect   9600 8-N-1    SCROLL   CAPS   NUM   Capture   Print echo
```

8.2.5.10 Step 10: Apply Authorization to VTY

The following command shows how to apply the authorization method (from Step 9) to VTY, which gives the user a privilege level of 15.

```
Configuration - HyperTerminal                                    _|□|×|
File  Edit  View  Call  Transfer  Help
D|☞| ⏺|⑤| □|🖺| ☎|

Router(config)#line vty 0 4
Router(config-line)#authorization exec ARR
Router(config-line)#exit
Router(config)#

Connected 1:08:53     Auto detect   9600 8-N-1    SCROLL   CAPS   NUM   Capture   Print echo
```

8.2.5.11 Step 11: Apply Authorization to the Console

To apply the authorization method, from Step 9, to the console line, issue the following command:

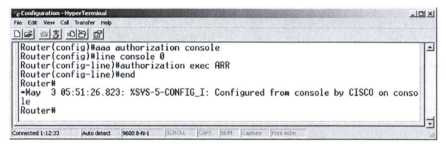

8.2.5.12 Step 12: Test the Console and Telnet Authorization

Next, issue the "exit" command. The username and password "CISCO" is given for user access verification. The default privilege level 15 is assigned to the user, which indicates that the user is authorized to execute all Cisco IOS commands on the router. To check the privilege level, use the following command:

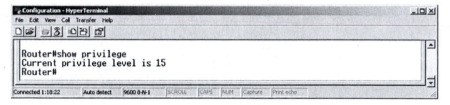

Next, telnet 150.1.1.1, an access verification message, appears because the authentication and authorization for VTY have been configured previously. Enter "CISCO" as the username and password; the privilege level of 15 is assigned directly to the user.

To verify that the user has privilege 15, use the "show privilege" command.

Finally, disconnect the Telnet session by issuing the exit command.

```
Configuration - HyperTerminal                                          _ |□| x|
File  Edit  View  Call  Transfer  Help
□|☞| ☞|⑧| ◻|⧄| ☞|
Router#exit                                                                 ▲

[Connection to 150.1.1.1 closed by foreign host]
Router#_
                                                                            ▼
Connected 1:22:31      Auto detect   9600 8-N-1   SCROLL   CAPS   NUM   Capture   Print echo
```

8.2.5.13 Step 13: Configure Console Logging

To move to configuration mode, use "*c*" alias of the "configure terminal" command. Next, enable logging by typing the "logging on" command. Then, use "logging console ?", which displays help on the available logging severity levels on the Cisco IOS router. There are eight levels, from 0 to 7. Level 0 logs only emergency events, and level 7 shows debugging messages as in the following commands:

```
Configuration - HyperTerminal                                          _|□| x|
File  Edit  View  Call  Transfer  Help
□|☞| ☞|⑧| ◻|⧄| ☞|
Router(config)#logging on                                                   ▲
Router(config)#logging console ?
  <0-7>          Logging severity level
  alerts         Immediate action needed              (severity=1)
  critical       Critical conditions                  (severity=2)
  debugging      Debugging messages                   (severity=7)
  emergencies    System is unusable                   (severity=0)
  errors         Error conditions                     (severity=3)
  filtered       Enable filtered logging
  guaranteed     Guarantee console messages
  informational  Informational messages               (severity=6)
  notifications  Normal but significant conditions    (severity=5)
  warnings       Warning conditions                   (severity=4)
  xml            Enable logging in XML
  <cr>

Router(config)#logging console _
                                                                            ▼
Connected 1:24:27      Auto detect   9600 8-N-1   SCROLL   CAPS   NUM   Capture   Print echo
```

The debugging logging level is a useful level that shows verbose information which is helpful during troubleshooting and maintenance. Use the "logging console 7" command to choose severity level 7 to show debugging messages on the console.

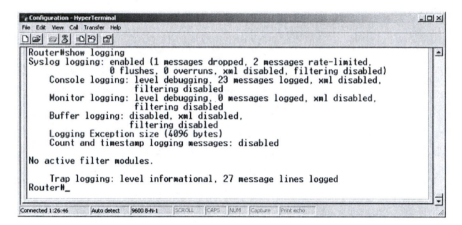

Exit the configuration mode and then use the "show logging" command to verify whether the console logging level is working.

8.3 Lab 8.2: Secure Network Services

8.3.1 Outcome

The learning objective of this exercise is to appreciate the security features of the Cisco router by securing network services.

8.3.2 Description

The default access method for router management and configuration is via the console port. Because the connection is directly connected to the console port, it is, relatively, a very secure method. However, the network devices are usually in a room that maintains very low temperature and is quite noisy, and hence the administrators prefer remote access to the devices. Consequently, a variety of remote interactive access protocols are supported on Cisco IOS routers, such as Telnet, SSH, HTTP, and HTTPS.

Perhaps Telnet protocol, described in RFC 854, is the most common protocol used to remotely connect to network devices. It is a client/server protocol that is assigned the standard TCP port 23 to provide remote login and access to the Command Line (CLI) of a remote host. The security vulnerability of Telnet is that it does not encrypt the data exchanged between its client and its server. Hence, it is possible for an adversary to eavesdrop on the traffic and extract sensitive information such as usernames and passwords.

The SSH protocol, described in RFC 4253, is designed as a replacement for Telnet to correct its main security shortcoming, which is sending data in plaintext. SSH is a client/server protocol assigned the standard TCP port 22. It offers a secure channel for remote login and access to CLI sessions. It uses public key cryptography, typically the RSA cryptographic algorithm, and symmetric key cryptographic algorithms to provide authentication, data confidentiality, and data integrity security services. By encrypting all its traffic, it effectively defends against several attacks, such as eavesdropping, session hijacking, and Man-in-the-Middle (MiM) attacks.

The HTTP (HyperText Transfer Protocol) protocol, described in RFC 26126, is the application layer protocol for the World Wide Web (WWW). It adopts the client/server architecture and is assigned the standard TCP port 80. An HTTP client, like a Web browser, sends a request message to an HTTP server to request resources, such as HTML files. The HTTP server returns a response message providing the requested resource. The security issue with HTTP is that all its traffic is plaintext, thus making it susceptible to eavesdropping attacks.

HTTP secure or HTTP over SSL (HTTPS), described in RFC 2818, is the secure alternative for HTTP. It is assigned the standard TCP port 443 and uses client/server architecture. HTTPS uses Secure Socket Layer/Transport Layer Protocol (SSL/TLS), described in RFC 5246, to create a secure channel between clients and servers over a public network such as the Internet. SSL/TLS has two main layers, the Handshake layer and the Record layer. In Handshake, the client and server negotiate the cipher suite, encryption and hash algorithms, and generate session keys using public key cryptography. The client authenticates the server using digital certificate technology. Then, the data encryption and decryption starts in the Record layer. Nowadays, HTTPS is quite pervasive and is used almost everywhere on the Web to provide efficient security and privacy solutions such as in e-transactions, mail exchange, and search engines.

This hands-on lab installs Telnet, SSH, HTTP, and HTTPS servers on the Cisco IOS router to demonstrate their security weakness or strength. It follows the offensive approach by launching eavesdropping and packet analysis attacks on these network services to extract sensitive information, such as usernames and passwords.

8.3.3 Experiment

To secure network services on the Cisco router, an experiment is conducted using Cisco router 2801 running OS 12.4. Below is a description and the steps of the experiment.

8.3.4 Network Architecture

The network architecture used in the experiment is illustrated in the following figure. A host is connected to the FastEthernet0/1 interface (Fa0/1) of the Cisco router through straight-through cables. The CommView sniffer is used to perform packet analysis and identify eavesdropping activities.

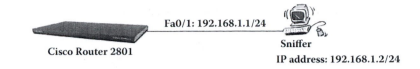

Cisco Router 2801   Fa0/1: 192.168.1.1/24

Sniffer
IP address: 192.168.1.2/24

8.3.5 Experiment Steps

The experiment consists of the following steps:

Step 1: Initialization of the PC and router.
Step 2: Sniff and analyze ICMP traffic.
Step 3: Sniff and analyze Telnet traffic.
Step 4: Sniff and analyze SSH traffic.
Step 5: Sniff and analyze HTTP traffic.
Step 6: Sniff and analyze HTTPS traffic.

8.3.5.1 Step 1: Initialization of the PC and Router

Assign the following network parameters to the PC:

■ IP address: 192.168.1.2
■ Subnet mask: 255.255.255.0
■ Default gateway: 192.168.1.1

To initialize the router, connect the PC to the Fa0/1 interface of the router using a straight-through cable. Next, connect the PC to the serial console of the router and start the configuration using the Hyper Terminal. To erase any previous configuration that has been made, use the following command:

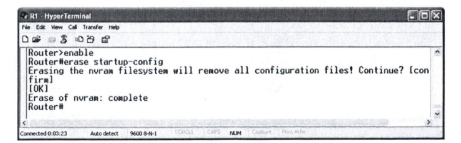

Use the "reload" command to reload the system and then disable the DNS lookup and Synchronize logging messages as shown in the following commands:

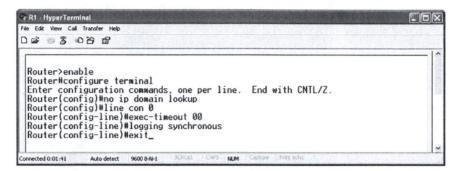

```
Router>enable
Router#configure terminal
Enter configuration commands, one per line.  End with CNTL/Z.
Router(config)#no ip domain lookup
Router(config)#line con 0
Router(config-line)#exec-timeout 00
Router(config-line)#logging synchronous
Router(config-line)#exit_
```

To view router interfaces, issue the following command:

```
Router(config)#do show ip int brief
Interface              IP-Address     OK? Method Status                    Prot
ocol
FastEthernet0/0        unassigned     YES unset  administratively down down
FastEthernet0/1        unassigned     YES unset  administratively down down
Serial0/2/0            unassigned     YES unset  administratively down down
Serial0/2/1            unassigned     YES unset  administratively down down
Router(config)#
```

To assign the IP address of 192.168.1.1 to the Fa0/1 interface, use the following command:

```
Router(config)#int fa0/1
Router(config-if)#ip address 192.168.1.1 255.255.255.0
Router(config-if)#no shutdown
Router(config-if)#exit
Router(config)#
-Apr 25 05:50:17.047: %LINK-3-UPDOWN: Interface FastEthernet0/1, changed state t
o up
-Apr 25 05:50:18.047: %LINEPROTO-5-UPDOWN: Line protocol on Interface FastEthern
et0/1, changed state to up
Router(config)#
-Apr 25 05:50:19.171: %LINK-3-UPDOWN: Interface FastEthernet0/1, changed state t
o up
Router(config)#_
```

Verify the IP assignment for the router interfaces using the following command:

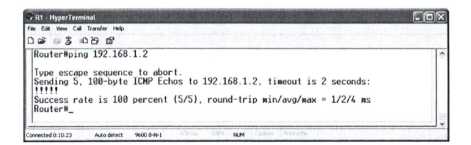

```
R1 - HyperTerminal
File  Edit  View  Call  Transfer  Help

Router(config)#do show ip int brief
Interface              IP-Address     OK? Method Status                Prot
ocol
FastEthernet0/0        unassigned     YES unset  administratively down down

FastEthernet0/1        192.168.1.1    YES manual up                    up

Serial0/2/0            unassigned     YES unset  administratively down down

Serial0/2/1            unassigned     YES unset  administratively down down

Router(config)#_

Connected 0:05:00    Auto detect    9600 8-N-1    SCROLL   CAPS   NUM   Capture   Print echo
```

The CommView sniffer is used in this lab to launch an eavesdropping attack on the different network protocols under study.

8.3.5.2 *Step 2: Sniff ICMP Traffic*

Ping the PC from the router to ensure interconnectivity, and sniff the ICMP echo and echo reply packets.

```
R1 - HyperTerminal
File  Edit  View  Call  Transfer  Help

Router#ping 192.168.1.2

Type escape sequence to abort.
Sending 5, 100-byte ICMP Echos to 192.168.1.2, timeout is 2 seconds:
!!!!!
Success rate is 100 percent (5/5), round-trip min/avg/max = 1/2/4 ms
Router#_

Connected 0:10:23    Auto detect    9600 8-N-1    SCROLL   CAPS   NUM   Capture   Print echo
```

The following screenshot shows the contents of the ICMP echo packet.

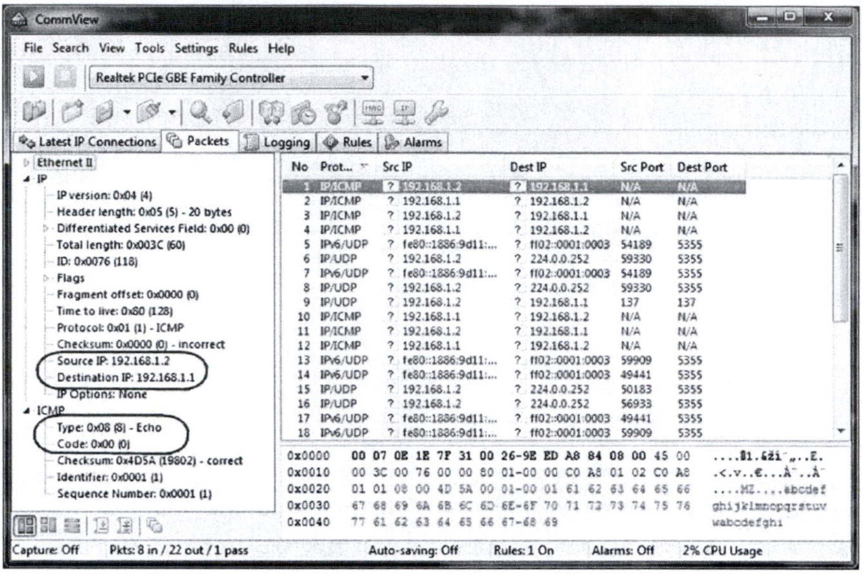

The next screenshot shows the contents of the ICMP echo reply packet.

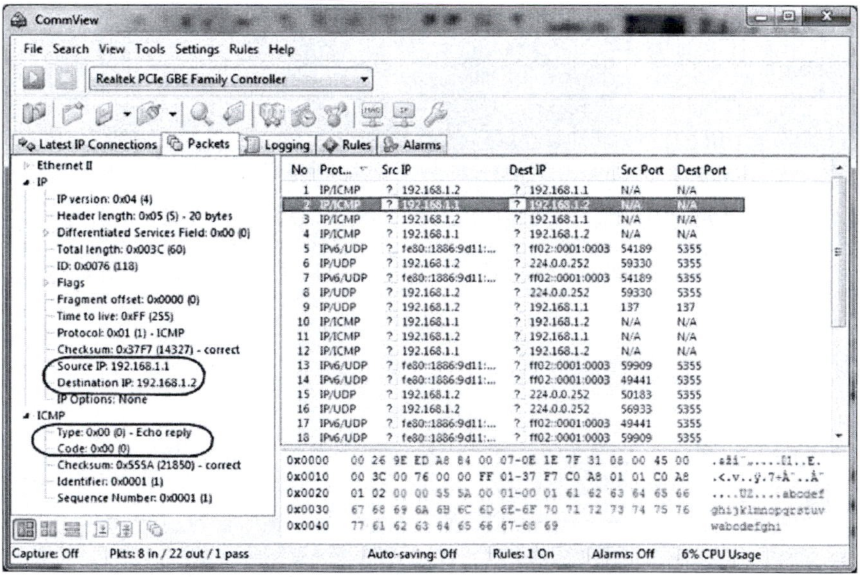

8.3.5.3 *Step 3: Sniff Telnet Traffic*

To configure Telnet authentication credentials, create a local database and assign it to the login service of the VTY (Telnet) line by entering the following commands:

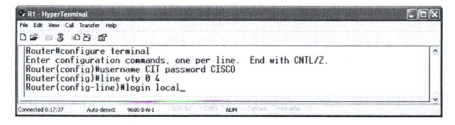

Telnet 192.168.1.1 (router) from the PC to generate Telnet traffic using Microsoft built-in Telnet client.

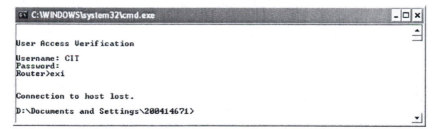

Once the user Access Verification window appears, enter the username as "CIT" and the password as "CISCO", as configured previously.

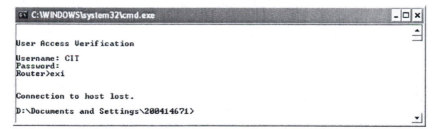

Sniff the Telnet packets on port 23. As demonstrated in the following series of screenshots, the Telnet traffic is not encrypted. By analyzing the traffic, it is easy to capture the Telnet username and password, which appear character by character. The TCP packet number 5, as shown in the next screenshot, contains the user access verification message prompt.

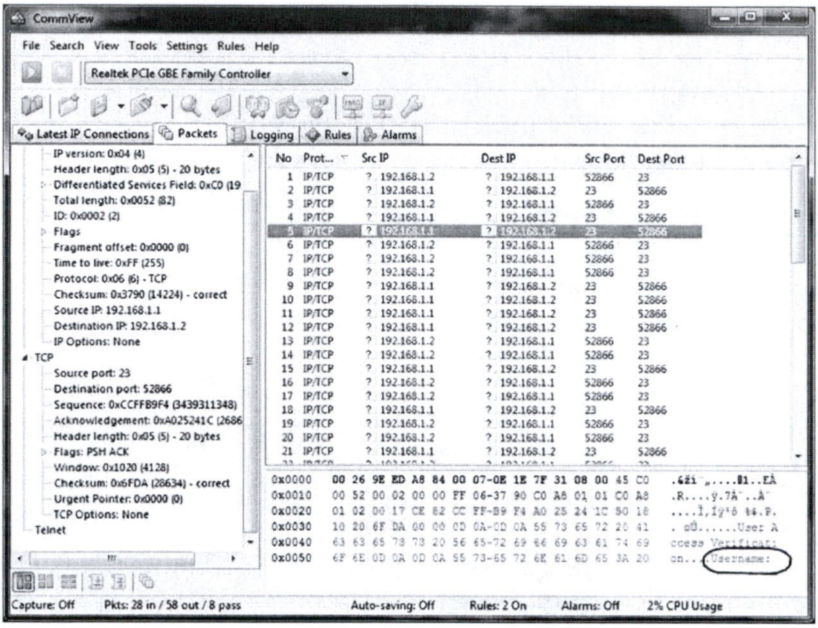

The TCP packet number 17, as shown in the next screen-shot, contains the first character of the username, which is "C".

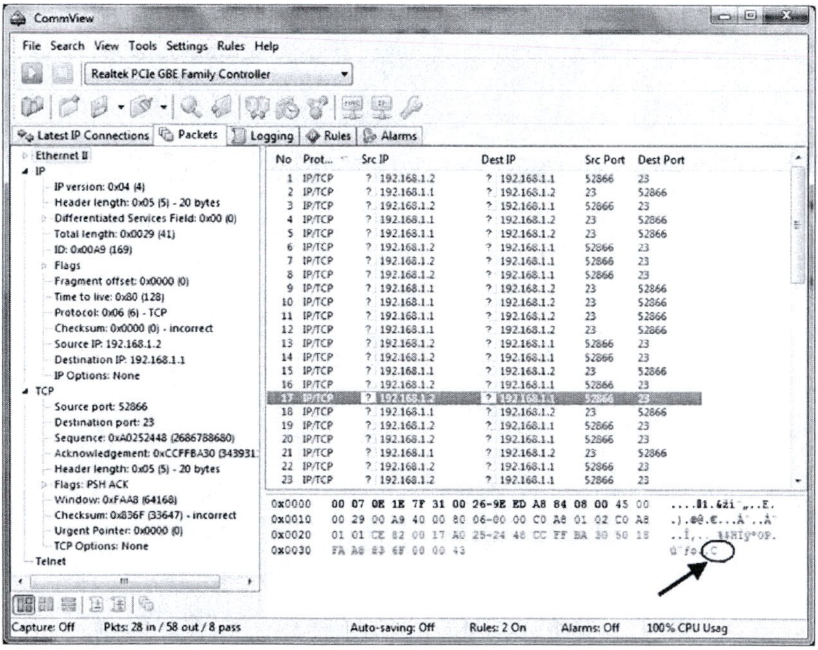

The TCP packet number 20, as shown next, contains the second character of the username, which is "I".

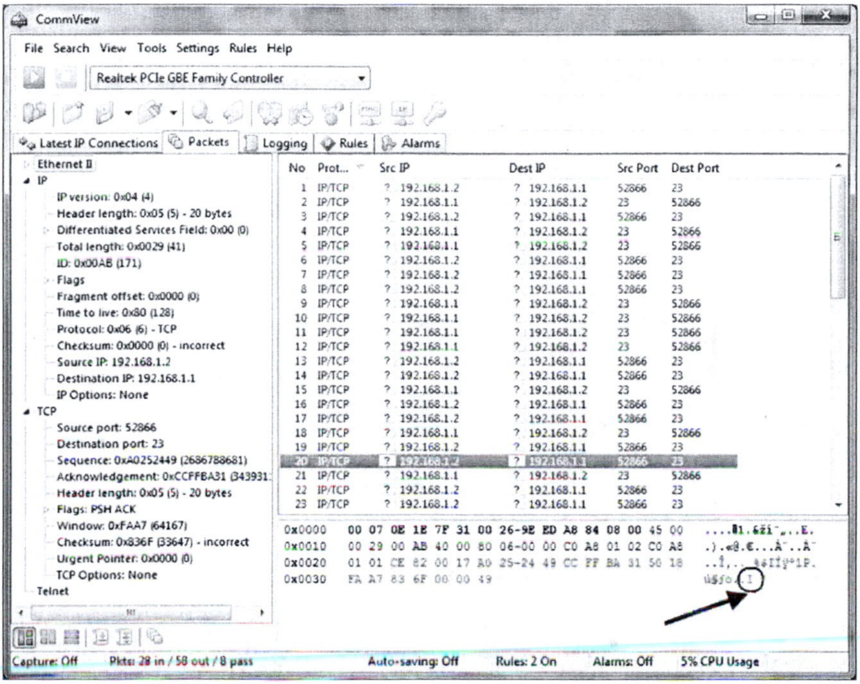

The consequent TCP packet displays the last character of the username, which is "T." Hence, the sniffed username is "CIT".

The TCP packet number 29, as shown in the subsequent screenshot, contains the first character of the user password, which is "C".

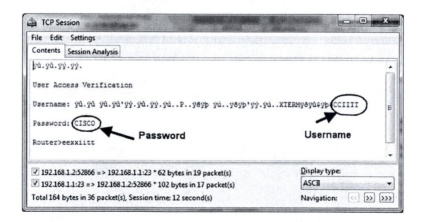

The subsequent packets contain the remaining characters of the password.

Using the CommView sniffer, the TCP session can be easily reconstructed to display the username and password in plaintext, as shown in the following screenshot.

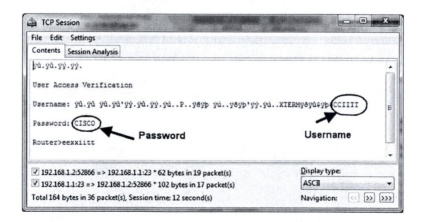

8.3.5.4 Step 4: Sniff SSH Traffic

To run SSH service on the router, a host name and a domain name are to be configured, as in the following commands. In addition, the RSA crypto keys must be generated with a modulus size of 512 bits, which is enough for the exercise at hand to ensure a quick key generation process. However, it is considered weak for an industry standard, which requires a modulus size of 1024 bits or even 2048 bits.

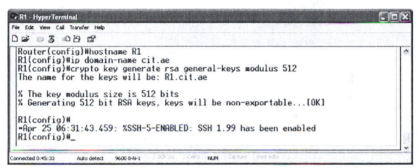

Launch the "Putty" application on the PC and enter the IP address 192.168.1.1 and TCP port 22 for the remote router, as shown in the following screenshot.

Click on the "Open" button and the connection will be established. Click "Yes" as shown next to add the SSH server key to the PuTTY cache.

Log in to the SSH server using the same authentication credentials of Telnet session, as shown below.

Sniff SSH packets and capture them using the CommView sniffer. The following screenshot shows that the SSH session is encrypted and, consequently, the attacker cannot make use of any captured packet.

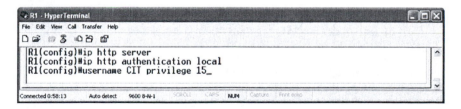

Therefore, the network administrator must replace the unsecure Telnet service by the secure SSH service to keep authentication and management data protected from attacks such as eavesdropping, session hijacking, and MiM attacks.

8.3.5.5 Step 5: Sniff HTTP Traffic

To run HTTP service on the router, specify the type of the authentication database, which is local in this experiment. It designates a privilege level of 15 for the user CIT.

```
R1(config)#ip http server
R1(config)#ip http authentication local
R1(config)#username CIT privilege 15_
```

Browse to the following URL: HTTP://192.168.1.1 on your PC and log in by entering "CIT" as the username and "CISCO" as the password, as shown below.

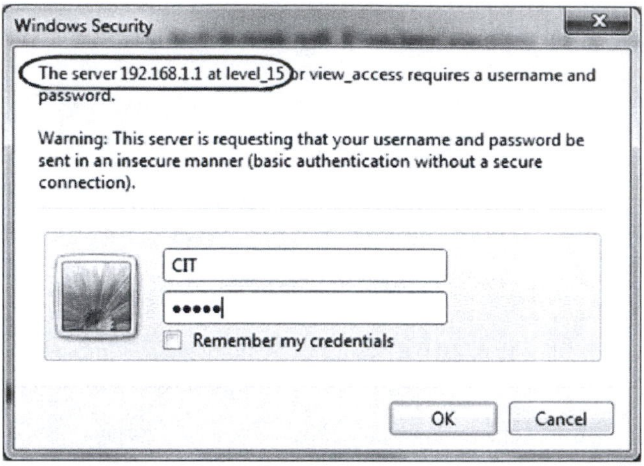

Click "OK" to get access to the router Web User Interface (WebUI), which can be used to perform most of the tasks that can be done with CLI, as shown in the following screenshot.

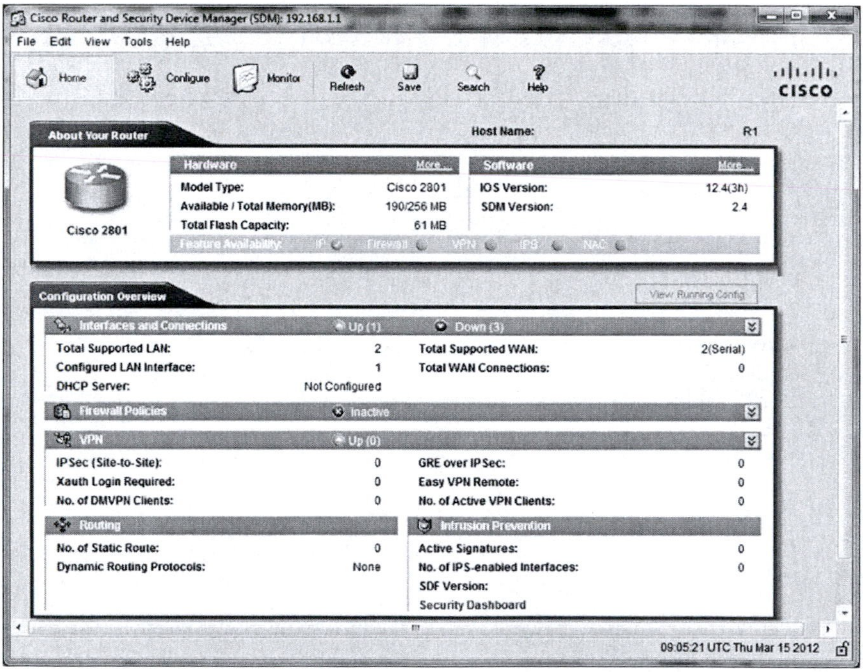

Sniff HTTP packets and analyze them to verify that the HTTP traffic is not encrypted. The selected packet displays the username and password explicitly in the HTTP header, as shown in the left pane of the next screen.

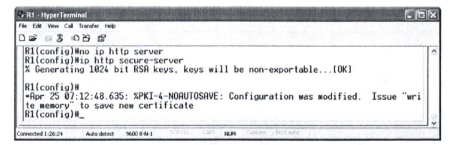

8.3.5.6 Step 6: Sniff HTTPS Traffic

To run the HTTPS service, the following commands are used, which will generate

- The required RSA keys of size 1024 bits in this example
- A new SSL certificate to authenticate the HTTPS server

```
R1(config)#no ip http server
R1(config)#ip http secure-server
% Generating 1024 bit RSA keys, keys will be non-exportable...[OK]

R1(config)#
*Apr 25 07:12:48.635: %PKI-4-NOAUTOSAVE: Configuration was modified.  Issue "wri
te memory" to save new certificate
R1(config)#_
```

From the HTTPS client (the PC), browse to the router Web server using the URL: HTTPS://192.168.1.1. It is important to notice that now HTTPS is used instead of HTTP, as shown in the following screenshot.

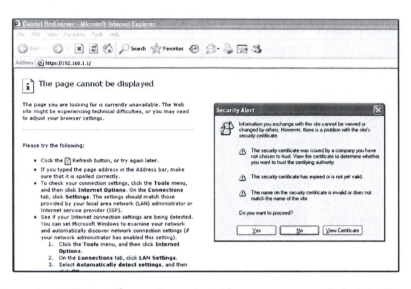

Once the SSL certificate Security Alert pops up, click "Yes" to accept the SSL security certificate. Type the needed username and password to access the router webpage with a privilege level of 15.

Sniff HTTPS packets on port 443 and analyze them. The whole HTTPS traffic on TCP port 443 is encrypted, as shown in the following screenshot. Consequently, this experiment demonstrates clearly that HTTPS must replace HTTP to secure access to the router WebUI.

8.4 Lab 8.3: Packet Filtering on a Border Router

8.4.1 Outcome

The learning objective of this exercise is for students to learn how to configure stateful packet filtering on a Cisco router.

8.4.2 Description

Packet filtering is a crucial responsibility for border routers, as they represent entry points to networks and to internal assets. Therefore, controlling traffic at these entry points is the first line of defense for the network infrastructure. On the other hand, successful attacks on border routers lead to serious security threats for the whole network.

The main mechanism used on a Cisco IOS router to implement packet filtering is the Access Control List (ACL). The ACL consists of three main parts, namely, action that can permit or deny packets, matching criteria, and direction, which is either *in* or *out*. The matching criteria define which fields of the packet header will be examined for making packet filtering decisions. Based on the matching criteria, ACLs are classified into two types: (1) Standard ACLs, which match on source IP address only; and (2) Extended ACLs, which match on source IP address, destination IP address, protocols, source port, destination port, and TCP flags.

It is important to implement RFC 1918 and RFC 2827 on the border router. This helps to protect against several well-known DoS (Denial-of-Service) attacks. RFC 1918 defines the ranges of private IP addresses that are not routable throughout any public network such as the Internet. Therefore, it is reserved for internal network usage. These private address ranges are as follows:

- Class A: 10.0.0.0–10.255.255.255
- Class B: 172.16.0.0–172.31.255.255
- Class C: 192.168.0.0–192.168.255.255

RFC 2827 talks about various ingress filtering methods to defeat DoS attacks using IP source address spoofing. The RFC advises that the ingress filtering policy of border routers has to block these private addresses, RFC 1918 addresses, on its external interfaces. In addition, one of the basic recommendations of RFC 2827 is to reject packets with source IP addresses that are the same as your network IP addresses. The only reason for that to happen is that an adversary has spoofed your own IP addresses to bypass your security measures or launch DoS attacks on your network. A famous example of this type of DoS attack is the Smurf DoS attack.

Whenever a packet filtering rule is configured, the border router acts as a firewall that splits the network into two segments: a *trusted segment*, which is the protected network, and the *untrusted segment,* which is the external network, such as the Internet. Most standard protocols, such as HTTP, SMTP, and FTP, return traffic from untrusted to trusted segments, which must be permitted to complete the TCP session. This can be achieved on the Cisco IOS router by employing Context Based Access Control (CBAC), which provides stateful packet filtering. CBAC creates a session table for connections passing across the router, from the trusted to the untrusted segment. The session table stores information such as source and destination IP addresses, source and destination ports, and the number of active sessions.

This hands-on lab exercise demonstrates how to implement packet filtering on a border router. The network architecture simulates a real-world network in which the border router is connected to a backbone router of an Internet Service Provider (ISP). For the sake of simplicity, the protected network on the trusted segment and the ISP network on the untrusted segment are simulated by two hosts. All the above-mentioned security measures are configured and tested thoroughly.

8.4.3 Experiment

To learn how to secure a border router and configure stateful packet filtering, an experiment is conducted using the Cisco router 2801 running OS 12.4 and Cisco Switch 3560. Below is a description and steps of the experiment.

8.4.4 Network Architecture

The following figure shows the network architecture of the experiment. As shown in the figure, an inside network will consist of an inside PC with IP address 184.1.1.2/24 connected to router FW via the Fa0/1 interface. The outside network consists of a backbone router BB1, which is supposed to be part of the ISP and an outside PC with IP address 10.1.1.2/24.

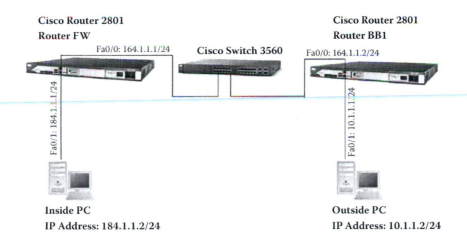

Cisco Router 2801
Router FW
Fa0/0: 164.1.1.1/24   Cisco Switch 3560   Fa0/0: 164.1.1.2/24
Cisco Router 2801
Router BB1

Fa0/1: 184.1.1.1/24

Fa0/1: 10.1.1.1/24

Inside PC
IP Address: 184.1.1.2/24

Outside PC
IP Address: 10.1.1.2/24

8.4.5 Experiment Steps

The experiment consists of the following steps:

    Step 1: Basic router set-up commands.
    Step 2: Enable buffered logging at debug level.
    Step 3: Initialize routers and PCs: IPs and hostnames.
    Step 4: Run dynamic routing: OSPF area 0 with redistribution.

Step 5: Run HTTP and Telnet servers on both routers.
Step 6: Implement the security policies on the border router.
Step 7: Test the security policies created in Step 6.

8.4.5.1 Step 1: Basic Router Set-Up Commands

Connect an inside PC to the serial console of the router through the HyperTerminal to get the Command Line Interface of router FW. Use the "enable" command for the router to move to the privileged EXEC mode. To disable the DNS lookup, use the "no ip domain lookup" command; and to synchronize the logging messages, enter the following commands:

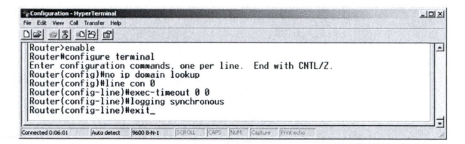

The same steps are repeated for router BB1 on the outside PC.

8.4.5.2 Step 2: Enable Buffered Logging at the Debug Level

In the configuration mode, enable logging with a logging severity of level 7. The accounting information is stored locally in a file on the router because a buffered logging type is chosen, as in the following commands:

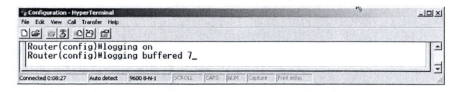

To confirm that the logging is working, use the "do show logging" command:

```
Configuration - HyperTerminal                                          _ |□| x|
File  Edit  View  Call  Transfer  Help
D|☞| ☜|☃| ▣|☝| ☞|

Router(config)#do show logging
Syslog logging: enabled (1 messages dropped, 2 messages rate-limited,
                0 flushes, 0 overruns, xml disabled, filtering disabled)
    Console logging: level debugging, 18 messages logged, xml disabled,
                     filtering disabled
    Monitor logging: level debugging, 0 messages logged, xml disabled,
                     filtering disabled
    Buffer logging: level debugging, 0 messages logged, xml disabled,
                    filtering disabled
    Logging Exception size (4096 bytes)
    Count and timestamp logging messages: disabled

No active filter modules.

    Trap logging: level informational, 21 message lines logged

Log Buffer (4096 bytes):
Router(config)#_

Connected 0:09:16    Auto detect   9600 8-N-1    SCROLL   CAPS   NUM   Capture   Print echo
```

Repeat Step 2 for router BB1.

8.4.5.3 *Step 3: Initialize Routers and PCs: IPs and Hostnames*

Assign the following network parameters for the PC of the inside network:

```
Internet Protocol (TCP/IP) Properties                            ? | x|

General |

You can get IP settings assigned automatically if your network supports
this capability. Otherwise, you need to ask your network administrator for
the appropriate IP settings.

  ○ Obtain an IP address automatically
  ◉ Use the following IP address:
    IP address:              184 . 1  . 1  . 2
    Subnet mask:            255 . 255 . 255 . 0
    Default gateway:         184 . 1  . 1  . 1|

  ○ Obtain DNS server address automatically
  ◉ Use the following DNS server addresses:
    Preferred DNS server:         .     .
    Alternate DNS server:         .     .

                                              Advanced...

                              OK            Cancel
```

Assign the following network parameters to the PC of the outside network:

- IP Address: 10.1.1.2
- Subnet mask: 255.255.255.0
- Default gateways: 10.1.1.1

The configuration steps for router FW are:

- Assign a name to the host, which is FW in our experiment.
- Create a Loopback interface to be used as an ID for the OSPF routing process.
- Assign the IP address 164.1.1.1 to the Fa0/0 interface of router FW.
- Assign the IP address 184.1.1.1 to the Fa0/1 interface of router FW.

```
router(config)#hostname FW
FW(config)#int loopback 0
FW(config-if)#ip address 150.1.1.1 255.255.255.0
FW(config-if)#int fa0/0
FW(config-if)#ip address 164.1.1.1 255.255.255.0
FW(config-if)#no sh
FW(config-if)#exit
FW(config)#int fa0/1
FW(config-if)#ip address 184.1.1.1 255.255.255.0
FW(config-if)#no sh
FW(config-if)#exit
```

To verify the configured addresses for router FW, type the following command:

```
FW#show ip int brief
Interface           IP-Address      OK? Method Status                     Protocol
FastEthernet0/0     164.1.1.1       YES manual up                         down
FastEthernet0/1     184.1.1.1       YES manual up                         down
Serial0/2/0         unassigned      YES unset  administratively down      down
Serial0/2/1         unassigned      YES unset  administratively down      down
Loopback0           150.1.1.1       YES manual up                         up
FW#
```

Similarly, the following steps ensue for router BB1:

- Assign a name to the host, which is BB1 in our experiment.
- Create a Loopback interface to be used as an ID for the OSPF routing process.
- Assign the IP address 164.1.1.2 to the Fa0/0 interface of router BB1.
- Assign the IP address 10.1.1.1 to the Fa0/1 interface of router BB1.

```
Configuration - HyperTerminal
File  Edit  View  Call  Transfer  Help

router(config)#hostname BB1
BB1(config)#int loopback 0
BB1(config-if)#ip address 150.1.2.2 255.255.255.0
BB1(config-if)#int fa0/0
BB1(config-if)#ip address 164.1.1.2 255.255.255.0
BB1(config-if)#no sh
BB1(config-if)#int fa0/1
BB1(config-if)#ip address 10.1.1.1 255.255.255.0
BB1(config-if)#no sh
BB1(config-if)#exit
BB1(config)#

Connected 0:39:00    Auto detect    9600 8-N-1    SCROLL    CAPS    NUM    Capture    Print echo
```

To display the addresses you just configured for router BB1 interface, type the following command:

```
Configuration - HyperTerminal
File  Edit  View  Call  Transfer  Help

BB1#show ip int brief
Interface              IP-Address    OK? Method Status                     Protocol
FastEthernet0/0        164.1.1.2     YES manual up                         down
FastEthernet0/1        10.1.1.1      YES manual up                         down
Serial0/2/0            unassigned    YES unset  administratively down      down
Serial0/2/1            unassigned    YES unset  administratively down      down
Loopback0              150.1.2.2     YES manual up                         up
BB1#_

Connected 0:39:47    Auto detect    9600 8-N-1    SCROLL    CAPS    NUM    Capture    Print echo
```

Test the connectivity of the network by first pinging the inside PC from router FW.

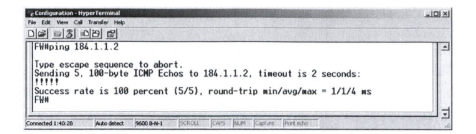

Next, ping the next hop of router FW that is 164.1.1.2, which should be successful, as in the following command:

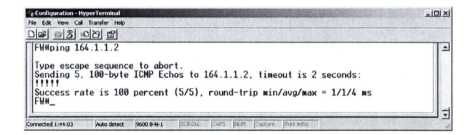

Next, ping the end of the outside network. This should not be successful, because no dynamic routing protocol, such as OSPF, was configured.

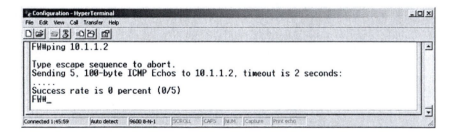

Finally, ping from the inside PC to the outside PC. This should not be successful because of the absence of a dynamic routing protocol, as in the following command:

```
C:\WINDOWS\system32\cmd.exe                                    _ |□| x|

D:\Documents and Settings\200414671>ping 10.1.1.2

Pinging 10.1.1.2 with 32 bytes of data:

Reply from 184.1.1.1: Destination host unreachable.
Reply from 184.1.1.1: Destination host unreachable.
Reply from 184.1.1.1: Destination host unreachable.
Reply from 184.1.1.1: Destination host unreachable.

Ping statistics for 10.1.1.2:
    Packets: Sent = 4, Received = 4, Lost = 0 (0% loss),
Approximate round trip times in milli-seconds:
    Minimum = 0ms, Maximum = 0ms, Average = 0ms

D:\Documents and Settings\200414671>
```

8.4.5.4 Step 4: Run Dynamic Routing: OSPF Area 0 with Redistribution

Routing is the process of selecting the best paths to different destinations on a network. There are two types of routing: static and dynamic. Static routing uses a manual configuration to specify paths to destinations. In our example, it is used on PCs when the default gateway is configured. On the other hand, dynamic routing achieves its purpose by populating a routing table with routes to directly connected networks. Then it learns dynamically about routes to other networks from the path advertisements of other routers that run the same dynamic routing protocol, such as: OSPF protocol, Routing Information Protocol (RIP), or Intermediate System to Intermediate System (IS-IS) protocol. Then, the router selects the best paths to different destinations based on a routing cost metric.

OSPF, described in RFC 2328, is a commonly used routing protocol for enterprise networks. It collects link state information from other routers to create a topology of the whole network, which helps to construct the routing table. The best routes are selected based on a shortest-path-first algorithm, also known as Dijkstra's algorithm. To assist administration and traffic optimization, OSPF splits the network into areas, where area 0 is considered the backbone area.

To run dynamic routing on router FW, the following steps are performed.

- Set the local process ID of the OSPF routing protocol to 1.
- Use Loopback interface as a router ID.
- Assign the interface of router FW to area 0 and redistribute routing advertisement to the directly connected networks, using the commands below:

```
Configuration - HyperTerminal
File  Edit  View  Call  Transfer  Help

FW(config)#router ospf 1
FW(config-router)#router-id 150.1.1.1
FW(config-router)#network 164.1.1.1 0.0.0.0 area 0
FW(config-router)#network 150.1.1.1 0.0.0.0 area 0
FW(config-router)#redistribute connected subnets
FW(config-router)#end
FW#

Connected 1:49:59      Auto detect    9600 8-N-1      SCROLL   CAPS   NUM   Capture   Print echo
```

Show the routing table in router FW using the "show ip route" command. The routing entries that start with "O" represent OSPF, while "C" stands for connected networks.

```
Configuration - HyperTerminal
File  Edit  View  Call  Transfer  Help

FW#show ip route
Codes: C - connected, S - static, R - RIP, M - mobile, B - BGP
       D - EIGRP, EX - EIGRP external, O - OSPF, IA - OSPF inter area
       N1 - OSPF NSSA external type 1, N2 - OSPF NSSA external type 2
       E1 - OSPF external type 1, E2 - OSPF external type 2
       i - IS-IS, su - IS-IS summary, L1 - IS-IS level-1, L2 - IS-IS level-2
       ia - IS-IS inter area, * - candidate default, U - per-user static route
       o - ODR, P - periodic downloaded static route

Gateway of last resort is not set

     184.1.0.0/24 is subnetted, 1 subnets
C       184.1.1.0 is directly connected, FastEthernet0/1
     10.0.0.0/24 is subnetted, 1 subnets
O E2    10.1.1.0 [110/20] via 164.1.1.2, 00:07:06, FastEthernet0/0
     164.1.0.0/24 is subnetted, 1 subnets
C       164.1.1.0 is directly connected, FastEthernet0/0
     150.1.0.0/24 is subnetted, 2 subnets
O E2    150.1.2.0 [110/20] via 164.1.1.2, 00:07:06, FastEthernet0/0
C       150.1.1.0 is directly connected, Loopback0
FW#_

Connected 2:09:12      Auto detect    9600 8-N-1      SCROLL   CAPS   NUM   Capture   Print echo
```

Configure dynamic routing on router BB1 by repeating the previous step for router FW but with corresponding network IP addresses, as in the following command:

```
Configuration - HyperTerminal                                    _|□|×|
File  Edit  View  Call  Transfer  Help
D|☞| ⯌|⅔| ⯌|🖻| 🖻|
 BB1(config)#router ospf 1
 BB1(config-router)#router-id 150.1.2.2
 BB1(config-router)#network 164.1.1.2 0.0.0.0 area 0
 BB1(config-router)#netw
 *May 31 05:59:33.019: %OSPF-5-ADJCHG: Process 1, Nbr 150.1.1.1 on FastEthernet0/
 0 from LOADING to FULL, Loading Done
 BB1(config-router)#network 150.1.1.2 0.0.0.0 area 0
 BB1(config-router)#redistribute connected subnets
 BB1(config-router)#end
 BB1#
Connected 2:02:08    Auto detect    9600 8-N-1    SCROLL    CAPS    NUM    Capture    Print echo
```

Show the routing table in router BB1 using the "show ip route" command:

```
Configuration - HyperTerminal                                    _|□|×|
File  Edit  View  Call  Transfer  Help
D|☞| ⯌|⅔| ⯌|🖻| 🖻|
 BB1#show ip route
 Codes: C - connected, S - static, R - RIP, M - mobile, B - BGP
        D - EIGRP, EX - EIGRP external, O - OSPF, IA - OSPF inter area
        N1 - OSPF NSSA external type 1, N2 - OSPF NSSA external type 2
        E1 - OSPF external type 1, E2 - OSPF external type 2
        i - IS-IS, su - IS-IS summary, L1 - IS-IS level-1, L2 - IS-IS level-2
        ia - IS-IS inter area, * - candidate default, U - per-user static route
        o - ODR, P - periodic downloaded static route

 Gateway of last resort is not set

        184.1.0.0/24 is subnetted, 1 subnets
 O E2   184.1.1.0 [110/20] via 164.1.1.1, 00:02:28, FastEthernet0/0
        10.0.0.0/24 is subnetted, 1 subnets
 C      10.1.1.0 is directly connected, FastEthernet0/1
        164.1.0.0/24 is subnetted, 1 subnets                       →OSPF
 C      164.1.1.0 is directly connected, FastEthernet0/0
        150.1.0.0/16 is variably subnetted, 2 subnets, 2 masks
 C      150.1.2.0/24 is directly connected, Loopback0
 O      150.1.1.1/32 [110/2] via 164.1.1.1, 00:02:28, FastEthernet0/0
 BB1#_
Connected 2:04:42    Auto detect    9600 8-N-1    SCROLL    CAPS    NUM    Capture    Print echo
```

Test the connectivity of the network by pinging the inside PC from router BB1, which is successful because BB1 learns about the inside network from OSPF routing table entries.

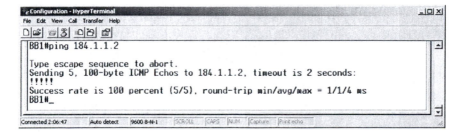

```
Configuration - HyperTerminal                                    _|□|×|
File  Edit  View  Call  Transfer  Help
D|☞| ⯌|⅔| ⯌|🖻| 🖻|
 BB1#ping 184.1.1.2

 Type escape sequence to abort.
 Sending 5, 100-byte ICMP Echos to 184.1.1.2, timeout is 2 seconds:
 !!!!!
 Success rate is 100 percent (5/5), round-trip min/avg/max = 1/1/4 ms
 BB1#_
Connected 2:06:47    Auto detect    9600 8-N-1    SCROLL    CAPS    NUM    Capture    Print echo
```

Then ping the loopback interface, which should be successful.

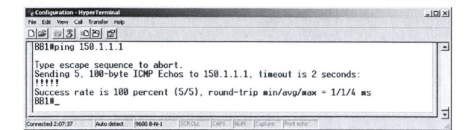

Next, ping 150.1.2.2 from router FW, which should be successful.

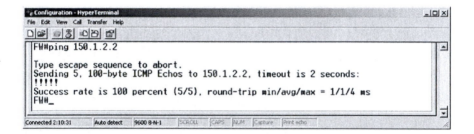

Next, ping the outside PC from router FW. This should be successful because the OSPF protocol is enabled.

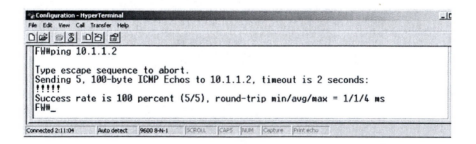

Finally, ping from the inside PC to the outside PC, which should be successful because the dynamic OSPF routing protocol is configured.

```
C:\WINDOWS\system32\cmd.exe                                       _|□|x|
D:\Documents and Settings\200414671>ping 10.1.1.2                   ▲
Pinging 10.1.1.2 with 32 bytes of data:                            ▬
Reply from 10.1.1.2: bytes=32 time=11ms TTL=126
Reply from 10.1.1.2: bytes=32 time<1ms TTL=126
Reply from 10.1.1.2: bytes=32 time<1ms TTL=126
Reply from 10.1.1.2: bytes=32 time<1ms TTL=126

Ping statistics for 10.1.1.2:
    Packets: Sent = 4, Received = 4, Lost = 0 (0% loss),
Approximate round trip times in milli-seconds:
    Minimum = 0ms, Maximum = 11ms, Average = 2ms

D:\Documents and Settings\200414671>                                ▼
```

This ensures that end-to-end communication is now established throughout the entire network.

8.4.5.5 Step 5: Run HTTP and Telnet Servers on Both Routers

Run HTTP and Telnet servers on router FW, using the following configuration steps:

■ Enable the HTTP server on the router through the "ip HTTP server" command.

■ Configure a username and password for Telnet authentication purposes.

■ Enable the Telnet service to allow a user to connect to the router through the VTY line.

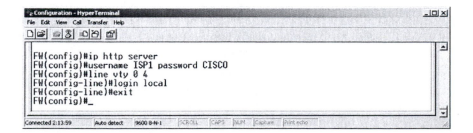

```
FW(config)#ip http server
FW(config)#username ISP1 password CISCO
FW(config)#line vty 0 4
FW(config-line)#login local
FW(config-line)#exit
FW(config)#_
```

Configure the HTTP and Telnet servers on router BB1; repeat the steps followed for router FW.

```
Configuration - HyperTerminal                                    _|□|x|
File  Edit  View  Call  Transfer  Help
□|☞| ☞|Ⅻ| ▢|☝| ☝|
BB1(config)#ip http server
BB1(config)#username ISP1 password CISCO
BB1(config)#line vty 0 4
BB1(config-line)#login local
BB1(config-line)#exit
BB1(config)#_
Connected 2:16:28   Auto detect  9600 8-N-1   SCROLL  CAPS  NUM  Capture  Print echo
```

Test the configuration of Step 5 with the following steps:

■ First, test the end-to-end connectivity by pinging the out-side PC from the inside PC (Ping 10.1.1.2). This should be successful.

```
C:\WINDOWS\system32\cmd.exe                                      _|□|x|
D:\Documents and Settings\200414671>ping 10.1.1.2

Pinging 10.1.1.2 with 32 bytes of data:

Reply from 10.1.1.2: bytes=32 time=11ms TTL=126
Reply from 10.1.1.2: bytes=32 time<1ms TTL=126
Reply from 10.1.1.2: bytes=32 time<1ms TTL=126
Reply from 10.1.1.2: bytes=32 time<1ms TTL=126

Ping statistics for 10.1.1.2:
    Packets: Sent = 4, Received = 4, Lost = 0 (0% loss),
Approximate round trip times in milli-seconds:
    Minimum = 0ms, Maximum = 11ms, Average = 2ms
D:\Documents and Settings\200414671>
```

■ Ping the inside PC from the outside PC (ping 184.1.1.2), which should be successful. Use a browser to navigate to router BB1 (HTTP://164.1.1.2). Similarly, browse from the outside PC to router FW (HTTP://164.1.1.1).
■ Telnet from the inside PC to router BB1 (telnet 164.1.1.2), which should be successful. User Access Verification is requested, for which the configured username and pass-word for router BB1 are used.

```
Telnet 164.1.1.2                                                 _|□|x|
User Access Verification

Username: ISP1
Password:
BB1>who
    Line        User       Host(s)          Idle       Location
   0 con 0                 idle             00:13:30
* vty 194      ISP1        idle             00:00:00  184.1.1.2

  Interface    User                 Mode        Idle    Peer Address

BB1>_
```

■ Use Telnet to connect from the outside PC to router FW (telnet 164.1.1.1). Next, from the inside PC, trace the route to the outside PC ("tracert 10.1.1.2"). Traceroute helps to check the number of hops that network traffic takes to reach its destination. Notice that there are three rows. In each row there is a column with a value that represents the number of stops along the route path. The other three columns are the time in milliseconds that is used while attempting to reach the destination. The last column is the IP address of the host that replied.

```
C:\WINDOWS\system32\cmd.exe                                    _|□|×|
Microsoft Windows XP [Version 5.1.2600]
(C) Copyright 1985-2001 Microsoft Corp.

D:\Documents and Settings\200414671>tracert 10.1.1.2

Tracing route to 10.1.1.2 over a maximum of 30 hops

  1     37 ms    <1 ms    <1 ms  184.1.1.1
  2    <1 ms     <1 ms    <1 ms  164.1.1.2
  3    <1 ms     <1 ms    <1 ms  10.1.1.2

Trace complete.
```

■ Next, from the outside PC, trace the route to the inside PC ("tracert 184.1.1.2"). Then trace the route from router FW to the outside PC ("traceroute 10.1.1.2").

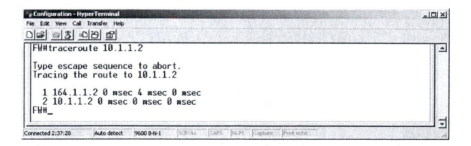

```
Configuration - HyperTerminal                                  _|□|×|
File  Edit  View  Call  Transfer  Help

FW#traceroute 10.1.1.2

Type escape sequence to abort.
Tracing the route to 10.1.1.2

  1 164.1.1.2 0 msec 4 msec 0 msec
  2 10.1.1.2 0 msec 0 msec 0 msec
FW#_

Connected 2:37:28    Auto detect    9600 8-N-1    SCROLL  CAPS  NUM  Capture  Print echo
```

■ Finally, trace the route from router BB1 to the inside PC ("traceroute 184.1.1.2").

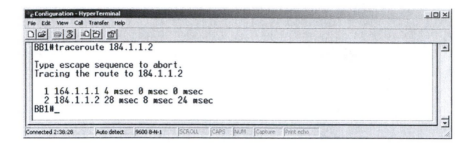

```
Configuration - HyperTerminal                                        _|□|x|
File  Edit  View  Call  Transfer  Help
D|☞| ☜|⥠| ⚏|🖰| 🖻|
 BB1#traceroute 184.1.1.2                                              ▲

 Type escape sequence to abort.
 Tracing the route to 184.1.1.2

   1 164.1.1.1 4 msec 0 msec 0 msec
   2 184.1.1.2 28 msec 8 msec 24 msec
 BB1#_
                                                                       ▼
Connected 2:38:28   Auto detect   9600 8-N-1   SCROLL  CAPS  NUM  Capture  Print echo
```

8.4.5.6 Step 6: Implement the Security Policies on Border Router FW

The following security policies are implemented on router FW:

1. *Security policy: Deny RFC 1918 addresses sourced from outside and log.* Use the extended access control list (INF) to match the source addresses that belong to the private addresses defined by RFC 1918.

```
Configuration - HyperTerminal                                        _|□|x|
File  Edit  View  Call  Transfer  Help
D|☞| ☜|⥠| ⚏|🖰| 🖻|
 FW(config)#ip access-list extended INF                               ▲
 FW(config-ext-nacl)#deny ip 10.0.0.0
 *Jun 11 04:20:39.107: %LINEPROTO-5-UPDOWN: Line protocol on Interface FastEthern
 et0/1, changed state to down
 FW(config-ext-nacl)#deny ip 10.0.0.0 0.255.255.255 any log
 FW(config-ext-nacl)#deny ip 172.16.0.0 0.15.255.255 any log
 FW(config-ext-nacl)#deny ip 192.168.0.0 0.0.255.255 any log_
                                                                       ▼
Connected 0:16:39   Auto detect   9600 8-N-1   SCROLL  CAPS  NUM  Capture  Print echo
```

2. *Security policy: Implement RFC 2827 and log using ingress traffic filtering.* To prevent a DoS attack that employs spoofed IP source addresses, a security measure must be implemented to block packets that claim to have IP source addresses similar to the internal network.

```
Configuration - HyperTerminal                                        _|□|x|
File  Edit  View  Call  Transfer  Help
D|☞| ☜|⥠| ⚏|🖰| 🖻|
 FW(config-ext-nacl)#deny ip 184.1.1.0 0.0.0.255 any log              ▲
 FW(config-ext-nacl)#deny ip 150.1.1.0 0.0.0.255 any log_
                                                                       ▼
Connected 0:18:30   Auto detect   9600 8-N-1   SCROLL  CAPS  NUM  Capture  Print echo
```

3. *Security policy: Inside can trace route to outside and log.*
   Allow the inside PC to trace the route to the outside network by permitting traceroute response messages to pass
   via the FW external interface. Microsoft uses an ICMP
   echo message for a request and an echo-reply message
   for a response, while Unix and Cisco routers use UDP for
   a request and time exceeded and unreachable port ICMP
   messages for a response.

```
FW(config-ext-nacl)#permit icmp any any time-exceeded log
FW(config-ext-nacl)#permit icmp any any port-unreachable log_
```

4. *Security policy: Inside can ping outside and log.* This can
   be achieved by accepting ICMP echo reply messages on
   the outside interface of the border router, using the following command:

```
FW(config-ext-nacl)#permit icmp any any echo-reply log_
```

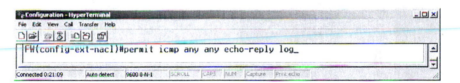

5. *Security policy: Permit necessary routing protocols and
   log.* OSPF routing advertisement and update message are
   allowed on the outside interface to populate the routing
   table with valid paths to destinations, using the following command:

```
FW(config-ext-nacl)#permit ospf any any log_
```

6. *Security policy: Deny all other traffic and log.* By denying
   the other traffic, the outside PC will be prohibited from

initiating any traffic that is not listed above in the ACL. This can be done using the following command:

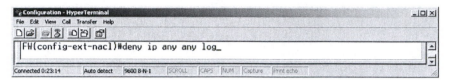

7. *Security policy: Inside can initiate TCP, UDP, and HTTP connection to outside.* Using Context-Based Access Control (CBAC), the outgoing TCP and UDP traffic is inspected. This allows the router to act as a stateful firewall, which permits the return traffic to pass via its external interface. Return traffic is related to an open outgoing TCP or UDP session. Configuration of CBAC is performed using the following command:

8. *Security policy: Apply to outside interface.* Without applying to the outside external interface, neither ACL nor CBAC will work. Notice that the CBAC direction is out while the ACL direction is in, as in the following command:

```
FW(config)#int fa0/0
FW(config-if)#ip access-group INF in
FW(config-if)#ip inspect CBAC out
FW(config-if)#end
```

8.4.5.7 Step 7: Test the Security Policies Created in Step 6

To test the ACL and the CBAC configuration, the following tests are conducted and the reason for each result is highlighted.

Ping from the inside PC to the outside PC (ping 10.1.1.2). This should not be successful because the echo reply comes from the outside IP address, which is a private address. The following ACL part explains the behavior.

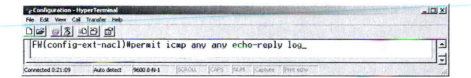

```
FW(config)#ip access-list extended INF
FW(config-ext-nacl)#deny ip 10.0.0.0
*Jun 11 04:20:39.107: %LINEPROTO-5-UPDOWN: Line protocol on Interface FastEthern
et0/1, changed state to down
FW(config-ext-nacl)#deny ip 10.0.0.0 0.255.255.255 any log
FW(config-ext-nacl)#deny ip 172.16.0.0 0.15.255.255 any log
FW(config-ext-nacl)#deny ip 192.168.0.0 0.0.255.255 any log_
```

Ping from the outside PC to the inside PC (Ping 184.1.1.2). This will not be successful because the echo comes from the outside IP address, which is a private address. The reason is as described above.

Ping from the inside PC to BB1 (Ping 164.1.1.2). This should be successful because echo reply traffic is permitted, as in the following ACL entry:

```
FW(config-ext-nacl)#permit icmp any any echo-reply log_
```

Ping from BB1 to the inside PC (Ping 184.1.1.2). This should not be successful because echo traffic is not allowed explicitly, as in the ACL entry below:

```
FW(config-ext-nacl)#deny ip any any log_
```

Next, browse from the inside PC to BB1 (HTTP://164.1.1.2). This will be successful because HTTP traffic is inspected by the following CBAC rule:

```
FW(config)#ip inspect name CBAC tcp
FW(config)#ip inspect name CBAC udp
FW(config)#ip inspect name CBAC http
```

Browse from the outside PC to FW (HTTP://164.1.1.2). This should not be successful because outside HTTP traffic is not allowed explicitly, as in the ACL entry below:

```
FW(config-ext-nacl)#deny ip any any log_
```

Next, use Telnet from the inside PC to BB1 (telnet 164.1.1.2). This should be successful because the TCP traffic is inspected statefully by the following CBAC rule:

```
FW(config)#ip inspect name CBAC tcp
FW(config)#ip inspect name CBAC udp
FW(config)#ip inspect name CBAC http_
```

Next, use Telnet from the outside PC to FW (telnet 164.1.1.1). This should not be successful because the outside Telnet traffic is not allowed by the following configured ACL entry:

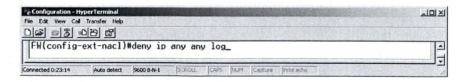

```
FW(config-ext-nacl)#deny ip any any log_
```

Trace the route from the inside PC to BB1 ("tracert 164.1.1.2"). This should be successful because the traceroute reply traffic (time exceeded and port unreachable) is permitted by the following ACL entry:

```
Configuration - HyperTerminal                                          _ |□| x|
File  Edit  View  Call  Transfer  Help
D|☞| ☞|♂| ☜|🖰| ☞|
FW(config-ext-nacl)#permit icmp any any time-exceeded log          ▲
FW(config-ext-nacl)#permit icmp any any port-unreachable log_
                                                                   ▼
Connected 0:20:01    Auto detect   9600 8-N-1   SCROLL  CAPS  NUM  Capture  Print echo
```

Next, trace the route from BB1 to the inside PC (traceroute 184.1.1.2). This should not be allowed because outside UDP traffic is prohibited by the following ACL entry:

```
Configuration - HyperTerminal                                          _ |□| x|
File  Edit  View  Call  Transfer  Help
D|☞| ☞|♂| ☜|🖰| ☞|
FW(config-ext-nacl)#deny ip any any log_                           ▲
                                                                   ▼
Connected 0:23:14    Auto detect   9600 8-N-1   SCROLL  CAPS  NUM  Capture  Print echo
```

8.5 Chapter Summary

The router on the border of the network represents a vulnerable entry point to the whole network, and hence its security is significant. In this chapter, various methods of securing the router were discussed, including the AAA model, securing network services, packet filtering, and stateful inspection. The AAA model authentication and authorization methods are executed to protect management access to the router from an unauthorized user. A sniffer application is used to demonstrate the need for disabling unsecured networks services such as Telnet and HTTP, and replacing them with secure network services such as SSH and HTTPS. Finally, packet filtering is implemented on the router to control the traffic flow based on the IP addresses, port numbers, and ICMP message types. Additionally, this chapter discussed the enhancement to the packet filtering technology through the use of CBAC as a stateful inspection engine.

Chapter 9

Site-to-Site VPN Tunnel Implementation against Eavesdropping Attacks

9.1 Introduction

A customary requirement for any multi-site network implementation is to have private communication channels between sites. The use of a dedicated leased line for the private connection is an obvious choice. Despite its security and performance advantages, this solution tends to be costly compared to the use of the Internet Protocol Security Virtual Private Network (IPsec VPN). The IPsec VPN is a private connection that provides a secure connection over a public or shared medium such as the Internet between two Local Area Networks (LANs) or a remote user and a LAN. Cryptographic techniques and protocols are employed to protect the privacy of traffic that flows between the VPN endpoints. The use of IPsec VPN for ensuring data privacy is an attractive solution because it uses the existing networking infrastructure that enables the Internet.

The IPsec VPN is an open standard that is defined by the Internet Engineering Task Force (IETF) to provide confidentiality, integrity, authentication, replay protection, and access control for network traffic. It is important to understand the relationship between different data privacy technologies such as IPsec VPN and Secure Socket Layer/Transport Layer Security (SSL/TLS). Primarily, IPsec VPN is a network layer security solution, while SSL/TLS is a transport layer security solution. Hence, SSL/TLS cannot hide the IP addresses of the communicating parties. In contrast, IPsec VPN has the capability to conceal IP addresses.

On the other hand, IPsec VPN and SSL/TLS share common features such as combining asymmetric and symmetric key cryptographic algorithms. Symmetric key cryptographic algorithms are fast and use small keys. However, the process of key generation, distribution, storage, and relocation is troublesome. On the other hand, the asymmetric key cryptographic algorithms solve the problem of key management by having two keys—a public key and a private key—but nevertheless are very slow.

An ingenious approach is to use both these methods, wherein asymmetric key cryptographic algorithms are used for key exchange and authentication and symmetric key cryptographic algorithms are used for data encryption. Consequently, both IPsec VPN and SSL/TLS have two main phases or layers. The first is used for key exchange and authentication, and the second is used for data encryption. These phases are

- Internet Security Association and Key Management Protocol (ISAKMP)/Internet Key Exchange (IKE) phase 1 and ISAKMP/IKE phase 2 for IPsec VPN
- Handshake and Record layers for SSL/TLS

A brief description of the main protocols, phases, modes, and types of VPN is presented.

9.1.1 IKE Protocol Phases

The IKE phase 1 is used mainly for session key exchange by means of Diffie–Hellman groups and authentication using pre-shared key or asymmetric key cryptographic algorithms. Other functions of this phase are to prepare key materials for IKE phase 2 and protect its own message using encryption and hash functions. This phase negotiates a Security Association (SA) called phase 1 SA. The SA is a unidirectional agreement between the IPsec VPN endpoints on the negotiated security parameters that will establish the VPN tunnel, including the applicable authentication method, encryption algorithm, and hash function. IKE phase 1 has two modes:

- Main Mode is a secure mode that involves peer identity protection and detailed negotiations.
- Aggressive Mode is the faster and less secure mode and offers no peer identity protection.

In IKE phase 2, data encryption and decryption are completed. The only mode that is available in this phase is the Quick Mode, which establishes two unidirectional phase 2 SAs. Each phase 2 unidirectional SA has an index called the Security Parameter Index (SPI). The negotiated phase 2 SA security parameters are as follows:

- IPsec protocols: Encapsulating Security Payload (ESP) or Authentication Header (AH).
- Encryption and hash function suite.
- The traffic that must be protected by the VPN tunnel.
- The Diffie–Hellman group if Perfect Forward Secrecy (PFS) is required. (PFS ensures that future keys are not derived from previous keys. Consequently, compromising a single key will only affect the data that is protected by that key.)

9.1.2 IPsec Modes

There are two IPsec modes: Tunnel Mode and Transport Mode. The Tunnel Mode protects the whole IP packet, starting from layer 3 of the ISO model (i.e., the Network layer) and up. This mode encapsulates the IP header and the payload, and it is the most commonly used mode. The Transport Mode protects layer 4 of the ISO model (i.e., the Transport layer) and up, and therefore it does not protect the IP header.

9.1.3 IPsec Protocols

The IPsec has two protocols: ESP (Encapsulating Security Payload) and AH (Authentication Header). The ESP uses port 50 and provides confidentiality, integrity, and authentication without protecting the IP header in the Transport Mode. Because of its data confidentiality security service, it is the most used IPsec protocol. The AH uses port 51 and provides integrity, authentication, and IP header protection. However, it does not provide data confidentiality security service, which makes it suitable for applications that require mainly authentication, such as IP routing message authentication.

9.1.4 VPN Types

There are mainly two types of VPNs: Site-to-Site VPN and Remote Access VPN. Site-to-Site VPN, or LAN-to-LAN VPN, provides data privacy for mission-critical traffic between networks at two sites. This chapter includes two hands-on labs to implement the Site-to-Site VPN. The first lab uses two Juniper Networks firewall appliances as VPN gateways to connect two sites, while Cisco firewall appliances are used in the second lab. The Remote Access VPN allows remote users to securely access the protected network resources of a central site. This will be the focus of Chapter 10.

IPsec VPN solutions implementation can be a challenging task for the beginner and even for the intermediate security engineer. It requires a clear understanding of several security technologies, algorithms, protocols, modes, and concepts. Moreover, the VPN configuration process tends to be lengthy and involves several steps, verification, and testing procedures. Moreover, there is no standard implementation practice for VPN across vendors. In view of these concerns, a key objective of this chapter is to explain the VPN implementation of two vendors who are leaders in the market (Juniper Networks and Cisco Microsystems) using various illustrations, screenshots, and configuration steps. This will help the reader form a rich understanding of VPN security solutions and the implementation process.

This chapter describes procedures to implement a VPN solution to establish secure communication between two remote sites. The process is explained within a lab set-up, and uses standards and best practices woven into a real-life scenario to enhance the comprehension of the reader.

The following hardware devices are used in the hands-on labs:

■ Juniper Networks SSG20 Wireless Appliance[*]: VPN gateway
■ Cisco Microsystems ASA Appliance[†]: VPN gateway

9.2 Lab 9.1: Site-to-Site VPN — First Implementation

9.2.1 Outcome

The learning objective of this lab is for students to learn how to implement a VPN (Virtual Private Network) tunnel between two sites using the Juniper VPN gateway.

---

[*] http://www.juniper.net
[†] http://www.cisco.com

9.2.2 Description

We present this exercise using a practical scenario to enrich
learning. The head office of a bank is located in Dubai City,
and there is a requirement to establish a secure communication link to a branch office located in Al-Ain, a city that is
about 160 kilometers from Dubai. The approach adopted to
establish this requirement is to create a private connection
between the two sites using VPN technology.

Each site (head office and branch) has a LAN (Local Area
Network) that connects computer hosts using switches within
a limited geographic area. For the sake of simplicity, each LAN
is represented by one host figure, as shown in the next figure.
A real-world implementation to relay data between these two
networks would require Wide Area Network (WAN) technologies to cover the broad area between Al-Ain and Dubai. For
our exercise, the WAN link is simulated by a crossover cable.
Alternatively, a switch and straight-through cables can serve
the same purpose.

To enable a private connection between the two sites, a
VPN gateway must be installed on each site. Usually, routers
and firewalls are used as VPN gateways; in this implementation, the Juniper Networks firewall appliance is used as a
VPN gateway for each site. The two VPN gateways negotiate IKE phase 1 Security Association to establish the VPN
tunnel. Then, they encrypt data using IKE phase 2 Security
Association parameters.

9.2.3 Experiment

The following figure shows the network architecture of the
experiment. Site 1, which represents Al-Ain, consists of a
host that is connected to a Cisco 3560 switch using a straight-
through cable. The switch is connected to the interface
Ethernet0/2 of the Juniper NetScreen firewall using a straight-
through cable. The same scenario is used at site 2, which

represents Dubai. The two sites are connected via the interface Ethernet0/3 of the Juniper NetScreen firewall using crossover cable where the tunnel will be implemented.

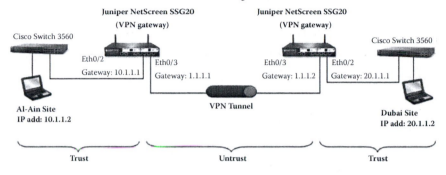

The experiment consists of the following steps:

Step 1: Reset the firewall to the default setting.

Step 2: Assign IP addresses of the machines and the firewall interfaces of both sites.

Step 3: Assign the network IP addresses of the two LANs (Al-Ain and Dubai) of both sites.

Step 4: Configure the VPN from the Al-Ain site to the Dubai site, and vice versa.

Step 5: Route from the Al-Ain site to the Dubai site, and vice versa.

Step 6: Set the policies for both sites.

Step 7: Ping from Al-Ain to Dubai, and vice versa, to test VPN tunnel establishment.

Step 8: Verify VPN tunnel establishment.

9.2.3.1 Step 1: Reset the Firewall to the Default Setting

We start the experiment by connecting a host to the serial console of the firewall for the Al-Ain site to access the Command Line Interface of the firewall through the hyper-terminal. Use "netscreen" for both Login ID and password. Next, enter "unset all". The following output is observed: "Erase all system config, are you sure [y/n]?" Affirm by typing "y"; then reset the system by typing "reset". The following output appears: "Configuration modified, save?", for which "n" is entered. Another question, "System reset, are you sure?", is asked, for which "y" is entered. Then, log in again using the default login ID and password, which is "netscreen". The same steps are repeated for the firewall for the Dubai site.

9.2.3.2 Step 2: Assign IP Addresses of the Machines and the Firewall Interfaces for Both Sites

To assign IP address to the machine and the firewall of the Al-Ain site, select "Use the following IP address" option and fill the entries as demonstrated in the next screenshot.

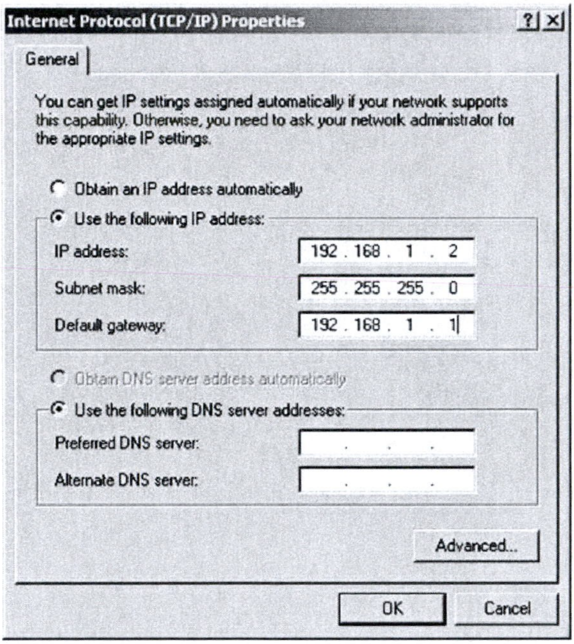

Next, open the Web User Interface (WebUI) of the Juniper Network device by entering "http://192.168.1.1." A list of interfaces appears:

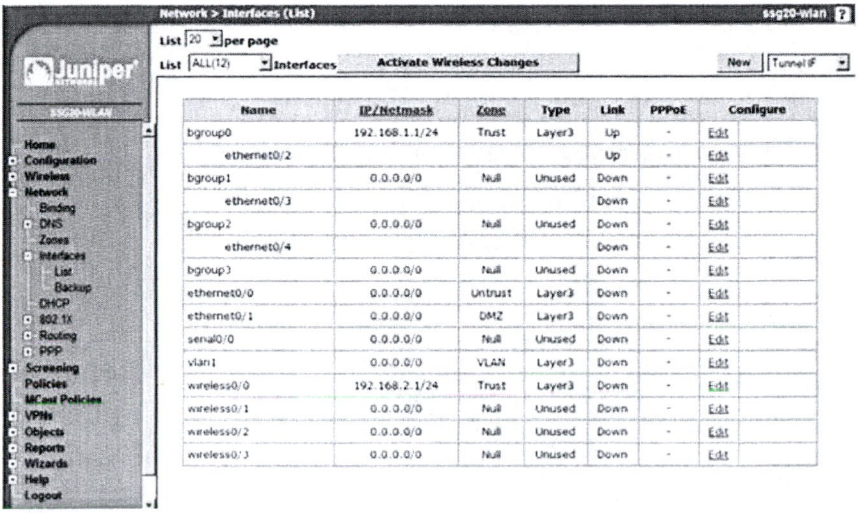

Next, click on the "Edit" link of the bgroup0 interface and complete the entries as shown in the next screenshot. The zone name is to be "Trust" for the Al-Ain site. The Interface Mode is "NAT," in which the firewall assigns public IP addresses to computers inside a private network. Select the services to be used; for example, "Web UI" allows the user to access the firewall configuration through the Web user interface. Click "Apply" and then "OK" to complete the configuration.

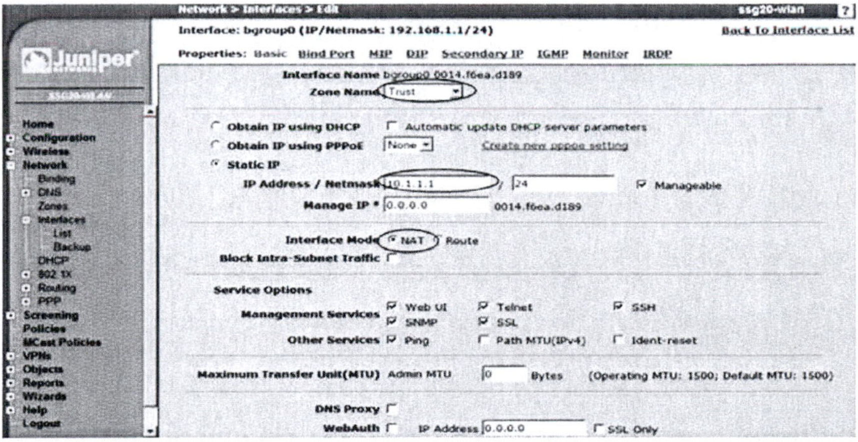

After changing the interface IP address, the Juniper WebUI automatically logs out. Therefore, change Al-Ain PC's IP address to 10.1.1.2/24, as shown below.

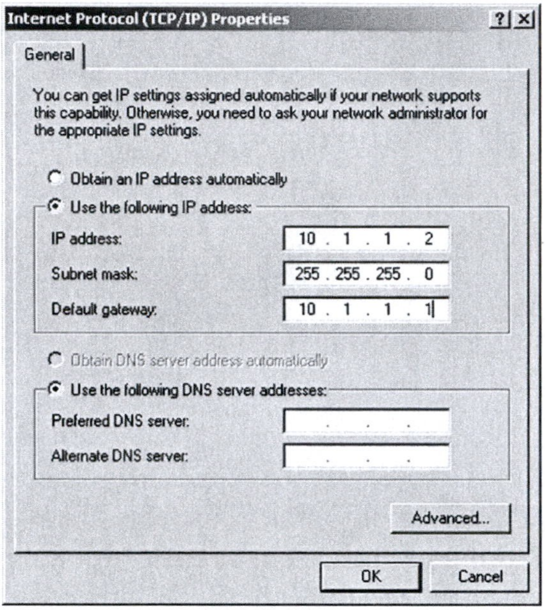

Launch the Web browser with the following URL— http://10.1.1.1—to access the Web user interface. Next, select "Network," then "Interfaces," and finally "List" to display the screen, as shown next.

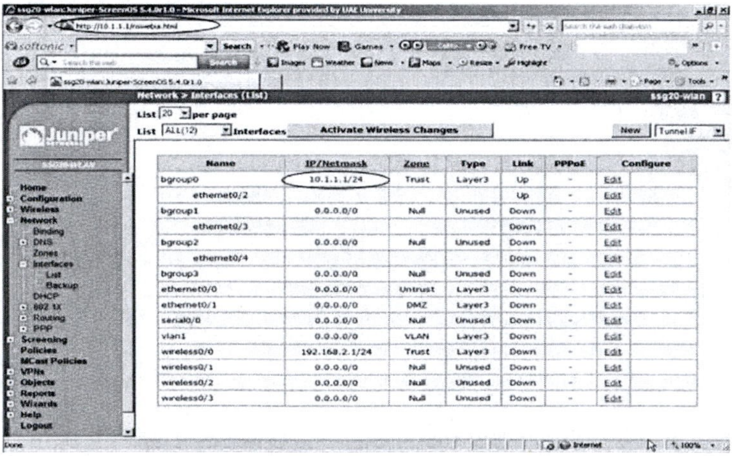

Click on the "Edit" link of bgroup1 interface and complete the entries, as shown in the following screenshot. The zone name will be "Untrust," in which the VPN tunnel will be created with the Dubai site. Select a service to use; for example, we enabled ping service to allow communication between the two sites, which will be done securely over the tunnel.

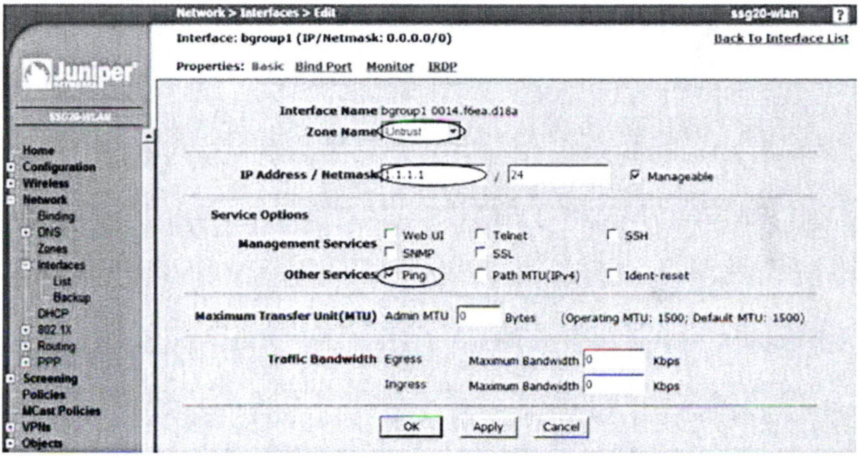

Click "Apply" and then "OK." The assigned IP addresses to the interfaces should look as shown below.

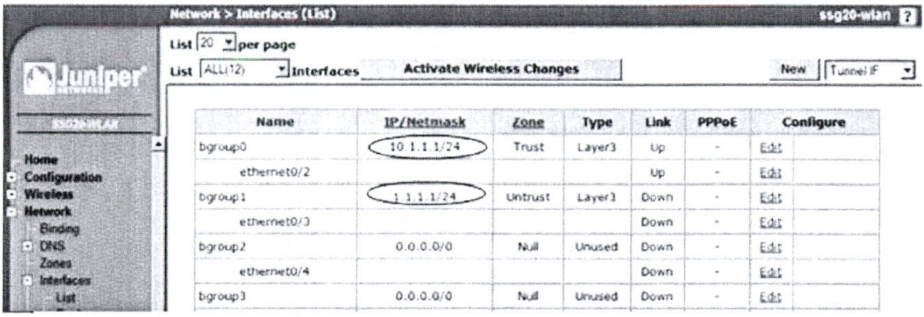

To assign an IP address to the machine and the firewall of the Dubai site, repeat the same steps as for the Al-Ain site. The firewall interface settings for the Dubai site are shown next.

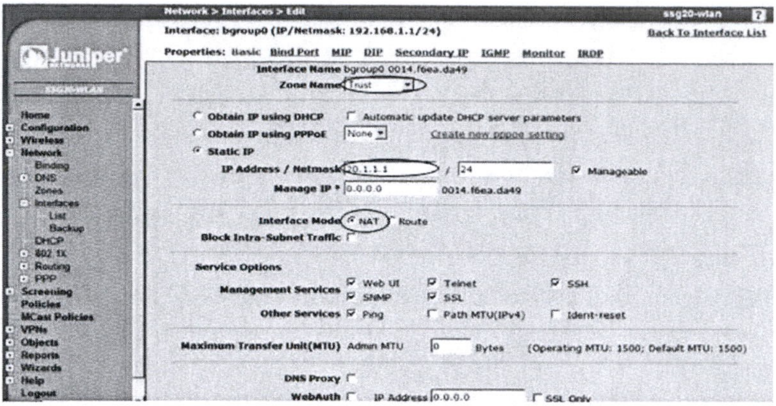

Click on the "Edit" link of bgroup0 interface and fill in the entries. The zone name will be "Trust" for the Dubai site and the interface mode is "NAT." Enable the services as was done for the Al-Ain site. Then click "Apply" and "OK."

Note: After changing the interface IP address, the NetScreen WebUI will automatically log out. The PC's IP address is to be changed to 20.1.1.2/24, as shown in the following screenshot.

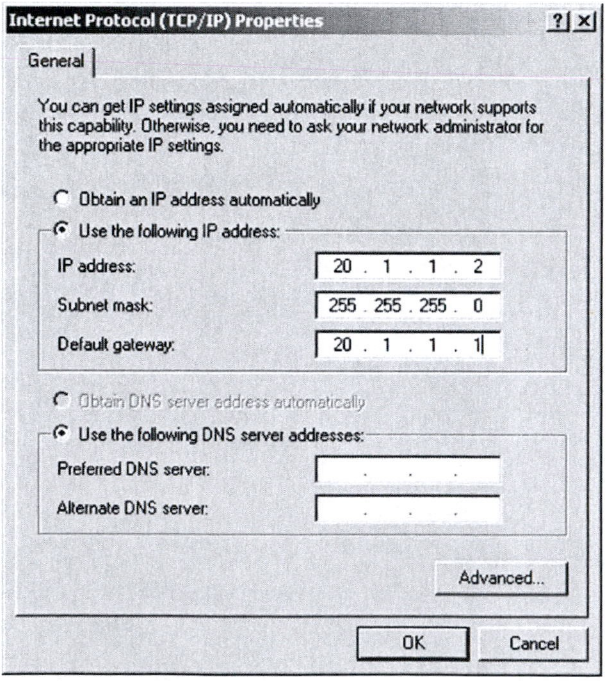

Next, launch the Web browser with the following URL, http://20.1.1.1, to access the Web user interface and select "Network," then "Interfaces," and finally "List," as shown in the following screenshot.

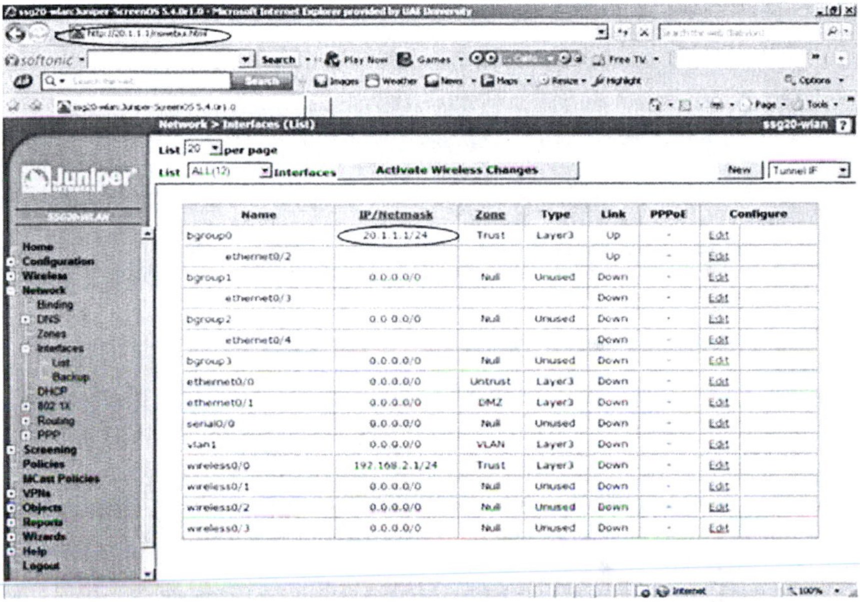

Click on the "Edit" link of bgroup1 interface and complete the entries as shown on the screen below. The zone name is set to "Untrust," in which the VPN tunnel is created with the Al-Ain site. Select a service to use; for example, we enabled ping service to allow communication between the two sites that will be done securely over the tunnel. Click "Apply" and then "OK."

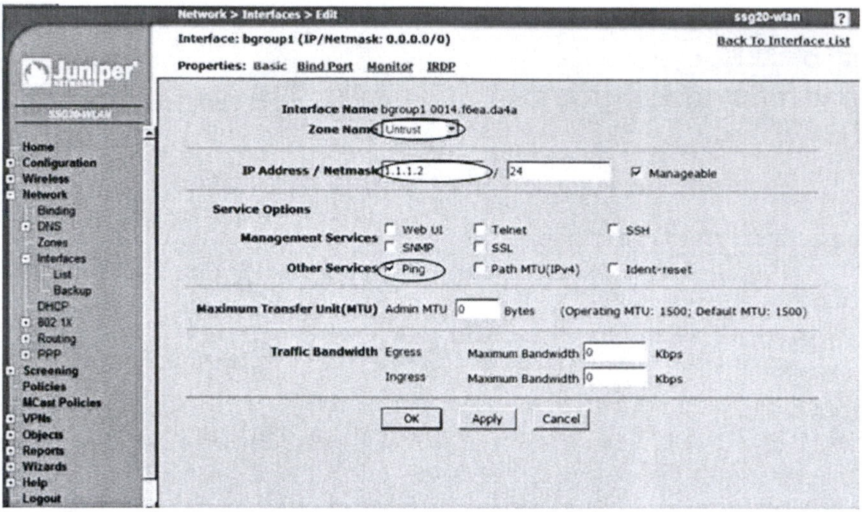

The resulting Dubai firewall interface final list is shown below.

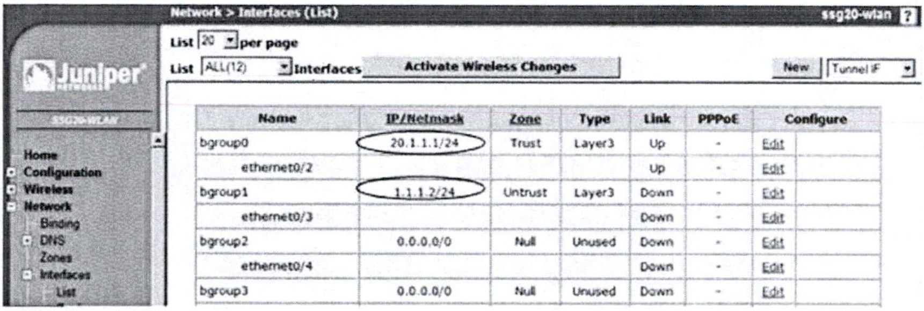

9.2.3.3 Step 3: Assign the Network IP Addresses of the Two LANs (Al-Ain and Dubai) for Both Sites

To assign the network addresses of Al-Ain site, select "Objects," then "Addresses," and finally "List." Fill the fields in the resulting screen as shown below.

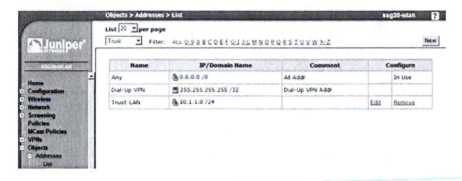

Clicking on the "OK" button results in the next screen.

Now click on the left drop-down menu and select the "Untrust" zone and then click on "New." Fill in the fields with appropriate values as shown in the following screenshot.

Click on the "OK" button; the network address of the "Untrust" zone is displayed as shown in the following screenshot.

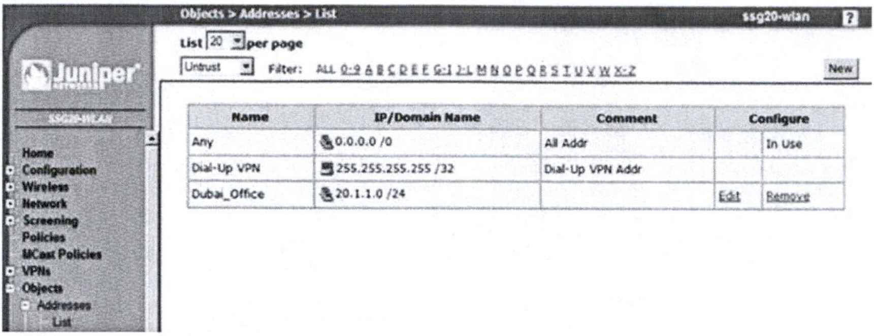

To assign the network addresses of the Dubai site, select "Objects," then "Addresses," and finally "List." Fill the fields with appropriate values as shown below.

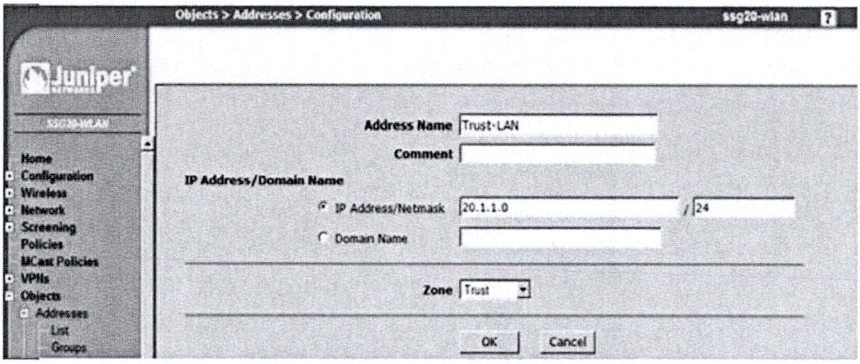

Click on the "OK" button, which results in the screenshot shown next.

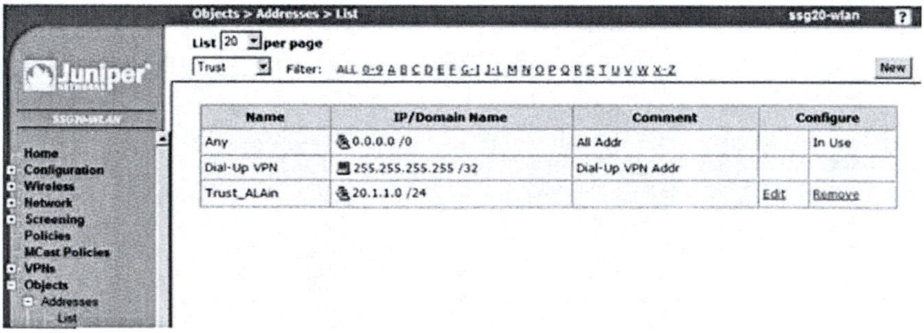

Click on the left drop-down menu and select the "Untrust" zone; then click on "New." Fill in the values of the fields as shown in the next screenshot.

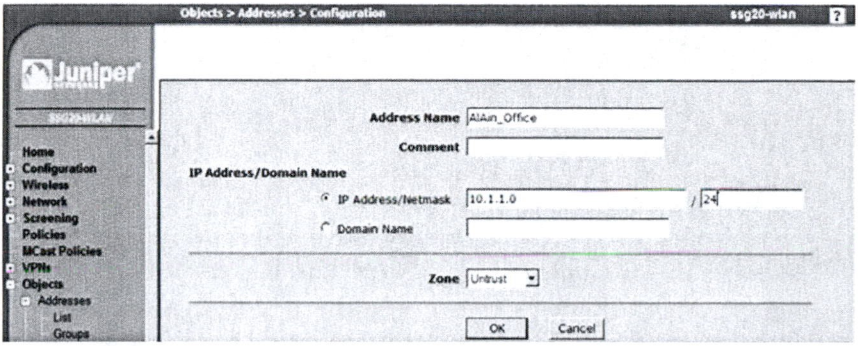

Click "OK"; the network address of the "Untrust" zone appears as shown in the screenshot below.

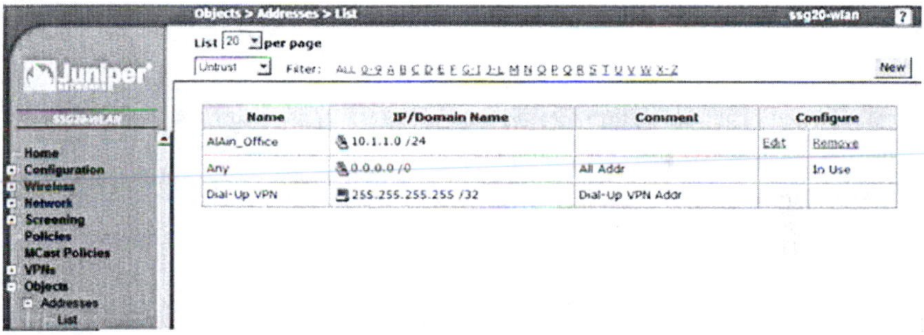

9.2.3.4 Step 4: Configure the VPN from the Al-Ain Site to the Dubai Site, and Vice Versa

To configure the VPN gateway from the Al-Ain site, navigate to "VPNs" and "AutoKey Advanced," then "Gateway," and finally "New". Enter the values as shown on the screen below. Type the name of the gateway To_Dubai site and select "Custom" for security level. Select "Static IP Address" for the remote gateway and enter the IP address of the gateway. Type the pre-shared key that is used for the authentication process between the two ends to identify each other. Select bgroub1 as Outgoing Interface where the VPN is implemented between the two ends.

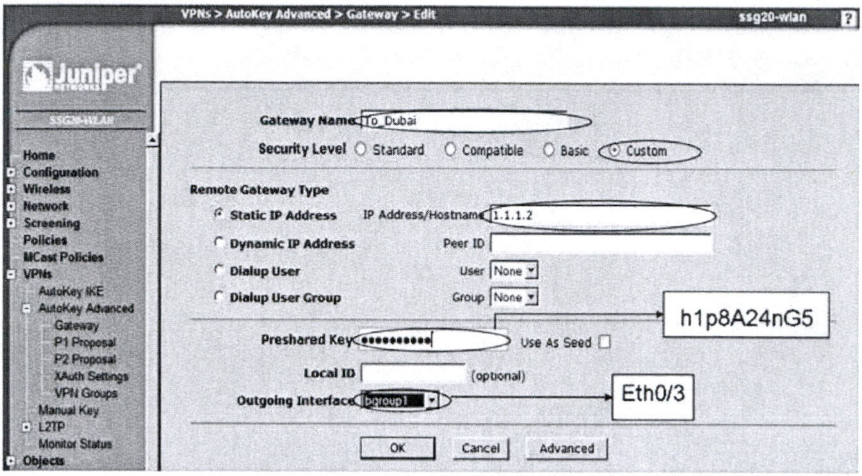

Click on the "Advanced" button to select the proposal of phase 1 for the Al-Ain site. The proposal consists of three algorithms. Diffie–Hellman Group 2 is the technique that allows the two ends to agree on the secret value; 3DES is the encryption algorithm that is used for encryption purposes, and SHA is used for data integrity purposes. Select Main Mode, which provides ID Protection, as shown in the following screenshot.

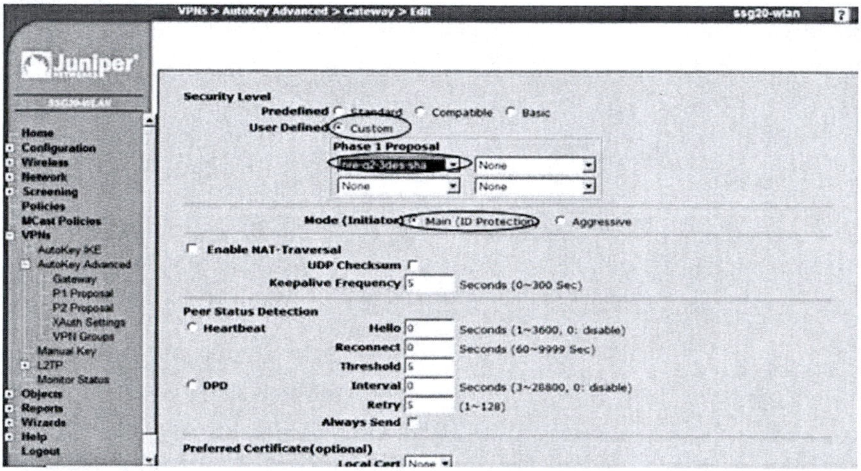

Click on the "Return" button to return to the basic gateway configuration page and then click on the "OK" button. Phase 1 creation is complete for the Al-Ain site, as shown below.

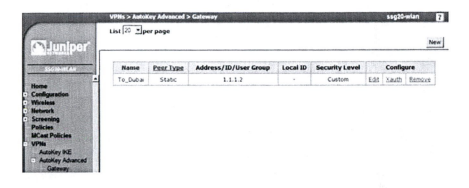

The phase 2 parameters are set automatically by selecting "VPNs," then "Auto IKE," and finally "New." Enter the values as shown on the following screen. Type in the VPN name and select a compatible choice as the security level. Select "Predefined" for the remote gateway and choose the To_Dubai gateway.

Click on the "OK" button to get the screen shown below (that is, the Al-Ain site VPN completed configuration).

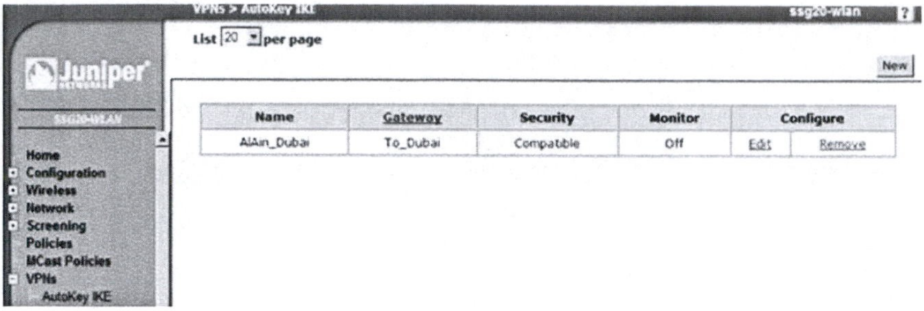

To configure the VPN from the Dubai site, go to "VPNs," then "AutoKey Advanced," then "Gateway," and finally "New." Enter the following entries as shown on the following screen: Type the name of the gateway To_Al-Ain site and select "Custom" for the security level. Select "Static IP Address" for the remote gateway and enter the IP address of the gateway. Type the same pre-shared key that is used for the authentication process on Al-Ain site. Select bgroub1 as the Outgoing Interface where the VPN will be implemented between the two ends.

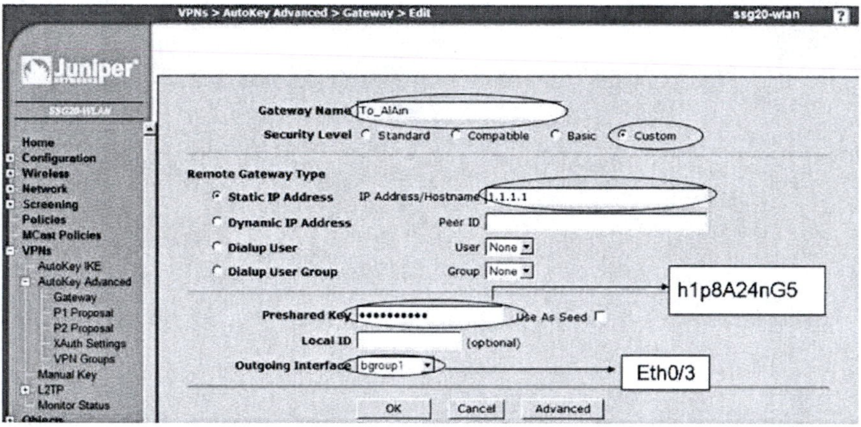

Click on the "Advanced" button and fill in the values as shown on the next screen. The phase 1 proposal consists of three algorithms: Diffie–Hellman Group 2, 3DES, and SHA. Select Main Mode for phase 1.

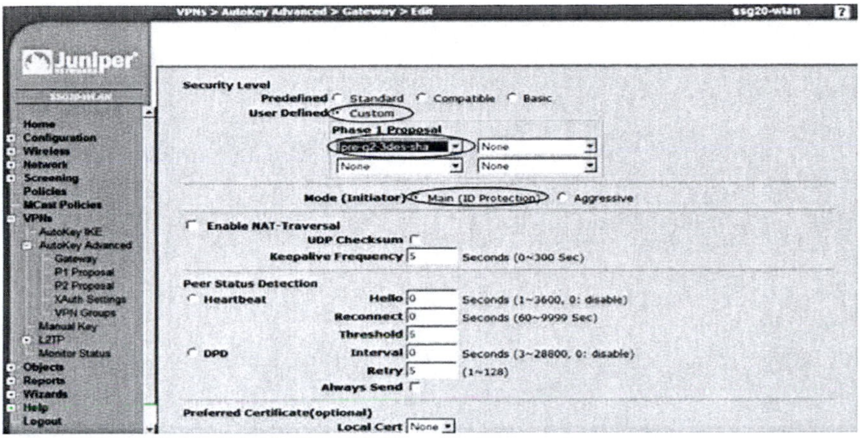

Click on the "Return" button to return to the basic gateway configuration page, then click "OK" so that phase 1 implementation is complete, as shown on the following screen.

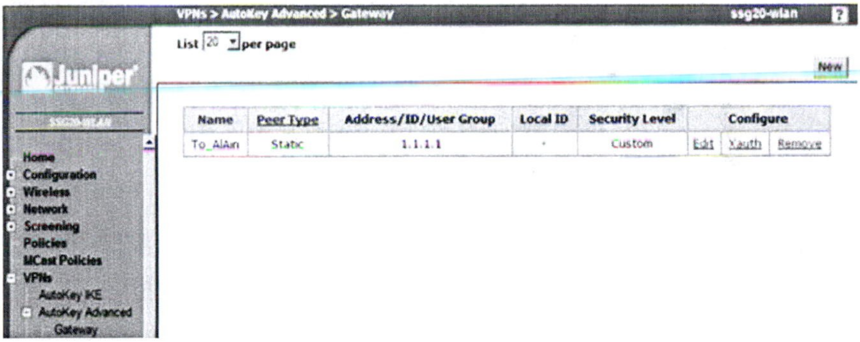

Select "VPNs," then "Auto IKE," and finally "New." Enter the values as shown on the next screen. Type the VPN name and select "compatible choice" as the security level. Select "Predefined" for remote gateway and choose the "To_AlAin gateway" that was previously configured.

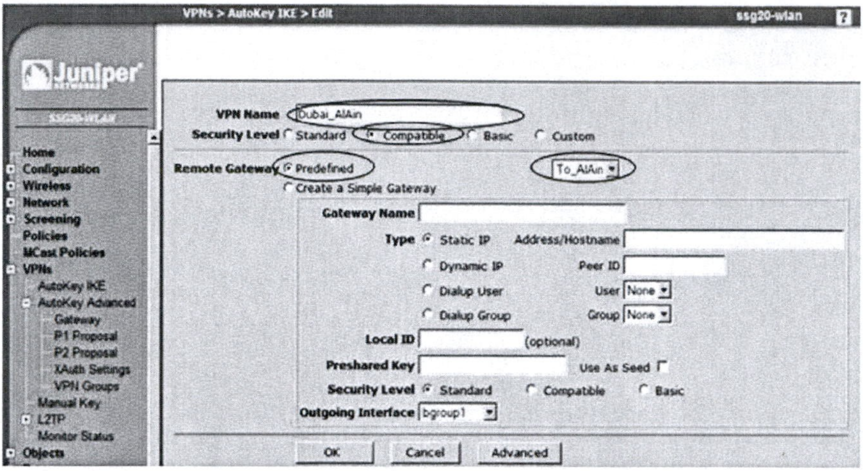

Click "OK" to complete Dubai site VPN configuration as shown on the following screen.

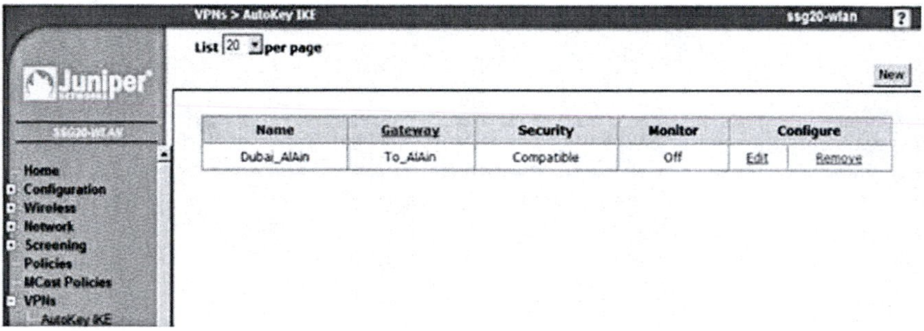

9.2.3.5 Step 5: Route from the Al-Ain Site to the Dubai Site Gateway, and Vice Versa

To route from the Al-Ain site to the Dubai site, select "Network," then "Routing," and finally "Destination." The routing configuration page will be displayed as shown below.

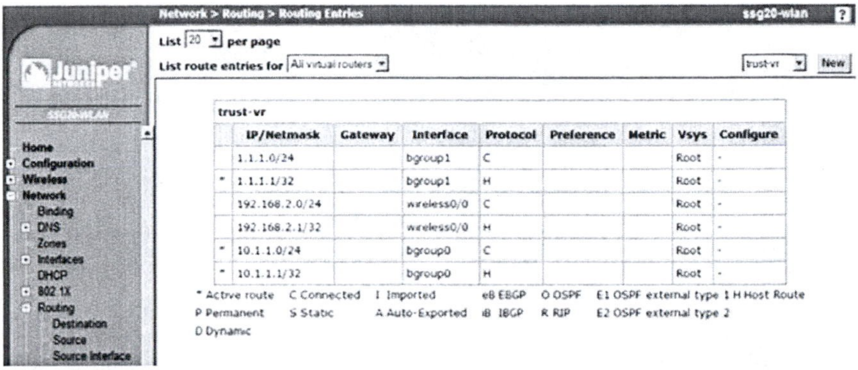

Network > Routing > Routing Entries ssg20-wlan [?]

List [20 ▼] per page
List route entries for [All virtual routers ▼]   [trust-vr ▼] New

trust-vr

	IP/Netmask	Gateway	Interface	Protocol	Preference	Metric	Vsys	Configure
	1.1.1.0/24		bgroup1	C			Root	-
*	1.1.1.1/32		bgroup1	H			Root	-
	192.168.2.0/24		wireless0/0	C			Root	-
	192.168.2.1/32		wireless0/0	H			Root	-
*	10.1.1.0/24		bgroup0	C			Root	-
*	10.1.1.1/32		bgroup0	H			Root	-

* Active route   C Connected   I Imported   eB EBGP   O OSPF   E1 OSPF external type 1 H Host Route
P Permanent   S Static   A Auto-Exported   iB IBGP   R RIP   E2 OSPF external type 2
D Dynamic

To create a default route toward the Dubai gateway, choose "trust-vr" from drop-down menu, then click on the "New" button, and fill in the fields as shown in the next screenshot.

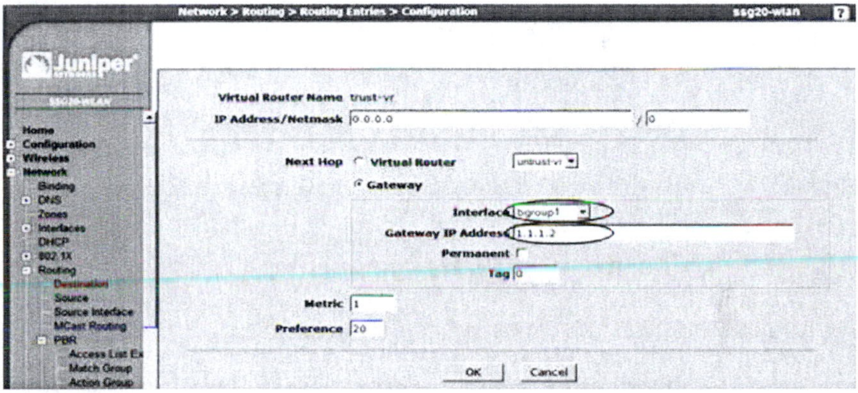

Network > Routing > Routing Entries > Configuration ssg20-wlan [?]

Virtual Router Name trust-vr
IP Address/Netmask 0.0.0.0   / 0

Next Hop ○ **Virtual Router** [untrust-vr ▼]
                   ⊙ **Gateway**

                   Interface [bgroup1 ▼]
                   Gateway IP Address 1.1.1.2
                   Permanent ☐
                   Tag 0

Metric 1
Preference 20

OK   Cancel

Click on the "OK" button; the routing entries should look as shown next.

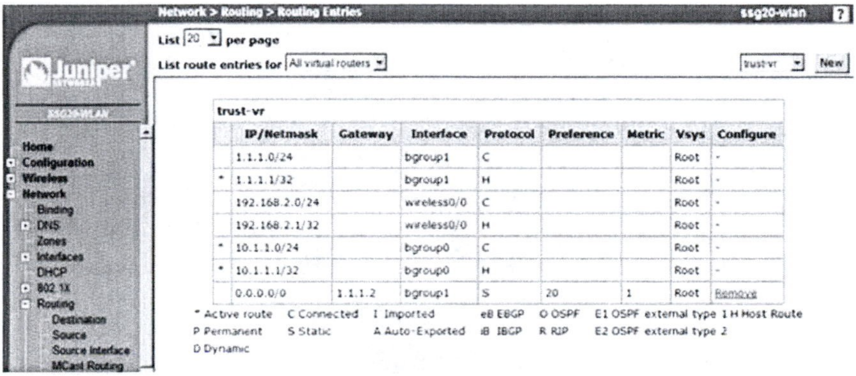

Network > Routing > Routing Entries ssg20-wlan [?]

List [20 ▼] per page
List route entries for [All virtual routers ▼]   [trust-vr ▼] New

trust-vr

	IP/Netmask	Gateway	Interface	Protocol	Preference	Metric	Vsys	Configure
	1.1.1.0/24		bgroup1	C			Root	-
*	1.1.1.1/32		bgroup1	H			Root	-
	192.168.2.0/24		wireless0/0	C			Root	-
	192.168.2.1/32		wireless0/0	H			Root	-
*	10.1.1.0/24		bgroup0	C			Root	-
*	10.1.1.1/32		bgroup0	H			Root	-
	0.0.0.0/0	1.1.1.2	bgroup1	S	20	1	Root	Remove

* Active route   C Connected   I Imported   eB EBGP   O OSPF   E1 OSPF external type 1 H Host Route
P Permanent   S Static   A Auto-Exported   iB IBGP   R RIP   E2 OSPF external type 2
D Dynamic

To route from the Dubai site to the Al-Ain site, select "Network," then "Routing," and finally "Destination." The routing configuration page is displayed. To create a default route toward the Al-Ain gateway, choose "trust-vr" from the drop-down menu; then click on the "New" button and fill in the fields as shown in the next screenshot.

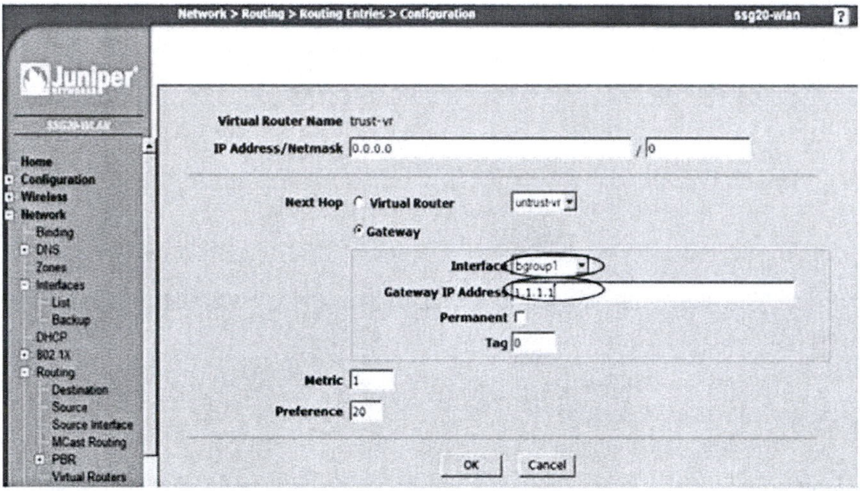

Click on the "OK" button; the routing entries should look as shown below.

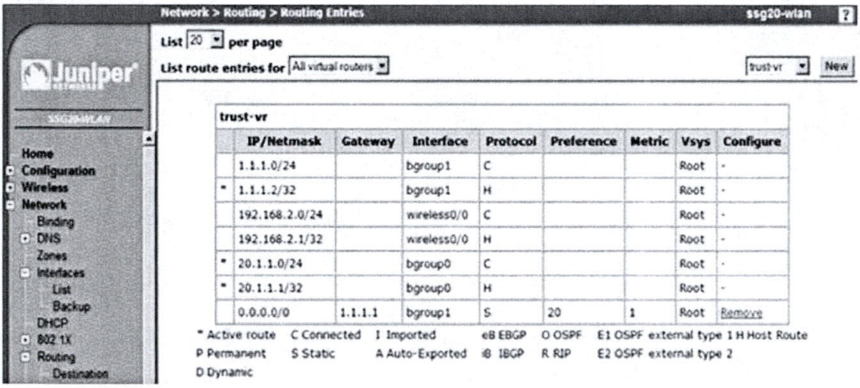

9.2.3.6 Step 6: Set the Policies for Both Sites

To set the policies from the Al-Ain site that allow the Al-Ain site to communicate with the Dubai site through the tunnel, select "Policies" and clear the default rules; then select the zones from the drop-down menu from trust zone to "Untrust" zone. Click on the "New" button and fill in the entries as shown on the next screen.

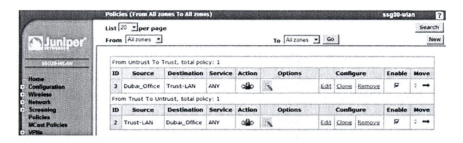

Enter the name of the policy, for example, To/From Dubai. Then specify the source and the preconfigured destination for the Al-Ain site. Select "Tunnel" for the action entry. Check the Modify matching bi-directional VPN policy, which will create a second policy for the other direction: from "Untrust" zone to trust zone.

Click on the "OK" button to get the two policies, as shown below.

To set the policies from the Dubai site that allow the Dubai site to communicate with the Al-Ain site through the tunnel, select "policies" and clear the default rules; then select the zones from the drop-down menu from trust zone to "Untrust" zone. Click on the "New" button and fill in the entries as shown in the following screenshot.

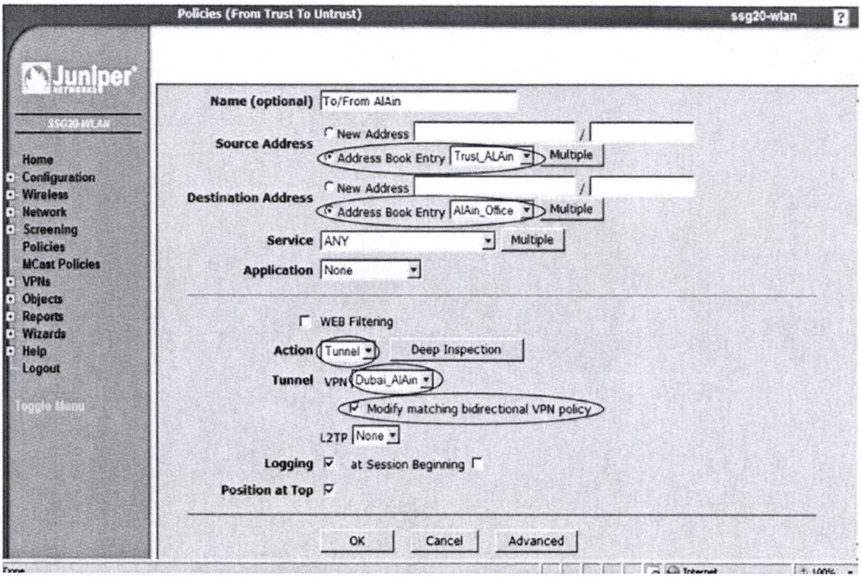

Enter the name of the policy, for example, To/From Al-Ain. Then specify the source and the destination that was precon-figured for the Dubai site. Select "Tunnel" for the action entry. Check the Modify matching bi-directional VPN policy that will create a second policy for the other direction: from "Untrust" zone to trust zone.

Click on the "OK" button to get the two policies, as shown next.

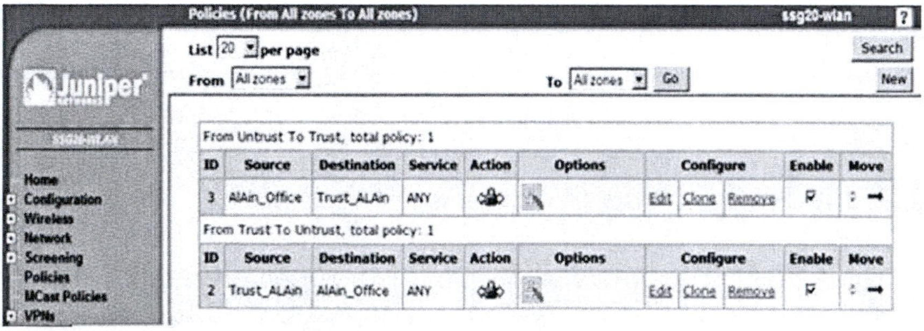

9.2.3.7 Step 7: Ping from Al-Ain to Dubai, and vice versa, to Test VPN Tunnel Establishment

Ping from Al-Ain to Dubai, which should be successful, as in the following command:

```
C:\WINDOWS\system32\cmd.exe                                      _|□| x|
Microsoft Windows XP [Version 5.1.2600]
(C) Copyright 1985-2001 Microsoft Corp.

D:\Documents and Settings\200414671>ping 20.1.1.2

Pinging 20.1.1.2 with 32 bytes of data:

Reply from 20.1.1.2: bytes=32 time=13ms TTL=126
Reply from 20.1.1.2: bytes=32 time=2ms TTL=126
Reply from 20.1.1.2: bytes=32 time=2ms TTL=126
Reply from 20.1.1.2: bytes=32 time=2ms TTL=126

Ping statistics for 20.1.1.2:
    Packets: Sent = 4, Received = 4, Lost = 0 (0% loss),
Approximate round trip times in milli-seconds:
    Minimum = 2ms, Maximum = 13ms, Average = 4ms
```

Ping from Dubai to Al-Ain, which should be successful. This confirms that the VPN tunnel is established in both directions.

9.2.3.8 Step 8: Verify VPN Tunnel Establishment

To verify the establishment of the tunnel between the two sites, analyze the security associations that are created after the negotiations between the two VPN gateways. Type the following command for the Al-Ain site.

```
configuration - HyperTerminal
File Edit View Call Transfer Help

ssg20-wlan-> get vpn
Name            Gateway           Mode RPlay 1st Proposal          Monitor Use Cnt
Interface
--------------- ----------------- ---- ----- -------------------- ------- -------
----------
AlAin_Dubai     T0_Dubai          tunl No    nopfs-esp-3des-sha    off     2
bgroup1
    Total Auto VPN: 1

Name        Gateway           Interface  Lcl SPI  Rmt SPI  Algorithm         Monitor
    Tunnel ID
----------- ----------------- ---------- -------- -------- ----------------- -------
----------
Total Manual VPN 0
ssg20-wlan-> _

Connected 2:01:39    Auto detect    9600 8-N-1    SCROLL    CAPS    NUM    Capture   Print echo
```

From the above output it is clear that the interface name is bgroup1 (Al-Ain_Dubai). The Gateway name is To_Dubai as it is configured by this name for the Al-Ain site. The IPsec mode is the tunnel mode, which encrypts the IP header and the payload so that the entire packet is protected. The 1st proposal is nopfs (no perfect forward secrecy), which means there would be no change to the key material in the future. ESP is a protocol that provides secure means for the packet by encrypting the entire IP packet and authenticates its content. 3DES is the encryption algorithm, and SHA is the data integrity algorithm that is used. The number of automatic VPNs is 1.

To study the security association parameters, use the command "get sa" as in the following, which shows two SAs, one per direction with the gateway IP address as 1.1.1.2 and the ISA KMP SHA 1UDP port as 500. The algorithms are 3DES for encryption and SHA1 for data integrity, and the SPI is the security parameter index, which is different for each security association.

```
configuration - HyperTerminal
File  Edit  View  Call  Transfer  Help

ssg20-wlan-> get sa
total configured sa: 1
HEX ID     Gateway          Port Algorithm      SPI         Life:sec kb Sta   PID vsys

00000001<           1.1.1.2  500 esp:3des/sha1 ebc80af8 2386 unlim A/-        2 0
00000001>           1.1.1.2  500 esp:3des/sha1 8a59a851 2386 unlim A/-        1 0
ssg20-wlan-> _

Connected 2:02:11    Auto detect    9600 8-N-1    SCROLL    CAPS   NUM    Capture   Print echo
```

To analyze the VPN establishment from the Dubai site, repeat the previous commands as in the following:

```
configuration - HyperTerminal
File  Edit  View  Call  Transfer  Help

ssg20-wlan-> get vpn
Name           Gateway           Mode RPlay 1st Proposal        Monitor Use Cnt
Interface
----------------  ----------------  ---- ----- -------------------- -------- -------
----------
Dubai_AlAin    To_AlAin          tunl No    nopfs-esp-3des-sha   off          2
bgroup1
  Total Auto VPN: 1
Name        Gateway           Interface  Lcl SPI  Rmt SPI  Algorithm          Monitor
  Tunnel ID
----------  ----------------  ---------  -------- -------- ------------------ -------
----------
Total Manual VPN 0
ssg20-wlan-> _

Connected 2:08:25    Auto detect    9600 8-N-1    SCROLL    CAPS   NUM    Capture   Print echo
```

```
configuration - HyperTerminal                                    _ □ ×
File  Edit  View  Call  Transfer  Help
 □ ☞  ⊜ ⅜  ⅰ□ ㉐  ☜

 ssg20-wlan-> get sa
 total configured sa: 1
 HEX ID    Gateway        Port Algorithm    SPI      Life:sec kb Sta   PID vsys

 00000001<     1.1.1.1    500 esp:3des/sha1 8a59a851 1981 unlim A/-      2 0
 00000001>     1.1.1.1    500 esp:3des/sha1 ebc80af8 1981 unlim A/-      1 0
 ssg20-wlan-> _

Connected 2:08:53    Auto detect   9600 8-N-1    SCROLL   CAPS  NUM   Capture  Print echo
```

9.3 Lab 9.2: Site-to-Site VPN — Second Implementation

9.3.1 Outcome

The learning objective of this exercise is for students to learn how to implement a VPN tunnel between two different sites using the Cisco VPN gateway.

9.3.2 Description

This hands-on lab scenario is similar to the previous lab, with the exception that it uses the Cisco VPN gateway instead of the Juniper VPN gateway.

9.3.3 Experiment

To learn how to implement a VPN tunnel between two different sites, an experiment is conducted using a Cisco ASA (Adaptive Security Appliance) running OS 7.0(7) and Cisco switch 3560.

The following figure shows the network architecture of the experiment. Site 1 represents Al-Ain and consists of a host that is connected to the GigabitEthernet0/1(Inside) interface of the Al-Ain ASA, while site 2 represents Dubai and is connected to the Gigabit Ethernet0/1 interface of the Dubai Cisco ASA. The two sites are connected via the interfaces Gigabit Ethernet0/0 (outside) of the Cisco ASA using crossover cable where the tunnel is to be implemented.

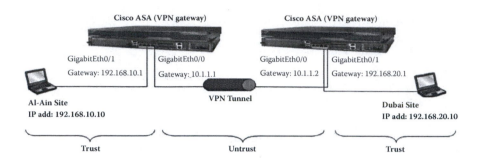

The experiment consists of the following steps:

Step 1: Reset the firewall to the default setting for both sites.

Step 2: Assign IP addresses of the machines and the firewall interfaces at both sites.

Step 3: Define the traffic that must be protected.

Step 4: Create a static route from the Al-Ain site to the Dubai site, and vice versa.

Step 5: Enable ISAKMP protocol at both sites.

Step 6: Define the phase 1 parameters of IKE.

Step 7: Define the pre-shared key that will be used by both sites.

Step 8: Define the IKE phase 2 parameters of the IPsec protocol.

Step 9: Bind the parameters of the two phases with each other.

Step 10: Apply the crypto map on the outside interface (GigabiteEthernet0/0).

Step 11: Ping from the Al-Ain site to the Dubai site, and vice versa.

Step 12: Study the parameters that are set in the security association.

9.3.3.1 *Step 1: Reset the Firewall to the Default Setting for Both Sites*

Connect a PC to the serial console of the firewall for the Al-Ain site through the HyperTerminal to get the Command

Line Interface of the firewall. Type "enable" at the prompt "ciscoasa>." Hit the Enter key for the password request and then provide the "configure" terminal command. Finally, enter "configure factory-default" to reset the system to its default setting.

9.3.3.2 Step 2: Assign IP Addresses to the Machines and the Firewall Interface at Both Sites

To rename and assign IP addresses to the firewall interfaces at the Al-Ain site, give a name to the host, such as ASA1. Assign an IP address to the GigabitEthernet0/0 interface and assign a name, such as "outside." Specify a security level of 0 for the interface, as in the following screenshot.

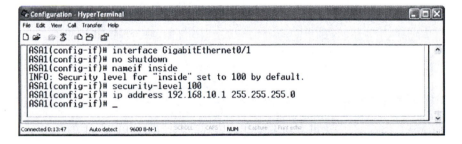

Assign an IP address to the GigabitEthernet0/1 interface and give it a name, such as "inside." Specify a security level of 100 for this interface, as in the following screenshot.

To rename and assign IP addresses to the firewall interface at the Dubai site, type the following commands:

```
Configuration - HyperTerminal                                          _|□|×|
File  Edit  View  Call  Transfer  Help
D|☞| ☜|⬚| ◻|🖺| 🖻|
ciscoasa(config)# hostname ASA2
ASA2(config)# interface GigabitEthernet0/0
ASA2(config-if)# no shutdown
ASA2(config-if)# nameif outside
INFO: Security level for "outside" set to 0 by default.
ASA2(config-if)# security-level 0
ASA2(config-if)# ip address 10.1.1.2 255.255.255.0
ASA2(config-if)# _

Connected 0:07:01    Auto detect    9600 8-N-1    SCROLL   CAPS   NUM   Capture   Print echo
```

Assign an IP address to the GigabitEthernet0/1 interface and give it a name, such as "inside."

```
Configuration - HyperTerminal                                          _|□|×|
File  Edit  View  Call  Transfer  Help
D|☞| ☜|⬚| ◻|🖺| 🖻|
ASA2(config-if)# interface GigabitEthernet0/1
ASA2(config-if)# no shutdown
ASA2(config-if)# nameif inside
INFO: Security level for "inside" set to 100 by default.
ASA2(config-if)# security-level 100
ASA2(config-if)# ip address 192.168.20.1 255.255.255.0
ASA2(config-if)# _

Connected 0:09:01    Auto detect    9600 8-N-1    SCROLL   CAPS   NUM   Capture   Print echo
```

9.3.3.3 Step 3: Define the Traffic that Must Be Protected

To protect the traffic between the two sites, create an access list on the Al-Ain site ASA by typing the following command:

```
ASA1 (config-if)# access-list PROXY_ACL extended
permit ip 192.168.10.0 255.255.255.0 192.168.20.0
255.255.255.0
```

Next, create an access list at the Dubai site ASA by typing the following command:

```
ASA2 (config-if)# access-list PROXY_ACL extended
permit ip 192.168.20.0 255.255.255.0 192.168.10.0
255.255.255.0
```

9.3.3.4 Step 4: Create a Static Route from the Al-Ain site to the Dubai site, and vice versa

To allow the Al-Ain site to communicate with the remote site, there should be a routing process because of the distance between the sites. Specify the gateway, which is ASA2, to the remote network address using the following command:

```
ASA1(config)# route outside 192.168.20.0 255.255.255.0 10.1.1.2 1_
```

To allow the Dubai site to communicate with the remote site, configure a similar static route, as in the following command:

```
ASA2(config)# route outside 192.168.10.0 255.255.255.0 10.1.1.1 1
ASA2(config)# _
```

9.3.3.5 Step 5: Enable IKE Protocol at Both Sites

To allow negotiation to occur between the two sites, enable IKE. It is a protocol that offers procedures of authentication between the communicated peers, generating keys and management for security association. Enter the following command for the Al-Ain site:

```
ASA1(config)# isakmp enable outside_
```

Similarly, for the Dubai site, repeat the same command:

```
ASA2(config)# isakmp enable outside
ASA2(config)# _
```

9.3.3.6 Step 6: Define the Phase 1 Parameters of IKE

To set the IKE parameters of the Al-Ain site, define the authentication methods, encryption, hash, Diffie–Hellman group, and lifetime as in the following:

```
Configuration - HyperTerminal
File  Edit  View  Call  Transfer  Help
ASA1(config)# isakmp policy 10 authentication pre-share
ASA1(config)# isakmp policy 10 encryption 3des
ASA1(config)# isakmp policy 10 hash md5
ASA1(config)# isakmp policy 10 group 2
ASA1(config)# isakmp policy 10 lifetime 86400_

Connected 0:22:49    Auto detect    9600 8-N-1    SCROLL    CAPS    NUM    Capture    Print echo
```

To set the IKE parameters for the Dubai site, repeat the above commands for the Dubai site:

```
Configuration - HyperTerminal
File  Edit  View  Call  Transfer  Help
ASA2(config)# isakmp policy 10 authentication pre-share
ASA2(config)# isakmp policy 10 encryption 3des
ASA2(config)# isakmp policy 10 hash md5
ASA2(config)# isakmp policy 10 group 2
ASA2(config)# isakmp policy 10 lifetime 86400_

Connected 0:20:42    Auto detect    9600 8-N-1    SCROLL    CAPS    NUM    Capture    Print echo
```

9.3.3.7 Step 7: Define the Pre-Shared Key that Will Be Used by Both Sites

Set the pre-shared key, which is a secret value that is exchanged in advance between the participants before any communication occurs. It is used for authentication between the two devices. To achieve this, type the following commands:

```
Configuration - HyperTerminal
File  Edit  View  Call  Transfer  Help
ASA1(config)# tunnel-group 10.1.1.2 type ipsec-l2l
ASA1(config)# tunnel-group 10.1.1.2 ipsec-attributes
ASA1(config-ipsec)# pre-shared-key CISCO
ASA1(config-ipsec)# _

Connected 0:26:41    Auto detect    9600 8-N-1    SCROLL    CAPS    NUM    Capture    Print echo
```

Be sure to use the same pre-shared key for the Dubai site as in the following commands:

```
ASA2(config)# tunnel-group 10.1.1.1 type ipsec-l2l
ASA2(config)# tunnel-group 10.1.1.1 ipsec-attributes
ASA2(config-ipsec)# pre-shared-key CISCO_
```

9.3.3.8 Step 8: Define the IKE Phase 2 Parameters of the IPsec Protocol

In this phase, negotiation of SA parameters and the match of the parameters between the peers take place. The parameters are encrypted using 3DES and authenticated using MD5 for Al-Ain.

```
ASA1(config-ipsec)# crypto ipsec transform-set 3DES_MD5 esp-3des esp-md5-hmac_
```

Similarly for the Dubai site, enter the same commands:

```
ASA2(config-ipsec)# crypto ipsec transform-set 3DES_MD5 esp-3des esp-md5-hmac
ASA2(config)# _
```

9.3.3.9 Step 9: Bind the Parameters of the Two Phases with Each Other

Use the "crypto map" command to bind the parameters of the two phases for the Al-Ain site. The "crypto map" defines the proxy-ACL, which identifies the protected traffic, the peer IP address, and phases transform set as in the following commands:

```
Configuration - HyperTerminal
File  Edit  View  Call  Transfer  Help
ASA1(config)# crypto map VPN 10 match address PROXY_ACL
ASA1(config)# crypto map VPN 10 set peer 10.1.1.2
ASA1(config)# crypto map VPN 10 set transform-set 3DES_MD5
ASA1(config)# _
Connected 0:32:33    Auto detect    9600 8-N-1    SCROLL    CAPS    NUM    Capture    Print echo
```

On the Dubai site, define another crypto map:

```
Configuration - HyperTerminal
File  Edit  View  Call  Transfer  Help
ASA2(config)# crypto map VPN 10 match address PROXY_ACL
ASA2(config)# crypto map VPN 10 set peer 10.1.1.1
ASA2(config)# crypto map VPN 10 set transform-set 3DES_MD5
ASA2(config)# _
Connected 0:29:54    Auto detect    9600 8-N-1    SCROLL    CAPS    NUM    Capture    Print echo
```

9.3.3.10 Step 10: Apply the Crypto Map on the Outside Interface (GigabitEthernet 0/0)

For the crypto map to function, it must be applied to the outside interface as in the following command on Al-Ain site:

```
Configuration - HyperTerminal
File  Edit  View  Call  Transfer  Help
ASA1(config)# crypto map VPN interface outside_
Connected 0:33:34    Auto detect    9600 8-N-1    SCROLL    CAPS    NUM    Capture    Print echo
```

Apply the crypto map on the outside interface of ASA2 on the Dubai site as in the following:

```
Configuration - HyperTerminal
File  Edit  View  Call  Transfer  Help
ASA2(config)# crypto map VPN interface outside_
Connected 0:31:57    Auto detect    9600 8-N-1    SCROLL    CAPS    NUM    Capture    Print echo
```

9.3.3.11 Step 11: Ping from the Al-Ain Site to the Dubai Site, and vice versa

To test the tunnel establishment, ping from Al-Ain to Dubai as in the following:

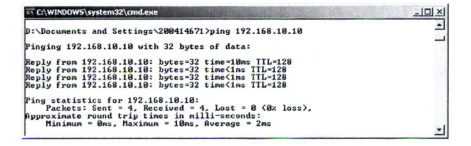

Next, ping from the Dubai site to the Al-Ain site as in the following:

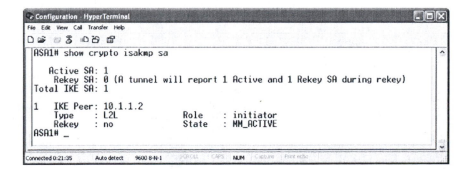

9.3.3.12 Step 12: Study the Parameters that Are Set in the Security Association

Use the "show crypto isakmp sa" command on the Al-Ain site to display the negotiated IKE phase 1 SA parameters, as in the following:

```
ASA1# show crypto isakmp sa

   Active SA: 1
     Rekey SA: 0 (A tunnel will report 1 Active and 1 Rekey SA during rekey)
Total IKE SA: 1

1   IKE Peer: 10.1.1.2
     Type    : L2L         Role    : initiator
     Rekey   : no          State   : MM_ACTIVE
ASA1# _
```

The previous command indicates that the number of active security associations is one. The IKE peer 10.1.1.2 is the gateway for the remote peer (Dubai site). The connection type is a LAN-to-LAN connection. The role of the Al-Ain appliance is that of an initiator of the connection with the remote peer.

The output of the same command on the Dubai site is the following:

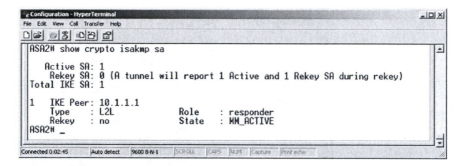

To display the IKE phase 2 security association, type the following command for the Al-Ain site: "show crypto ipsec sa".

```
Configuration - HyperTerminal
File  Edit  View  Call  Transfer  Help

ASA1# show crypto ipsec sa

      access-list PROXY_ACL permit ip 192.168.10.0 255.255.255.0 192.168.20.0 25
5.255.255.0
      local ident (addr/mask/prot/port): (192.168.10.0/255.255.255.0/0/0)
      remote ident (addr/mask/prot/port): (192.168.20.0/255.255.255.0/0/0)
      current_peer: 10.1.1.2

      #pkts encaps: 11, #pkts encrypt: 11, #pkts digest: 11
      #pkts decaps: 10, #pkts decrypt: 10, #pkts verify: 10
      #pkts compressed: 0, #pkts decompressed: 0
      #pkts not compressed: 11, #pkts comp failed: 0, #pkts decomp failed: 0
      #send errors: 0, #recv errors: 0

      local crypto endpt.: 10.1.1.1, remote crypto endpt.: 10.1.1.2

      path mtu 1500, ipsec overhead 58, media mtu 1500
      current outbound spi: AE650A1B

    inbound esp sas:
      spi: 0x5F78A223 (1601741347)
         transform: esp-3des esp-md5-hmac none
         in use settings ={L2L, Tunnel, }
         slot: 0, conn_id: 1, crypto-map: VPN
         sa timing: remaining key lifetime (kB/sec): (3824999/28048)
<--- More --->_

Connected 0:25:08      Auto detect    9600 8-N-1    SCROLL   CAPS   NUM   Capture   Print echo
```

```
 Configuration - HyperTerminal                                    _ □ X
File  Edit  View  Call  Transfer  Help
 D ☞  ☜ ⅋  ⏚ 🗐 ☞
         IV size: 8 bytes
         replay detection support: Y
     outbound esp sas:
       spi: 0xAE650A1B (2925857307)
           transform: esp-3des esp-md5-hmac none
           in use settings =(L2L, Tunnel, )
           slot: 0, conn_id: 1, crypto-map: VPN
           sa timing: remaining key lifetime (kB/sec): (3824999/27998)
           IV size: 8 bytes
           replay detection support: Y

ASA1# _

Connected 0:25:53      Auto detect   9600 8-N-1    SCROLL    CAPS   NUM   Capture  Print echo
```

The output of the above command indicates that the number of encapsulated, encrypted, and digested packets is 11. The number of decapsulated, decrypted, and verified packets is 10. The number of compressed and decompressed packets is 0. The IPsec mode is the tunnel mode. There are two SAs, one inbound and one outbound. Every SA has its own SPI. A similar output will appear for the Dubai site, as in the following:

```
 Configuration - HyperTerminal                                    _ □ X
File  Edit  View  Call  Transfer  Help
 D ☞  ☜ ⅋  ⏚ 🗐 ☞
ASA2# show crypto ipsec sa
interface: outside
     Crypto map tag: VPN, seq num: 10, local addr: 10.1.1.2

       access-list PROXY_ACL permit ip 192.168.20.0 255.255.255.0 192.168.10.0 25
5.255.255.0
       local ident (addr/mask/prot/port): (192.168.20.0/255.255.255.0/0/0)
       remote ident (addr/mask/prot/port): (192.168.10.0/255.255.255.0/0/0)
       current_peer: 10.1.1.1

       #pkts encaps: 10, #pkts encrypt: 10, #pkts digest: 10
       #pkts decaps: 11, #pkts decrypt: 11, #pkts verify: 11
       #pkts compressed: 0, #pkts decompressed: 0
       #pkts not compressed: 10, #pkts comp failed: 0, #pkts decomp failed: 0
       #send errors: 0, #recv errors: 0

       local crypto endpt.: 10.1.1.2, remote crypto endpt.: 10.1.1.1

       path mtu 1500, ipsec overhead 58, media mtu 1500
       current outbound spi: 5F78A223

     inbound esp sas:
       spi: 0xAE650A1B (2925857307)
           transform: esp-3des esp-md5-hmac none
           in use settings =(L2L, Tunnel, )
           slot: 0, conn_id: 1, crypto-map: VPN
           sa timing: remaining key lifetime (kB/sec): (4274999/27546)
<--- More --->_

Connected 0:04:23      Auto detect   9600 8-N-1    SCROLL    CAPS   NUM   Capture  Print echo
```

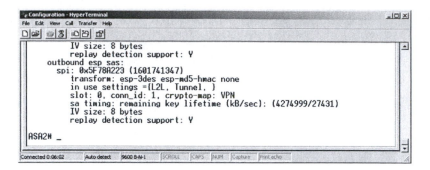

To view more details of the VPN tunnel, type the following command for both sites:

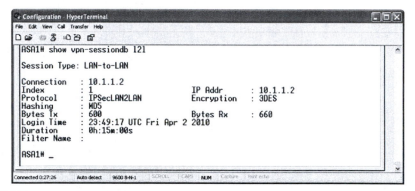

Several parameters of the session that occurred between the peers are displayed, such as Session Type: LAN-to-LAN. The connection is established with the other peer 10.1.1.2. The encryption and hashing algorithms are displayed, and the login time and the duration of the session are also displayed. Similar output can be obtained for the Dubai site as in the following:

9.4 Chapter Summary

IPsec VPN solutions implementation can be a very tedious task. Consequently, making the VPN part of the network security solutions is a challenging task for the beginner and even for the intermediate security engineer. Accordingly, a key objective of this chapter was to explain VPN implementation as clearly as possible using various illustrations, screenshots, and configuration steps. This chapter provided a basic overview of VPN technology and briefly explained how it works. In addition, it presented a comparison between IKE protocol phases, IPsec modes, IPsec protocols, and VPN types. The chapter focused mainly on site-to-site IPsec VPN architecture. The deployment scenarios and implementation guidelines were explained using security products from two leaders in the field, namely, Juniper Networks and Cisco Microsystems.

Chapter 10

Remote Access VPN Tunnel Implementation against Eavesdropping Attacks

10.1 Introduction

Any time and anywhere, connectivity, which enables seamless communication, is an important catalyst for successful business and scientific solutions. There is an increasing demand for this kind of connectivity, but there is also growing concern about the privacy of information in such networks. As this demand is being met, information security and privacy are an evident challenge that must be effectively tackled. The Remote Access IPsec VPN (Virtual Private Network) is increasingly proving to be the most effective solution for data privacy on the Internet. This chapter provides a comprehensive explanation of the Remote Access IPsec VPN security solution that allows remote users behind a remote VPN client to access data and network resources of a central site securely through a VPN tunnel. Being an Internet-based technology, it offers a scalable, low-cost, anywhere and any time solution for small, medium, and large businesses.

The Remote Access VPN is crucial for any enterprise network security design, mainly because of the growing off-site applications that require secure access to critical in-house network resources. A typical use case of the Remote Access IPsec VPN is when employees want to access their office computers while traveling. Despite secure access to network resources that the Remote Access VPN provides, it often opens the door to serious threats. A possible infiltration method is when an infected remote system compromises the security measures of the protected network. Consequently, "Network Admission Control" (NAC) or compliance scanning is performed on the remote user machine. This ensures that the machine is free of malware or any malicious code and is fully compliant with the protected network's security policies. Additionally, the VPN encrypted traffic is treated as trusted traffic and therefore it bypasses the protected network firewall security policies by default. To combat this threat, a firewall must be installed after the VPN gateway to execute the security policies on the VPN decrypted traffic. This necessitates having the VPN solution as part of a comprehensive security solution that also includes a firewall and intrusion protection system.

As in the previous chapter, two Remote Access IPsec VPN solutions are implemented here. This gives a clear idea about the main components involved in the VPN tunnel set-up process.

The following hardware and software tools are needed to complete the configuration tasks:

■ Juniper Networks SSG20 Wireless Appliance[*]: VPN gateway
■ Juniper Networks Remote Access VPN Client[†]: VPN client

---

[*] http://www.juniper.net
[†] http://www.juniper.net

■ Cisco Microsystems ASA Appliance*: VPN gateway
■ Cisco Microsystems Remote Access VPN Client†: VPN client

10.2 Lab 10.1: Remote Access VPN — First Implementation

10.2.1 Outcome

The learning objective of this exercise is for students to learn how to implement Remote Access VPN using Juniper technology.

10.2.2 Description

Unlike site-to-site VPNs, which require at least two VPN gateways, the two main components that constitute the Remote Access IPsec VPN network are a software component called the Remote Access VPN client and a VPN gateway, also called a Remote Access VPN server.

First, the software component called the Remote Access VPN client is installed successfully on the client machine before any attempt is made to connect to the central site network. The basic role of the VPN client is to receive security policies from the second component (the VPN server). Current desktop operating systems such as Windows, Linux, Macintosh, and Solaris provide a built-in version of the remote VPN client. Here, we use Juniper software for the VPN client. A significant advantage of using a Remote Access VPN is that the set-up and configuration of a Remote Access VPN client are extremely minimal.

The second component, which is the VPN gateway (server), is usually a hardware component. Its role is very similar to the VPN gateway of the site-to-site VPN; however, it requires the

---

* http://www.cisco.com
† http://www.cisco.com

remote user to provide the necessary authentication credentials before establishing the VPN tunnel.

The configuration steps of both Remote Access VPN components are explained in the "Experiment" section (Section 10.2.3). In addition, the necessary testing procedures are conducted to confirm that the VPN tunnel is established and working as desired.

10.2.3 Experiment

The configuration steps for the Remote Access VPN are conducted using Juniper NetScreen SSG20 running ScreenOS 5.4.0r1.0 and Juniper NetScreen Remote VPN Client.

The next figure illustrates the network architecture of the experiment designed for three users to access the internal network remotely through the VPN as an example. The three users are connected to the "Untrust" zone on Ethernet0/3.

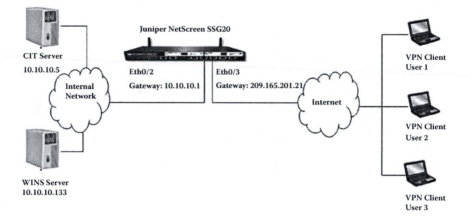

The experiment consists of the following steps:

Step 1: Reset the firewall to the default setting.
Step 2: Assign IP addresses of the machines and the firewall interfaces.
Step 3: Create users.

Step 4: Configure the phase 1 proposal.

Step 5: Configure the phase 2 proposal.

Step 6: Create the security policy.

Step 7: Configure the NetScreen remote VPN client and test the connectivity.

Step 8: Verify VPN tunnel establishment.

10.2.3.1 Step 1: Reset the Firewall to the Default Setting

Refer to Step 1 in the first lab for Site-to-Site VPN (Lab 9.1) using the Juniper network firewall.

10.2.3.2 Step 2: Assign IP Addresses to the Machines and the Firewall Interface

Refer to Step 1 in the first lab for site-to-site VPN (Lab 9.1) using the Juniper network firewall until the screen for configuring the firewall is displayed.

Here, IP addresses are assigned to the firewall interface. First, click on "Network," then "Interfaces," and finally "Lists" to view the screen shown in the following.

Name	IP/Netmask	Zone	Type	Link	PPPoE	Configure
bgroup0	192.168.1.1/24	Trust	Layer3	Up	-	Edit
ethernet0/2				Up	-	Edit
ethernet0/3				Down	-	Edit
ethernet0/4				Down	-	Edit
bgroup1	0.0.0.0/0	Null	Unused	Down	-	Edit
bgroup2	0.0.0.0/0	Null	Unused	Down	-	Edit
bgroup3	0.0.0.0/0	Null	Unused	Down	-	Edit

Network > Interfaces (List) — ssg20-wlan. List 20 per page. List ALL(12) Interfaces. Activate Wireless Changes. New / Tunnel IF. Juniper. Home, Configuration, Wireless, Network (Binding, DNS, Zones, Interfaces, List).

The default IP address assigned to the bgroup0 interface is 192.168.1.1. Before assigning the IP addresses to the interfaces, the Ethernet interfaces are split into different "bgroups" as shown next.

Name	IP/Netmask	Zone	Type	Link	PPPoE	Configure
bgroup0	192.168.1.1/24	Trust	Layer3	Up	-	Edit
ethernet0/2				Up	-	Edit
bgroup1	0.0.0.0/0	Null	Unused	Down	-	Edit
ethernet0/3				Down	-	Edit
bgroup2	0.0.0.0/0	Null	Unused	Down	-	Edit
ethernet0/4				Down	-	Edit
bgroup3	0.0.0.0/0	Null	Unused	Down	-	Edit
ethernet0/0	0.0.0.0/0	Untrust	Layer3	Down	-	Edit
ethernet0/1	0.0.0.0/0	DMZ	Layer3	Down	-	Edit
serial0/0	0.0.0.0/0	Null	Unused	Down	-	Edit
vlan1	0.0.0.0/0	VLAN	Layer3	Down	-	Edit
wireless0/0	192.168.2.1/24	Trust	Layer3	Down	-	Edit
wireless0/1	0.0.0.0/0	Null	Unused	Down	-	Edit
wireless0/2	0.0.0.0/0	Null	Unused	Down	-	Edit
wireless0/3	0.0.0.0/0	Null	Unused	Down	-	Edit

Click on the "Edit" link of the bgroup0 interface and fill in the values as shown next. Make sure to have the zone name as "Trust" and the interface mode as "NAT." Enable the services to use in this zone (for example, WebUI), which allows the user to access the firewall configuration using the Web user interface through eth0/2. Confirm the setting by clicking "Apply" and then "OK."

After the interface IP address is changed, Juniper's WebUI automatically logs out. Therefore, change the PC IP address to 10.10.10.2/24 to maintain connectivity, as shown in the following.

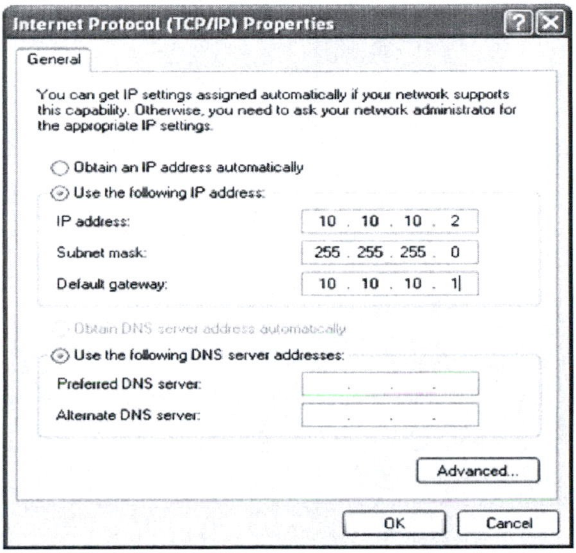

Use a Web browser to navigate to http://10.10.10.1 to access the Web user interface. Select "Network," then "Interfaces," and finally "List," which displays the screen shown next.

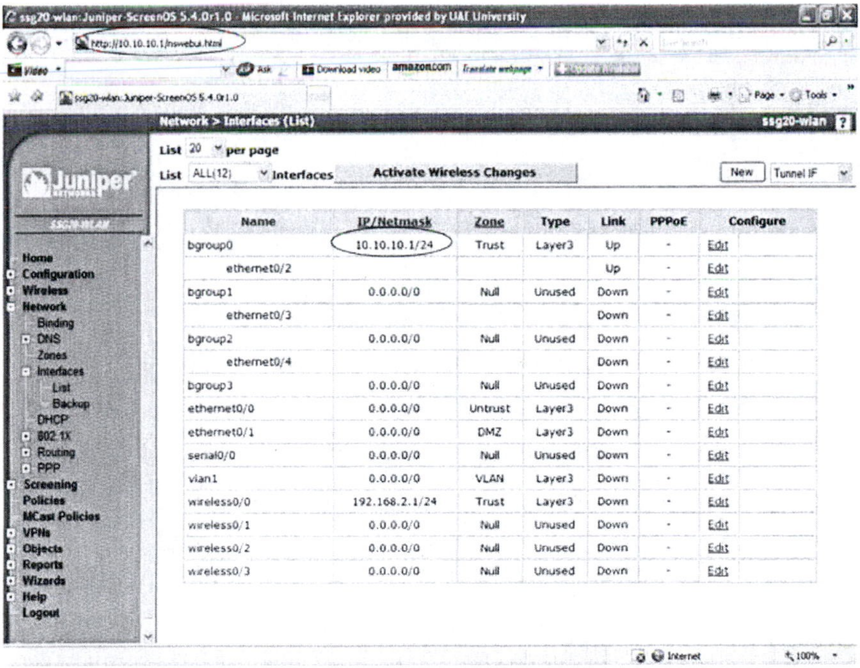

Click on the "Edit" link of the bgroup1 interface and fill in the values as shown in the following . The zone name is "Untrust" where the remote users are trying to access the trusted zone through the VPN tunnel that will be created. Enable the services to use in this zone by clicking "Apply" and then "OK." The configured IP addresses are assigned to the interfaces eth0/2 and eth0/3.

To create the network IP address of the server that the remote users will connect to, navigate to "Objects," then "Address," and finally "List.". Click on "New", as indicated in the following.

Fill in the values as shown in next. Give the address a name, which is "CIT" in our example, so that it facilitates choosing the destination address during policy setting. Then enter the IP address and the Netmask, and finally select "Trust" zone from the drop-down menu and confirm by clicking "OK."

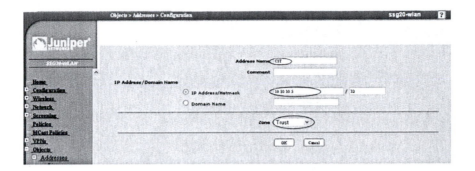

10.2.3.3 Step 3: Create Users

To create the users for remote connection over the VPN, navigate to "Objects," then "Users," and finally "Local." Click on "New" as indicated in the following.

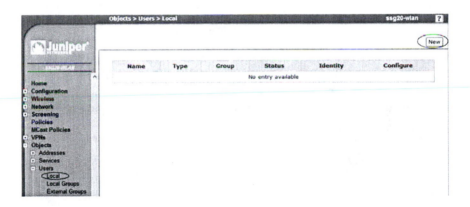

NetScreen provides various types of users, and each type has its own features. Enter the username and enable the status for the user. Next, select the user type, which is "IKE User" that uses the local database provided by the NetScreen device. Select the "Simple Identity" option and enter the Identity of the user, which is "CITUser@cit.com." Confirm the settings by clicking "OK" as shown in the following.

Now create two more users with XAuth type, to ensure that users are challenged to authenticate themselves with the user-name and password for establishing a connection. The screens are shown in the next two screenshots for the first and second XAuth users.

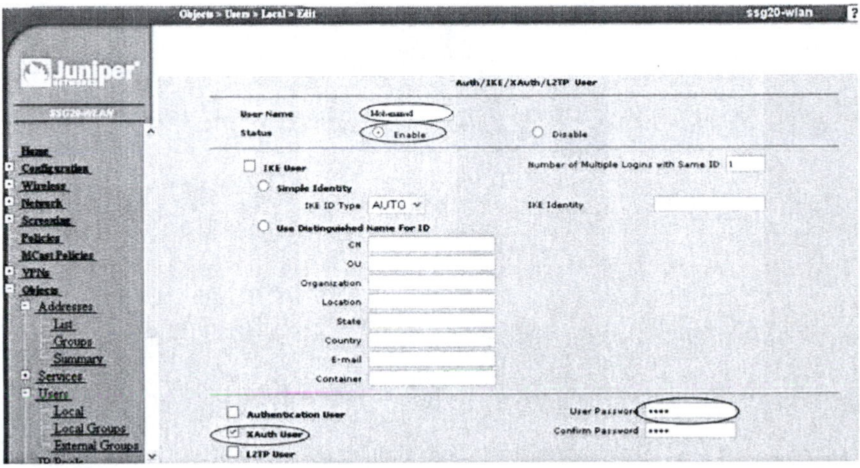

Next, create a group for the users that were created. Navigate to "Objects" and then "User Groups," and finally "Local." Provide a group name and then select the members in the "Available Members" area and add them to the text area of "Group Members." Confirm by clicking "OK" as shown in the next screenshot

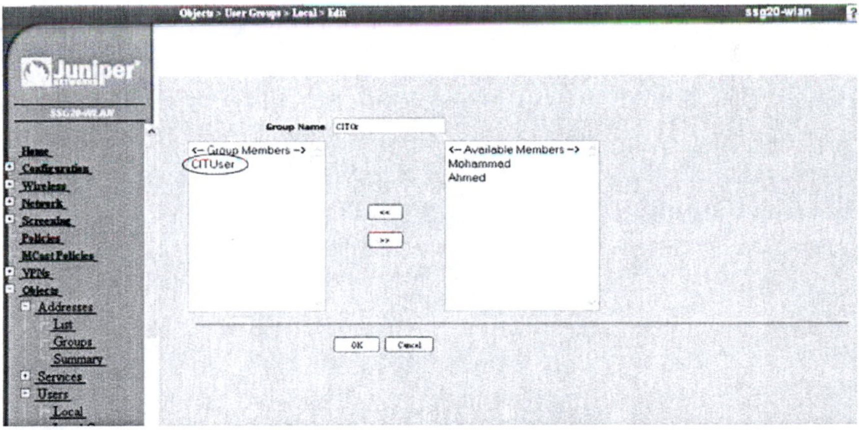

The group is created with its members as shown in the following.

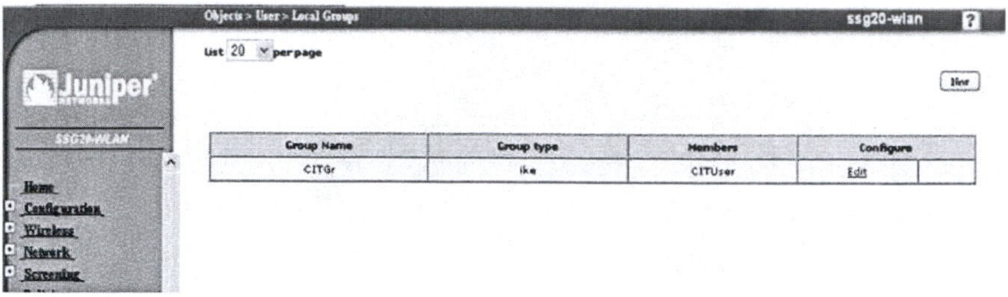

10.2.3.4 Step 4: Configure the Phase 1 Proposal

To create the phase 1 proposal, as indicated in the next screenshot, first navigate to "VPNs," then "AutoKey Advanced," and next "Gateway" (AutoKey is the automated key exchange and negotiation with certificate or pre-shared key used by the Internet Key Exchange protocol). Next, click on "New" and type the name of the gateway. Choose the security level as "Custom" and also choose the type of the remote gateway as "Dialup User Group"; then select the group from the drop-down menu. Provide a pre-shared key ("12345678" in our example). Select the outgoing interface, which is the "Untrust" interface (bgroub1) (see next screen).

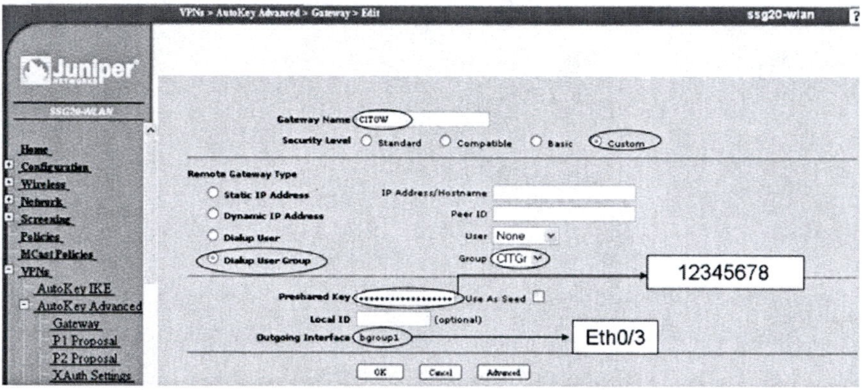

Next, click on the "Advanced" button; the resulting screen is shown in the following (i.e., VPN gateway advanced configure Phase 1).

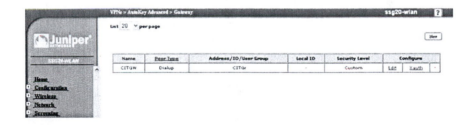

Specify phase 1 parameters by choosing "Custom" as the security level. Next, choose the proposal of phase 1 from the drop-down menu. It consists of three algorithms. The first one is Diffie–Hellman Group 2, which is used for the agreement on the secret key between the two ends. The second algorithm is 3DES, which is used for encryption purposes. The third algorithm is SHA, which is used for authentication purposes. Select the aggressive mode and click "Return"; then confirm by clicking "OK" to complete the steps of phase 1 creation as shown below (VPN gateway phase 1 completed).

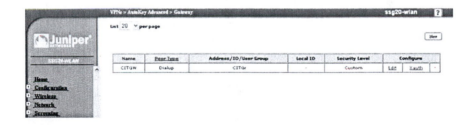

Because Xauth users are configured, the Xauth server must be enabled. To enable this, click on the "Xauth" link and select "XauthServer"; then select "Local Authentication" and select the "Allow Any" option. Confirm by clicking "OK." The Xauth server settings are shown below.

10.2.3.5 Step 5: Configure the Phase 2 Proposal

As illustrated in the following phase 2 basic configuration, create the phase 2 proposal by navigating to "VPNs" and then "AutoKey IKE" and click on "New." Type the VPN name as "CITVPN" and Select "Custom" as the security level. Select "Predefined" for Remote Gateway and then choose the gateway from the drop-down menu.

Next, click on "Advanced"; the resulting screen (the VPN gateway phase 2 advanced configuration) is

Now specify phase 2 parameters by selecting "Custom" for the security level. Next, choose the phase 2 proposal from the drop-down menu. It consists of an ESP protocol, a 3DES algorithm, and an SHA hash algorithm. Select "Tunnel Zone" for "Bind to"; then select "Untrust" from the drop-down menu. Click "Return" to confirm settings. Next, click "OK" to complete the phase 2 creation as shown below for the VPN gateway phase 2 completed.

10.2.3.6 Step 6: Create the Security Policy

To enable users to connect remotely, a security policy is configured by navigating to "Policies." Then select the "Zones" drop-down menu from "Untrust" to "Trust" and click on "New." Next, complete the entries as shown in the following security policy creation screen.

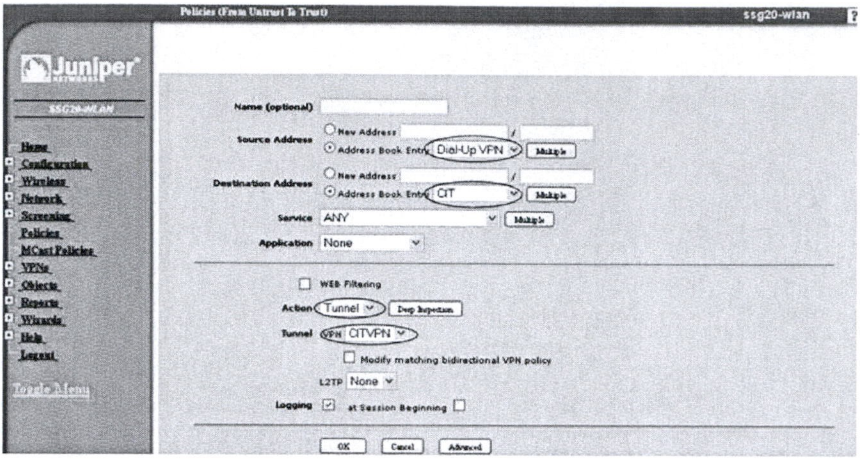

Specify the source address as "Dial-Up VPN" for the remote users, which is the "Untrust" side. Specify the destination address as "CIT," which is the "Trust" side that the remote user will connect to. The action of the policy should be "Tunnel," and the tunnel field is the preconfigured VPN, which is "CITVPN." Confirm settings by clicking "OK."

10.2.3.7 Step 7: Configure the Juniper NetScreen Remote VPN Client and Test the Connectivity

Install the NetScreen remote VPN client software on the client machine and launch the software to configure it. First, click on the "New" connection button and type the name of the connection as "CIT." For the Connection Security area, select the "Secure" option; for the "Remote Party Identity and Addressing," select IP Address as the "ID Type." Then type the IP address. Finally, enable "Use Secure Gateway Tunnel" and type the IP address of the remote gateway. The Juniper NetScreen remote VPN client configuration is shown below.

Now expand the tree of the CIT connection and click on "Security Policy." Choose the "Aggressive Mode" for "Phase 1 Negotiation Mode" to match the VPN gateway configuration.

Select "My Identity" and then choose the "ID Type" as the "E-mail" address from the drop-down menu. Type the e-mail address, which should be identical to the one you configured in the firewall: CITUser@cit.com.

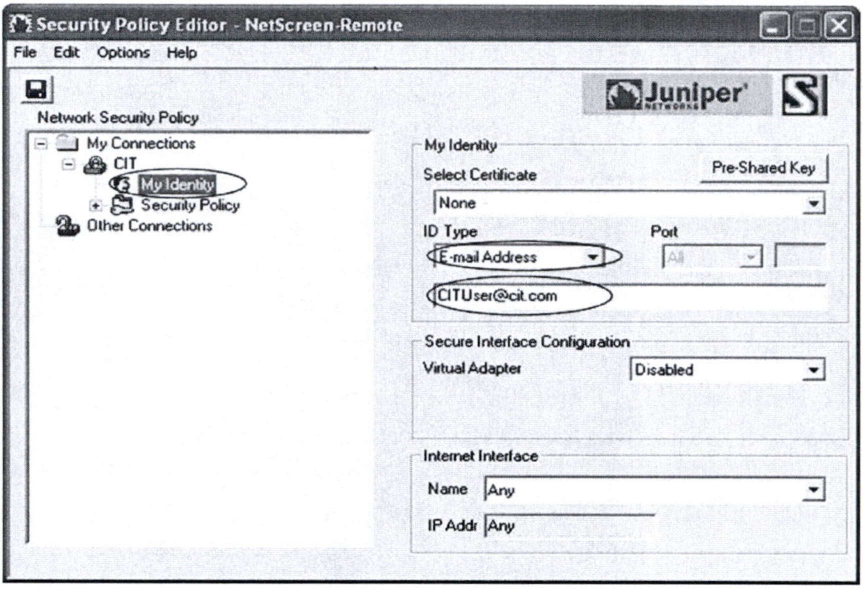

Next, click on the "Pre-shared Key" button, and then enter the key used in the VPN gateway configuration, which was "12345678", and click "OK" to complete the configuration as shown below.

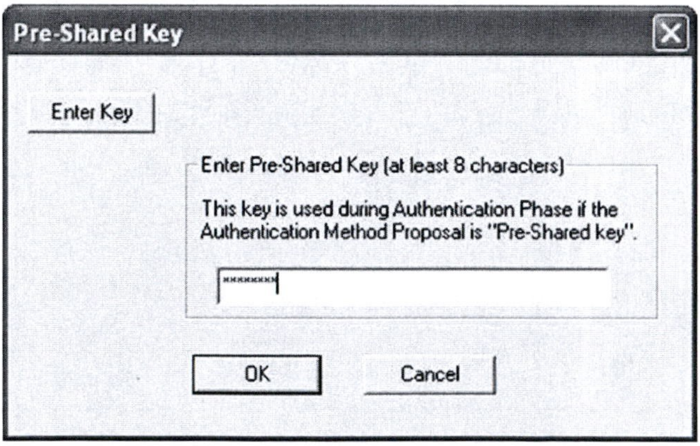

Now select "Security Policy," then "Authentication Phase 1," and finally "Proposal 1." Choose "Pre-shared Key Extended Authentication" for "Authentication Method," and choose "Triple DES" for the encryption algorithm. Then choose "SHA-1" for the Hash algorithm, and finally choose "Diffie-Hellman Group 2" for "Key Group." The choices are shown below.

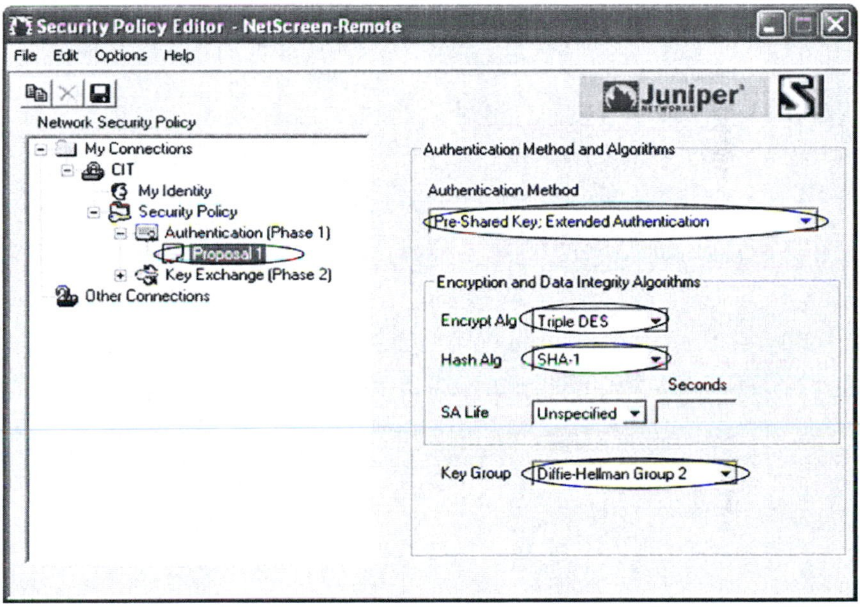

Next, select "Proposal 1" for "Key Exchange (Phase 2)" and enable the encapsulation protocol. Then choose "Triple DES" for the encryption algorithm and choose "SHA-1" for the Hash algorithm. Finally, choose "Tunnel" for Encapsulation, as shown below (Phase 2 Proposal 1).

Create a second proposal in "Key Exchange Phase 2" and enable the encapsulation protocol. Choose "Triple DES" for the encryption algorithm and then choose "MD5" for the hash algorithm. Finally, choose "Tunnel" for Encapsulation as shown in the following (Phase 2 Proposal 2).

Next, create a third proposal in "Key Exchange Phase 2" and enable the encapsulation protocol. Choose "DES" for the encryption algorithm and choose "SHA-1" for the hash algorithm. Finally, choose "Tunnel" for Encapsulation as shown below (Phase 2 Proposal 3).

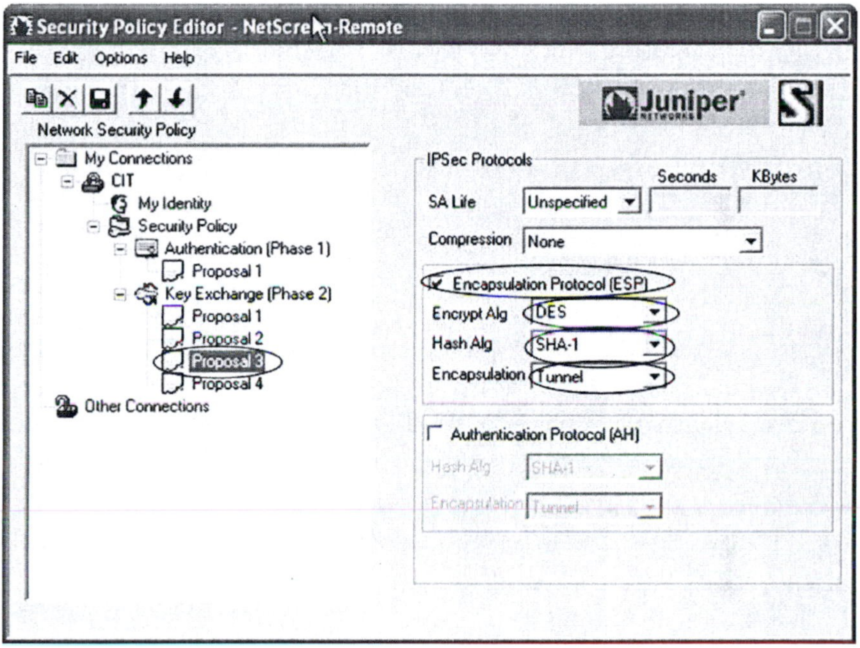

Now create the fourth proposal in "Key Exchange Phase 2" and enable the encapsulation protocol. Choose "DES" for the encryption algorithm and then choose "MD5" for the hash algorithm. Finally, choose "Tunnel" for Encapsulation as shown in the next screen (Phase 2 Proposal 4).

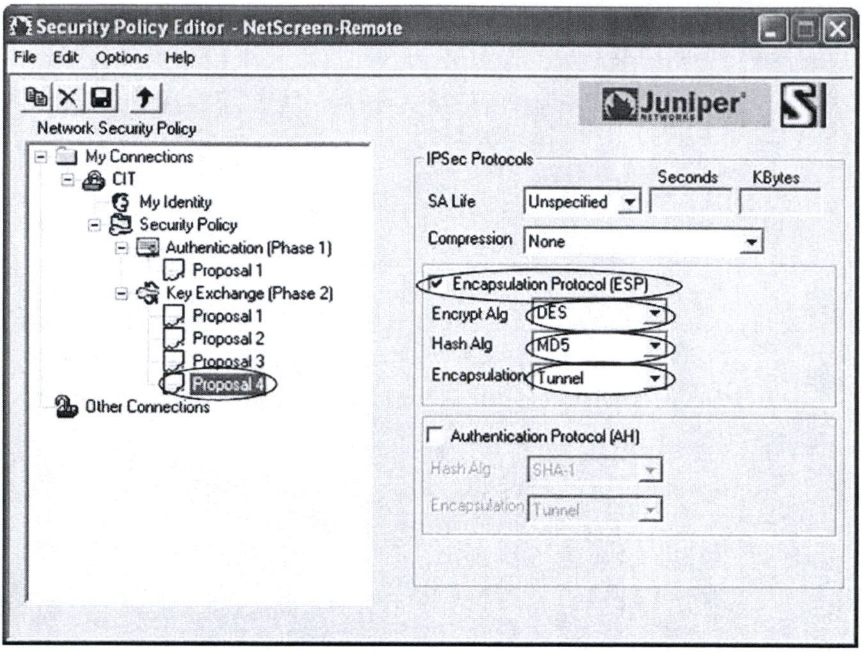

Finally, click on the "Save" icon (the floppy disk icon), then right-click on Juniper NetScreen remote VPN client and select "Connect." A User Authentication window appears, as shown in the following screenshot. Enter the username and password that was configured before (Xauth user configuration) and confirm by clicking "OK" (as shown).

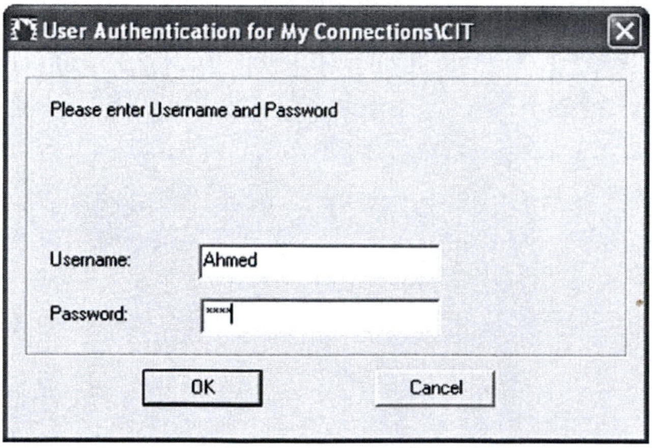

An indication of a successful connection with the remote destination is shown, depicted in the following.

```
┌─────────────────────────────────────────────┐
│ ▣ Manual Connection Status        ─ □ ✕      │
├─────────────────────────────────────────────┤
│                                               │
│  Successfully connected to My Connections\CIT │
│                                               │
│                                               │
│              ┌──────────────┐                 │
│              │      OK      │                 │
│              └──────────────┘                 │
└─────────────────────────────────────────────┘
```

The log viewer records all the negotiations that occurred over the VPN tunnel. The next screen represents the log entries of the remote VPN client. As shown, the initiation of phase 1 started from the remote user who was Ahmed to the gateway 209.165.201.21. Then a response was received from his peer. After exchanging the proposal of phase 1, the second phase started from the remote user (209.165.201.19) to negotiate with his peer on the proposal of the second phase. The last entry indicates the successful connection.

```
┌──────────────────────────────────────────────────────────────────────────────────────┐
│ ▣ Log Viewer - NetScreen-Remote                                          ─ □ ✕        │
├──────────────────────────────────────────────────────────────────────────────────────┤
│  │ Clear │ Freeze │ Save Log │ Print │ Close │                                          │
├──────────────────────────────────────────────────────────────────────────────────────┤
│ 5-11: 22:27:59.940                                                                     │
│ 5-11: 22:27:59.940 My Connections\CIT - Initiating IKE Phase 1 (IP ADDR=209.165.201.21)│
│ 5-11: 22:28:00.191 My Connections\CIT - SENDING>>>> ISAKMP OAK AG (SA, KE, NON, ID, VID 6x) │
│ 5-11: 22:28:00.251 My Connections\CIT - RECEIVED<<< ISAKMP OAK AG (SA, VID 4x, KE, NON, ID, HASH) │
│ 5-11: 22:28:00.251 My Connections\CIT - Peer supports Dead Peer Detection Version 1.0  │
│ 5-11: 22:28:00.251 My Connections\CIT - Dead Peer Detection enabled                    │
│ 5-11: 22:28:00.371 My Connections\CIT - SENDING>>>> ISAKMP OAK AG *(HASH, NOTIFY:STATUS_REPLAY_STATUS, NOTIFY:STATUS_INITIAL_CONTACT) │
│ 5-11: 22:28:00.371 My Connections\CIT - Established IKE SA                             │
│ 5-11: 22:28:00.371 My Connections\CIT -   MY COOKIE 1 ba 7 f5 27 75 f0 9b              │
│ 5-11: 22:28:00.371 My Connections\CIT -   HIS COOKIE 20 31 c8 eb 5c b4 b6 22           │
│ 5-11: 22:28:00.371 My Connections\CIT - RECEIVED<<< ISAKMP OAK TRANS *(HASH, ATTR)     │
│ 5-11: 22:28:06.570 My Connections\CIT - RECEIVED<<< ISAKMP OAK TRANS *(Retransmission) │
│ 5-11: 22:28:12.589 My Connections\CIT - RECEIVED<<< ISAKMP OAK TRANS *(Retransmission) │
│ 5-11: 22:28:18.597 My Connections\CIT - RECEIVED<<< ISAKMP OAK TRANS *(Retransmission) │
│ 5-11: 22:28:24.616 My Connections\CIT - RECEIVED<<< ISAKMP OAK TRANS *(Retransmission) │
│ 5-11: 22:28:30.625 My Connections\CIT - RECEIVED<<< ISAKMP OAK TRANS *(Retransmission) │
│ 5-11: 22:28:36.643 My Connections\CIT - RECEIVED<<< ISAKMP OAK TRANS *(Retransmission) │
│ 5-11: 22:28:42.662 My Connections\CIT - RECEIVED<<< ISAKMP OAK TRANS *(Retransmission) │
│ 5-11: 22:28:48.670 My Connections\CIT - RECEIVED<<< ISAKMP OAK TRANS *(Retransmission) │
│ 5-11: 22:28:54.689 My Connections\CIT - RECEIVED<<< ISAKMP OAK TRANS *(Retransmission) │
│ 5-11: 22:29:00.698 My Connections\CIT - RECEIVED<<< ISAKMP OAK TRANS *(Retransmission) │
│ 5-11: 22:29:06.716 My Connections\CIT - RECEIVED<<< ISAKMP OAK TRANS *(HASH, ATTR)     │
│ 5-11: 22:29:12.735 My Connections\CIT - RECEIVED<<< ISAKMP OAK TRANS *(Retransmission) │
│ 5-11: 22:29:16.460 My Connections\CIT - SENDING>>>> ISAKMP OAK TRANS *(HASH, ATTR)     │
│ 5-11: 22:29:16.470 My Connections\CIT - RECEIVED<<< ISAKMP OAK TRANS *(HASH, ATTR)     │
│ 5-11: 22:29:16.470 My Connections\CIT - IKE Extended Authentication successful.        │
│ 5-11: 22:29:16.470 My Connections\CIT - Setting compliance status to OK.               │
│ 5-11: 22:29:16.470 My Connections\CIT - Calling UpdateBypassRecordsForCompliance - OK  │
│ 5-11: 22:29:16.470 My Connections\CIT - SENDING>>>> ISAKMP OAK TRANS *(HASH, ATTR)     │
│ 5-11: 22:29:16.721 My Connections\CIT - Initiating IKE Phase 2 with Client IDs (message id: 18665A21) │
│ 5-11: 22:29:16.721 My Connections\CIT -   Initiator = IP ADDR=209.165.201.19, prot = 0 port = 0 │
│ 5-11: 22:29:16.721 My Connections\CIT -   Responder = IP ADDR=10.10.10.5, prot = 0 port = 0 │
│ 5-11: 22:29:16.721 My Connections\CIT - SENDING>>>> ISAKMP OAK QM *(HASH, SA, NON, ID 2x) │
│ 5-11: 22:29:16.741 My Connections\CIT - RECEIVED<<< ISAKMP OAK QM *(HASH, SA, NON, ID 2x, NOTIFY:STATUS_RESP_LIFETIME) │
│ 5-11: 22:29:16.741 My Connections\CIT - Filter entry 3 added  SECURE  209.165.201.019&255.255.255.255  010.010.010.005&255.255.255.255  209.165.201.021 │
│ 5-11: 22:29:16.741 My Connections\CIT - SENDING>>>> ISAKMP OAK QM *(HASH)              │
│ 5-11: 22:29:16.741 My Connections\CIT - Loading IPSec SA (Message ID = 18665A21 OUTBOUND SPI = CC9C7EDB INBOUND SPI = D20C07DA) │
│ 5-11: 22:29:16.741                                                                     │
│ ◄                                                                               ►       │
└──────────────────────────────────────────────────────────────────────────────────────┘
```

To see the details of remote VPN tunnel establishment in the firewall appliance, navigate to "Reports," then "System Log," and then "Event" as shown below.

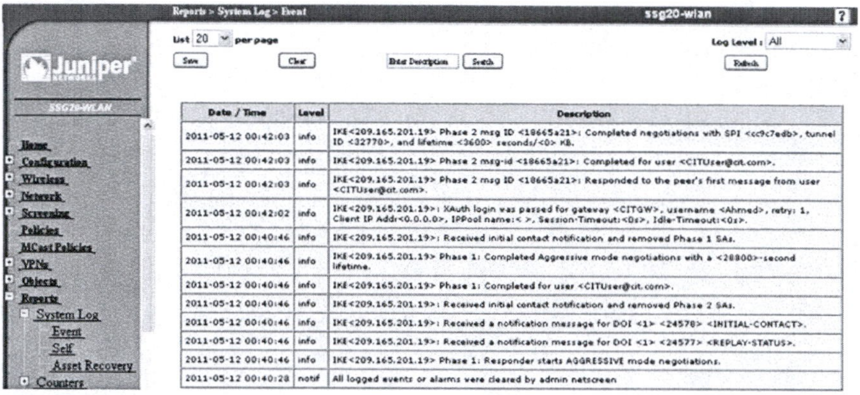

To test the connectivity between the two peers, a ping command to 10.10.10.5 is issued from the remote user machine. The command and reply of the peer are as follows:

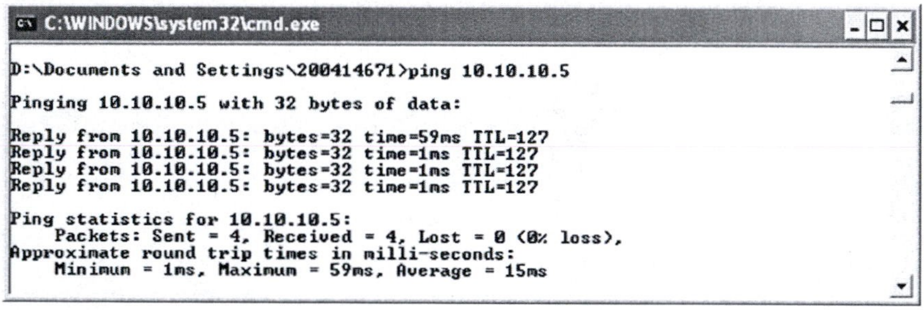

```
D:\Documents and Settings\200414671>ping 10.10.10.5

Pinging 10.10.10.5 with 32 bytes of data:

Reply from 10.10.10.5: bytes=32 time=59ms TTL=127
Reply from 10.10.10.5: bytes=32 time=1ms TTL=127
Reply from 10.10.10.5: bytes=32 time=1ms TTL=127
Reply from 10.10.10.5: bytes=32 time=1ms TTL=127

Ping statistics for 10.10.10.5:
    Packets: Sent = 4, Received = 4, Lost = 0 (0% loss),
Approximate round trip times in milli-seconds:
    Minimum = 1ms, Maximum = 59ms, Average = 15ms
```

To view the ICMP packets resulting from pinging 10.10.10.5, click on "Traffic Log" in the policy window. The resultant screen is:

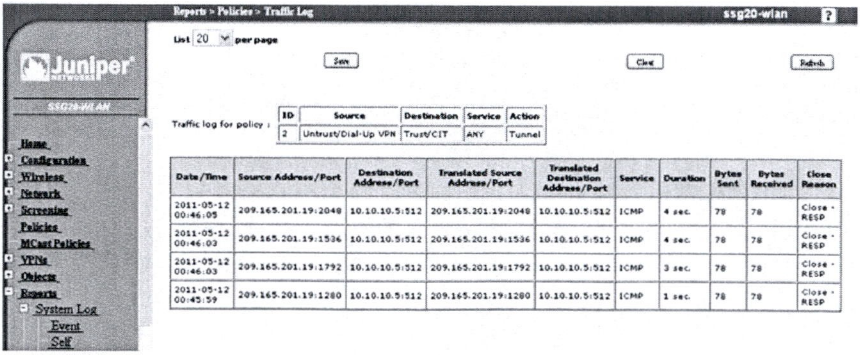

10.2.3.8 *Step 8: Verify VPN Tunnel Establishment*

To analyze tunnel establishment, check the VPN sessions with the following command:

```
Configuration - HyperTerminal                                                _ □ ×
File  Edit  View  Call  Transfer  Help
□ ☞  ●  3  ⅅ  🖹  🖻

ssg20-wlan-> get vpn
Name            Gateway           Mode RPlay 1st Proposal           Monitor Use Cnt
Interface
----------------  ----------------  ----  -----  --------------------  -------  -------
----------
CITVPN          CITGW             tunl No    nopfs-esp-3des-sha    off          1
bgroup1
  Total Auto VPN: 1

Name            Gateway           Interface  Lcl SPI  Rmt SPI  Algorithm         Monitor
  Tunnel ID
----------  ----------------  ----------  --------  --------  -----------------  -------
----------
Total Manual VPN 0
ssg20-wlan-> _

Connected 0:41:32      Auto detect    9600 8-N-1    SCROLL    CAPS   NUM   Capture   Print echo
```

Various parameters are displayed, such as "Name Interface," which is bgroup1 (CITVPN). The "Gateway" appears as "CITGW." The mode is the tunnel mode, which encrypts the IP header and the payload so that the entire packet is protected. The first proposal is nopfs (no perfect forward secrecy), which means that there would be no change of the key in the future. ESP (Encapsulating Security Payload) is the protocol, 3DES is the encryption algorithm, and SHA is the authentication algorithm that is used. The total automatic VPN is 1.

To study the Security Association parameters, type the command "get sa":

```
Configuration - HyperTerminal                                                _ □ ×
File  Edit  View  Call  Transfer  Help
□ ☞  ●  3  ⅅ  🖹  🖻

ssg20-wlan-> get sa
total configured sa: 2
HEX ID      Gateway         Port Algorithm     SPI      Life:sec kb Sta   PID vsys

00000002<         0.0.0.0   500 esp:3des/sha1 00000000 expir unlim I/I     2 0
00000002>         0.0.0.0   500 esp:3des/sha1 00000000 expir unlim I/I    -1 0
00008002< 209.165.201.19    500 esp:3des/sha1 cc9c7edb  3319 unlim A/-     2 0
00008002> 209.165.201.19    500 esp:3des/sha1 d20c07da  3319 unlim A/-    -1 0
ssg20-wlan-> _

Connected 0:41:58      Auto detect    9600 8-N-1    SCROLL    CAPS   NUM   Capture   Print echo
```

The output indicates that the number of configured sa is two. The Gateway IP address is 209.165.201.19 and the IKE UDP port is 500. Algorithms are 3des for encryption and sha-1 for authentication. The SPI is the security parameter index. There are two SPI, one for each sa.

10.3 Lab 10.2: Remote Access VPN — Second Implementation

10.3.1 Outcome

The learning objective of this exercise is for students to learn how to implement Remote Access VPN using Cisco technology.

10.3.2 Description

The scenario for this lab is similar to the one explained in Lab 10.1, with the exception of using different equipment.

10.3.3 Experiment

To explain how to configure Remote Access VPN, an experiment is conducted using the Cisco Adaptive Security appliance and Cisco VPN client.

The following figure shows the network architecture of the experiment. Three users are trying to access the internal network remotely through the VPN tunnel that is configured in the Cisco ASA (Adaptive Security Appliance) running OS 7.0(7). The three users are connected to the outside interface GigabitEthernet0/0.

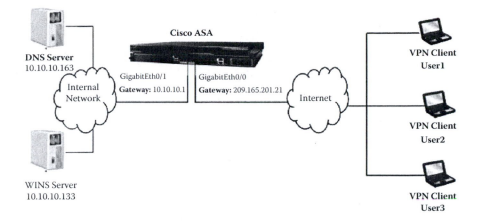

The experiment consists of the following steps:

Step 1: Reset the firewall to the default setting.

Step 2: Assign IP addresses to the machines and the firewall interfaces.

Step 3: Choose the VPN tunnel type that is remote access and select the remote access clients.

Step 4: Specify the VPN tunnel group name and authentication method.

Step 5: Configure user accounts.

Step 6: Configure the pool of addresses.

Step 7: Configure the client attributes.

Step 8: Configure the IKE policy.

Step 9: Configure IPsec encryption and authentication parameters.

Step 10: Address translation exception and split tunneling.

Step 11: Install Cisco VPN client software.

Step 12: Launch the software and test the connectivity.

Step 13: Verify VPN tunnel establishment.

Step 14: Monitor the VPN tunnel in the ASA.

10.3.3.1 Step 1: Reset the Firewall to the Default Setting

To start the exercise, we reset the firewall to the default setting. For this, connect the PC to the serial console of the firewall through the HyperTerminal to get the command line interface of the firewall. Provide the "enable" command at the prompt "ciscoasa>" and then hit the "Enter" key for the password request. Finally, enter the command "configure factory-default".

10.3.3.2 Step 2: Assign IP Addresses to the Machines and the Firewall Interfaces

To assign an IP address to the machines and the firewall, repeat Step 2 in Lab 9.1 of Chapter 9, but with the network parameters shown below.

Complete the IP assignment by clicking the "OK" button and then connect the PC to the management port of the firewall to start the configuration using straight-through cables. Launch a Web browser, and in the URL address field, navigate to https://192.168.1.1 to open the Web user interface (WebUI). The Adaptive Security Device Manager (ADSM) of the ASA is displayed as shown in the following.

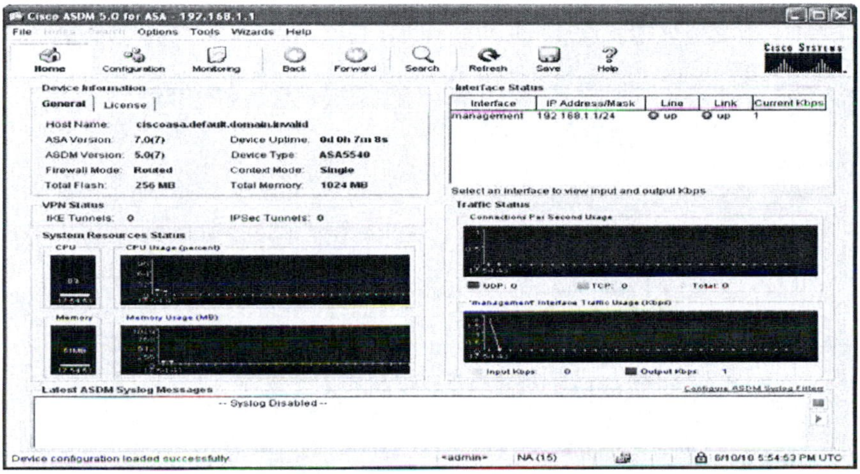

Click on the "Configuration" tab to get a display of all the interfaces of the firewall as shown in next screen.

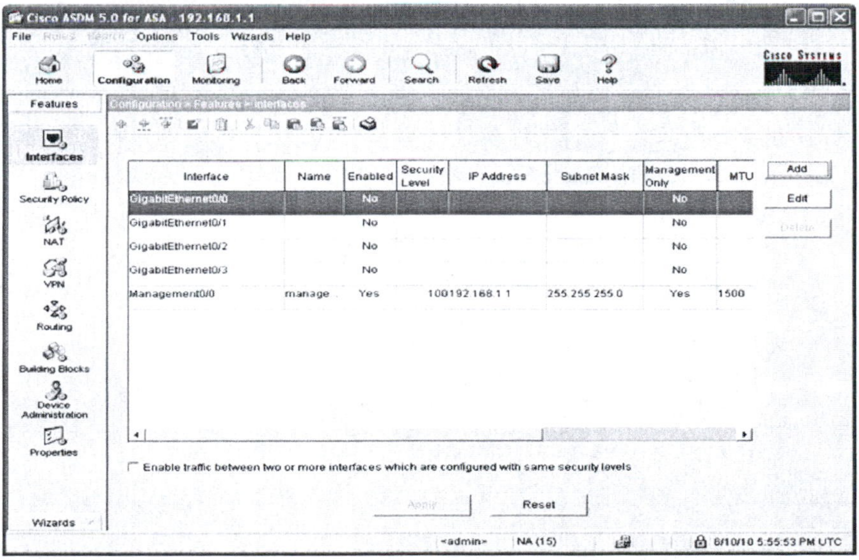

Now, select GigabitEthernet0/0 as the outside interface with a security level of 0, and click the "Edit" button to assign an IP address for it, as shown below.

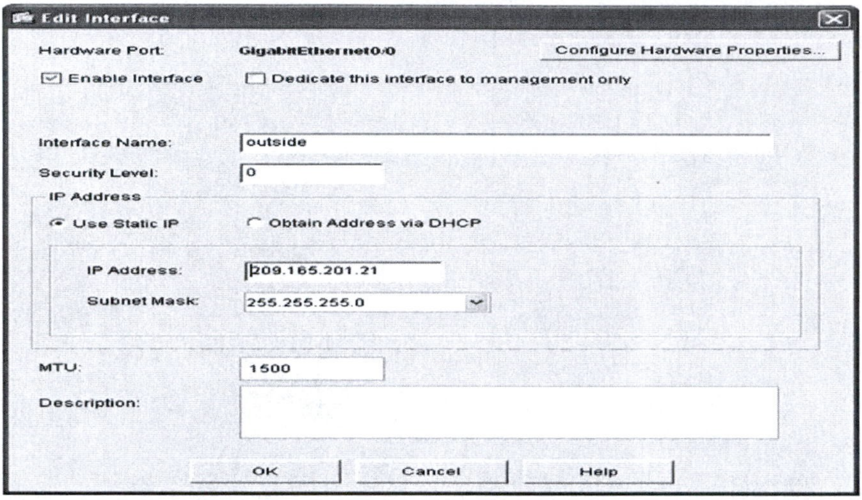

To confirm the setting, click the "OK" button, which ensures that the interface will be assigned to the specified IP address, as shown in the next screen.

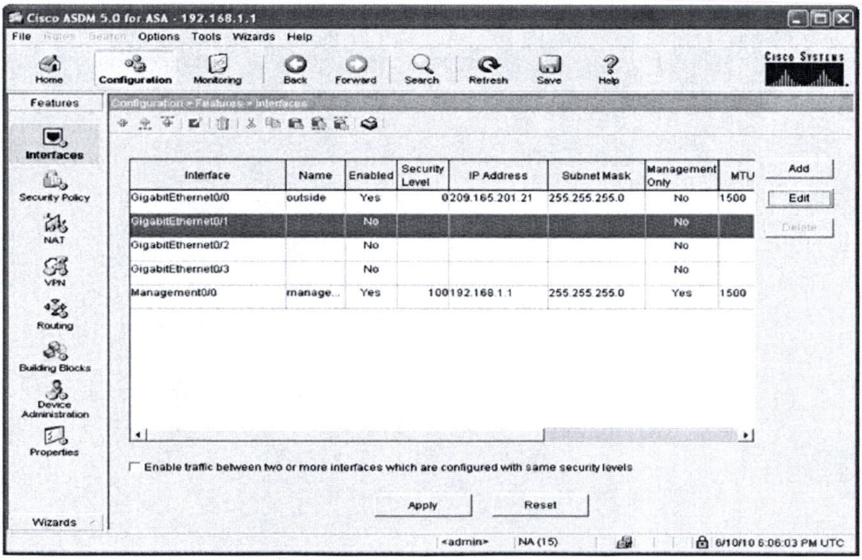

Repeat the previous steps with the interface GigabitEthernet0/1, which will be the inside interface, as shown next.

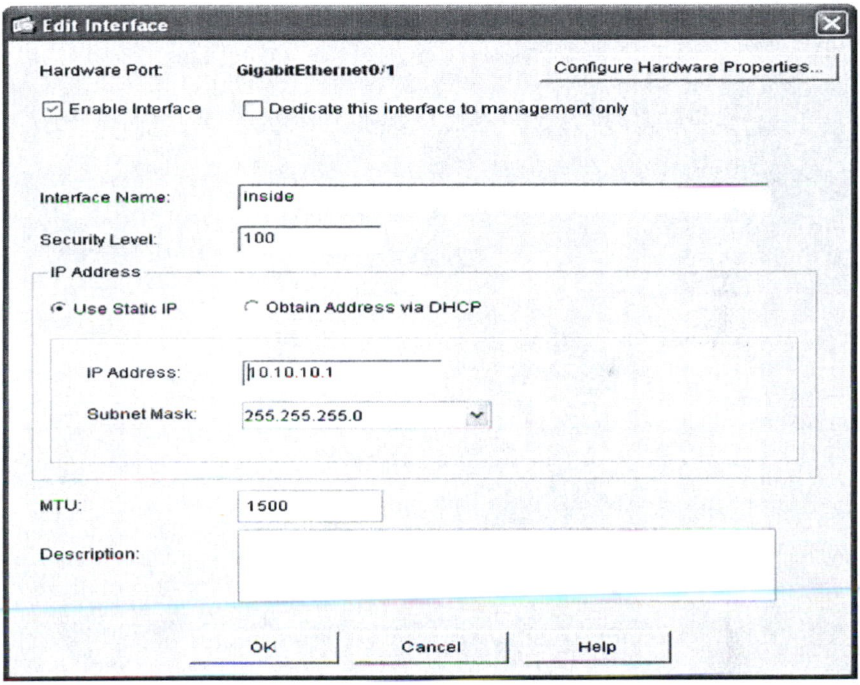

10.3.3.3 Step 3: Choose the VPN Tunnel Type that Is Remote Access and Select the Remote Access Clients

From the wizard's drop-down menu, choose the VPN wizard option, and the window shown below is displayed.

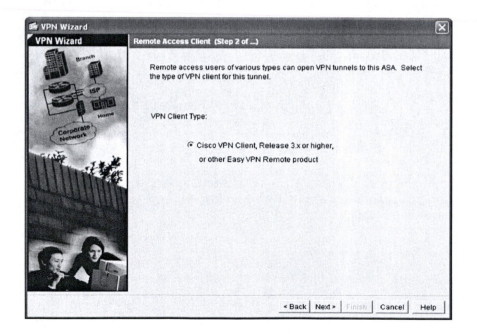

Select "Remote Access" type and choose the outside interface from the drop-down menu as the "VPN Tunnel Interface." Then click on the "Next" button and select "VPN clients" as shown in the next screenshot. Finally, click on the "Next" button.

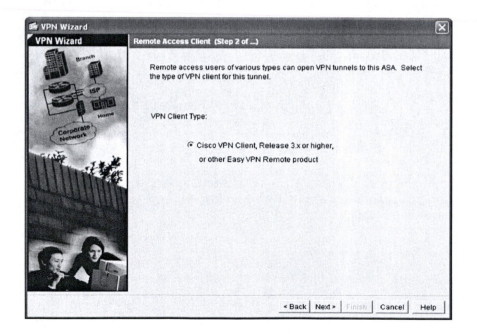

10.3.3.4 Step 4: Specify the VPN Tunnel Group Name and Authentication Method

Type the name of the tunnel group for the remote users and select the pre-shared key option as an authentication method, as shown in the following screenshot.

Click on the "Next" button and specify the user authentication database by clicking on the radio button. In our scenario, we will select the local user database, as shown in the next screenshot, and click "Next."

10.3.3.5 Step 5: Configure User Accounts

Type the username and password to be added to the local authentication database as a new entry; then click on the "Add" button as shown below.

Repeat the previous step if more than one user needs to be configured (as shown in the next screenshot) and click on the "Next" button.

10.3.3.6 Step 6: Configure the Pool of Addresses

Type the pool name or choose a preconfigured one from the drop-down menu. Next, type the start range of the pool and the end of the range, and enter the subnet mask and click "Next" as shown in the following screenshot.

10.3.3.7 Step 7: Configure the Client Attributes

Enter the optional network configuration information that would be pushed to remote clients (as shown below) and click on the "Next" button.

10.3.3.8 Step 8: Configure the IKE Policy

Configure the IKE Phase 1 proposal by selecting the encryption algorithm, authentication algorithm, and Diffie–Hellman group for SA negotiation, as shown in the following window, and click on the "Next" button.

10.3.3.9 Step 9: Configure IPsec Encryption and Authentication Parameters

For IKE Phase 2 configuration, choose the encryption algorithm as 3DES and the authentication algorithm as SHA, as shown next.

10.3.3.10 Step 10: Address Translation Exception and Split Tunneling

Network Address Translation is used to hide the internal network IP address from being exposed externally, as shown below.

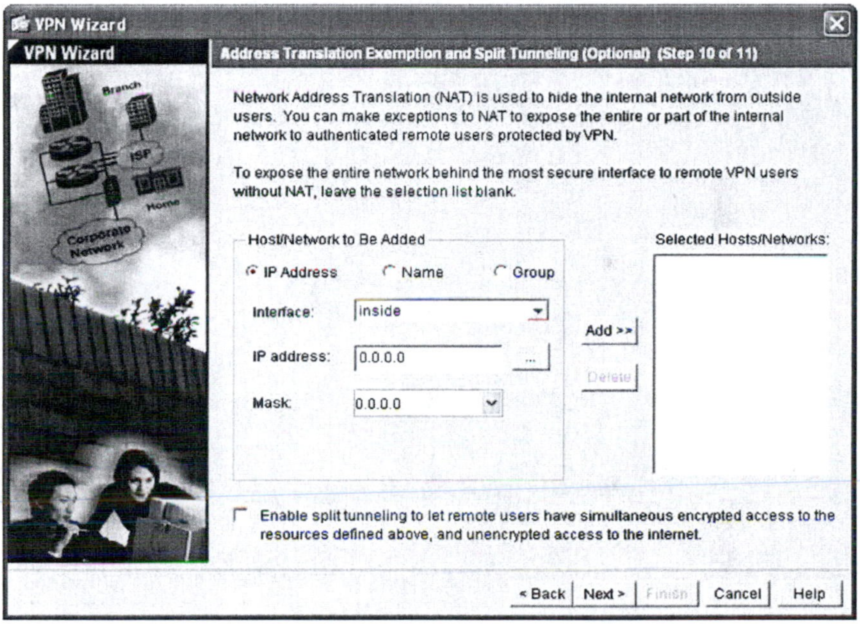

Exceptions can be made by identifying local hosts and networks whose addresses will not be translated. In addition, split tunneling can be enabled to allow unencrypted user access to the Internet. Finally, click on the "Next" button to get the confirmation window shown below and then click "Finish."

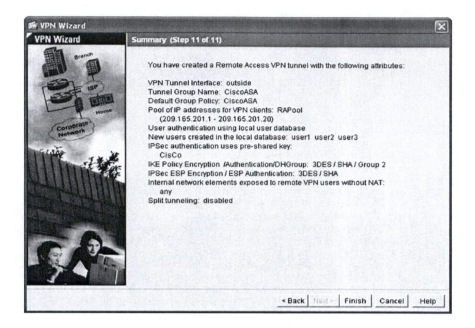

10.3.3.11 Step 11: Install Cisco VPN Client Software

Install the VPN client on the machine that is connected to the outside interface. Double-click on the "Local Area Connection" icon (not the Cisco System VPN Adapter) as shown next.

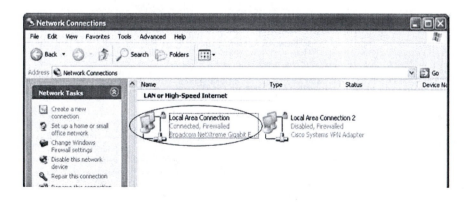

Assign the machine with the following IP address: 209.165.201.19, as below.

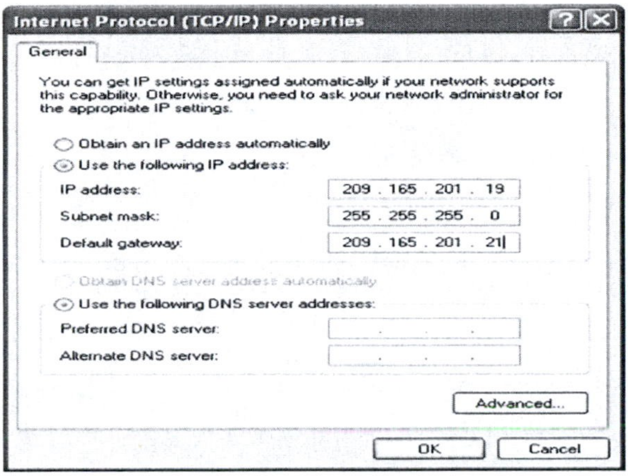

10.3.3.12 Step 12: Launch the Software and Test the Connectivity

First, run the Cisco system VPN client. Create a new connection by clicking on the "New" icon. Fill in the entries of the "Connection Entry" window, enter the name for the connection, and type the IP address of the VPN server, which is 209.165.201.21. Next, type the name of the group tunnel and the password, which is the pre-shared key configured for remote access VPN in ASA. The details are shown below.

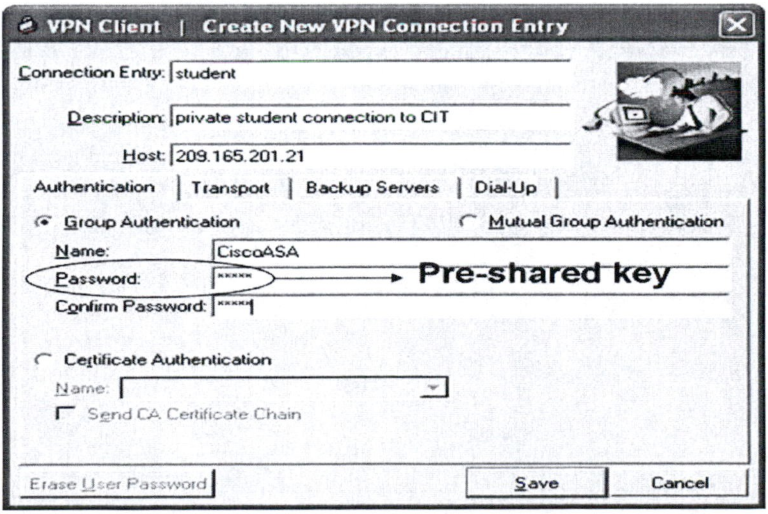

Next, click on the "Transport" tab and select "Enable Transparent Tunneling," which allows encrypted IPsec traffic to pass through network address translation/port address translation (NAT/PAT) devices such as firewalls. Next, select IPsec over UDP (NAT/PAT), as shown on the next screen.

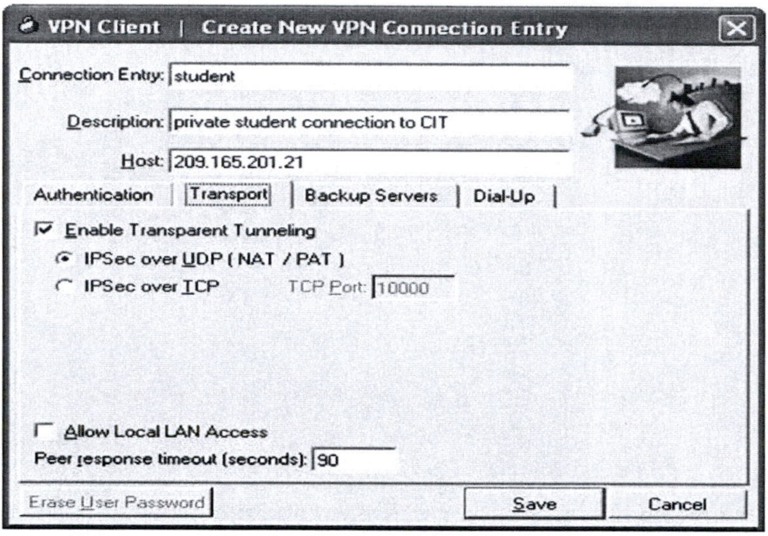

Click the "Save" button, so that the connection will be created, as shown next.

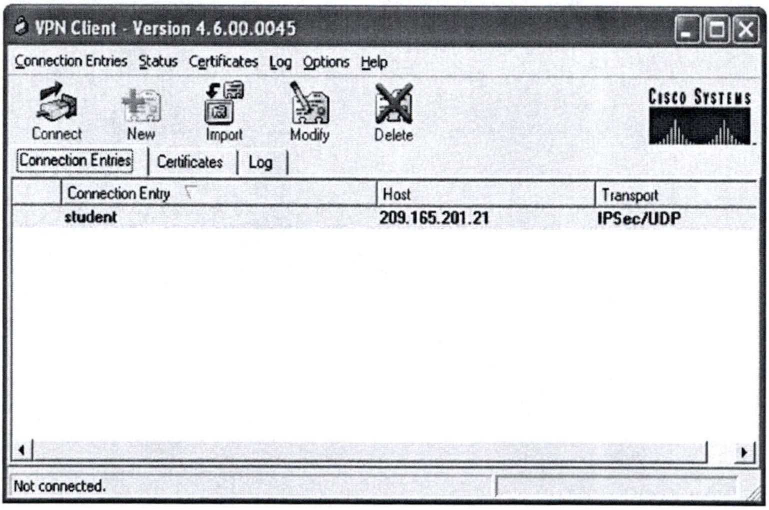

To test the connectivity of the network, ping 209.165.201.21 from the client host. This must be successful, as in the following command.

```
C:\WINDOWS\system32\cmd.exe                                    - □ ×

Microsoft Windows XP [Version 5.1.2600]
(C) Copyright 1985-2001 Microsoft Corp.

C:\Documents and Settings\Administrator>ping 209.165.201.21

Pinging 209.165.201.21 with 32 bytes of data:

Reply from 209.165.201.21: bytes=32 time<1ms TTL=255
Reply from 209.165.201.21: bytes=32 time<1ms TTL=255
Reply from 209.165.201.21: bytes=32 time<1ms TTL=255
Reply from 209.165.201.21: bytes=32 time<1ms TTL=255

Ping statistics for 209.165.201.21:
    Packets: Sent = 4, Received = 4, Lost = 0 (0% loss),
Approximate round trip times in milli-seconds:
    Minimum = 0ms, Maximum = 0ms, Average = 0ms
```

Go to the "Options" menu on the VPN client and select preferences, as shown in the following screen, to get more options.

```
VPN Client - Version 4.6.00.0045                              _ □ ×

Connection Entries  Status  Certificates  Log  Options  Help
                                         Application Launcher...              CISCO SYSTEMS
    Connect      New      Import    M     Windows Logon Properties...
                                         Stateful Firewall (Always On)
Connection Entries | Certificates | Log
                                         Simple Mode              Ctrl+M
    Connection Entry                     Preferences...                      Transport
    student                                                                  IPSec/UDP
```

Select the following "Preferences": "Save window settings," "Enable tool tips," "Enable connect history display," and "Enable accessibility options," as shown below.

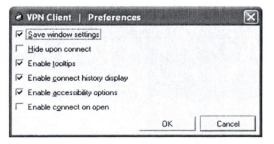

Next, click on the "Connect" button, which pops up a user authentication window, as shown in the following screen.

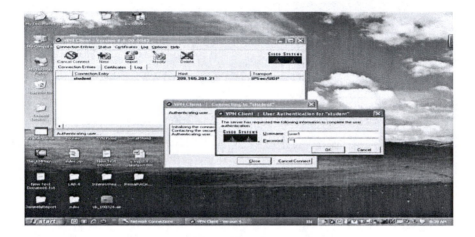

Fill in the username and the password fields as user1 and 123 as configured in this example, and click the "OK" button. The connection will be initialized, and the negotiation of security policies will be started, as shown in the following screenshot.

⚫ VPN Client	Connecting to "student"	☒

Securing communications channel...

Connect History

Initializing the connection...
Contacting the security gateway at 209.165.201.21...
Authenticating user...
Contacting the security gateway at 209.165.201.21...
Negotiating security policies...
Securing communications channel...

Close | Cancel Connect

Once the user is connected to the VPN gateway, another pop-up window will appear confirming that the connection is established, as shown in the following screenshot.

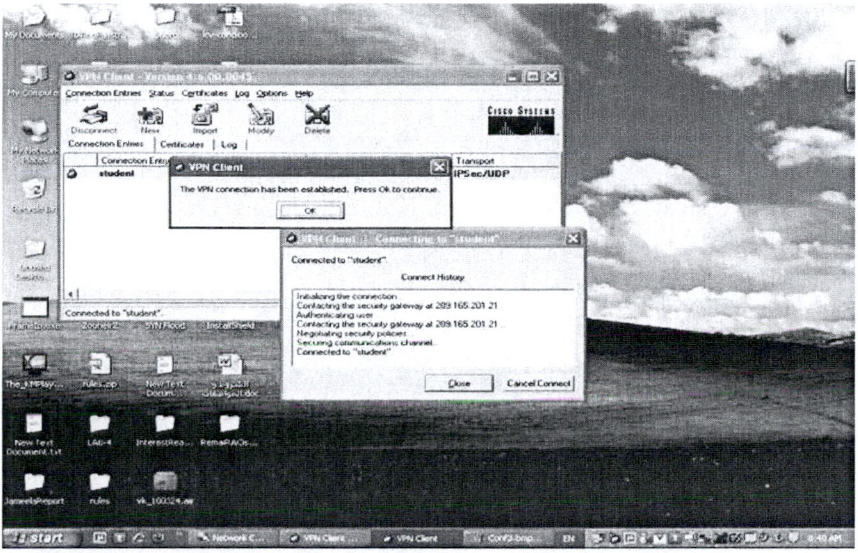

To view more details of the VPN tunnel, go to the "Status" menu and select "Statistics" on the VPN client. As shown in the next screenshot, the remote client got an IP address from the preconfigured pool and it is 209.165.201.1. The new connection, "student" information is displayed. The number of encrypted packets is 78, and the encryption and authentication algorithms are 3-DES and SHA-1, respectively.

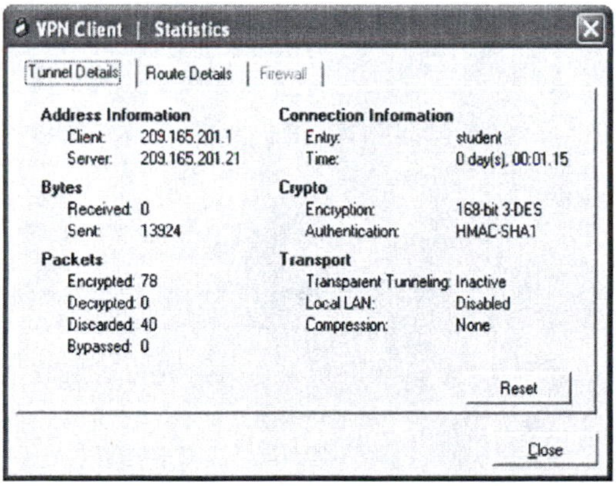

To view the details of the remote client IP address, type the "ipconfig" command as below, to see the IP address that has been assigned to the user from the address pool on the VPN gateway.

```
C:\WINDOWS\system32\cmd.exe                                    _ □ ×
D:\Documents and Settings\200414671>ipconfig

Windows IP Configuration

Ethernet adapter Local Area Connection:

        Connection-specific DNS Suffix  . :
        IP Address. . . . . . . . . . . : 209.165.201.19
        Subnet Mask . . . . . . . . . . : 255.255.255.0
        Default Gateway . . . . . . . . : 209.165.201.21
Ethernet adapter Wireless Network Connection:

        Media State . . . . . . . . . . : Media disconnected
Ethernet adapter Local Area Connection 6:

        Connection-specific DNS Suffix  . :
        IP Address. . . . . . . . . . . : 209.165.201.1
        Subnet Mask . . . . . . . . . . : 255.255.255.0
        Default Gateway . . . . . . . . : 209.165.201.1
D:\Documents and Settings\200414671>
```

10.3.3.13 Step 13: Verify VPN Tunnel Establishment

On the ASA, use the "show crypto isakmp sa" command to display the negotiated IKE phase 1 SA parameters, as in the following:

```
Configuration - HyperTerminal                                   _ □ ×
File  Edit  View  Call  Transfer  Help

ciscoasa# show crypto isakmp sa

   Active SA: 1
   Rekey SA: 0 (A tunnel will report 1 Active and 1 Rekey SA during rekey)
Total IKE SA: 1

1   IKE Peer: 209.165.201.19
    Type    : user         Role  : responder
    Rekey   : no           State : AM_ACTIVE
ciscoasa# _

Connected 0:38:20    Auto detect    9600 8-N-1    SCROLL    CAPS    NUM    Capture    Print echo
```

It is noticed that the number of active security associations is 1, the IKE peer is 209.165.201.19, the connection type is Remote Access VPN (user), the role of the remote user is responder, and the IKE phase 1 mode is aggressive as denoted by the "State : AM-ACTIVE."

To display the IKE Phase 2 security association, type the following command: "show crypto ipsec sa".

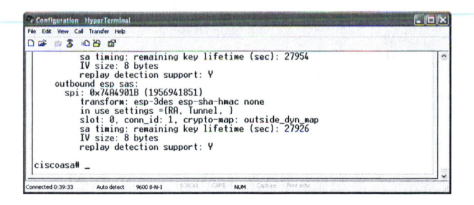

It is noticed that the current number of encapsulated, encrypted, and digested packets is 0; the number of de-capsulated, decrypted, and verified packets is 255; the number of compressed and decompressed packets is 0; the IPsec mode is the tunnel mode; and there are two SAs, one inbound and one outbound and each SA has its own SPI.

To view more details of the VPN tunnel, type the following command:

```
Configuration - HyperTerminal
File  Edit  View  Call  Transfer  Help

ciscoasa# show vpn-session remote

Session Type: Remote

Username      : user1
Index         : 1
Assigned IP   : 209.165.201.1          Public IP   : 209.165.201.19
Protocol      : IPSec                  Encryption  : 3DES
Hashing       : SHA1
Bytes Tx      : 23755                  Bytes Rx    : 0
Client Type   : WinNT                  Client Ver  : 4.6.00.0045
Tunnel Group  : CiscoASA
Login Time    : 23:13:13 UTC Sat May 21 2011
Duration      : 0h:15m:25s
Filter Name   :

ciscoasa# _

Connected 0:40:45      Auto detect    9600 8-N-1    SCROLL  CAPS  NUM  Capture  Print echo
```

Several parameters of the session that has occurred between the peers are displayed, such as Session Type is Remote, the username is user1 and its assigned IP address is 209.165.201.1, the user protocol is Ipsec, and encryption and hash algorithms are 3DES and SHA1, respectively. The Tunnel Group name is Cisco ASA, and the login time and duration of the session are specified.

10.3.3.14 Step 14: Monitor the VPN Tunnel in the ASA

To monitor the sessions in detail, click on the "Monitoring" tab and from the VPN statistics tree, select the "Sessions" sub-tree. The next screenshot shows session details such as the username, which is user1; its tunnel group Cisco ASA; the assigned IP address of the remote user; the IPsec protocol used; the encryption algorithm; and the time the user logged in.

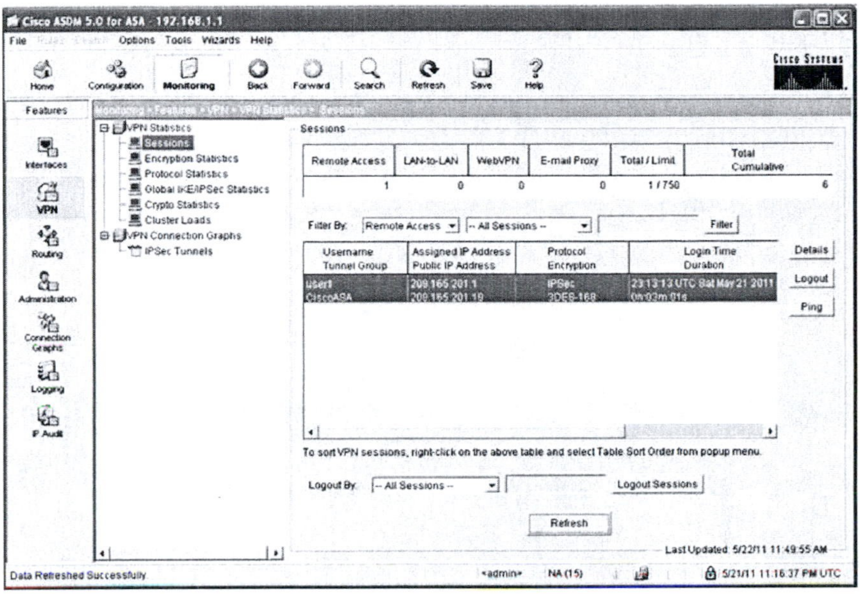

To view more details, click on the "Details" button. The next screenshot displays the details of phase 1 and phase 2 security associations. In addition, the encryption and hash algorithm are being used in each phase

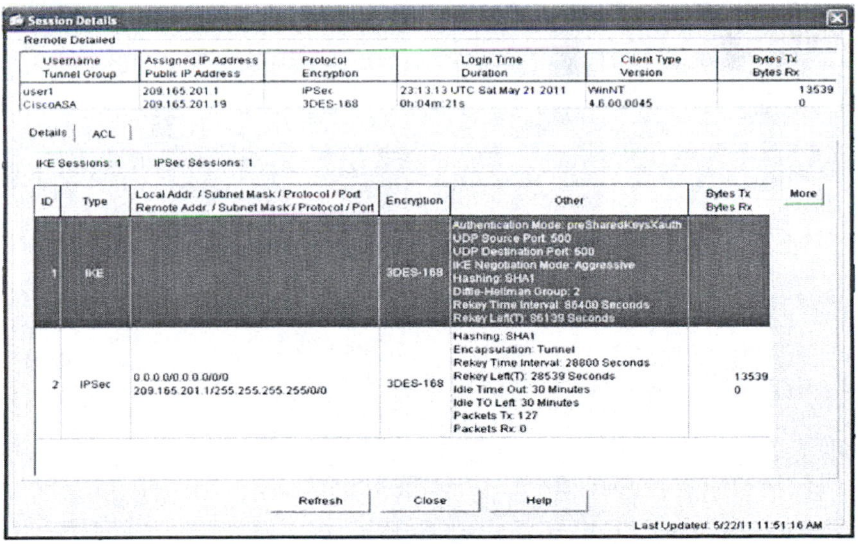

By clicking on the "More" button while selecting the IKE Phase 1 line, the details of IKE SAs will appear as shown in the following screenshot, which displays the IKE peer 209.165.201.19; the type of the peer, which is user; the role she plays, which is responder; the encryption; and the hash algorithms, which are 3DES and SHA. The mode is aggressive; in addition, the authentication method is pre-shared.

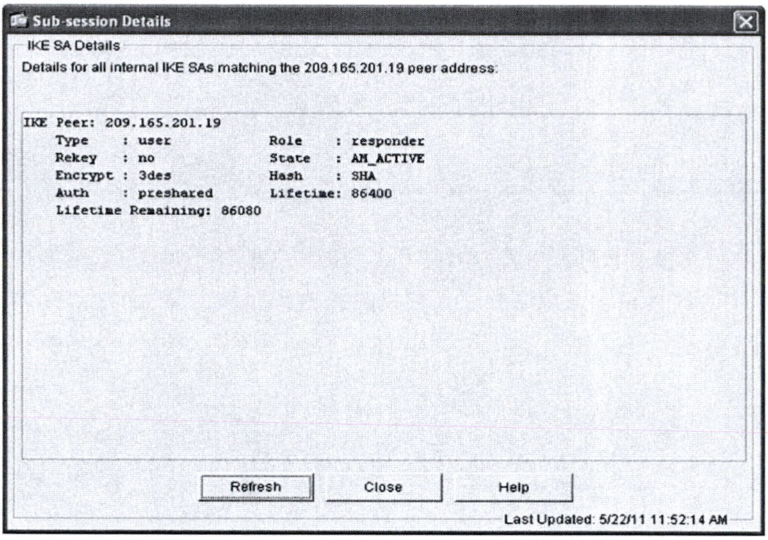

```
┌─────────────────────────────────────────────────────────────────┐
│ ▒ Sub-session Details                                        [X] │
│  ─IKE SA Details────────────────────────────────────────────     │
│   Details for all internal IKE SAs matching the 209.165.201.19 peer address: │
│                                                                   │
│   IKE Peer: 209.165.201.19                                        │
│        Type    : user        Role    : responder                 │
│        Rekey   : no          State   : AM_ACTIVE                  │
│        Encrypt : 3des        Hash    : SHA                        │
│        Auth    : preshared   Lifetime: 86400                      │
│        Lifetime Remaining: 86080                                  │
│                                                                   │
│                                                                   │
│             ┌──────────┐   ┌──────────┐   ┌──────────┐           │
│             │ Refresh  │   │  Close   │   │  Help    │           │
│             └──────────┘   └──────────┘   └──────────┘           │
│                              Last Updated: 5/22/11 11:52:14 AM    │
└─────────────────────────────────────────────────────────────────┘
```

Next, select the other sub-trees to learn more about the encryption statistics. There is one active session that is using the 3DES encryption algorithm 100% of the time as shown on the following screen.

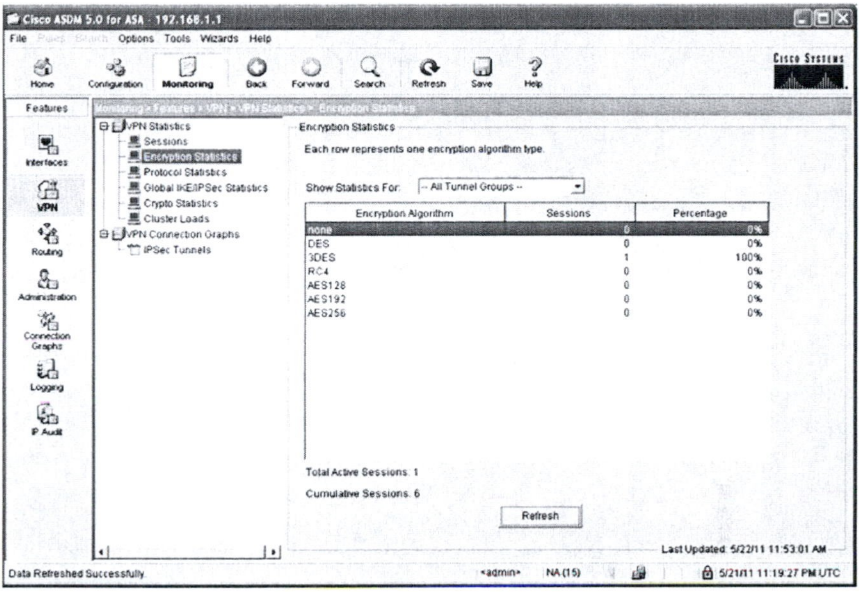

Select the Protocol statistics sub-tree to view the details of the protocol used. There is an active session working on the IPsec protocol 100% of the time, as shown below.

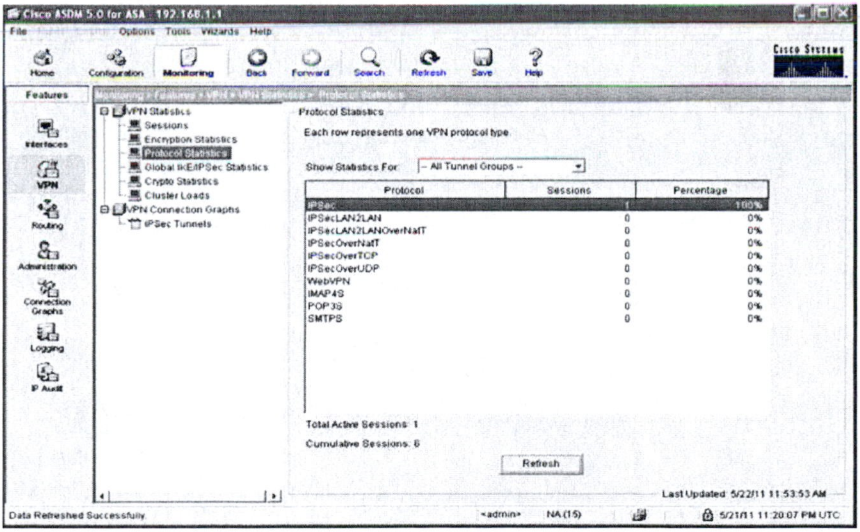

From the Global IKE/IPsec Statistics sub-tree, the number of active tunnels is 1 and the previous tunnels are 6. There are 111

IP packets and 3 In Drop Packets. Moreover, there are 109 Out Packets and 0 Out Drop Packets, as shown in the following.

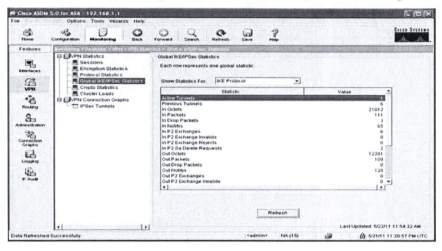

Select the Crypto Statistics sub-tree and analyze its statistics. There are 102 requests to encrypt packet and encapsulate packet, and 98 decrypt and de-capsulate packet requests. There are 231 HMAC calculation requests, 7 requests of SA creation, and 6 SA deletion requests. Furthermore, there are 12 requests of next phase key allocation, as shown below.

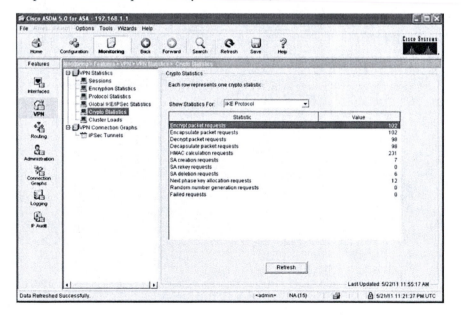

To view the VPN tunnel information in graphical form, select "VPN Connection Graph" and then "IPsec tunnels" to get the window shown below:

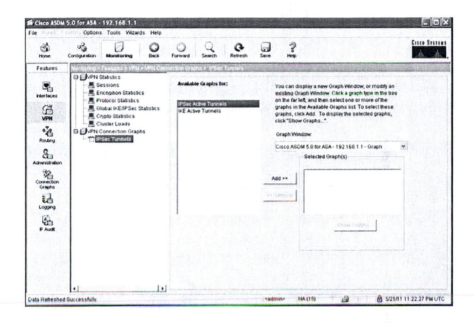

From the text area of available graphs, select "IPsec Active tunnel" and click the "Add" button to get the window shown below. Repeat the previous step with the IKE active tunnels, so that the IKE and IPsec active tunnels information will be shown in a graph.

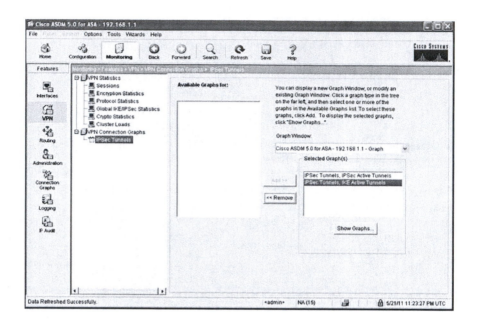

Click "Show Graphs" and the stable straight green line indicates that the tunnel is still active, as shown in the following window.

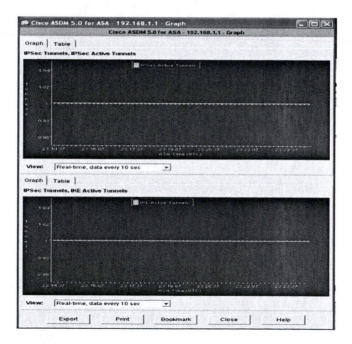

10.4 Chapter Summary

As demand for anywhere, any time remote access continues to grow, the Remote Access IPsec VPN has increasingly proven to be the most effective solution for data privacy on the Internet. This chapter presented a comprehensive explanation of the Remote Access IPsec VPN security solution and covered implementation details of the main components that make up a Remote Access IPsec VPN, which are the Remote Access VPN Client and the Remote Access VPN Server. It is divided into two sections: discussion of features and configuration based on Juniper Networks NetScreen firewall appliance, followed by implementation using Cisco Microsystems Adaptive Security Appliance. Throughout this chapter, the core concepts of Remote Access IPsec VPN, such as IKE Phase 1 SA negotiation and IKE Phase 2 packet statistics, were examined and analyzed thoroughly.

Index